CW01468089

WHO'S WHO OF LINCOLN CITY FC

1993-2016

BY GARY HUTCHINSON

Who's who of Lincoln City 1993-2016

FIRST EDITION

First Published November 2016

Copyright Gary Hutchinson / Cecil Anthony Geoffrey Publishing

Cecil Anthony Geoffrey Publishing, Kemp House, 160 City Road, London, EC1V 2NX

All rights reserved. No part of this publication may be reproduced, stored in a retrieval system or transmitted in any form, or by means electronic, mechanical, photocopying, recording or otherwise without permission in writing from the publisher

All endeavour has been made to ensure stats are correct at time of going to press

UTFI

CECIL ANTHONY GEOFFREY

Bibliography & Acknowledgements

Thanks to the following website and publications which helped with the research of this book.

www.soccerbase.com

www.wikipedia.com

www.redimps.com

Lincoln City FC: The Official History, Ian & Donald Nannestad

City's Centenary, John Vickers

Who's Who of Lincoln City 1892-1994, Donald and Ian Nannestad

The Imps Match day Magazine (1993-2016)

Deranged Ferret (Bates, Parle, Stow, Bride, Barwise, Clarke, Hutchinson)

The Lincolnshire Echo

BBC Sports & BBC News Website

Photographs by Graham Burrell

Thanks to Daren Dykes for starting it all off

Thanks to Bradley Wood, Paul Farman, Peter Gain, Marcus Stergiopolous, and Gijsbert Bos

Thanks to Mum, Dad, Mo, Paul, Mel, Isaac and Daisy Rae.

Thanks to all those who contributed with articles and in discussions on LCB

Thanks to you for buying it

Finally thanks to Danny and Nicky Cowley for finally giving Imps fans some hope after a decade of despair

For Fe

Without her, I'd still be playing FIFA on the sofa

Contents

Foreword – by Grant Brown

I had two thoughts when I was asked to write the foreword for this book. My first thought was, how do you even start to write a foreword? I was worried I'd make a balls up of it, but I really wanted to give it a go. I felt thrilled to be asked, whenever I get asked to do anything associated with the club it brings back very fond memories of my time there which I will always treasure. That was enough to get me over my fears!

Lincoln City has been a part of my life for so long now. I remember the first person I ever met from the Imps, it was quite fittingly the legendary manager Colin Murphy. He came over to Leicester to meet up with me. He was a big character and I instantly liked him and knew I would enjoy playing for him. The players were all very welcoming too. I thought maybe Lincoln would be good place to get some games, if only I knew how many I'd get!

As this book deals with players I'll talk about a couple of them. David Puttnam is worth a mention, he arrived a few weeks after I did. Putters was the best crosser of the ball that I played with. He could run at full pace down the left wing and deliver a pinpoint cross without breaking stride. He was a good player but picked up a bad Achilles injury which restricted his career, and that was a real shame.

Mind you, he enjoyed a Thursday night out at his local on the outskirts of Leicester, so was sometimes not at his best on a Friday morning. Friday used to be a light training session so he could get away with it, until we started to do team shape work on a Friday instead. He hoped we would attack down the right side so he didn't have to do much, but we thought it would be funny to keep giving him the ball, the look on his face when the ball kept going down his side was a picture.

This book deals with all players, from record appearance holders to those who only had a handful of outings. Joe Allon was one I remember well; he was a bit of a lad who never got going as a player for Lincoln. He certainly made an impression on the dressing room and the physio room though. He had a problem with haemorrhoids while at the club and it was not an uncommon sight to see him knelt on all fours on the treatment table with his pants around his knees, shouting for the physio Mark Hudson to apply his ointment. I can tell you that is not a pretty sight; neither Joe nor his farmers!!!

The football club isn't all about the players though, it's about the characters that a book often won't mention. Dawn Cussens is the only full time member of staff who was always at the club whilst I was there. She has been an outstandingly loyal employee, and a good friend. There's also Ashton family, George, Doreen and Chris. They've been a constant too, their whole lives seem to revolve around their beloved football club. Of course, I must mention Barry Clements even after retiring as groundsman, he's been there for the current ground staff to pick his brains and also to support his team. Players come and go and make up part of a football club, but people like those I've mentioned are a constant, and are just as much a part of Lincoln City as any player.

Another constant has been the quality and loyalty of the fans, home and away. I remember celebrating with the fans back at the start of my Imps career on a wet Tuesday night in Stockport when Gordon Hobson scored a delightful curling equaliser to grab a point. It was just like the great support we took to Barnet twenty years later when Jon Nolan grabbed a last gasp equaliser sending our fans into wild celebrations. Twenty years apart but exactly the same passion and the same pride. I'd bet a few fans were at both games as well. Again, it is fans as much as staff and players that make up the whole spectrum of a football club.

I am one of the few who have been lucky enough to play for Lincoln, and manage them for a short spell as well. I didn't enjoy having to take over from John Schofield in 2007 who was, and still is, a good friend of mine but I enjoyed working with the players who were a good group. We came very close to beating a very good Peterborough side in, conceding a late goal to give Posh the draw. We then went to Brentford and defended well for most of the game before conceding a late goal to lose 1-0.

Results weren't good enough during my short spells as manager. After taking over from Steve Tilson we did register one win against Alfreton, despite a good performances against Cambridge United away. We had a good performance at Mansfield Town at home after I took over from David Holdsworth, but I didn't pick up another win. I enjoyed my times in charge of the 1st team, my only regret is that we didn't win more games.

I couldn't write a short piece without mentioning that wonderful day I became the record appearance holder at Lincoln. It was a such a very proud moment for me and my family. To receive a memento from the club, presented by Tony Emery, was a great honour. Tony had held the record before me and it made the occasion even more special to have him there. The game itself? It wasn't the greatest spectacle! It was an LDV Vans Trophy game at Sincil Bank, not a very prestigious game at all, but at least it wasn't against Derby under-23's! Lee Thorpe grabbed a hat-trick to win us the tie and put further gloss on a lovely evening.

Lincoln City has been such a big part of my life for so long, and I'm delighted I got to write the opening for this book. I'll know a lot of the players mentioned, I may have coached them, I may have captained them or I may just have played with them. One or two I may even have played against as well! If you don't agree with everything that's written please remember I've only written the foreword, they're not my opinions after this first bit finishes! You'll have to hunt down Gary, the author if you think he's been too harsh on your favourite player. I just hope he hasn't been too harsh on me, because even now I still have a strong tackle that I'm not afraid to use!

Enjoy the book,

Grant

Preface

Welcome, and thank you for buying my book. Firstly thank you to Grant Brown for writing a foreword. There could be nobody more suitable than a man who played in 469 games for Lincoln City, and took control as caretaker manager more times than I care to remember. This book is all about the good, the bad, the average and unique. Grant Brown is unique.

Secondly thank you, I appreciate the fact you find what I've written worth reading, even though I suspect as a City fan you'll probably buy anything written about the club. I know I would have bought this book, if I hadn't written it of course.

I've wanted to write a book about Lincoln City my whole life. I have a virtually complete manuscript for a story covering my spell as Poacher the Imp and telling the demise and hopefully rise of the club I love. I never thought I'd actually get published, when I started writing it twelve years ago there was only just such as thing as the internet and publishing was much harder to get into.

I've been writing about Lincoln City for the last twenty years. I started with a few letters to the Lincolnshire Echo, mainly defending the negative football of John Beck. Eventually I began to contribute to the Imps fanzine 'Deranged Ferret', at first a few articles but most recently as it's full-time editor.

From there I edited a Lincoln City website, and when I got bored of that I moved on to blogging for Sky Sports. They weren't interested when we got relegated so for a short while I sat around staring at my laptop wondering where to vent my opinions. Then came Lincoln City Banter on Facebook, courtesy of Paul Dawson. It is a medium whereby you can offer opinion, but can't remain nameless and therefore have to think through what you write. Or not in some cases. essentially I always wanted to offer opinion and perspective on our football club, and whichever medium allowed me to do it most effectively I pursued with vigour.

Most recently I've been writing my own blog, the Stacey West Blog which was a finalist in the 'best new blog' category at the prestigious Football Blogging Awards 2016. It was such an honour to travel to Old Trafford for the award ceremony in November 2016, and although I didn't win the big prize it was a great night. If you're reading this you've probably read the blog anyway, but if not it's www.staceywest.co.uk

I find writing therapeutic and rewarding, I'd much rather create something for other people to enjoy than sit around playing on the PlayStation. At least that's how I feel now, perhaps if I felt that way all the time this wouldn't be my first Lincoln City book! I can guarantee it won't be my last, the (provisionally titled) Mascot Diaries will be out for Christmas 2017 (cynical I know, but that's life) and after that I do have at least one more planned.

It was whilst writing a feature for my blog about obscure past players that the idea for this first book came into my mind. I was researching a player called Daren Dykes, and it occurred to me that despite many fans being unable to recall him, at some point he had played on the Sincil Bank turf, he had represented the club we all love. From him I moved on to Martin Garratt, and I discovered his sad story. Due to his passing I opted not to blog about him as a 'failed Imp', but I became convinced that behind a lot of these players there is a story. I'm not telling it here, you'll have to flick to 'D' or 'G' to read about those two players.

It was then I decided to follow on the excellent work done by Ian and Donald Nannestad twenty-two years ago, and chart every player to have represented the Imps. I'm not quite as meticulous as those guys though, I'm afraid there is no appendices for players who only played friendlies. The game has changed so much since 1994 that to list everyone who featured in non-competitive matches would take an age. It would read like a modern day phone book with trialist after trialist trying to stake a claim for a contract. Nope, I decided to focus purely on those players who have made a competitive appearance for us only, so my apologies to all the Jamie Sherlock types out there

My book does differ from theirs significantly though, because rather than just talk about who a player played for and what they achieved, I've tried to look at what they brought to he club and what made them unique. A player such as Jefferson Louis deserves more than just eighty lines of previous clubs, I think he needs explaining in more detail.

Although history will show people like Drewe Broughton represented the club, I wanted to ensure that it would also be able to reference what I felt their contribution to be. Just because a player pulled on the red and white doesn't mean they are popular, nor does it mean they actually did anything. Ben Hutchinson must appear in this book because he played, but I think it only fair for fans to know the bigger picture. The worst fans in the world we might be, but I want to ensure fans of the future know the total sum of his contribution. Or rather, lack of it.

So, that's the book and how I came to write it, but what about my devotion to Lincoln City? We've all got a different story and at the end of the book you'll read about a handful more who have contributed in some way. My own story starts in October of 1986 when my Dad caught me swearing somewhere in rural Lincolnshire. As punishment, I was taken to watch Lincoln instead of spending the afternoon with my friends. We lost 4-1 at home to Hartlepool but it was the start of a romance that will outlast any other.

I don't know what it first was that attracted me to Lincoln City. Sincil Bank seemed packed that day (it wasn't), and apart from me everyone could swear as much as they wanted. My Dad even swore, and on the way home he bought me sweets so I wouldn't tell Mum. Maybe it was the bribery that sold me on days at the football.

Maybe it was time spent with my Dad, and in turn for a short while my Granddad too. My old man worked hard and there wasn't always a lot of time for me and my brother, but afternoons at the football became 'me and Dad' time. I loved connecting with him and even today it gives us something to talk (and argue) about. We still go together some matches, he holds a season ticket for 2016/17 which is his first ever. I hope his unusual optimism is an indication of what is to come!

The Nannestad's started their book with a brief history of Lincoln City, so for the next few pages I would like you to indulge me as I briefly cover the last twenty-three years in about six pages.

So, our journey starts in the 1993-94 season. It was the first spell as manager for Keith Alexander, and he was a trailblazer even then as the first full time black football manager. The football he played was nice and neat passing as well, something we hadn't been used to for a long while. It wasn't always successful though and despite two Coca Cola cup matches with Everton and an FA Cup tie with Bolton, he only lasted one season. Results tailed off after Sam Ellis came on board to help out, and it was former player Big Sam who replaced Keith in the summer of 1994.

Big Sam was a popular player at Sincil Bank, but perhaps not so popular as manager. He did have managerial experience though, unlike his predecessor. He had taken Blackpool into the bottom four of the Football League, but after successful re-election they stormed to the Third Division and avoided relegation. He'd also served as assistant to Peter Reid at Manchester City before coming to help Keith, and eventually succeeding him.

Things didn't start brilliantly, after a 2-1 win over Exeter City the Imps lost four straight games. Although our league form was decidedly average, we managed a run in the cup under Ellis, after 184 minutes of football against Crystal Palace we were leading 1-0. A late, late aggregate equaliser left us with extra time to face, and they went on to win 3-1 over two legs. We also made the FA Cup third round, losing to the same opposition 5-1 at Selhurst Park.

Sam liked to play really direct football, and his short tenure saw an immediate return to the long ball tactics. He brought in old so-called experienced players like Trevor Hebberd and Steve Foley, who failed to produce the goods for City.

He also played some of the most promising players we had out of position, namely Matt Carbon and Ben Dixon. Both had represented England as youths but neither was utilised regularly in the position they preferred to play in.

The following season he had an atrocious start once again, an opening day victory over Preston wasn't backed up by solid performances. Signings such as Gary Megson simply didn't bring anything to the team and after three more defeats and a draw he was sacked. In his final game we lost 3-1 to Barnet, and Steve Wicks was sat watching in the stands in a pattern that was to repeat itself just forty-two days' layer.

Technically Steve Wicks was only the Head Coach, as John Reames retained control over off the field matters, or to put it a better way John Reames kept his hands on the purse strings.

That being the case it might be harsh to criticise Wicks for his transfer dealings, but swapping Dean West for Kevin Hulme was a monumental error, and as a man who liked to play football it does seem odd he chose to get rid of David Puttnam.

The football under Wicks was attractive even if it didn't bear fruit in terms of results. When Wicks was unceremoniously dumped after getting his second point against Scarborough he had fans on his side. It was common knowledge he was going prior to the Scarborough game; John Beck was in the stands in another show of professionalism. Fans chanted his name, but to no avail. He was predictably sacked after just seven league games.

In fairness to Wicks it is worth noting that he won one match, a 4-3 victory in the Autoglass Windscreens Shield against Rochdale. With a league win ratio of 0% he does statistically rank as the worst manager we've had in the spell this book covers but that would be very harsh given some of the clowns that we've seen since.

After Lincoln he went to work as head scout at Newcastle United, whom he advised to come back to Lincoln and sign Darren Huckerby a few weeks later. By that time the City manager was the divisive John Beck. I could write a book about John Beck and perhaps one day I will. Instead I have to sum up his contribution and legacy to Lincoln City in just a few paragraphs.

Under Beck we immediately changed from a passing team back to our familiar long ball style. Whatever results that brought us were irrelevant to some. If a player didn't fit the Beck mould then he was out on his ear, Paul Mudd being one who suffered almost immediately.

John Beck's team were not popular with some fans, and certainly not with opposition teams. We were direct, but we were incredibly hard and rarely tried to indulge in the finer arts of the beautiful game. Beck would try all manner of spoiling tactics, long grass in his favourite area of the pitch 'danger alley', so those big balls would settle quicker for his wide men. He kept us up playing ugly, and then he proceeded to build a promotion winning team playing ugly.

He would give specific orders and once subbed Mark Hone minutes after bringing him on for not following instructions. To some he was a thug and a bully, to others he was way ahead of his time in terms of the science behind his approach. Whatever he was he built the team that won us automatic promotion in 1998, and gave us the one season of third tier football I've had the pleasure of watching.

By the time we were promoted he was gone. He had a long running clash of personalities with John Reames, and after two written warnings over his conduct he took an unauthorised holiday after a 0-0 draw with his old side Cambridge. He was sacked and his assistant Shane Westley stepped up to take over the helm. He guided us into Division Two before also being dismissed, and finally John Reames took charge of everything from team selection to transfer dealings.

Mr Reames divided opinion at times, but I think looking back he did a fantastic amount for the club. Taking over as manager might not have seemed like his smartest move, but he did pick up a Manager of the Month award, and his win ratio is significantly better than David Holdsworth, Steve Tilson and Chris Sutton. He did all this against a backdrop of relegation, albeit relegation from one of the toughest third tiers in history. Fulham, Stoke, Reading and Manchester City were all opponents at the Bank as we crashed to relegation.

After a spell of treading water back in the basement division he stepped down and let veteran striker Phil Stant take over. It was June 2000. Just a few months later he left the club he loved, for good.

John Reames should now be remembered fondly, he was the first chairman to employ a black full time manager in Keith Alexander, and upon resigning he left £400,000 worth of shares to the supporters' trust for the well-being of the club. He might not always have been a popular figure, but sometimes in order to be a good boss you have to take a lot of stick.

Stant's reign was brief. Off the field we'd been suffering financial issues, and Mr Reames shares helped the Supporters Trust take over the club. No sooner had that happened than Stant and his assistant George Foster were gone. Their spell in charge might have been brief, but it was also terrible and we'd gone from an aspiring Division Two side to real relegation candidates. The football was dire and crowds were dropping.

Former Grimsby Town manager Alan Buckley took over but once again his reign was brief. He started well with two away wins, something we hadn't managed in eleven months, but despite the quality of football improving the quality of results did not. Buckley has the worst win ratio outside of Steve Wicks. Before long we weren't just battling relegation, we were battling for financial survival as well. The collapse of ITV Digital had his us hard financially, and ominously administration beckoned.

Buckley brought Keith Alexander back to the club, and it was Keith who stepped up when Buckley was dismissed at the end of the 2001/02 season. We'd scraped survival by the skin of our teeth, but there was a real chance we could go broke in the summer. We entered administration and let most of the playing staff go. The aim was to kick off the following season, and then to finish 22nd or above.

Of course, I don't need to tell you the next four years under Keith Alexander were the best times to support Lincoln City since the early 1980's. Keith instilled a belief in his patchwork squad that we hadn't seen before and he galvanised the city as we strode through the season to our first ever major final, the play-off final at the Millennium Stadium. I'm only giving you a brief overview here, but very few Imps fans will forget the elation of that day in Cardiff, having been so close to folding twelve months earlier. Graham Lloyd's book 'One Hell of a Season' covers it very well, if you feel like some extra reading.

For another three years Keith assembled the best side I've ever watched at Lincoln. Players like Peter Gain, Gary Taylor-Fletcher, Richard Butcher, and Simon Yeo thrilled us and had us on the edge of our seats. It wasn't always pretty, but it wasn't the ugly side of the game we'd shown under Beck. We could be direct, but we had some really good football players as well.

When Keith fell ill in November of 2003 the whole City held its collective breath. It showed the character and strength of the man that he was able not only to recover from his cerebral aneurism, but he could return and lead us to further play-off matches.

Keith was always on the search for a striker, he always insisted with goals in the team you had a chance. As you read through this list of players you'll see just how many strikers he tried and tested, many without success!

Keith left the club in 2006, always just one step away from achieving what he wanted to achieve. A change in the boardroom had seen a restructuring and the joint chairmen of Steff Wright and Ray Trew suspended Keith in January 2006. He was quickly reinstated but the ripples caused a lot of unpleasantness and nobody blamed Keith when he left for Peterborough. It was a sad day for the club, and a sad day for the City.

For the first six months of the following season John Schofield and John Deehan got the side that Keith built playing some of the best football we've seen in years. Jamie Forrester and Mark Stallard formed a frightening partnership and scored goals for fun. In a mad October we beat Barnet 5-0, Rochdale 7-1, and Swindon Town 1-0 away to go top of the League. It seemed like we'd hit gold.

Then the decline started. Firstly clubs seem to find us out, and we scraped into the play-offs for the fifth successive year but were unsurprisingly beaten by Bristol Rovers. A summer of discontent followed, the signings we'd hoped for didn't arrived and by October 2008 the management duo were gone. Their final game was a dismal hammering on TV against MK Dons.

The whirlwind Peter Jackson was next up, a man so full of hot air I felt tempted to tie a basket to his feet to get an aerial view of the City. He kept us up and he tried a lot of youth players, which are two things I will give him credit for. He also survived a cancer battle as manager as well which we were all thankful for.

The problem was he was a bad manager. He signed the Magnificent Seven, a collection of players he said would fire us to the next level. They didn't. Two of those players were Kevin Gall and David Graham, and they scored zero goals between them. His leading scorer was Romanian Adrian Patulea, a player who couldn't get a game half the time. After a little under two years the self-promoting manager was gone, but not without the heartfelt TV interview and warm wishes you'd expect from such a strong self-publicist.

Next came Chris Sutton. He took over when we were 22nd and guided us to 19th, which he saw as some sort of achievement, although we did feature in the third round of the FA Cup. The following season despite spending a huge sum on players like Carayol and Jarrett, he resigned. Just a few games into the season he was unhappy at not being given FA Cup money to spend and he walked out after our 0-0 draw with Burton Albion.

Next came Steve Tilson. He completed the destruction started by Peter Jackson, he refused to play experienced players with fire in their bellies such as Scott Kerr, preferring to draft in an endless supply of players on short term contracts or loan players. Some, like Stephen Hunt and Ashley Grimes were very good, others such as Elliot Parrish and Pat Kanyucka were not. Needing just three points from mid-March we collected one and were relegated on the final day of the season.

Everything Keith Alexander had worked hard on had been destroyed by three incompetent managers. We were a team of loan players, has-beens and never-have beens, devoid of cohesion, devoid of hope and crucially devoid of money. The future looked bleak in 2002, it looked just as bleak in the summer of 2011.

Since relegation we've only really held our own. Steve Tilson lasted a year, David Holdsworth came in and used more players in a season than the Nannestad's had to write about over a hundred-year period. We flirted with further relegation and scraped absolute rock bottom. Steff Wright was long gone, handing the poisoned and badly managed chalice over to Bob Dorrian.

The last eighteen months have seen us start to make our comeback. Clive Nates has been brought in as an investor and Mr Dorrian has managed to steer the good ship Lincoln City away from the rocks and back out towards open sea. Chris Moyses took over as manager and worked for free to help put the club back on the right course. His contacts across Lincoln helped garner support for a club that had seemingly lost the support of local people. The final piece of the jigsaw arrived in May 2016, with Danny Cowley and his brother Nicky taking over as managers. At the time of writing we sit second in the National League, the brothers have a win ratio that is better than any of the other) in the last twenty years and financially we appear to be out of the woods thanks to Clive Nates and Bob Dorrian. Crowds are up, optimism is up and there seems like no better time to stick a book out!

Anyway, I think it is time to let you crack on with the book. I want you to be aware there is a lot of opinion in here, mainly mine. I've tried to give a fair and balanced view of most players. The stats for Imps appearances include cup matches, but I can't be held responsible if they're slightly out. I have checked them through two independent sources although at times those sources disagreed so I plumped for the most reliable! I used a cut-off point of October 31st 2016, so Theo Robinson (if you're reading this) please don't contact me and try to claim a couple of goals. As an appendices, I've included a few interviews I've done with Imps and ex-Imps recently. I've also spoken to Gijsbert Bos and Daren Dykes exclusively for this book.

If you want me to sign a copy or anything like that I'd be absolutely delighted to feel important for a few seconds. I'm usually milling around the bar at the ground before a game, but make sure you bring a pen, and the book (obviously). I won't sign body parts or babies or anything like that though. Unless you bring a pint of Fosters with you.

From Charlee Adams to Adi Yussuf I hope you find a picture building up of Lincoln City Football Club. There's a hundred different stories in here trying to bubble out, from match-fixing to the England Disability team, from play-off finals to drug smuggling. I hope you find this so much more than just a list of players who represented our club.

Most of all I hope you enjoy reading it just half as much as I enjoyed writing it.

Gaz

Adams – Austin

Adams, Charlee
(2014, 2014-2015)
Midfielder, 28 Apps 2 Goals
Born 16th Feb 1995
*2013-2016 Birmingham, **2014** Imps (loan), 2014 Imps (loan) 2016 Kilmarnock (loan)*

Stylish midfielder Adams signed on loan from Birmingham in January 2014 for three months. He impressed in his 14 starts and after completion of his first spell he returned to Lincoln in November 2014. He scored two spectacular goals against Grimsby and Aldershot, both goals getting an awful lot of hits on YouTube for their audacious execution. Returned to Birmingham in March 2015 and has since signed on loan for Kilmarnock.

Adams was highly rated at City but a recent injury at Kilmarnock will no doubt put his development on hold. I wouldn't be surprised if he doesn't eventually go on to play Championship football on a regular basis.

Adams, Nathan
(2008-2010)
Forward, 0 (5) Apps 0 Goals
Born 6th October 1991
2008 Imps (trainee), 2010 Stamford (loan), 2010 Stamford, 2011 Lincoln Moorlands railway, 2012 Lincoln Utd, 2015 Spalding

Former youth team player Nathan Adams made just 5 appearances as a substitute for City without registering a goal. He made his debut in a 1-0 defeat by Exeter City and despite earning a full time deal never managed to break into the first team. His contract was terminated by mutual consent in December 2010 as Chris Sutton culled his squad. He went on to feature in the lower leagues for a host of sides including Lincoln Utd.

Agogo Junior
(1999-2000)
Forward, 3 Apps 1 Goal
Born 1st August 1979
1997–2000 Sheffield Wednesday 2 (0), 1999 Oldham Athletic (loan) 2 (0), 1999 Chester City (loan) 10 (6), 1999 Chesterfield (loan) 4 (0), 1999–2000 Imps (loan), 2000 Chicago Fire 1 (0), 2000–2001 Colorado Rapids 32 (11), 2001 San Jose Earthquakes 14 (4), 2002 Queens Park Rangers 2 (0), 2002– 2003 Barnet 39 (19), 2003–2006 Bristol Rovers 126 (41), 2006–2008 Nottingham Forest 64 (20), 2008–2009 Zamalek SC 15 (4), 2009–2011 Apollon Limassol 24 (6), 2011–2012 Hibernian 12 (1)

Well-travelled Ghanain striker Junior Agogo signed for City on loan from Sheffield Wednesday in 1999. He had previously scored against Lincoln while on loan at Chester. He made an immediate impact scoring on his Imps debut against Shrewsbury but only featured twice more, all three games ending in defeat for City. After a spell in America he picked his career up with prolific spells at Bristol Rovers and Barnet before a couple of seasons with Nottingham Forest. He did return to Sincil Bank with Bristol Rovers in January of 2005, scoring an equaliser in a 1-1 draw before being sent off for making an obscene gesture in his celebration.

16

Ainsworth, Gareth
(1995-1997)
Forward, 97 Apps 41 Goals
Born 10th May 1973
1991–1992 Northwich Victoria 14 (4), 1992 Preston North End 5 (0), 1992–1993 Cambridge United 4 (1), 1992–1993 Northwich Victoria (loan) 5 (0), 1993–1995 Preston North End 82 (12), 1995–1997 Imps, 1997–1998 Port Vale 54 (10), 1998–2003 Wimbledon 36 (6), 2002 Preston North End (loan) 5 (1), 2002–2003 Walsall (loan) 5 (1), 2003 Cardiff City 9 (0), 2003–2010 Queens Park Rangers 141 (36), 2009–2010 Wycombe Wanderers (loan) 2 (0), 2010–2013 Wycombe Wanderers 112 (16)

Gareth Ainsworth was an Imps hero for his goal average of one every two games and his all action committed performances. He had followed manager John Beck from Cambridge to Preston North End and again followed Beck to Sincil Bank for a fee of £25,000 in November of 1995. He made his Imps debut in a 2-1 win at Mansfield and scored his first goals for the club a fortnight later in a 2-0 win at Torquay. He swiftly became a firm fan's favourite due to his on-pitch prowess and his immense personality off the field. He would ensure he always acknowledged the fans in an era where it wasn't common place.

He was ever present in the 1996-97 season during which the Imps missed out on the play-offs on the final day. He formed a formidable front line with veteran striker Phil Stant and towering Dutchman Gjisbert Bos. A Coca Cola cup run ensued with Ainsworth scoring at Premier League Southampton in the third round, and again in the home replay which the Saints won 3-1. His displays and regular goals were earning him a reputation and it was widely expected he would move on to bigger and better things. Despite being a hero Ainsworth wanted to progress, and the more cynical fan noted that his move didn't happen whilst season ticket sales were going on. However a firm offer from Wigan Athletic ahead of the 1997/98 season indicated his Sincil Bank days were numbered. The first few games of the season Ainsworth was subject to some horrific tackling and often had two men marking him. There would have been fear in the board room that the most saleable asset could get injured and leave in the summer on a Bosman free transfer.

A few weeks in to the following season the inevitable happened. After signing off from Sincil Bank with a hat trick against Scarborough, he earned himself a £500,000 move to Port Vale with the Wigan offer rejected. After just 53 appearances for Vale, Premier League Wimbledon paid £2m for his services.

During his time at Lincoln, Ainsworth was twice voted as the Player of the Year and in 2007 was voted fourth in a poll to find the 100 greatest Imps players of all time.

In recent years he has taken over as manager of Wycombe Wanderers with some success, and is a cult figure wherever he has played his football. At Lincoln, he will always be remembered fondly as 'winding, blinding Gareth Ainsworth'.

Alcide, Colin
(1995-1999)
Forward 119 (22) Apps, 31 Goals
Born 14th April 1972
1991–1992 Emley, 1992–1993 Altrincham 3 (0), 1994–1995 Emley, 1995–1999 Imps, 1999 Hull City (loan) 3 (1), 1999 Hull City 24 (3), 1999–2001 York City 53 (7), 2001–2002 Cambridge United 8 (0), 2002–2003 Gainsborough Trinity, 2002–2003 Exeter City 1 (0), 2004–2005 TNS 2 (0), 2004–2005 Ashton United 11 (2)

Bustling striker Alcide arrived from non-league Emley shortly after manager John Beck took over at Sincil Bank. Alcide was a classic John Beck style centre forward, big and uncompromising. As we took to knocking balls long the figure of Alcide was often seen rising high for a flick on. His goal ratio wasn't the best, it took him three months to find the net for City before he finally broke his duck in a 4-2 home defeat by Wigan. On the final day of the 1995-96 season he bagged a brace as City ran out 5-0 winners over Torquay.

He missed just four games of the 1996-97 season and was occasionally amongst the goals, most notably on the score sheet in a 4-1 demolition of Manchester City in the Coca Cola Cup. He saw promotion the season after with Lincoln and played half a season in the third tier before John Reames took over from Shane Westley. Alcide was the subject of bids from Plymouth Argyle and Colchester Utd in January 1999, and both bids were accepted by manager John Reames. An agents representitve then got involved and demanded a percentage of the sale to force the moves through. Both collapsed.

As Lincoln tried to play a bit more football he was loaned out to fourth tier side Hull in February 1999. He returned for one game, a 1-0 defeat by Fulham before his move to Hull was made permanent.

Allon, Joe
(1995)
Forward 4 (1) Apps 0 Goals
Born 12th November 1966
1984–1987 Newcastle United 9 (2), 1987–1988 Swansea City 34 (12), 1988–1991 Hartlepool United 112 (48), 1991–1992 Chelsea 14 (2), 1992 Port Vale (loan) 6 (0), 1992–1994 Brentford 45 (19), 1993 Southend United (loan) 3 (0), 1994–1995 Port Vale 23 (9), 1995 Imps, 1995–1998 Hartlepool United 56 (19)

Well-travelled striker Joe Allon arrived at Sincil Bank ahead of the 1995-96 season. He had some pedigree and Imps fans expected a goal machine. He'd made his name at Hartlepool before earning a move to top flight Chelsea, and although that didn't pan out much was expected of him. However, after just four starts for City he left to return to his native North east.

Of those four starts he didn't finish a single game. He was subbed in all three league games and sent off in his solitary league cup appearance. Of course after he left he managed to score against the Imps for Hartlepool. He went from being 'Super Joe Allon' to 'Goofy Joe Allon' in just a few short months, although I think the Super Joe tag was more optimism than fact.

Allon was one of a number of talented goal scorers who suffered dry runs when turning out for the Imps, like Phil Stant before him and Leo Fortune-West after him.

Almond, Louis
(2012)
Forward 3 (2) Apps 1 Goal
Born 5th Jan 1992
2009–2014 Blackpool 1 (0), 2010 Cheltenham Town (loan) 4 (0), 2011 Barrow (loan) 20 (2), 2011–2012 Barrow (loan) 23 (1), 2012 Imps (loan), 2012–2013 Barrow (loan) 11 (2), 2013 Hyde (loan) 13 (2), 2013–2014 Hyde (loan) 28 (1), 2014 Hyde 1 (0), 2015–2016 Southport 59 (17), 2016 Tranmere Rovers 5 (0)

Almond was a striker initially brought in from Blackpool as David Holdsworth looked to find a formula that could keep us in the National League. He scored a last-minute equaliser on his Imps debut against Braintree on Valentine's Day in 2012 after coming off the bench. After just 3 starts and another appearance from the bench he went back to Blackpool and signed a new one year deal. He dropped into the non-league game but has recently shown good form at Southport which earned him a surprise move to promotion chasing Tranmere Rovers.

Amoo, Ryan
(2006-2008)
Midfielder 51 (12) Apps, 3 Goals
Born 11 Oct, 1983
2000–2004 Aston Villa 0 (0), 2004 Northampton Town (loan) 1 (0), 2004–2005 Northampton Town 5 (0), 2005 Highfield Rangers, 2005–2006 Barrow Town, 2006–2008 Imps, 2008–2009 Barwell, 2009 Thurnby Rangers, 2009 Stamford, 2009–2010 Thurnby Rangers, 2010 Solihull Moors, 2010 Halesowen Town, 2010-2011 Solihull Moors 3 (0), 2011 Thurnby Nirvana

Imps of a certain age will remember the chant 'Amoo, Amoo, Amoo is on fire'. For one game he certainly was on fire scoring twice two days before Christmas in 2006 to cancel out a Peter Gain strike for Posh. Amoo was a cult hero, loved by some Imps fans for his one superb display.

He came to City from the non-league scene having served his apprenticeship with Villa and then having a short spell with Northampton. It was there he managed to indulge himself in an 11-month relationship with reality TV star Jade Goody. By the time he arrived at Sincil Bank he was better known for his choice of female partner than he was for his footballing prowess. He was a slightly built wide player who came billed as having a nice touch and turn of pace, but failed to impress himself on any match he played in, bar one.

His other Lincoln goal came in a 1-1 draw with Macclesfield in October 2007 to earn the last point John Schofield registered as manager. When Schofield left Amoo found his chances more than limited and he was on his way. He has done the rounds in the Midlands non-league scene since turning out for Solihull Moors amongst others but despite those two goals at Peterborough he never showed anything else to warrant a third crack at league football. He may have drifted off into obscurity, but every so often an Imps fan is reminded of that two-goal showing against Peterborough Utd, where for 90 minutes Amoo was on fire.

Anderson, Harry
(2016- Current)
Midfielder 9 (5) Apps 4 Goals
Born 9th January 1997
2015 Peterborough United 14 (0), 2016 Braintree Town (loan) 2 (0), 2016 St Albans City (loan) 11 (1), 2016 Imps

Harry Anderson is currently on-loan from Peterborough United, and is fast developing into a key player for City. He has a direct style of play which involves running at defenders and all-too often beating them for both pace and power. He's already weighed in with four goals this campaign, and any success in the National League in 2016/17 will be dependent on retaining his services into the New Year. He dropped out of the side for a short while at the beginning of the season to give him a rest, but since his return he has looked as sharp as a razor and twice as dangerous.

Anderson has been passed to play in the FA Cup by his parent club which could be a signal of their intention to let him remain out on loan, but the presence of Barry Fry at a recent game shows he is still on their radar, and if his performance levels remain the same as the first part of the season then it might be hard for Peterborough not to take him back.

Anderson, Joe
(2009-2011)
Defender 46 (4) Apps 0 Goals
Born 13th October 1989
2008–2010 Fulham 0 (0), 2009 Woking (loan) 14 (1), 2010–2011 Imps, 2011–2012 AFC Hornchurch 40 (1), 2012–2013 Billericay Town 18 (0), 2013 Cambridge United 5 (0), 2013 Bromley 144 (6)

Full back arrived courtesy of Chris Sutton's contacts originally on loan from Fulham. After a successful loan spell, he made his move permanent in July 2010. He was in the side that lost 3-0 to Aldershot on the last day of that season to be relegated to the National League, as well as featuring in the 6-0 reverse at home to Rotherham and the 4-0 drubbing at home to Gillingham.

Unsurprisingly he was released by Steve Tilson as we dropped into the National League. Ironically it is in the National League he has discovered his best form, currently featuring for Bromley.

Anderson, Tom
(2014)
Defender 6 Apps 1 Goal
Born 2nd September 1993
2012 Burnley 0 (0), 2012–2013 Barrow (loan) 18 (0), 2013 Hyde (loan) 4 (0), 2013–2014 FC Halifax Town (loan) 1 (0), 2014 Imps (loan), 2014–2015 Carlisle United (loan) 8 (0), 2016 Chesterfield (loan) 18 (0), 2016 Chesterfield (loan) 9 (0)

Anderson signed on loan at the beginning of the 2014/15 season towards the end of Gary Simpson's reign as manager. A towering centre half, he helped Lincoln to two clean sheets during his tenure and even weighed in with a goal in a 1-1 draw with Gateshead. Upon completion of his loan spell he returned to Burnley and has since spent time out on loan in the Football League for Carlisle and latterly Chesterfield.

Anyon, Joe
(2010-2012)
Goalkeeper 64 Appearances, 0 Goals
Born 29th December 1986
2004–2010, Port Vale 109 (0), 2005 Stafford Rangers (loan) 5 (0), 2005 Stafford Rangers (loan) 5 (0), 2005 Harrogate Town (loan) 2 (0), 2006 Harrogate Town (loan) 9 (0), 2010–2012 Imps, 2011 Morecambe (loan) 4 (0), 2012–2014 Shrewsbury Town 11 (0), 2013 Macclesfield Town (loan) 0 (0), 2015 Crewe Alexandra 0 (0), 2015 Scunthorpe United 8 (0)

Talented keeper Anyon was signed as a replacement for the departing Rob Burch but fell out of favour once Chris Sutton left as manager. He was in goal the night we lost 5-0 at home to Bury which prompted him to fall further out of favour with Steve Tilson. He was guilty of several errors in his early Imps career which cost him dearly in terms of starts later in the season.

He was kept on the bench whilst a succession of young keepers failed miserably to keep us in the league, even spending time out on loan at Morecombe. Upon relegation, he still wasn't fancied and was farmed out on loan to Shrewsbury until the completion of his contract. He's recently been back up keeper to League One high-flyers Scunthorpe United.

Appleton, Michael
(1995)
Midfielder 5 Apps 0 Goals
Born 4ᵗʰ December 1975
1994–1997 Manchester United 0 (0), 1995 Wimbledon (loan) 0 (0), 1995 Imps (loan), 1997 Grimsby Town (loan) 10 (3), 1997–2001 Preston North End 121 (12), 2001–2003 West Bromwich Albion 33 (0)

Appleton was a midfielder signed from Manchester Utd on loan to get first team football. He made five uninspiring appearances before returning to Old Trafford. His career was cut short by a knee injury and he has since moved into management with several clubs including Blackpool, Blackburn and Oxford where he is managing at the time of writing.

Arnaud, Jean
(2011)
Defender 0 (1) Apps 0 Goals
Born 7ᵗʰ April 1987
2011 Imps, 2012 KVK Tienen

French defender Arnaud was signed by beleaguered manager Steve Tilson to try and stop the flow of goals that was to ultimately cost him his job. He made his only appearance as a 63ʳᵈ minute substitute in a 4-0 defeat away at Tamworth that signalled the end of Tilson, and ultimately the end of Arnaud. Later linked up with former Imps team mates Jean-Francois Christophe and Francis Laurent in Belgium.

If all he did was help cost Steve Tilson his job, then he deserves his place in history.

Arnold, Nathan
(2016- Current)
Midfielder 18 Apps 5 Goals
Born 26ᵗʰ July 1987
2005–2009 Mansfield Town 104 (13), 2009–2010 Hyde United 35 (9), 2010–2013 Alfreton Town 109 (23), 2013–2015 Cambridge United 35 (3), 2014–2015 Grimsby Town (loan) 35 (6), 2015–2016 Grimsby Town 40 (8), 2016 Imps

Nathan Arnold is an experienced and talented wide player who raised a few eyebrows by turning down a contract in the Football League with Grimsby to sign for Lincoln. One thing the Imps have lacked in recent years are wide men, especially wide men who perform at their best consistently. In Nathan Arnold, we have a dedicated and experienced professional who not only can switch wings but also lifts the younger players around him.

He has a keen eye for goal too and is averaging around one every three games for City which is as good a return as he's had all through his career. He isn't your stereotypical footballer; he owns a hairdressing salon in Grimsby and comes across as a shy and thoughtful individual. When he is on the ball though, he can be devastating and Grimsby fans were genuinely gutted that he opted to sign for The Imps.

Having tasted success at National League level he knows what is required and aside from missing two games through injury it's no surprise he's been one of the first names on the team sheet every week.

Arthur, Koby
(2014)
Midfielder 2 (4) Apps 0 Goals
Born 31ˢᵗ January 1996
2013 Birmingham City 12 (0), 2014 Imps, 2014 Cheltenham Town (loan) 7 (3), 2016 Cheltenham Town (loan) 1 (0)

Arthur joined on loan from Birmingham along with Charlee Adams and Nick Townsend initially on a month-long loan. Whilst he showed glimpses of his class he only started two games for City and was brought off at half time in both. He returned to Birmingham after a month and has since spent time on loan at Cheltenham. He's still rated as one for the future.

Asamoah, Derek
(2005-2006)
Forward 32 (11) Apps, 2 Goals
Born 1ˢᵗ May 1981
2000–2001 Slough Town 8 (3), 2001–2004 Northampton Town 112 (30), 2004–2005 Mansfield Town 30 (5), 2005–2006 Imps 2006 Chester City (loan) 17 (8), 2006–2007 Shrewsbury Town 39 (10), 2007–2009 OGC Nice 0 (0), 2009 Hamilton Academicals 3 (0), 2009–2010 Lokomotiv Sofia 36 (13), 2011–2012 Pohang Steelers 56 (13), 2013 Daegu FC 33 (4), 2014–2016 Carlisle United 67 (10)

Asamoah signed for the Imps after falling out with then Mansfield Town boss Carlton Palmer. He was lightening quick and showed lots of promise but struggled badly with finding the back of the net. Both his goals came at Sincil Bank, one in a 2-1 win over Oxford and another in a 3-1 win against Chester. His performance in that game prompted Chester to take him on loan where he scored four times as many goals in just 17 games as he managed in 43 for Lincoln. Since then he's played in a couple of different countries and represented Ghana four times, scoring once.

Asamoah always threatened to be a potent force in League Two for City, but he was found wanting when we needed him most. He was quick, one of the quickest players I've ever seen for Lincoln. He did seem to have just pace in his locker though, and a lack of end product contributed to his abysmally low goal count.

When he left Keith Alexander echoed my comments; "I'm sorry to see him go as he's been a good servant to the club, albeit at times you want more of an end product. He's a crowd pleaser and a likeable lad and I wish him all the best."

Audel, Thierry
(2014, 2014)
Defender 18 Apps 3 Goals
Born 15ᵗʰ Jan 1987
2006–2007 Auxerre 0 (0), 2007 Izola 0 (0), 2007–2010 Triestina 6 (1), 2008–2009, San Marino (loan), 2010–2012 Pisa 29 (0), 2013 Macclesfield Town 19 (1), 2013–2015 Crewe Alexandra 4 (0), 2014 Imps, 2014–2015 Imps (loan) 3 (0), 2015Macclesfield Town 12 (2), 2015 Notts County 16 (1)

6'2 French defender Audel first signed on loan for City in January of 2013. He made his Imps debut in a 3-1 win over Halifax and notched his first Imps goal a couple of games later in a 4-3 win at Hyde Utd. Audel quickly endeared himself to fans who clamoured to have him sign permanently although he did look a cut above the National League. He started the next season for Crewe but fell out of favour after a 6-1 thumping by MK Dons.

He returned to City on loan shortly afterwards under Gary Simpson but his second spell wasn't as fruitful. In just his second game the Imps drew 3-3 with Forest Green in a match that lost Simpson his job, and after two more defeat Audel left as well. He spent time on loan at Macclesfield in the National League before securing league football with Notts County.

Austin, Kevin
(1996-1999)
Defender 145 (1) Apps 2 Goals
Born 12th February 1973
1992–1993 Saffron Walden Town 8 (0), 1993–1996 Leyton Orient 109 (3), 1996–1999 Imps, 1999–2001 Barnsley 3 (0), 2000–2000 Brentford (loan) 3 (0), 2001–2002 Cambridge United 6 (0), 2001–2002 Kettering Town 3 (0), 2002–2004 Bristol Rovers 56 (0), 2004–2008 Swansea City 117 (0), 2008–2010Chesterfield 54 (0), 2010–2011Darlington 12 (0), 2011 Boston United (loan) 14 (0), 2011–2012 Boston United 25 (0)

Kevin Austin was arguably one of the best full backs to ply his trade at Sincil Bank in a generation. Whilst at Leyton Orient he had featured in a documentary called 'Club for a Quid' that ultimately ruined the career of manager John Sitton.

He was signed for £30,000 by John Beck as part of a 'buy me a player' campaign and he always looked destined to bigger and better things. He made his debut in a 2-1 defeat at lowly Torquay in a season where Lincoln missed out on the play-offs by just a point. Austin had it all, pace and power with a fearsome tackle to match. He was on the pitch for the Coca Cola cup wins over Man City and he was part of the team that took Premier League Southampton back to Sincil Bank.

The following season he was a key player in our automatic promotion charge. John Beck's team at the time was built on strength and the ability to defend as if their lives depended on it and Austin looked every inch the leader and inspiration behind the clubs rise. Whilst in the third tier he scored what turned out to be the winning goal in our 2-1 home win over Manchester City, but could not stop the Imps sliding back into the basement division. He was only sent off once in his Imps career, a 76th minute dismissal in a tempestuous 3-2 defeat at Notts County during which former Imp Gary Strodder was sent off for punching Tony Battersby.

It came as no surprise when he secured a move to Barnsley on a Bosman after three stellar years playing for Lincoln and many fans felt that he'd quickly ascend the divisions in the same way Gareth Ainsworth did. Disaster struck in only his third game for Barnsley, ironically back at Sincil Bank in the Coca Cola cup. He suffered an Achilles tendon injury in a challenge with Peter Gain that ruled him out for the season and he never returned the same player. He had a plethora of clubs, most notably Swansea but was never able to recapture the scintillating form that had him voted at number 56 in the Imps all-time top 100 legends.

Tim Priestley's view

"Super, super Kev, super, super Kev, super, super Kev, super Kevin Austin!"

Any regular watchers of the Imps in the mid to late nineties will remember, with fondness, our colossus at the back. Brought in by John Beck amid scenes of collection buckets being passed around to fund his transfer from Leyton Orient, Kevin made an immediate impact at Sincil Bank. The man was an Everest. He commanded the back line, subdued forwards and would see the ball out to safety, blocking opposing players like a lion imposing itself on a mouse. Let's not forget that he wasn't just a barricade of muscle and flesh. He could pass, had pace and a steady temperament. In short, he was one of the best defenders to grace the hallowed turf – held in the same regard by the faithful as Thompson, Peake, Walling and McAuley.

Surprisingly for a tall defender, he scored few goals at a time when Lincoln relied on set-pieces. One of them would come against Manchester City at a time when we were in the same division. However, he should be remembered more for the goal he prevented that evening at Sincil Bank. The ball was going in, but 'the doorman' seemingly defied gravity to clear it from the goal line. His stay at Lincoln would span 128 games before a transfer (on a Bosman) to Barnsley. Sadly, he would injure his Achilles tendon (ironically playing against us) which curbed his pace and performance. A single international cap for Trinidad and Tobago and appearances with Cambridge, Bristol Rovers and Swansea followed but the injury betrayed his potential. Super Kev playing at the top level? Would have been a solid possibility.

Austin, Mitchell
(2014)
Forward 4 (2) Apps 0 Goals
Born 3rd April 1991
2010-2013 Stalybridge Celtic 69 (10), 2013- 2015 Cambridge Utd 9 (0), 2014 Imps (loan), 2014 Brackley (loan) 9 (2), 2014-2015 Southport (loan) 8 (0), 2015-2016 Central Coast 23 (5), 2016 - Melbourne Victory

Australian forward Austin signed on loan towards the end of the 2013-2014 season from fellow National League side Cambridge United. He made four appearances, two as a substitute without having any significant impact before returning to The U's. After a short spell at Southport he returned to his native Australia where he currently plays for Melbourne Victory under Kevin Muscat.

Bacon – Butcher

Bacon, Danny
(2005-2007)
Forward 1 (2) Apps 0 Goals
Born 20th September 1980
1998–2003 Mansfield Town 44 (4), 2003–2005 Hucknall Town 83 (30). 2005–2007 Imps, 2005–2006 Burton Albion (loan) 5 (0), 2006–2007 Worksop Town (loan) 10 (2), 2007 Hednesford Town 13 (0), 2007–2009 Hucknall Town 28 (8)

Forward Bacon spent his early years at Mansfield Town before dropping into the non-league scene with Hucknall. A goal every two and a half games prompted Keith Alexander to take a punt on him in 2005. He featured in the season opener at Notts County and as a substitute in the fine 5-1 win against Crewe Alexandra in the Carling Cup.

He then picked up an injury whilst out on loan at Burton Albion, a broken leg which ruled him out for the season. Once he regained fitness Keith gave him another chance and another 1 year deal. He picked up another injury after a clash with Jason Lee and he simply couldn't bounce back from that. He eventually left by mutual consent in 2007 without another appearance to his name, and spent the rest of his career drifting around the non-league scene in the Midlands.

Bailey, Dennis
(1998)
Forward 1 (4) Apps 0 Goals
Born 13th December 1965
1986–1987 Fulham 0 (0), 1987 Farnborough Town 16 (3), 1987–1989 Crystal Palace 5 (1), 1989 Bristol Rovers (loan) 17 (9), 1989–1991 Birmingham City 75 (23), 1991 Bristol Rovers (loan) 6 (1), 1991–1995 Queens Park Rangers 40 (10), 1993–1994 Charlton Athletic (loan) 4 (0), 1994 Watford (loan) 8 (4), 1995 Brentford (loan) 6 (3), 1995–1998 Gillingham 88 (11), 1998 Imps, 1998–1999 Farnborough Town 30 (13), 1999 Cheltenham Town 8 (2), 1999–2001 Forest Green Rovers 60 (9), 2001 Aberystwyth Town, 2001–2002 Tamworth 7 (2), 2002–2003 Stafford Rangers 30 (12), 2003–2004 Moor Green 24 (3)

To give him his full name, Dennis Lincoln Bailey was perhaps best known for scoring a hat trick against Manchester United for QPR prior to arriving at Sincil Bank. He is still the last player to have scored a hat trick at Old Trafford and come away on the winning side, QPR running out 4-1 winners. He came to Lincoln towards the end of the 1998 season to bolster our play off ambitions. He made just one start and came off the bench four times. He was initially credited with scoring the final goal in our 2-2 draw with Darlington which not only secured a play-off spot but left us in with a shout of automatic promotion. In recent years, the goal has been credited to Terry Fleming, not the first time Terry has been involved in a case of mistaken identity! His last appearance was as a 90th minute substitute in the 2-1 win over Brighton that saw us seal automatic promotion.

Bailey, Mark
(2001-2004)
Defender 109 (2) Apps 4 Goals
Born 12th August 1976

1994–1997 Stoke City 0 (0), 1996–1999 Rochdale 67 (1), 1999–2000 Winsford United, 1999–2000 Lancaster City, 1999–2001 Northwich Victoria 61 (2), 2001–2004 Imps, 2004–2006Macclesfield Town 26 (2), 2006–2007 Peterborough United 0 (0), 2006–2007 Stafford Rangers 2 (0)

Former Stoke City trainee Mark Bailey was arguably the best right back of a generation to ply his trade at Sincil Bank. He was the definition of a box to box player with the ability to get up and down the line for 90 minutes. He could deliver a decent ball for a centre forward but was equally as adept at booting a flash winger into the advertising hoardings and winning the ball at the same time.

He signed for Lincoln from Northwich Victoria having played there under Keith Alexander and he served his former manager well in an Imps shirt. He survived those dark days of administration and went on to be an integral part of the Imps team that made the 2003 play-off final. He was also instrumental in taking us to the semi-finals the year after and even scored to put us ahead on aggregate in the second leg against Huddersfield.

Bails has become the benchmark by which Lincoln full-backs are measured by fans of a certain age. Bradley Wood is as close to Bailey as we have, but as yet Wood hasn't scored from inside his own half, as Bailey did away at Carlisle.

He left after the failure to make the finals and in June of 2004 he signed for Macclesfield Town. Injuries hampered his career there and he was unlucky to miss out on a play-off final appearance as Macclesfield lost to the Imps in the semi-final. He joined up with former manager Keith Alexander for a third time in 2006 signing a month to month deal with Peterborough, but only appeared twice before retiring from the game.

Baker, Nathan
(2009-2010)
Defender 17 (1) Apps 0 Goals
Born 23rd April 1991
2009 Aston Villa 80 (0), 2009–2010 Imps (loan), 2011 Millwall (loan) 6 (0), 2015–2016 Bristol City (loan) 36 (1)

Young defender Nathan Baker signed on loan from Aston Villa along with team mates Chris Herd and Eric Lichaj. He was one of the loan generation that Chris Sutton used to just keep us in the league in the 2009/10 season. He made 18 first team appearances and looked useful if not a little naïve at times. Since Lincoln he has represented England up to Under-21 level and played over 80 senior games for Aston Villa and he looks to have a bright future ahead of him.

Bannister, Gary
(1994-1995)
Forward 29 (5) Apps 8 Goals
Born 22nd July 1960
1978–1981 Coventry City 22 (3), 1980 Detroit Express (loan) 22 (10), 1981–1984 Sheffield Wednesday 118 (55), 1984–1988 Queens Park Rangers 136 (56), 1988–1990 Coventry City 43 (11), 1990–1992West Bromwich Albion 72 (18), 1992 Oxford United (loan) 10 (2), 1992–1993 Nottingham Forest 31 (8), 1993Stoke City 15 (2), 1993–1994 Hong Kong Rangers, 1994–1995 Imps, 1995–1996 Darlington 41 (10)

Veteran forward who came to the club towards the end of a successful career in top flight football. Despite not troubling the international scene Bannister was a feared striker in Division One during the 1980's with prolific spells at Sheff Weds, QPR and a short stay at Coventry. He continued to score well in the lower divisions and even when he reached us he was still sharp in front of goal.

On his arrival manager Sam Ellis commented that; "Gary has scored goals consistently throughout his career and is an important addition to the squad". A satisfactory return of a goal every three games or so was adequate if not spectacular for a player nearing the end of his career. He netted on the day the Linpave Stand (now the Coop Stand) opened as we beat Hartlepool 3-0. He managed another season after Sincil Bank at Darlington where he was unsurprisingly amongst the goals. Spent time in property development in Cornwall after he finished playing.

Baraclough, Ian
(1992-1994)
Defender 86 (5) Apps 11 Goals
Born 4th December 1970
1988–1991 Leicester City 0 (0), 1990 Wigan Athletic (loan) 9 (2), 1990 Grimsby Town (loan) 4 (0), 1991–1992 Grimsby Town 1 (0), 1992–1994 Imps, 1994–1995Mansfield Town 47 (5), 1995–1998 Notts County 111 (10), 1998–2001 Queens Park Rangers 125 (12), 2001–2004 Notts County 101 (18), 2004–2008 Scunthorpe United 134 (18)

Barraclough could operate in defence or midfield and offered an imposing figure wherever he played. He stood at 6'1 but could get up and down the left flank as mobile as any full back. Signed for us from Grimsby after a short loan spell and went on to make over 90 appearances for the club. It came as some shock when he was allowed to leave for Mansfield Town, but the run of games at Sincil Bank helped set him up for a stellar career at Notts County and Queens Park Rangers.

After his playing career, he moved into coaching under Nigel Adkins at Scunthorpe United and eventually succeeded him as manager. He also manager Sligo Rovers and Motherwell before taking on the assistant manager role at Oldham Athletic. Whilst at Scunthorpe he was one of a few select managers who appeared as an item in the popular online FIFA Ultimate Team mode.

Barnett, David
(1999-2000)
Defender 25 (2) Apps 4 Goals
Born 16th April 1967
1985–1986 Boldmere St. Michaels, 1986–1987 Alvechurch, 1987–1988 Windsor & Eton, 1988–1989 Colchester United 20 (0), 1989 Edmonton Brickmen, 1989–1990 West Bromwich Albion 0 (0), 1990 Walsall 5 (0), 1990–1992 Kidderminster Harriers 39 (4), 1992–1994 Barnet 59 (3), 1993 Birmingham City (loan) 2 (0), 1994–1997 Birmingham City 44 (0), 1997–1998 Dunfermline Athletic 21 (1), 1998 Port Vale (loan) 9 (1) 1998–1999 Port Vale 27 (0), 1999–2000 Imps, 2000 Forest Green Rovers (loan) 3 (0), 2001 Halesowen Town

A classic journeyman centre half signed in the close season of 1999/00 season as we dropped back into the basement division. Originally nicknamed 'psycho' by Colchester fans after being sent off twice in his first seven matches he ended up as an uninspiring defender. Came to Lincoln towards the end of his career and lacked both pace and direction. Scored four times for City including a late equaliser in the FA Cup tie with Luton in 1999. As we struggled to make an impact in the league he was farmed out to Forest Green before leaving at the end of his contract.

Dave Barnett never looked like being the answer to our problems, even if that problem was how to keep a seat warm on the bench. Described by Deranged Ferret at the time thus; "To say he once played at a higher level makes the mind boggle. To be brutally honest he has proved to be a nightmare making mistake after mistake and has been one of the main reasons behind City's awful goals conceded record." Damning stuff.

Barnett, Jason
(1995 – 2002)
Defender 218 (20) Apps, 6 Goals
Born 21st April 1976
1994–1995 Wolverhampton Wanderers 0 (0), 1995–2002 Imps, 2002 Lincoln United

Very much a one club man and a name that often goes unnoticed when talking about former Imps stalwarts. Playing over 200 games for one club should almost entitle you to a place in folklore but Jason Barnett rarely gets mentioned as a great. He was a lynchpin of the John Beck 'up and at them' side of 1996, forever punching the ball down the line into danger alley. He loved a tackle and he loved a chase, but a lack of goals and threat going forward means he didn't get noticed as much as maybe he should.

He always had rumours of a move to a bigger club surrounding him but he always stayed true to Lincoln City, eventually leaving as the club entered administration. Suffered from being a good player in a bad side towards the end of his Imps career which is a real shame. Stayed in the City after he finished with the Imps, playing for Lincoln United and working for a taxi rank in town.

Apparently singing 'He's a baby' at him in a taxi rank does not have the same affect as singing in to him from the terraces, so just for reference I wouldn't try it.

Barraclough, Bradley
(2011-2013)
Forward 4 (9) Apps 0 Goals
Born 26th May 1989
2011 Imps, 2011 Buxton (loan), 2012 Gainsborough Trinity (loan), 2013 Gainsborough Trinity, 2014 Bradford Park Avenue, 2015 Spalding

Young forward Barraclough came to Lincoln in the summer of 2011 after we dropped out of the league. Initially he looked to have a lot of promise all packaged up with pace as a condiment. He struggled to impress himself on games when given a chance and he ended up at Buxton on loan. Once Steve Tilson left Bradley never found a way back and he drifted into the lower reaches of the non-league scene.

Bassele, Aristede
(2012)
Midfield 1 (1) Apps 0 Goals
Born 15th June 1994
2012 Hayes and Yeading 4 (0), 2012 Imps (loan), 2014- Welling 26 (2)

One of the enormous numbers of average or non-descript players signed by David Holdsworth in an attempt to keep us in the National League. Came on in the last minute of a 3-2 home win against Hereford and then started the next match, a 2-0 home defeat by Woking. Came off at half time and wasn't seen at Sincil Bank again. Most recently been kicking around Welling's reserve team. If they've got one.

Battersby, Tony
(1998-2002)
Forward 108 (39) Apps 26 Goals
Born 30th August 1975
1993–1996 Sheffield United 10 (1), 1994–1995 Southend United (loan) 8 (1), 1995 BK-IFK (loan) 18 (24), 1995–1997 Notts County 39 (8), 1996–1998 Bury 48 (8), 1998–2003 Imps, 1999–2000 Northampton Town (loan) 3 (1), 2002–2003 Boston United 11 (1), 2002–2003Hucknall Town 1 (1), 2002–2003 Rushden & Diamonds 5 (0), 2002–2004 Stevenage Borough 19 (6), 2003–2004 Gravesend & Northfleet 1 (0), 2003–2004 Cambridge City 6 (1), 2004–2005 King's Lynn 12 (4), 2004–2006 Grays Athletic 34 (9), 2005–2006 AFC Wimbledon 7 (1), 2006–2007 Chelmsford City 9 (0), 2006–2007 Welling United (loan) 13 (2)

I was excited by the arrival of Tony Battersby. On the computer game 'Championship Manager' he had been rated a £2.2m when at Notts County, and when the Imps paid out a record fee for him I expected big things. At first he seemed an inspired signing. Tony Battersby definitely had ability and was prone to the odd moment of absolute genius. Those moments were rare, and the longer he stayed the rarer thay became. His goals weren't enough to keep us in the third tier, but he did seem to have enough in his locker to help us get promoted back up.

He didn't, and as his Imps career bumbled along it became clear he was in decline from the moment he signed for the club. He weighed in with a goal here and another one there but he never made a significant enough impact to be anything other than a squad player. Towards the end of his time with Lincoln he looked unfit and short on motivation and it wasn't a surprise when his contract was terminated in October 2002. To cement his position as a pantomime villain he immediately signed for rivals Boston United, and so began his one-man tour of every non-league club in the country. I'm sure if you were to look him up today he would still be putting in an appearance he and there at a John Smiths Paint League Division Six outfit. He might even be playing for your pub team. For now.

Chris Gooding's view

1998 to 1999 as a Lincoln City fan was a season that stands out on many levels, embarking on a season in League One after a deserved promotion under guidance of Shane Westley. Albeit most of the hard work previously done by Manager John Beck before his sacking which in my opinion was not about football matters.

That summer was an important one for Lincoln as we entered a league that was full of clubs such as Manchester City, Stoke City, Preston North End and most notably Kevin Keegan's Fulham team whose front line included ex Newcastle and England striker Peter Beardsley.

For mighty Imps to survive they needed to show intent in Player recruitment and my theory was backed by the £75,000 arrival of Tony Battersby from Bury. Tony was seen at the time as the potent striker that was to score goals to ensure an immediate return to League Two was not on the cards. To many fans of clubs at our level, spending money that is to go down in history books as a record transfer fee, your instant reaction is you're securing a ready-made player that's going to hit the ground running.

With Tony Battersby this was not the case, he flattered to deceive on many occasions and whilst I can't say he was a bad player, I can't say he was money well spent either because I don't know. Any player that plays 130 games for a team, must have had something about them to keep getting on the team sheet. In his case being picked by 3 different Managers in his Lincoln tenure. Although the appointment of Alan Buckley certainly helped Tony get to that mark by instantly giving him an improved 3-year contract which would have surprised many fans.

In my opinion he would usually start a game relatively slow, some neat and nice touches to get you interested. You would think here is the Battersby we want to see before swiftly returning to type by retreating from games. This is what I found the most difficult thing to understand because it was clear that he had a football brain, he could thread a through ball to a teammate on a sixpence but glaringly, if he'd had the desire to be involved for the full 90 minutes then I believe we would be talking about Tony Battersby in a different light. Footballers that can do that usually are much sought after and would find themselves moving up the football pyramid, toward the most lucrative league of them all, the Premiership.

Tony's career didn't find its way to the promised land, it rapidly went the other way. The sacking of a clear fan in Alan Buckley and the appointment of Keith Alexander saw Tony's time at Lincoln come to abrupt end which I suspect was partly down to the state of the finance of the club. I believe Keith already knew as his role as Assistant Manager previously under Alan, he was never going to be the player a record transfer player should be and the decision was made.

After Lincoln, I never did follow his career but a quick glance of his Wikipedia tells you the same. There are managers who obviously see something and in his later career, his tour of the Lincolnshire non-league scene testifies to this. Tony Battersby will be a mystery and after all this time, I still don't know.

Beardsley, Jason
(2011-2012)
Defender 0 (1) Apps 0 Goals
Born 12th July 1989
2007–2009 Derby County 0 (0), 2008 Notts County (loan) 11 (0), 2010 FC Tampa Bay 0 (0), 2010–2011 Macclesfield Town 0 (0), 2010 Eastwood Town (loan) 2 (0), 2011 Mickleover Sports, 2011 Stafford Rangers 0 (0), 2011–2012 Imps, 2012–2013 Uttoxeter Town, 2013 Eastwood Town, 2013 Worcester City 2 (0)

Jason Beardsley played just 30 minutes of football for Lincoln coming on in the 60th minute of a Boxing Day clash with Grimsby Town. Within just a minute of coming on Liam Hearn scored the winner for Grimsby. Like most of Holdsworth's loan signings Beardsley wasn't seen at Sincil Bank again and drifted into non-league football.

Beevers, Lee
(2005-2009, 2015- Current)
Defender 229 (16) Apps 11 Goals
Born 4th December 1983
2001–2003 Ipswich Town 0 (0), 2003 Boston United (loan) 1 (0), 2003–2005 Boston United 71 (3), 2004–2009 Imps, 2009–2011 Colchester United 23 (0), 2011–2012 Walsall 35 (0), 2012–2015 Mansfield Town 97 (3), 2015 Imps

Of all the current squad Lee Beevers is one of the most experienced having not only made almost 250 appearances for Lincoln, but also having played at a good standard in the Football League. He caught the eye whilst playing for county rivals Boston United after starting out at Ipswich as a youth. His impressive performances convinced a promotion chasing Keith Alexander to spend an 'undisclosed amount' to bring him to Sincil Bank. Although primarily a right back Lee found himself employed all across the defence, often in the left back position. Whilst employed out of position he still put in committed and full-bloodied performances. He continued to do the same after Keith left, and looked perhaps his most settled whilst playing under Peter Jackson.

All good things must come to an end and eventually Beevers opted to sign for Colchester, which represented a climb up the football ladder for him. He always committed himself to City and left having made over 170 outings in an Imps shirt.

In May of 2015 Lee signed a new 2-year deal with City after being released by Mansfield Town. He was the second ex-Stag to join in a week, teammate Matt Rhead also putting pen to paper on a deal. Beevers arrival was thought by some to be no more than to offer cover for the defensive positions, assuming he would be past his best. A difficult 2015/16 season saw him utilised at left back, and although he performed adequately, it did look like his last season at National League level. The arrival of Danny and Nicky Cowley changed all that, and at the start of the 2016/17 season he began to show the sort of form he had exhibited the very first time he played for Lincoln. He slotted in at his preferred right back and was a revelation, prompting many fans to favour keeping Bradley Wood in midfield to allow Beevers a run in the team. Indeed, when he was dropped and Tom Champion came into the side, the Imps went on a losing run. When Lee was restored to the team we went on yet another unbeaten run.

Tragically Lee suffered a ruptured patella tendon during our home win against Boreham Wood in October 2016, an injury that looks set to rule him out for the remainder of the season. His experience and knowledge will still doubtless prove useful off the pitch as he takes the long road to recovery.

Oscar Chamberlain's view

When I started my Sports Journalism degree back in 2008, one of the first assignments given to me was to interview a professional athlete. It was quite a daunting task because I had never done anything like that before and I didn't know any professional athletes or how to go about contacting them.

After a few failed attempts to find a suitable interviewee, a friend of mine offered to contact Lee Beevers and ask him if he'd be willing to help. Much to my surprise, Lee called me the next day and we arranged to meet at Sincil Bank later that week so that I could speak to him.

I remember being extremely concerned about asking the wrong question or making a fool of myself. After all, this was a professional footballer who had been interviewed by 'real' journalists and now he was speaking to a clueless student who was struggling to get his Dictaphone to work properly.

I needn't have worried. Lee wasn't at all bothered by the fact that I wasn't a proper journalist and he was happy to talk about his career to date, his ambitions for the future and Lincoln City in general.

It was a genuine pleasure speaking to him and he certainly compares favourably to some of the footballers I have spoken to since. He was easy-going, humble and seemed to be genuinely interested in the course I was doing and my ambition to work as a commentator.

When I left he said that he'd been impressed by the way I'd conducted the interview (I'm sure he wasn't, but it was a nice thing for him to say!), wished me luck for the future and even offered to give me a lift back to the University.

I spent no more than 30-40 minutes with him and he probably never gave it another thought but as far as I was concerned it was the start of my career in the media, even if it was just a bit of course work.

I'll always be grateful to Lee for taking the time to speak to me when he didn't have to. It says a lot about the kind of person he is and I imagine that he is a great influence on the younger players now that he is back at the club again.

He is probably one of the more versatile players that I've seen at Sincil Bank since I started watching the Imps in 2002. Capable of playing across the back four, he was named 'player of the season' playing predominantly at right-back in 2007 and was described as the 'best left-back in League Two' by Peter Jackson a little over a year later. John Ward even used him as a holding midfielder during his spell at Colchester in 2010 while Danny Cowley called him 'irreplaceable' and compared him to an iPhone 6.

He's played in League One for Colchester and Walsall and at international level for the Welsh U21s but I believe he could have achieved even more had he not suffered big injuries at crucial times in his career. It is a real shame that he may miss the rest of the current campaign because he deserves the chance to be part of a successful Lincoln side after so many years of great service.

Bencherif, Hamza
(2007, 2014-2015)
Midfielder 54 (1) Apps 7 Goals
Born 2nd February 1988
2006–2009 Nottingham Forest 0 (0), 2007 Imps (loan), 2009–2011 Macclesfield Town 60 (16), 2011–2013 Notts County 31 (2), 2013–2014 Plymouth Argyle 9 (0), 2014 JS Kabylie 12 (0), 2014–2015 Imps, 2015–2016 FC Halifax Town 41 (0), 2016 Wrexham 14 (1)

Big Algerian Hamza Bencherif first turned up at Sincil Bank in 2007 on loan from Forest. He was brought in by John Schofield just a few games before he lost his job, but he kept his place for the first few games of Peter Jackson's reign. He impressed in his 12-game spell as a powerful and commanding presence, and despite being linked with him after his loan spell he didn't return immediately. Instead he went off to Macclesfield, Notts County and Plymouth Argyle.

He was brought back by Gary Simpson ahead of the 2014-15 season after a spell on trial at Cambridge United, with devastating effect. He scored four in five games early in the season, one a superb last minute winner in a scintillating local derby with Grimsby. His versatility meant he could feature across the defence or in midfield although he looked much stronger when operating in front of the defence.

He had a solid season despite Gary Simpson leaving and Chris Moyses coming in, but at the end of the season he opted to sign for ambitious FC Halifax along with team mate Jordan Burrow. That move didn't work out as Halifax were relegted, but the powerful midfielder was able to stay in our division. Since leaving Sincil Bank he's only scored one goal, a long-range strike against Lincoln for current club Wrexham.

Bennett, Lee
(2009-2010)
Midfielder 0 (1) Apps 0 Goals
Born 19th September 1990
2009–2010 Imps, 2010 FriskaViljor 9 (2), 2010–2011 Ossett Albion, 2011 FriskaViljor 3 (6), 2011–2012 Frickley Athletic, 2011–2012 Glasshoughton Welfare, 2012–2013 Ossett Town, 2012-2015 Athersley Recreation, 2015 Pontefract Collieries, 2015-2016 Shaw Lane Aquaforce, 2016 Buxton

Barnsley-born Bennett joined the Imps on a 2-year scholarship after starting out with Ossett Albion. After impressing with the youths and the reserves he was awarded a squad number, making his debut against Bradford City as a 90th minute substitute for Stefan Oakes. He made the bench just once more before moving to the Swedish third division with FriskaViljor.

Bermingham, Karl
(2005)
Forward 0 (2) Apps 0 Goals
Born 6th October 1985
2003–2006 Manchester City 0 (0), 2005 Imps (loan), 2005 Burnley (loan) 4 (0), 2006–2007 Newry City 5 (4), 2007 Derry City 0 (0), 2007–2008 Waterford United 42 (8), 2009–2010 Monaghan United 54 (27), 2011Shelbourne 15 (1), 2012Longford Town 27 (3)

Manchester City youth striker Bermingham was one of numerous players brought in by Keith Alexander with a view to scoring a few goals. Unfortunately, he didn't get any chance to shine with just two half-hour substitute appearances in defeats against Rochdale (1-3) and Wycombe (2-3). After a short unsuccessful loan spell with Burnley he moved back to his native Ireland where he enjoyed a particularly prolific stint with Monaghan United.

Like players such as Neale Fenn and Chris Fagan, Bermingham suffered from coming into lower league football from a top-flight academy and simply not adjusting adequately to the physicality of the game. There was little doubting his ability but in the bruising world of League Two he just looked out of his depth.

Betts, Robert
(2001)
Midfielder 1 (3) Apps 0 Goals
Born 21st December 1981
1997–1998 Doncaster Rovers 3 (0), 1998–2003 Coventry City 13 (0), 2000–2001 Plymouth Argyle (loan) 4 (0), 2001–2002 Imps (loan), 2003–2004 Rochdale 5 (2), 2003–2004 Kidderminster Harriers 9 (0), 2003–2004 Hereford United 8 (0), 2004–2005 Racing Club Warwick, 2004–2005 Forest Green Rovers 3 (0), 2004–2006 Racing Club Warwick, 2006–2008 Quorn

Midfielder Betts joined on loan from Coventry at the beginning of the 2001/02 season under Alan Buckley. He started his first game, a home match with Oxford, but lasted just 45 minutes before being replaced by Dave Cameron. He made three further substitute appearances totalling just under 30 minutes without managing to make a name for himself.

He was rated by Coventry and played 12 times for them on his return before dropping down the leagues. Robert Betts is a name I doubt you'll remember when you've finished the book, and there's good reason for that.

Bimson, Stuart
(1996-2003)
Defender 180 (21) Apps 4 Goals
1986–1987 Prescot Cables, 1987–1989 Ellesmere Port & Neston, 1988–1991 Southport 94 (1), 1991–1995 Macclesfield Town 102 (2), 1994–1997 Bury 36 (0), 1996–2003 Imps, 2003–2005 Cambridge United 43 (0), 2004–2005 Accrington Stanley (loan) 6 (0), 2005–2006 Canvey Island 22 (0), 2006–2007 Chelmsford City 2 (0), 2006–2008 Bedford Town

I use the phrase 'uncomplicated' a couple of times in this book. It's a phrase I like to think looks favourably on players who may have lacked certain techniques or facets to their game, but who I still want to heap praise on. In that respect Stuart Bimson was definitely 'uncomplicated', in every positive sense of the word.

He spent seven years menacingly prowling up and down the line at City. He originally came in as cover for the injured Jon Whitney, and made 13 appearances in the 1996/97 team before losing his spot towards the end of the season. However, he forced his way into the team after we were promoted, and he went on to make over 200 appearances for City in a strong career. He survived the administration scare and developed into an integral part of the side pushing for promotion the season after.

Bimson was well known for his corners, often trying to score directly from the kick. Many fans expected an effort at goal every time we got a corner, and it added to his popularity no end.

Bimson was a great leader and organiser for the younger players and during John Reames spell as manager his influence was incredibly important. As part of the five-man defence that Keith built in 2002/03 he was crucial not only for getting up and down the line, but also for encouraging younger players and putting his experience to good use. Yes he was uncomplicated, but he did the simple things well and he did them right. His penultimate game at Sincil Bank could have ended badly for him, he gave away a penalty as we trailed Torquay 1-0. If they'd scored we would have missed out on the play-offs, but they missed and the rest is history.

In that season he also scored a penalty at the KC Stadium as we became the first team to beat Hull City in their new home. He gave us a 1-0 win in a memorable match against the now-Premier Legaue giants.

He was the only squad player to leave after that play-off final against Bournemouth, the lure of a two-year deal at Cambridge was too much to turn down, and it brought the curtain down on seven years as a City player. He played just 25 times for Cambridge before dropping into the Conference with Accrington Stanley. In 2006 he replaced another former Imp, Nicky Platneuar as manager of Lewes, but recently he's been coaching at Southend's centre of excellence.

Birch, Gary
(2005-2007)
Forward 28 (15) Apps 10 Goals
Born 8th October 1981
1998–2004 Walsall 48 (7), 2001 Exeter City (loan) 24 (2), 2001–2002Nuneaton Borough (loan) 5 (3), 2004 Barnsley (loan) 8 (2), 2004–2005 Kidderminster Harriers 14 (3), 2005–2007 Imps, 2006 Tamworth (loan) 1 (0), 2006Hucknall Town (loan) 1 (0), 2007–2008 AFC Telford United 22 (6), 2007 Rushall Olympic (loan) 6 (4), 2008–2012 Chasetown 127 (40)

Gary Birch had an electric start to his Lincoln City career as he scored five goals in his first five appearances, culminating in a brace against Crewe in a 5-1 win. If that was to endear him to Imps fans, then his barren run afterwards had the opposite effect. He hadn't ever really been prolific prior to joining City so to see him go seven games drawing a blank wasn't a surprise. A brace in a 2-0 win over Stockport went some way to putting him back on the map, but he managed just three more after that. His final game was the 1-0 play-off semi-final loss at home to Grimsby. Despite having a 2 year deal he didn't play for City again and was released after two loan spells.

Birch might feel a little hard done by not to be remembered fondly by Imps fans averaging a goal every three starts but his lack of mobility and long barren spells meant he wasn't able to write his name into Imps folklore. He out-scored Simon Yeo in his first season, but playing in a side that ultimately failed to make the play-off final probably means he won't be remembered for the right things.

Birley, Matt
(2006-2007)
Midfielder 3 (1) Apps 0 Goals
Born 26th July 1986
2005–2007 Birmingham City 1 (0), 2006–2007 Imps (loan), 2007–2008 Bromsgrove Rovers, 2008–2009 Tamworth 7 (2), 2009 King's Lynn 6 (0), 2009–2013 Worcester City, 2013 Solihull Moors 0 (0)

Midfield man Matthew Birley signed on loan from Birmingham under the watchful eye of John Schofield and John Deehan for two months. He made three starts before dropping to the bench, his last Imps outing was as an 88th minute substitute in a 2-0 win against Grimsby at Sincil Bank. After his Imps spell he drifted into non-league football.

Black, Kingsley
(2001-2002)
Winger 38 (3) Apps 5 Goals
Born 22nd June 1968
1987–1991 Luton Town 127 (26), 1991–1995Nottingham Forest 98 (14), 1994 Sheffield United (loan) 11 (2), 1995 Millwall (loan) 3 (1), 1996–2001 Grimsby Town 141 (8), Imps (loan), 2001-2002 Imps

Kingsley Black had a good career. At Luton Town, he was renowned as a speedy winger with the ability to find a telling cross. He cost Forest £1.5m in 1991 which was a tidy fee in those days. He represented his country 30 times and made himself a hero at Blundell Park. When Lennie Lawrence released him Grimsby fans were surprised, and a little irate as he joined us.

Sadly, we never got to see the flying winger that convinced Brian Clough to part with so much money. We saw the slower version, still able but not entirely willing most of the time. He did score twice in a 2-2 draw at Carlisle, but those performances were few and far between. As the club slid towards administration Black was seen as an expensive luxury that we could ill afford. His goals meant very little, despite hitting five he never scored in a Lincoln win. It was a shame as in his heyday Black was an exciting and vibrant player who stood out playing for Luton Town, where he is still regarded as a hero.

He agreed a severance package in October 2002 as Keith Alexander was starting to implement his master plan. Black sloped off, never to be remembered in the annals of Imps history. The sad decline of a once pacey and flamboyant winger.

Blackwood, Michael
(2004-2005)
Defender 6 (4) Apps 0 Goals
Born 30th September 1979
1998–2000 Aston Villa 0 (0), 1999 Chester City (loan) 9 (2), 2000–2002 Wrexham 46 (2), 2002 Worcester City 7 (0), 2002–2003, Stevenage Borough 18 (2), 2003 Halesowen Town 7 (2), 2003–2004 Telford United 35 (3), 2004–2005 Imps, 2005–2008 Kidderminster Harriers 100 (4), 2008 Oxford United (loan) 7 (0), 2008–2009 Mansfield Town 25 (3), 2009 Tamworth (loan) 9 (0), 2009–2010 Tamworth 22 (2), 2010–2011 Brackley Town, 2010–2011 Solihull Moors (loan) 5 (0), 2011–2014 Solihull Moors 84 (3)

Former Aston Villa trainee Blackwood signed in the close season of 2004 having made his name at Wrexham. He arrived as an attacking full back and made his debut in the season opener, a 1-0 win at Shrewsbury.

Unfortunately, he ruptured an abdominal muscle in late August of that season as was ruled out for four months. He came back in January of 2005 but by then Kevin Sandwith had made the left back spot his own. He struggled to even hold a place on the bench as we chased down a third consecutive play-off spot and he left by mutual consent in May.

Blackwood was unlucky as he had seemed to be a fast and energetic defender who might have also been deployed in an advanced midfield role. Football sometimes deals players a rough hand, and that injury coincided with a resurgent Lincoln pushing up the league.

Blissett, Nathan
(2015-2016)
Forward 1 (2) Apps 0 Goals
Born 29th July 1990
2011–2012 Romulus 34 (13), 2012–2015 Kidderminster Harriers 59 (12), 2013 Cambridge United (loan) 7 (2), 2013–2014 Hednesford Town (loan) 10 (4), 2014 Bristol Rovers (loan) 8 (3), 2014–2016 Bristol Rovers 20 (2), 2015 Tranmere Rovers (loan) 5 (1), 2015 Imps (loan), 2016 Torquay United 16 (7)

The nephew of former England international Luther, Nathan signed for the Imps the same day that Liam Hearn decided he wanted some time at Barrow. He came in having scored goals at Kidderminster and to a lesser extent at Bristol Rovers, but he never looked at ease in a Lincoln shirt. It was intended he play off Matt Rhead in the role vacated by Hearn. Two draws and a defeat in his three blank outings convinced Chris Moyses that there was no point in chasing the player further. Most recently he's been playing for Torquay with limited success.

Bloomer, Matthew
(2003-2006)
Defender 67 (38) Apps, 4 Goals
Born 3rd November 1978
1997–2001 Grimsby Town 12 (0), 2001–2003 Hull City 3 (0), 2002 Imps (loan), 2002 Telford United (loan) 13 (0), 2003–2006 Imps, 2006 Grimsby Town (loan) 3 (0), 2006 Cambridge United (loan) 8 (0), 2006–2007 Cambridge United 17 (0), 2007 Grimsby Town 9 (0), 2007–2009 Boston United 40 (0), 2009–2016 Harrogate Town 232 (2), 2016 Cleethorpes Town 12 (0)

Matt Bloomer was a versatile defender who operated primarily as a right back. Alan Buckley first brought him in on loan towards the end of the 2001/02 season. He played in the penultimate game of the campaign in the 1-1 draw with Rochdale that was preceded by a fans march around Lincoln.

In January of 2003 Keith Alexander brought him back to the club from non-league exile with Telford. He came to act as cover for his back five and with his versatility he was able to do that comfortably. He was in and out of the team as suspensions and injuries affected the other players, but he struggled to force himself into the first team on a consistent basis.

He did manage to feature more regularly the season after, even bagging a goal in the 3-1 FA Cup win over Brighton. His versatility was often his undoing as he flitted between midfield and defence without managing to make a single position his. He often had to battle Richard Liburd and Mark Bailey for a starting spot, and although he played regularly towards the end of the season it was usually in an un-favoured central role.

The next season saw him play much more regularly after replacing veteran Dean West at right back. He never shook the tag of utility man though, often covering anywhere across the defence. He had an absolute stinker in March 2005 against Nathan Tyson and Wycombe, coming off after 48 minutes having been directly at fault for two of Tyson's three goals. He'd started that game at centre half covering for the injured captain Paul Morgan. He dropped to the bench for the remainder of the season, appearing as a 94th minute substitute in the play-off final against Southend. As a striker. We didn't score and went on to lose 2-0.

He featured as a 33rd minute sub for an injured Lee Beevers in our 3-0 defeat at Grimsby Town on December 28th, and just five days later he was starting for Grimsby after completing a loan deal. He only played once more for Lincoln in a 1-1 draw with Bury.

Bloomer filled a role without ever making himself indispensable to Keith Alexander. His ability to play a number of positions adequately ensured he kept getting a run out, but a lack of outright excellence in any one position meant he was often yo-yoing between the bench and the first team.

Bonne, Macauley
(2016)
Forward 5 (2) apps 1 Goal
Born 26th October 1995
2013 Colchester United 59 (6) 2016 Imps (loan)

Zimbabwe born Bonne signed on loan early in the 2016/17 campaign in the wake of Jonny Margetts surprise move to Scunthorpe. Highly-rated Bonne had almost 60 League One appearances under his belt for Colchester and he made an immediate impact scoring the winning goal away at Tranmere to put City top of the table. A clash of heads against Barrow left him suffering concussion, and he didn't impress in the remainder of his loan spell.

Undoubtedly a player that will have a decent career in the bottom two divisions of league football with his pace and eye for goal. He has appeared for his country's under-23 team and even registered a goal as they lost 2-1 to Morocco.

Bore, Peter
(2012-2013)
Defender 16 (3) Apps 2 Goals
Born 4th November 1987

2006–2011 Grimsby Town 153 (15), 2008 York City (loan) 4 (0), 2011–2012 Harrogate Town 22 (3), 2012–2013 Imps, 2013 Gateshead 10 (0), 2013–2014 Boston United 12 (1), 2013–2014 Spalding United (loan) 8 (0), 2014 King's Lynn Town 11 (3), 2014 Spalding United 12 (2), 2016 Cleethorpes Town 0 (0)

Bore was a former Grimsby Town midfielder brought in by David Holdsworth to try and help us stay in the National League. His time with the Imps wasn't particularly fruitful as he struggled to hold down a first team place due to injuries.

He made his debut in a 3-3 draw with Braintree and went on to represent the Imps 19 times. He scored twice against Tamworth (4-0) and Ebbsfleet (3-2). The following season his chances were even more limited and his last outing was at Walsall as we ran out 3-2 winners in the FA Cup. He signed for Gateshead before dropping further down into the non-league scene.

Bos, Gjisbert
(1996-97)
Forward 35 (5) Apps 10 Goals
Born 22nd February 1973
1994–1996 IJsselmeervogels 36 (16), 1996–1997 Imps, 1997 Gateshead (loan) 10 (8), 1997–1998 Rotherham United 18 (4), 1998 Walsall (loan) 0 (0), 1998–1999, IJsselmeervogels 15 (7), 1999–2000 SV Huizen 24 (9), 2000–2001 Nunspeet 20 (10), 2001–2003 GVVV, 2003–2004 SDC Putten, 2004 VV Eemdijk

Bos signed from the Dutch League for John Beck in 1996 and set about making himself something of a cult hero. He wasn't inconspicuous on the field as he stood six feet four and towered above most other players. He was a typical John Beck centre forward, tall and a target for those balls whipped in from 'danger alley'.

Bos might just have been another centre forward with a less than one in three strike rate, but two goals he scored will remain long in the memories of City fans. He notched one in the first leg of our magnificent Coca Cola Cup win against Man City which meant we took a three-goal advantage to Maine Road.

In the return leg, we expected an onslaught, but as early as the 17th minute Bos capitalised on a mistake in the Man City defence to give us a precious away goal. He came off at half time as Man City needed to score four, but instead we kept a clean sheet and set up a tie against Premier League Southampton.

Carl Cort joined on loan in February of 1997 and Gijsbert Bos was dropped. He never regained his place in the side and he joined Gateshead on loan before being shipped off to Rotherham. It doesn't matter what else he did or who else he played for. He will always be the guy who scored a winning goal at Maine Road for Lincoln City.

Bound, Matthew
(1995)
Defender 4 (1) Apps 0 Goals
Born 6th November 1972
1991–1994 Southampton 5 (0), 1993 Hull City (loan) 7 (1), 1994–1997 Stockport County 44 (5), 1995 Imps (loan), 1997–2002 Swansea City 176 (10), 2001–2002 Oxford United (loan) 8 (0), 2002–2004

Oxford United 92 (2), 2004–2006 Weymouth 81 (16), 2006–2007 Eastleigh 33 (4), 2009 Weymouth 3 (0)

Defender Bound joined on loan from Stockport in late 1995. After a spell with Stockport County he was looking for a run of games and appeared five times for the Imps. City conceded 15 goals in his five games and he soon found himself back at his parent club. Went on to have a good career with Swansea.

Boyce, Andrew
(2012-2014)
Defender 66 Apps 5 Goals
Born 5th November 1989
2008–2009 Doncaster Rovers 0 (0), 2008–2009 Worksop Town (loan), 2009 King's Lynn 18 (0), 2009–2012 Gainsborough Trinity 71 (8), 2012–2014 Imps, 2013 Scunthorpe United (loan) 2 (0), 2014–2016 Scunthorpe United 29 (1), 2014 Grimsby Town (loan) 13 (0), 2014 Grimsby Town (loan) 6 (0), 2015 Hartlepool United (loan) 8 (0), 2016 Notts County (loan) 3 (0), 2016 Grimsby Town

Big defender Andrew Boyce joined after leading Gainsborough Trinity to the National League North play-off final. He immediately commanded a first team spot and notched two goals in his first four games as an Imp. He was a tremendously popular player despite being part of a defence that found clean sheets incredibly hard to come by. His prowess in and around the opposition penalty area made him a real danger from set pieces and he always turned in good, honest performances.

He was virtually ever present in the 2012/13 season and when he signed another one year deal it was seen as quite a coup for Lincoln as he had been linked with a move away from Sincil Bank. He wasn't able to stop the Imps tumbling down the league under Gary Simpson, and after conceding nine goals in two games (5-0 Plymouth, 4-1 Forest Green) he was shipped out on loan to League Two Scunthorpe before signing permanently for them on January 6th. He wasn't able to cement a place in their first team though and he surprisingly ended the season lining up for Grimsby Town, where he was a member of the side beaten in the play-off semi-finals by Gateshead. Recently linked up with Grimsby again in League Two.

Charlie Russell's view

Andrew Boyce will always be one of my favourite players to have played their trade at Sincil Bank.

Following a three-year spell at Gainsborough Trinity we snapped the talented centre back up in 2012.

When Boyce first joined I had a season ticket at the time and I remember there being a number of stand out players in the side including: Jamie Taylor, Tom Miller and Paul Farman whilst there was also some stand out players on the other end of the spectrum such as Gomez Dali, who I don't think we need to go into details with.

Boyce was another name to add to our list of star players at the time, a reason why he went on to make so many appearances in his first season at the club.

A strong centre half Boyce was a player I would look up to as I was also playing the position at the time for local side, Ruskington Lions. Regularly tweeting Boyce, he would reply to me about Lincoln and also provided me with advice on how to become a better player in certain situation, something I believe every footballer should do, interacting with their fans.

The former Doncaster Rovers youngster gave me a signed pair of his boots which he wore for Gainsborough in a play off final, something I have treasured and have on display in my house to this day.

With regular impressive performances, there was obviously going to be some interest from the Football League, which is why he got the move to Scunthorpe.

I will always remember Boyce for the passion he would show for Lincoln and the time he had for the Imps following, something his former teammate, Paul Farman does to this day!

A number of fans were angered by his choice to join Grimsby Town on loan and then permanently this season but I feel that we should be proud to have a player come from Sincil Bank to go and achieve things for his career in a higher league, plus who knows with promotion looking strong this season we could always tempt him back?

Recently, I was lucky enough to interview my Imps hero, something I am very proud of and when I spoke to Gary about the book I was very keen to get myself involved by writing about Boyce.

Brabin, Gary
(1998-1999)
Midfielder 4 (1) Apps 0 Goals
Born 9th December 1970
1989–1991 Stockport County 2 (0), 1991 Gateshead (loan) 10 (0), 1991Gateshead 2 (0), 1991–1994 Runcorn 98 (10), 1994–1996 Doncaster Rovers 59 (11), 1996Bury 5 (0)1996–1999, Blackpool 50 (2), 1998–1999 Imps (loan) 4 (0), 1999–2001 Hull City 95 (9), 2001 Boston United 1 (0), 2001–2002 Torquay United 6 (0), 2002 Chester City 16 (3), 2002–2004 The New Saints 48 (7), 2005–2006 Halifax Town 4 (1), 2006 Southport 14 (0), 2006–2007 Burscough 12 (3), 2007–2008 The New Saints 2 (0)

Brabin was a somewhat robust midfielder signed on loan in 1998 shortly after chairman John Reames took over as manager. He was a team mate of Bruce Grobbelaar for his two games, then lasted a further three games before heading off back to Blackpool. With his added steel, we only lost once in five games and despite appearing a little portly he wasn't that bad.

The season afterwards Brabin signed for Hull City and managed to spoil any reputation he may have had with Lincoln by getting sent off in our derby match at Sincil Bank. Whilst his strength and bravery helped him in a Lincoln shirt, his thuggery and vicious nature damaged him in amber and black. In recent years, he moved into management and hasn't helped himself by being an outspoken critic of Lincoln. He was last seen sloping off to the job centre shortly after we beat his Tranmere side 1-0.

Bradley, Shayne
(2003)
Forward 3 Apps 1 Goal
Born 8th December 1979
1998–2000 Southampton 4 (0), 1999 Swindon Town (loan) 7 (0), 1999 Exeter City (loan) 8 (1), 2000–2002 Mansfield Town 47 (11), 2002–2003 Eastwood Town, 2002–2003 Chesterfield 9 (2), 2003 Imps (loan)

Bradley was one of a high number of strikers signed on loan by Keith Alexander to try and find goals in our first play-off season. Dene Cropper and Simon Yeo weren't prolific by any means (at that time) and Bradley seemed to fit the bill having scored a few for Mansfield Town the season prior to joining us. He had struggled with injuries and had fallen out of favour at Chesterfield after being sent off three minutes after coming on as a sub against his old side Mansfield Two for spitting at Rhys Day.

He started two games, a 3-0 win over Hartlepool and a solid 1-0 away win at Southend before picking up an injury. He sat out most of March before hitting a 15th minute winner in a home tie with Kidderminster Harriers. He was out again before the next match, withdrawn prior to kick off against Bristol Rovers after a warm up injury. He returned to Chesterfield but was forced to retire before making another appearance.

Had he not suffered injuries I think Shayne Bradley could have been a strong lower-league striker. He had all the necessary attributes as he was big, strong and could finish when needed to. He was the classic League Two forward with less finesse and more bustle than most, but sadly injury put paid to what could have been a promising career though. Mind you he did manage a ratio of one goal in three games for Lincoln which is certainly better than a lot of players we could mention (*cough* Drewe *cough* Broughton)

Branston, Guy
(1999)
Defender 6 Apps 0 Goals
Born 9th January 1979
1997–1999 Leicester City 0 (0), 1997 Rushden & Diamonds (loan), 1998 Colchester United (loan) 12 (1), 1998 Colchester United (loan) 1 (0), 1998–1999 Plymouth Argyle (loan) 7 (1), 1999 Rushden & Diamonds (loan), 1999 Imps (loan), 1999 Rotherham United (loan) 5 (0), 1999–2004 Rotherham United 99 (13), 2003 Wycombe Wanderers (loan) 9 (0), 2004 Peterborough United (loan) 14 (0), 2004–2005 Sheffield Wednesday 11 (0), 2004–2005 Peterborough United (loan) 4 (1), 2005–2006 Oldham Athletic 45 (2), 2006–2007 Peterborough United 26 (0), 2007 Rochdale (loan) 4 (0), 2007 Northampton Town (loan) 3 (0), 2008 Notts County 1 (0), 2008–2009 Kettering Town 39 (0), 2009–2010 Burton Albion 19 (0), 2010 Torquay United (loan) 16 (0), 2010–2011 Torquay United 45 (2), 2011–2012 Bradford City 16 (1), 2011 Rotherham United (loan) 2 (0), 2012–2013 Aldershot Town 3 (0), 2012 Bristol Rovers (loan) 4 (1), 2013–2014 Plymouth Argyle 31 (0)

The stereotypical lower league journeyman, Branston made a good living from being a tough and uncompromising defender who was never afraid to stick a boot or a head in where he might get injured. He featured for City relatively early in his career, playing four league games and two cup games whilst on loan from Leicester City. He impressed enough in an Imps shirt to give an indication of the career he might go on to have.

After City, he went on to make his name at Rotherham, winning promotion with them the same season he played for City and then cementing a place in their defence (when he wasn't suspended) for over 100 games. He later lined up against Lincoln for Peterborough, Torquay, Burton and Kettering to name a few.

After his playing career ended he worked behind the scenes for Notts County and more recently Nuneaton Town.

Bright, Kris
(2014)
Forward 7 Apps 2 Goals
Born 5th September 1986

2004–2005 Waitakere City 22 (30), 2005–2006 New Zealand Knights 11 (1), 2006–2007 Fortuna Sittard 11 (1), 2007–2008 Kristiansund 24 (28), 2009 Panserraikos 7 (1), 2009–2010 Shrewsbury Town 27 (3), 2011 Budapest Honvéd 10 (2), Balzan Youths 11 (5), 2012 Bryne FK 12 (4), FC Haka 13 (3), 2013 IFK Mariehamn 23 (9), 2014 Imps, 2015 Bharat FC 17 (6), 2015–2016 Bidvest Wits 3 (1), 2016 Linfield FC 4 (0)

New Zealand international Bright signed for City on a short-term contract at the end of the 2013/14 season. He was already known to Imps fans having scored one of his three Shrewsbury Town goals against us. He was tall and athletic and had scored regularly in his career, just not at Football League level.

He scored on his debut, a 2-1 home defeat by Welling but was sent off in his second appearance against Braintree by referee Amy Fearn. He drew a blank for five games before scoring again in his last outing, a 3-3 draw with Barnet. Lincoln only lost one game in which he played so he proved to be something of a good omen. Last heard of playing for Linfield in the Irish league.

Brightwell, David
(1995)
Defender 7 Apps 0 Goals
Born 7th January 1971
1988–1995 Manchester City 43 (1), 1991 Chester City (loan) 6 (0), 1995 Imps (loan), 1995 Stoke City (loan) 1 (0), 1995 Bradford City (loan) 1 (0), 1995–1997 Bradford City 23 (0), 1996–1997 Blackpool (loan) 2 (0), 1997–1998 Northampton Town 35 (1), 1998–2000 Carlisle United 78 (4), 2000–2001 Hull City 27 (2), 2001–2002 Darlington 36 (0)

David Brightwell made 43 league appearances for Man City early in his career, and looked set to forge a partnership with brother Ian Brightwell who went on to make over 350. However, he started to drift down the leagues and ended up on loan with Lincoln in 1995 for a handful of games. There wasn't an opportunity to sign him and after five defeats in his seven outings there probably wasn't a great deal of desire to either. His only Imps win came on his debut, a superb 2-1 victory over Preston North End on the opening day of the season. He returned to Man City upon completion of his loan.

Latterly in his career he played a major part in one of the greatest football stories ever told. Whilst playing for Carlisle they needed a win over Plymouth on the last day of the season to remain in the Football League. Plymouth took the lead and it was Brightwell who equalised for the Cumbrians. That set up goal keeper Jimmy Glass to score a dramatic 90th minute winner to secure a fairy-tale finish to the season.

Brough, Patrick
(2016)
Midfield 4 Apps 0 Goals
Born 20th February 1996
2013 Carlisle United 38 (0), 2016 Imps (loan)

Unremarkable young defender who joined on a month loan in January 2016 to aid Chris Moyses' push towards a play-off spot. Played in three defeats and a disappointing draw against Halifax Town before returning to Carlisle to resume his fledgling career. Having just turned 20 I'm sure he will have more opportunities to make a name for himself, although so far in the 2015/16 season he has just one outing in his locker, Carlisle's 5-4 Football League Trophy win over Oldham.

Broughton, Drewe
(2010-2011)
Forward 16 (15) Apps 0 Goals
Born 25th October 1978
1996–1998 Norwich City 9 (1), 1997 Wigan Athletic (loan) 4 (0), 1998 Brentford 1 (0), 1998–2001 Peterborough United 35 (8), 2000 Nuneaton Borough (loan) 10 (2), 2000 Dagenham & Redbridge (loan) 9 (5), 2000–2001 Stevenage Borough (loan) 4 (3), 2001 Kidderminster Harriers (loan) 19 (7), 2001–2003 Kidderminster Harriers 75 (12), 2003–2005 Southend United 44 (2), 2004 Rushden & Diamonds (loan) 21 (6), 2004–2005 Wycombe Wanderers (loan) 3 (0), 2005–2006Rushden &Diamonds 37 (10), 2006–2007Chester City 14 (2), 2006–2007 Boston United (loan) 25 (8), 2007–2008 Milton Keynes Dons 13 (0), 2008 Wrexham (loan) 16 (2), 2008–2010 Rotherham United 57 (9), 2010 Imps (loan) (0), 2010–2011 Imps, 2011 AFC Wimbledon (loan) 8 (2), 2011 Alfreton Town 2 (1), 2011–2012Thurrock 10 (1), 2012 Arlesey Town 2 (1),2012 Darlington 11 (1)

Drewe Broughton's reputation suggested he was a hard man who knew occasionally where the net was. He had scored against Lincoln and had also turned out for Boston so there was little chance of him gaining a lot of support when he first joined. A run of goals might have helped, but they didn't come either. He'd spent his career getting more bookings than goals every season and in a Lincoln shirt he didn't change his ways. At least elsewhere he'd managed to score some goals because in an Imps shirt he only ever got booked, and even then it wasn't as much as before. His total input into our survival was absolutely nothing at all. When we needed a goal, he wasn't there. When we needed a target man to hold the ball up and flick it on, he wasn't there. When we needed a hard-nut centre forward to put himself about, he wasn't there.

By mid-season he wasn't at Lincoln at all, he was out on loan scoring goals for Wimbledon in the league below us. By the time his couple of goals had added to their promotion party he was back in our squad (not scoring) as we went down and Wimbledon replaced us.

He made a brief comeback with Darlington, scoring once, getting booked three times and getting sent off twice. He did get a second chance on the Sincil Bank turf, his Darlo side running out 5-0 losers in a rare rampant win for David Holdsworth. In his final game for Darlington he lasted just 40 minutes before being sent off. There ended the career of a man who shouldn't ever have been mentioned again in the annals of Imps history, but thanks to me you've had to endure him all over again (see also Dali, Gomez and Kanyucka, Pat)

Brown, Aaron
(2008-2010)
Defender 51 (10) Apps, 3 Goals
Born 14th March 1980
1998–2004 Bristol City 160 (12), 2000 Exeter City (loan) 5 (1), 2004–2006 Queens Park Rangers 3 (0), 2005 Torquay United (loan) 5 (0), 2005 Cheltenham Town (loan) 3 (0), 2005–2006 Swindon Town (loan) 8 (0), 2006–2007 Swindon Town 49 (4), 2007–2008 Gillingham 11 (1), 2008–2010 Imps, 2010 Wrexham 8 (1), 2010–2012 Darlington 70 (2), 2012–2014 Bath City 58 (1), 2014 Hungerford Town 0 (0), 2014-2015 Weston-super-Mare 23 (1), 2015 Paulton Rovers

Aaron Brown joined as one of Peter Jackson's Magnificent Seven in the summer of 2008. He had the right sort of experience having served Bristol City and Swindon well in a solid career. He came in as a left back but he was much more attack focused than he was defensively minded. He was quick and could get up and down the line but during his City tenure he was often found wanting in his defensive duties.

He made his Imps debut in the opening day 1-0 defeat at Rotherham and went on to make 41 appearances in his first season. When Peter Jackson was sacked the following season Brown fell out of favour and was loaned to Burton Albion by Chris Sutton. He returned briefly to score in the 3-1 FA Cup win at Telford before his contract was terminated by mutual consent in February 2010.

I for one was sad to see Brown leave as I think as a wide midfield player he had a lot to offer at League Two level. He signed for relegated Wrexham in the Blue Square Premier and then moved on to Darlington. He featured for Darlington in a return to Sincil Bank as the Imps ran out 5-0 winners.

Brown, Grant
(1989-2002)
Defender 458 (7) Appearances 18 Goals
Born 19th November 1969
1988–1989 Leicester City 14 (0), 1989–2002 Imps, 2002–2003 Telford United 35 (0), 2003–2005 Alfreton Town 83 (1), 2005, Worksop Town 0 (0), 2005–2006 Grantham Town 42 (6)

A Who's who of Lincoln City is a vehicle to track all the weird, wonderful and woeful players we've had over the years. For players like Grant Brown trying to sum up their contribution in a couple of paragraphs is nothing short of insulting.

Here's the facts. Grant signed for City in the late 80's from Leicester and went on to enjoy 13 years playing in the Imps defence. He earned the nickname 'hoof' for his fondness of booting the ball as far away from the goal as he possibly could. He survived manager after manager, from John Beck to Phil Stant, from John Reames to Steve Wicks. All the while he was doing the basics right, if the ball came near his feet he kicked it away. If it came near his head, he headed it away. If it came anywhere else, he shifted it onto his feet or head to get rid. He was the stereotypical lower league defender, not usually one to nutmeg an opponent or go on a mazy run, but never one to shirk a tackle either.

As the years passed by the appearances racked up and Grant went from simple defender to become part of the furniture. He was nicknamed Mr Lincoln City for his unwavering devotion to the club, always signing new deals when put in front of him. Everyone was delighted when he finally broke the appearances record. Looking back the £60,000 it cost to sign him has been repaid ten-fold.

All good things must come to an end and his reign at the heart of the Imps defence finished as we entered administration in 2002. In a cruel twist of irony he won the Player of the Year award just before leaving the club. There simply wasn't enough money to sustain the squad and Grant left along with several the first team. He ended his playing days in the non-league scene, finally hanging up his boots in 2006 after a spell at Grantham Town.

However, by that time he was already back in the fold at Sincil Bank having taken over youth team responsibilities in 2005. He eventually found himself as caretaker boss after the sacking of John Schofield and John Deehan. It was a role he was to find himself in again as managers came and went, but he remained loyal and dedicated to our club. At various points, he acted as assistant manager too, significantly as Chris Moyses assistant in the 2015/16 season.

Following the departure of Chris Moyses in mid-2016 Grant Brown left the club to seek pastures new. In all he had given 24 years as player and official to the club and he will always be a true club legend. His unswerving dedication and robust, no-nonsense approach to playing meant he will be forever remembered as 'Hoof' Grant Brown, Mr Lincoln City himself.

In 2007 he was voted third in a poll to find the greatest Imps players of all time. This was the highest placing for any player featured in this book. Who better to write a foreword for it?

Brown, Nathaniel
(2005-2008, 2013-2016)
Defender 192 (9) Apps 11 Goals
Born 15th June 1981
2000–2005 Huddersfield Town 76 (0), 2005–2008 Imps, 2008–2009 Wrexham 7 (0), 2008–2009 Macclesfield Town (loan) 30 (6), 2009–2013 Macclesfield Town 141 (8), 2013 Imps (loan) 10 (0), 2013-2016 Imps 85 (2), 2015-2016 FC Halifax Town (loan) 4 (0), 2016 Harrogate Town (loan) 0 (0), 2016 Boston United 0 (0)

Nat originally arrived from Huddersfield in the immediate aftermath of our play-off defeat by Southend. The aim was to help us kick on and end three years of play-off hurt, and Nat had experience having won a final with Huddersfield two years before. He was injured playing for Huddersfield against Lincoln in the infamous 'Pawel Abbott offside' match of 2005, and only returned after their two-legged win over us in the semi-finals.

Brown showed himself to be a competent if not outstanding centre back over a three-year period. He chipped in with a few goals as Keith often liked to use his big defenders as strikers from time to time. He finished his first full season at the Bank with eight goals to his name.

Injury ruled him out of the start of the next campaign and his first appearance was as a 20th minute sub for Adie Moses as we won 5-0 away at Barnet. Once he got in he retained his place in the side, until a tangle with Liam Dickinson of Stockport earned him his first Imps red card in April. He was in the side that finished our play-off assault in the two-legged mauling at the hands of Bristol Rovers.

He struggled to make an impact under Peter Jackson and was released at the end of the 2007/08 season, first linking up with Wrexham before re-joining Keith Alexander at Macclesfield, where ironically he also rediscovered his goal scoring touch hitting three goals in his first three games.

No sooner had former Macclesfield assistant Gary Simpson took over at Lincoln in 2013, he signed Nat Brown initially on loan. He was signed permanently at the start of the following season. I'm sure the aim was to recreate some of the spirit the Imps had under Simmo and Big Keith, but sadly Nat wasn't the same player he had been. He may have still had the bandage on his permanently injured wrist, but the similarities ended there.

He featured regularly under Simpson until his dismissal, and then he featured for Chris Moyses. It was clear his days were numbered though, and after only two appearances the following season he was allowed to join numerous lower league sides on loan until he was released.

Brown, Simon
(1997-1998)
Goalkeeper 1 Apps 0 Goals
Born 5th December 1976
1996–1999 Tottenham Hotspur 0 (0), 1997–1998 Imps (loan), 1998 Fulham (loan) 0 (0), 1998 Kingstonian (loan) 3 (0), 1999 Aylesbury United (loan) 12 (0), 1999–2004 Colchester United 140 (0), 2004–2007 Hibernian 49 (0), 2007–2009 Brentford 27 (0), 2008–2009 Darlington (loan) 22 (0), 2009–2010 Northampton Town 2 (0), 2010–2012 Cambridge United 49 (0), 2012 Welling United 1 (0)

Simon Brown is the Alan Judge of the 1990's. In the 80's Alan Judge played two games for Lincoln, one of them a 7-0 defeat by Derby. His Imps career never recovered but he had a few good years playing in goal for Oxford and Hereford. Poor old Simon arrived just in time for our 5-1 festive hammering at Peterborough in 1997. He never pulled an Imps shirt on again and was sent packing back to Spurs. After us he had a decent career as a reliable keeper for Colchester and Scottish Premier League Hibernian.

Brown, Steve
(1995-1998)
Forward 52 (30) Apps, 9 Goals
Born 6th December 1973
1992–1993 Southend United 10 (2), 1993–1994 Colchester United 62 (17), 1994–1995 Gillingham 9 (2), 1995–1998 Imps, 1998–1999 Macclesfield Town 2 (0), 1999–2001 Dover Athletic 57 (12)

Steve Brown enjoyed a goal ever three games ratio at Colchester and it was hoped he could recreate that form for Steve Wicks. Sadly, Wicks only lasted a few weeks before being replaced by John Beck. Beck liked Brown's enthusiasm and attitude, which overshadowed the distinct lack of goals.

Brown was popular with the fans as well and he became something of a cult hero for a while. A winner away at Northampton helped secure that cult status as well as further goals against Fulham and Wigan as John Beck steered us away from the relegation spots. He had a never say die attitude that means he is recalled just as fondly now, twenty years after kicking his first ball in anger for us.

Brown was famous for once playing in a pair of trainers belonging to groundsman Nigel Dennis and dating a page three girl. However, his popularity off the pitch wasn't matched by a goal return on it. He had further committed outings without a high goal return until our promotion to the third tier in 1998. Once we went up he was deemed surplus to requirements and he left the club in the summer.

Buckley, Adam
(2001-2003)
Midfielder 23 (18) Apps 1 Goal
Born 2nd August 1979
1996–1997 West Bromwich Albion 0 (0), 1997–2001 Grimsby Town 15 (0), 2001–2003 Imps

I'm not going to write too much about Buckley. Arrived on his father's coat tails as he had at Grimsby and went on to make over 40 uninspiring, tepid appearances in a Lincoln shirt. For a short spell, he kept the insanely talented Peter Gain out of the team, a crime I never forgave him for.

Another crime he didn't get forgiven for was theft from his team mates. After just six appearances in our first play-off season he was arrested at the ground on suspicion of stealing from his team mates. Just a month later he was sentenced to 120 hours' community service for his crimes and he left the club.

He played for a variety of non-league sides locally after his professional career ended but I haven't listed them as I don't want to waste words on an instantly forgettable player from Lincoln's history. If they're sixth tier or lower and within commuting distance from Lincoln, then he probably played for them at some point. I bet he got changed on his own though.

Bullock, Tony
(2001)
Goalkeeper 2 Apps 0 Goals

Born 18th February 1972

1992–1993 Northwich Victoria 37 (0), 1992–1993 Hyde United (loan) 3 (0), 1996–1997 Leek Town, 1997–2000 Barnsley 38 (0), 2000–2001 Macclesfield Town 24 (0), 2001 Imps, 2001–2003 Ross County 69 (0), 2003–2005 Dundee United 31 (0), 2005–2006 Gillingham 6 (0), 2006–2007 St Mirren 29 (0), 2007–2009 Ross County 40 (0), 2009 Montrose 16 (0), 2009–2010 Dundee 19 (0), 2010–2012 Livingston 34 (0), 2012–2013 Arbroath 10 (0), 2013–2014 Airdrieonians 0 (0)

Goalkeeper signed towards the end of the 2001 season to give some competition to Alan Marriott. Played twice in defeats against Hartlepool (0-1) and Cheltenham (1-2) but didn't appear again and ended up playing for a handful of Scottish clubs including Dundee United and St Mirren.

Burch, Rob
(2008-2010)
Goalkeeper 100 Apps 0 Goals
Born 8th October 1983

2002–2007 Tottenham Hotspur 0 (0), 2003 Woking (loan) 6 (0), 2004 Stevenage Borough (loan) 2 (0), 2004–2005 West Ham United (loan) 0 (0), 2005 Stevenage Borough (loan) 1 (0), 2005 Bristol City (loan), 0 (0), 2007 Barnet (loan) 6 (0), 2007–2008 Sheffield Wednesday 2 (0), 2008–2010 Imps, 2010–2012 Notts County 15 (0)

Rob Burch was a good goal keeper, of that there is no doubt. He arrived as part of the much heralded 'Magnificent Seven', and of the seven he was the only one who was even close to magnificent. However his spell at Lincoln will always be sullied a little by the circumstances of his arrival.

The facts: He was a tall and commanding keeper who it was thought might have a good few years ahead of him once he left City. He was a safe pair of hands in Peter Jackson's spell as manager, something that was needed given the frailties of the defence. The trouble was Alan Marriott had to make way for him, and Alan Marriott was only one year away from a testimonial.

It is harsh on a player that he is judged by who he replaced and not on his own steam, but whereas Marriott stayed loyal to the club when his stock rose, Burch did not. After Jackson was dismissed he saw out the season before leaving on a free transfer to Notts County. Maybe he could sense what was coming. Things never worked out for him at County though and after just 15 league appearances in two years he was replaced.

Burridge, John
(1993-1994)
Goalkeeper 4 Apps 0 Goals
Born 3rd 12th 1951

1969–1971 Workington 27 (0, 1971, Blackpool (loan) 3 (0), 1971–1975 Blackpool 131 (0), 1975–1978 Aston Villa 65 (0), 1978 Southend United (loan) 6 (0), 1978–1980 Crystal Palace 88 (0), 1980–1982 Queens Park Rangers 39 (0), 1982–1984 Wolverhampton Wanderers 74 (0), 1984 Derby County (loan) 6 (0), 1984–1987 Sheffield United 109 (0), 1987–1989 Southampton 62 (0), 1989–1991 Newcastle United 67 (0), 1991–1993 Hibernian 65 (0), 1993 Newcastle United 0 (0), 1993 Scarborough 3 (0), 1993–1994 Imps, 1994 Enfield 0 (0), 1994, Aberdeen 3 (0), 1994 Newcastle United 0 (0), 1994 Dunfermline Athletic 0 (0), 1994 Dumbarton 3 (0), 1994 Falkirk 3 (0), 1994–1995 Manchester City 4 (0), 1995Notts County 0 (0), 1995Witton Albion 0 (0), 1995 Darlington 3 (0), 1995–1996 Grimsby Town 0 (0), 1996 Gateshead 0 (0), 1996 Northampton Town 0 (0), 1996 Queen of the South 6 (0), 1996Purfleet 0 (0), 1996 Blyth Spartans 0 (0), 1996 Scarborough 0 (0), 1997 Blyth Spartans 0 (0)

Just look at that list of clubs. I spent more minutes typing that than John Burridge spent playing for Lincoln. This is probably the only player who will have a shorter write-up than list of former clubs. He kept one clean sheet in a 2-0 win over Scunthorpe before letting in a goal a game until he left in early 1994 to tour the world through the medium of goal keeping. I've dragged this out and his list of clubs is still longer than his pen picture. Madness.

Burrow, Jordan
(2014-2015)
Forward 29 (11) Apps 10 Goals
Born 12th September 1992
2011 Chesterfield 0 (0), 2011 Boston United (loan) 8 (2), 2012–2013 Morecambe 51 (5), 2013–2014 Stevenage 20 (2), 2014–2015 Imps 2015 Halifax Town 52 (14)

Former Chesterfield trainee Burrow signed for City from Stevenage in 2014 to play for Gary Simpson. Burrow was rated as a good prospect and he had a decent game to goals return. Scored to put us 3-0 up against Forest Green in a match we went on to draw 3-3 that ultimately cost Gary Simpson his job.

He found himself a first team regular by the end of the season after scoring a brace against Nuneaton and again against Braintree to give us 3-1 wins. At the end of the season the decision was made not to retain his services and he followed Hamza Bencherif to ambitious Halifax Town where he managed 14 goals as they were relegated.

Bush, Chris
(2013, 2015-2016)
Defender 31 (3) Apps 2 Goals
Born 12th July 1992
2010–2011 Brentford 0 (0), 2010 Salisbury City (loan) 7 (0), 2010 Woking (loan) 4 (0), 2010–2011 AFC Wimbledon (loan) 13 (0), 2011 Thurrock (loan) 8 (0), 2011–2012 AFC Wimbledon 22 (0), 2012–2013 Gateshead 20 (1), 2013 Imps (loan), 2013 Hereford United (loan) 6 (0), 2013–2014 Hereford United 42 (3), 2014–2015 Welling United 33 (4), 2015–2016 Imps, 2016 Chelmsford

Defender Bush first came to City on loan in 2013, but after ending up on the end of three defeats and 10 goals he returned to Gateshead.

He was back again in the close season of 2015/16, signed by Chris Moyses along with Luke Waterfall and Callum Howe to ensure competition for places across the back. He lost his place in the first team at Christmas but fought back and returned with a winning goal and man of the match display at home to Guiseley. His appearances triggered a clause in his contract for an extra year, but Danny Cowley didn't fancy him and he dropped down a division early in the next season to play for Chelmsford City.

Butcher, Richard
(2002-2005, 2005, 2009-2010)
Midfielder 129 (14) Apps 14 Goals
Born 22nd January 1981
1999–2000 Northampton Town 0 (0), 2000–2001 Rushden & Diamonds 0 (0), 2001–2002 Kettering Town 44 (13), 2002–2005 Imps, 2005–2006 Oldham Athletic 36 (4), 2005 Imps (loan), 2006–2007 Peterborough United 43 (4), 2007–2009 Notts County 80 (18), 2009–2010 Imps, 2010 Macclesfield Town (loan) 8 (2), 2010–2011 Macclesfield Town 7 (1)

When writing about 95% of this book I was having to recall and research players about whom I knew very little. Occasionally I've could write about my favourite players, the ones who have thrilled me in the red and white, the ones I respected and the ones who gave everything for the club. They're the very best bits to write.

Then there are two people all in a category of their own, Keith Alexander and of course Richard Butcher. I'm going to 'break cover' a little here and make this entry as personal as I can.

Shortly after Butch signed I knew he'd be a favourite of mine. He had some real ability and played with passion and dedication whenever he wore a Lincoln shirt. He had the privilege of playing in a semi-successful team and that added to his persona. He was at Lincoln when everything was right, 2003-2005.

When he left, he was one of the only players who went with good wishes and no animosity at all. He didn't take more money at the same level, he looked to progress himself and push on with his career. Stepping up to Oldham was a good career move.

When it didn't work out there he came back home to further cement his legacy. It might only have been on loan but he came back to aid a cause, even earning us a point with a goal at Orient. If money had been no object I wonder if we could have bought him back, there and then. Keith Alexander speculated to that end in his programme notes for the MK Dons FA Cup clash; "Richard Butcher went back to Oldham purely and simply because of the money involved. He was a player we didn't want to let go in the summer but he went higher up for a lot more money than we could afford to pay. That was understandable but he came back and did a good job for us during his month loan and hopefully at some stage in the future we might be able to get him back permanently. I know the lad is desperate to come back and he could go on and help us to achieve what we're trying to achieve."

He didn't come back, at least not whilst Keith was in charge. He wound up playing for Notts County, and whilst there I interviewed Butch over social media for the lincolncity-mad website. It's been taken down now and sadly I have no copy of the interview, but we spoke about his times at Lincoln. He said he always thought he might come back and play for City again one day, but at the time didn't want quoting.

When he did come back for Peter Jackson I was over the moon. I knew we weren't just getting a good player, we were getting a club legend back, a player who would be motivated by the right things. We he wore red and white you knew his head wouldn't drop and he'd fight for the cause. We were in a bit of a rut at that time and Richard Butcher had only played in successful Imps teams.

His return wasn't a fairy-tale and after just three months Chris Sutton came in, and within three more moved Butch on. He went to join Macclesfield Town after a short loan spell. That one move by Sutton angered me more than anything he did.

Butch passed far too young, just a few days into January 2011. It is one of those 'Diana' moments for me. I will always remember where I was the moment I heard Richard Butcher had passed away. We didn't just lose an ex-Imp; we didn't just lose a key figure from our history. We lost a good, honest man who approached life in the correct way.

I could talk about his goal at Bournemouth that set up that final day clash with Torquay. I could talk about his goal in the play-off semi-final against Huddersfield that gave us belief that we might make a second final. I won't though, I'll just remember the all-round Lincoln City hero taken from us far too soon.

Cameron – Cunningham

Cameron, Dave
(2000-2002)
Forward 39 (34) Apps 11 Goals
Born 24th August 1975
1994–1995 Falkirk 0 (0), 1995–1996 East Stirlingshire 8 (0), 1998–1999 St Mirren 10 (2), 1999–2000 Brighton & Hove Albion 17 (0), 2000 Worthing, 2000–2002 Imps, 2002–2003 Chester City 15 (2), 2002 Droylsden (loan), 2003 Telford United (loan) 6 (0), 2003 Tamworth, 2003–2004 Halifax Town 9 (1), 2004–2006 Droylsden, 2006–2008 Rhyl 48 (12), 2008 Bradford Park Avenue 0 (0)

Dave Cameron initially came on to Lincoln's radar as his Brighton side drew 2-2 with us in 1999, and after his release he came on trial. He made a notable debut in the 4-4 friendly draw with a strong Middlesbrough side, and he signed shortly after. His Imps career started well with goals against Torquay and his old side Brighton.

Cameron had a robust and uncomplicated style of play, and whilst he started very well for City he faded after an October injury. As Phil Stant moved on and Alan Buckley took over he found himself in and out of the team with Lee Thorpe often preferred. He started our 2001/02 season in a rich vein of form scoring four in ten matches, but goals didn't come regularly enough and good performances were all-too sporadic.

He went three and a half months without a goal before grabbing us an equaliser in the penultimate away game with Kidderminster to earn a 1-1 draw. He played on that emotional day in 2002 against Rochdale when the fear of losing the club altogether was looming large.

He left at the end of the season as most of the squad disbanded in the face of administration, and struggled to have any impact at clubs for the rest of his career. Most recently he's been coaching with Droylsden, and not running the country. That's another Dave Cameron.

Camm, Mark
(2000-2004)
Midfielder 13 (27) Apps, 0 Goals
Born 1st October 1980
1999-2000 Sheffield United 0 (0), 2000–2004 Imps, 2002–2003 Gainsborough Trinity (loan) 10 (1), 2003 King's Lynn (loan) 14 (2), 2004-2009 King's Lynn 209 (4), 2009-2010 Boston United 19 (1), 2010 Worksop Town, 2010–2011 Frickley Athletic, 2010 Rainworth Miners Welfare (loan), 2011 Belper Town 0 (0), 2011–2013 Rainworth Miners Welfare

Camm was a former Sheffield United youth who signed for City under Phil Stant in the summer of 2000. In four seasons with Lincoln he only ever featured as a covering player, managing just 40 outings in four years, with 27 of those coming as a substitute.

Booked for City once in a 2001 FA Cup tie with Bury in which Dave Cameron scored a rare Lincoln goal. He played a few times in the play-off season of 2002/03, last appearing for Lincoln just before Christmas of 2002. I think the best word to describe Mark Camm in a Lincoln shirt would be unremarkable.

52

Campbell, David
(1994)
Midfielder 3 (2) Apps 1 Goal
Born 2nd June 1965
1984–1987 Nottingham Forest 41 (3), 1987 Notts County (loan) 18 (2), 1987–1989 Charlton Athletic 30 (1), 1989 Plymouth Argyle (loan) 1 (0), 1989–1990 Bradford City 35 (4), 1990–1991 Derry City (loan) 5 (0), 1991–1992 Shamrock Rovers 31 (5), 1992 Cliftonville (loan) 4 (0), 1992 Rotherham United 1 (0), 1992–1993 Burnley 8 (0), 1993–1994 Imps (loan), 1994 Portadown 7 (2), 1994 Wigan Athletic 7 (0), 1995 Cambridge United 1 (0)

Campbell looked to have a good career ahead of him, he made his Northern Ireland debut in Mexico 86 after a good season with Nottingham Forest, where he broke through in a midfield also containing Neil Webb and Steve Hodge. Unfortunately, his end product often lacked and Brian Clough first dropped him, and then loaned him to Notts County. After joining Bradford and losing his Northern Ireland place in 1988 he floated around a few clubs before settling at Burnley. He had an injury hit spell there and joined us in February of 1994 on loan.

He scored in a 3-1 home win over Hereford but eventually dropped to the bench, and hadn't done enough on expiry of his loan to earn him a second look. Campbell was a player who showed a great amount of promise early in his career but ended up struggling with form and injuries.

Caprice, Jake
(2014-2015)
Defender 34 (4) Apps 0 Goals
Born 11th November 1992
2011–2012 Crystal Palace 0 (0), 2012–2014 Blackpool 0 (0), 2012–2013 Dagenham & Redbridge (loan) 8 (0), 2013 St Mirren (loan) 6 (0), 2014 Tamworth (loan) 12 (0), 2014–2015 Imps, 2015 Woking 54 (0)

Caprice was a pacey full back who signed for City under Gary Simpson. He suffered an injury which kept him out of the side for Simpson's dismissal, but he returned under Chris Moyses to make 34 appearances in a Lincoln side that once again found itself battling against relegation.

Despite his talent he wasn't able to earn himself a new contract and he moved to Woking once his Imps time was up. Was part of the Woking team that beat Lincoln twice the following season, and recently gained an England C call up after Imp Sam Habergham withdrew from the squad. Jake is a player I expect to see more of in Ihe future.

Carayol, Mustapha
(2010-2011)
Midfielder 28 (9) Apps, 4 Goals
Born 4th September 1988

2007–2008 Milton Keynes Dons 0 (0), 2007–2008 Crawley Town (loan) 25 (2), 2008–2010 Torquay United 50 (6), 2009 Kettering Town (loan), 2010–2011 Imps, 2011–2012 Bristol Rovers 30 (4), 2012–2016 Middlesbrough 50 (11), 2015 Brighton & Hove Albion (loan) 5 (0), 2015–2016 Huddersfield Town (loan) 15 (3), 2016 Leeds United (loan) 12 (1), 2016 Nottingham Forest 1 (0)

Carayol was one of those insanely frustrating footballers who had so much to offer but simply didn't produce when it was needed. After a goal-less first season with Torquay he began to impress, catching the eye of Chris Sutton as we ran out 3-2 winners at Plainmoor in March 2010.

He agreed terms with Sutton in the summer although due to Carayol being under the age of 24 the fee was decided by a tribunal. In August, it was announced that a deal had been struck between the two clubs with Lincoln paying £35,000. He scored on his debut, in the opening game of the season, in a 2–1 loss away at Rotherham United.

It has been rumoured that the deal to bring Carayol included much more than just a big fee. We allegedly haemorrhaged money in 2010/11 due to all sorts of different deals whereby players had houses and accommodation paid for over and above their wages. Was Carayol one of those players? Who knows?

As our miserable 2010–11 season progressed, Carayol began to suffer from injuries which saw him restricted to 37 appearance in all competitions. Despite his obvious ability he often went missing in games, just like Dany N'Guessan before him. He only played four games in that horrible final run in, and was absent as we slipped out of the league. Carayol's future at City was doubt after a clause was activated on relegation that gave him freedom to quit the club, and he left in May 2011. He had been one of the higher earners at the club and contracts such as his were part of the reason the club suffered so badly financially when they were relegated.

Since then he's done alright but I find it hard to celebrate a player whom has since proven he had bags of ability, but wasn't able to show the sort of fight that might have kept us in the league.

Carbon, Matthew
(1993-1996, 2003)
Defender 78 (6) Apps, 11 Goals
Born 8th June 1975
1993–1996 Imps), 1996–1998 Derby County 20 (0), 1998–2001 West Bromwich Albion 113 (5), 2001–2004 Walsall 55 (2), 2003 Lincoln City (loan) 1 (0), 2004–2006 Barnsley 50 (1), 2006–2007 New Zealand Knights 0 (0), 2007–2008 Milton Keynes Dons 3 (0)

Carbon came off the same talent conveyor belt as Ben Dixon and Darren Huckerby, under the watchful eye of Keith Alexander, and when Keith progressed to team manager he brought Matt Carbon through with him. When he first emerged, he was a powerful and commanding defender and it was widely assumed he would go on and have a decent career. After scoring 10 league goals in 66 starts and surviving Alexander, Sam Ellis and Steve Wicks he was sold to Derby County for £385,000.

The money was used in part by John Beck to build the side that eventually won us promotion, and that may have been the end of the Imps story for Matt Carbon. However, a return for former manager Keith Alexander meant a brief return to the club for his former pupil.

In October 2003 after a spell out with injury he left Division One (now the Championship) side Walsall for a spell on loan with Lincoln. Injuries continued to hit him and he made just one appearance for City in a 3-0 defeat at York. He returned to Walsall and by the end of the season was featuring regularly for them in the second tier.

Carr, Darren
(2001)
Defender 3 (0) Apps 0 Goals
Born 4ᵗʰ September 1968
1986-1987 Bristol Rovers, 1987-1988 Newport County, 1988-1990 Sheffield United, 1990-1993 Crewe Alexandra 1993-1998 Chesterfield, 1998-1999 Gillingham, 1999-2001 Brighton & Hove Albion 2001 Rotherham United (loan), 2001 Imps (loan), 2001 Carlisle United (loan), 2001-2002 Dover Athletic 2002-2002 Rushden & Diamonds, 2002 Bath City

Defender signed on loan for three games as Alan Buckley battled relegation in the 2001/02 season. Kept a clean sheet in his first game but couldn't repeat that feat and he wound up leaving.

Perhaps better known to Imps fan for an alleged clash with Jason Lee in the aftermath of an early nineties visit by Crewe. Apparently Jason had to be restrained to stop him going after Carr in the dressing room. Before his Lincoln stint he also featured in the Chesterfield side that almost made the FA Cup final in 1996/97 alongside former Imps Andy Leaning and Tony Lormor. Works as a plasterer now in Bristol.

Carruthers, Martin
(2004-2005)
Forward 8 (4) Apps 0 Goals
Born 7ᵗʰ August 1972
1990–1993 Aston Villa 4 (0), 1992 Hull City (loan) 13 (6), 1993–1996 Stoke City 91 (13), 1996–1999 Peterborough United 67 (21), 1999 York City (loan) 6 (0), 1999 Darlington 17 (2), 1999 Southend United (loan) 5 (3), 1999–2001 Southend United 65 (23), 2001–2003 Scunthorpe United 86 (34), 2003–2004 Macclesfield Town 39 (8), 2004 Boston United 6 (0), 2004–2005 Imps, 2005 Cambridge United (loan) 5 (0), 2005–2006 Grantham Town, 2006 Ilkeston Town (loan), 2006–2008 Ilkeston Town, 2008–2011 Arnold Town, 2012 Basford United

Martin Carruthers scored goals more or less everywhere he played. After a fairly prolific spell at Peterborough in the late 90's he had another prolific spell at Southend before scoring almost one in two for Scunthorpe United. In 2003/04 he found the net a few times for Macclesfield. Then he moved to Lincoln.

Lincoln can often be a curse on certain strikers (see Allon, Joe and Fortune-West, Leo), players who have a reputation for scoring goals simply can't do it at Sincil Bank. Carruthers was one of those players. In his short spell with us he didn't score a single goal. 2004/05 was a tough season for him though and it proved to be his last in professional football. He started with Boston (0 goals), moved to us (0 goals) and finished with a loan spell at Cambridge (0 goals). Had he been with us 12 months or 24 months earlier I think we would have had a gem, but unfortunately those legs couldn't power him through one more prolific season.

Carson, Trevor
(2011)
Goalkeeper 16 Apps 0 Goals
Born 5ᵗʰ May 1988
2006–2012 Sunderland 0 (0), 2008–2009 Chesterfield (loan) 18 (0), 2011 Imps (loan), 2011 Brentford (loan) 1 (0), 2011 Bury (loan) 8 (0), 2012 Hull City (loan) 0 (0), 2012 Bury (loan) 9 (0), 2012–2014 Bury

44 (0), 2013–2014 Portsmouth (loan) 37 (0), 2014–2015 Cheltenham Town 46 (0), 2015 Hartlepool United 43 (0)

The day Trevor Carson was born was one of the greatest days of this writers' life, the day we beat Wycombe 2-1 to return to the Football League. It was almost poetic that 23 years later he should play a crucial role is us dropping back into the non-league pyramid.

Carson is a good goal keeper, and back when he signed on loan from Sunderland that was evident. Steve Bruce loaned him to Steve Tilson to help us secure those precious points we needed to remain a league club. He made his debut in a 4-3 win at Stockport that gave us the edge over our relegation rivals and was a lynchpin in a side that began to amass points and climb away from the relegation spots.

He was in goal the day we beat Southend to all-but assure safety, and he was in the sticks the night we got one point against Macclesfield when a win would have seen us safe. It seemed certain that with his safe hands we'd grab those extra points. After all he'd kept five clean sheets which was no mean feat with a defence as flimsy as wet toilet paper in front of him.

Only we didn't get the points we needed, because immediately after a 2-1 defeat at Stevenage Steve Bruce recalled him, and then loaned him back out to Brentford. Heartbreakingly he played one game for Brentford. One game. In the meantime, Steve Tilson brought in a young lad called Elliott Parish who wore gloves made of butter and we lost every game through until the end of the season, sealing our relegation on the final day. Thanks Steve Bruce, I'm glad you never won an England cap now.

Caton, James
(2016)
Midfielder 8 (4) Apps 3 Goals
Born 4th January 1994
2012–2014 Blackpool 2 (0), 2013 Accrington Stanley (loan) 2 (0), 2014 Chester (loan) 1 (1), 2014– 2016 Shrewsbury Town 2 (0), 2015 Southport (loan) 4 (0), 2015 Mansfield Town (loan) 0 (0), 2015– 2016 Wrexham (loan) 4 (0), 2016 Imps (loan) 12 (3), 2016 Southport 12 (1)

Most fans will remember James Caton as a tricky and fast wide player who could cut inside at will. He joined on loan from Shrewsbury towards the end of Chris Moyses reign as City boss and oozed quality. In eight starts he managed three goals, one an absolute stunner against Eastleigh in a fine 3-0 win. On expiry of his loan he was linked with Lincoln but a change of manager suggested he might end up elsewhere.

Danny Cowley brought him back in on trial throughout the close season of 2016/17 and it seemed a deal was in the offing. He appeared in most of the pre-season friendlies and it was a case of 'when' he signed rather than 'if'. However, at the eleventh hour he was told there was no deal with Nathan Arnold coming in instead. A devastated Caton ended up at struggling Southport.

Champion, Tom
(2016)
Midfielder 3 (2) Apps 0 Goals
Born 15th May 1986

2004–2005 Barnet 7 (0), 2005 Wealdstone (loan) 0 (0), 2005–2010 Bishop's Stortford 114 (4), 2010 Braintree Town 0 (0), 2010–2013 Dartford 117 (5), 2013–2015 Cambridge United 81 (1), 2015 Barnet 27 (0) 2016 Imps (loan)

Tom Champion arrived with the billing of a commanding and combative midfielder who had experienced success at this level with Cambridge United, where he was highly thought of. He immediately dropped into the first team for the 0-0 draw with Solihull Moors which ended the Imps five match winning streak. Fans were on his back and further outings against Dover and Barrow ended in defeats, and Champion became the scapegoat. He dropped out of the side and returned from the bench for the away trip to Bromley where less than ten minutes after coming on he gave the ball away twice to allow Bromley to equalise. Recalled by Barnet before his loan spell had expired to prevent further damage to his confidence.

Chandler, Dean
(1997-1998)
Defender 1 Apps 0 Goals
Born 6th May 1986
1994–1997 Charlton Athletic 3 (0), 1997 Torquay United (loan) 3 (0), 1997–1998 Imps, 1997–1998 Yeovil Town (loan) 9 (1), 1998 Chesham United, 1998 Slough Town 0 (0), 1998–2000 Yeovil Town 37 (1), 2000–2001 Slough Town 2 (0), 2001 Woking 14 (0), 2001–2003 Purfleet 62 (0), 2003 Thurrock, 2003–2004 Ford United 45 (0), 2004–2005 East Thurrock United[1] 14 (3), 2005–2006 Leyton[1] 20 (2), 2006–2006 Heybridge Swifts, 200?–2007 East Thurrock United, 2007 Redbridge

Chandler began his career as a trainee with Charlton Athletic, Prior to coming to Lincoln Chandler along with Lee Bowyer was found to have tested positive for cannabis after a training ground check. Chandler was banned, and upon his return found it difficult to break into the Charlton first team. He signed for Lincoln after a three-game spell at Torquay and played one game, ending up on the losing side against Burnley. He looked out of his depth and gave away two penalties. He never got near the first team again.

In 2004 Chandler made his debut for the England Learning Disability team, playing in a 16–0 win against Sweden. He was sent off in his next match against Brazil for violent conduct.

Christophe, Jean-Francois
(2011-2012)
Midfielder 27 (5) Apps 2 Goals
Born 27th June 1987
2007 RC Lens 2007–2008 Portsmouth 1 (0), 2007–2008 Bournemouth (loan) 11 (1), 2008 Yeovil Town (loan) 5 (0), 2008 Southend United (loan) 14 (1), 2008–2010 Southend United 55 (4), 2010 Oldham Athletic 1 (0), 2010–2011 Compiègne 3 (0), 2011–2012 Imps, 2012–2013 Tienen 15 (4), 2013 Avion 12 (1), 2013–2015 Boussu Dour Borinage 17 (3), 2015-2016 Arras Football Association, 2016 US Vimy

Christophe was a battling midfielder brought in to give us some steel as we contended with teams in the Blue Square Premier. He was well known to Steve Tilson having played 14 games for him in 2008 at Southend, including the FA Cup third round draw with Chelsea, and the subsequent replay they lost 4-1.

It was clear to see what he could bring to the side; the idea of Jean-Francois Christophe was very appealing. A big and combative midfielder who could physically dominate the midfield as well as get forward. It never really panned out like that.

He didn't immediately endear himself to home fans getting sent off in his home debut as we slipped to Kettering at Sincil Bank. It was only after Tilson left that we began to see glimpses of the big Frenchman's potential. He scored a 22nd minute winner at home to Barrow, and followed it up a few weeks later with a goal against Southport at Sincil Bank. Sadly, he never found the consistency that might have helped as we battled against a slide down the table.

He made his last home appearance in March of 2012 as a demonstration took place outside the ground, and his final performance came away at Fleetwood in the much referenced 2-2 draw in which Jamie Vardy scored twice.

He spent some time at Tienen in Belgium after Lincoln, hooking up with Francis Laurent and Jean Arnaud.

Clapham, Jamie
(2010-2011)
Defender 23 (5) Apps 2 Goals
Born 7th December 1975
1994–1998 Tottenham Hotspur 1 (0), 1997 Leyton Orient (loan) 6 (0), 1997 Bristol Rovers (loan) 5 (0), 1998 Ipswich Town (loan) 12 (0), 1998–2003 Ipswich Town 195 (8), 2003–2006 Birmingham City 84 (1), 2006–2008 Wolverhampton Wanderers 26 (0), 2007 Leeds United (loan) 13 (0), 2008 Leicester City 11 (0), 2008–2010 Notts County 70 (3), 2010–2011 Imps, 2011 Kettering Town 3 (0)

Jamie Clapham was the one that slipped through the net, a Lincoln-born youngster who somehow found his way to Tottenham instead of our own youth set up. In March 1998, he cost Ipswich £300,000 and after five good years at Portman Road Birmingham decided to outlay £1.3m for him. It's fair to say Clapham was a decent player.

By the time he finally returned to his hometown club he had obviously played his best football, and he came in at a time of absolute carnage and disarray. Chris Sutton brought him in and then left, and Steve Tilson took up the reigns. Mix this with a battle against injury you'd expect any 35-year-old pro to have, and you get a potential for a disaster of a stay.

If you take league position into account then Clapham didn't have the best of times at Lincoln, but I always thought he had the experience and ability to help keep us in the league. If we could have seen a bit more of him on the pitch his calming influence might (I stress might) have helped those younger players who didn't seem to have the heart for the fight.

He missed almost all of that dreadful run-in, returning half fit for the 3-0 trouncing by Aldershot. He wasn't there as we lost 4-0 to Gillingham, or 6-0 to Rotherham or even 5-1 to Shrewsbury. Could he have made a difference? Could he have helped secure those two points that would have kept us up? Who knows. One thing is for sure, it wasn't the veteran defenders fault we went down.

Clarke, David
(1987-1993)
Defender 199 (15) Apps 7 Goals
Born 3rd December 1964

1982–1987 Notts County 123 (7), 1987–1994 Imps, 1993–1994 Doncaster Rovers 16 (0), 1994–1995 Gainsborough Trinity 1 (0)

I haven't had to write about many of the GMVC winning players here, and it seems unusual to be writing about Dave Clarke. I remember him from my earliest games, and that seems a lifetime ago now!

Clarke was a skilful left back who joined City in our Conference season from Notts County. It was a big decision in the summer of 1987 to drop out of the Football League to join the newly relegated Imps. He made a goal scoring debut against Stafford Rangers in September 1987, and went on to make 30 league appearances as we secured promotion back to the league at the first attempt.

Prior to his life as an Imp he had been a really promising full back, capped by England Youths in 1983/84. His ability shone through in that first season as well, he was composed and cultured at all times.

Following our promotion, he stayed around for five and a half seasons. His tenure was often interrupted by injuries, but every time he came back and dropped comfortably back into the side. He hit both goals in our two legged Littlewoods Cup tie with Southampton in our first season back, and a winner in front of over 6,000 against Peterborough the season after.

The 1990/91 season was a non-starter as injury restricted him to just 14 league appearances, but he had two more solid seasons after that at left back. However, he couldn't go on bouncing back for ever, and just seven outings under Keith Alexander spelled the end for the popular defender. He made his last appearance in October 1993 as we lost 2-1 to Doncaster Rovers, and was released after spending the majority of the season injured.After Lincoln he tried to get his career back on track with Doncaster Rovers, but his body had simply taken too much punishment.

Even now when discussing the best Lincoln side of the last thirty years the name of Dave Clarke often pops up. He was reliable, steady and always put his body on the line for the team.

Clarke, Jamie
(2009-2010)
Forward 17 (6) Apps 4 Goals
Born 11th September 1988
2007–2009 Blackburn Rovers 0 (0), 2008 Accrington Stanley (loan) 16 (5), 2009 Rotherham United 11 (2), 2009–2010 Imps

Jamie Clarke signed in June 2009 after he agreed terms with manager Peter Jackson. He was a cult hero from the start having previously scored a hat trick past county rivals Grimsby whilst playing for Accrington. Changes in management didn't do Clarke any favours though as Chris Sutton seemed hell-bent on dismantling the squad the Jackson had thrown together.

Ironically towards the end of his Imps spell he started finding the net, one in the FA Cup first round against Telford and then a brace away at Northwich to give us a third-round tie with Bolton. His reward was omission from the side from early December and he didn't get to play in the match his goals earned for us. Clarke left City by mutual consent on 29 January 2010 after scoring just one league goal in addition to those FA Cup strikes.

Clarke, Shane
(2006-2010)
Midfielder 51 (24) Apps 0 Goals
Born 7th November 1987
2006–2010 Imps, 2010 Gateshead 1 (0), 2010–2011 Boston United 9 (1), 2011–2013 Gainsborough Trinity 51 (6), 2013–2014 Worksop Town, 2014 Tamworth 36 (7), 2016 Boston United

Shane is a product of the club's centre of excellence and was one of five players who accepted a three-year scholarship with the Imps at the start of the 2004/05 season. Of those five, three would go on to forge good professional careers: Jack Hobbs, Scott Loach and Clarke.

He started his Imps career with a bit of controversy, he was red-carded for a last-minute lunge on Mark Hudson in a 3–1 home defeat to Rotherham United which resulted in a three-match ban.

He stayed with City for four more years, getting plenty of game time under Peter Jackson who (to his credit) did have a policy of giving youth a chance. However once hatchet man Chris Sutton came in, everyone's days were numbered. In May 2010, Clarke was placed on the transfer list by Sutton and on 31st August 2010 agreed a deal with the club to have his contract cancelled.

Most recently he signed for Boston United but suffered an injury really early in his spell. He is often seen at Sincil Bank, most recently in the stands as we beat North Ferriby 6-1.

Clucas, Sam
(2009-2010)
Midfielder 1 Apps 0 Goals
Born 25th September 1990
2009–2010 Imps, 2010–2011 Jerez Industrial, 2011–2013 Hereford United 58 (8), 2013–2014 Mansfield Town 43 (8), 2014–2015 Chesterfield 41 (9), 2015 Hull City 51 (6)

Lincoln born, he spent 6 years with Leicester City before dropping down to play for Nettleham. Peter Jackson signed him up as one for the future and he made his Imps debut against Darlington in the Football League Trophy. He was replaced in that game by former Glenn Hoddle pupil Chris Fagan. The game resulted in a 1-0 defeat and saw Peter Jackson dismissed.

Chris Sutton came in bemoaning his luck at the squad he inherited. He signed lots of young players from the top flight such as Matt Saunders, Adam Watts, and Michael Uwezu. The name of Sam Clucas didn't feature on any of his team sheets and the youngster was released into obscurity at the end of July 2010 with just a solitary appearance to his name.

Oh no, wait. He wasn't released into obscurity at all. He went off to the Glenn Hoddle Spanish Soccer School and then.... well then he's not done badly has he?

He's since gone on to play in all five divisions climbing the ranks quickly. He's garnered a reputation as a goal scoring midfielder who should have a long and stellar career in the top two divisions. He is currently a Premier League player featuring regularly for Hull City. What of Saunders, Watts, and Uwezu? Luckily you have this book so you can find out.

Quite unfairly Chris Sutton is often berated for letting Clucas go, and whilst on the face of it the decision seemed ludicrous, at the time Clucas wasn't achieving what he could. The stay with Glenn Hoddle made the player what he is today, so credit for that.

Cobb, Frazer
(2012-2013)
Midfielder 0 (1) Apps 0 Goals
Born 5th September 1993
2012-2013 Imps

Midfielder who made one appearance for City after coming through the youth ranks. Played as 10 man Hayes and Yeading beat us 1-0 at the Bank under David Holdsworth. I'm sure Frazer is a nice guy, but I really can't write anymore about him.

Colman-Carr, Luca
(2008-2010)
Defender 0 (2) Apps 0 Goals
Born 11th January 1991
2009–2010 Imps, 2010 Arundel, 2012 Pagham, 2015 Molesey, 2015 Petersfield Town 1 (0)

Colman-Carr was offered a scholarship with the Imps in May 2008. In April 2009, he was handed a first team squad number and found himself making his Football League debut as a 70th-minute substitute for Stefan Oakes in the 2–0 home defeat to Aldershot.

He began the 2009–10 season in Peter Jackson's match day squad, appearing from the bench as a last-minute replacement for Joe Heath in the 1–0 opening day home victory over Barnet in August 2009. He was an unused sub in seven of the next eight fixtures. However, after the appointment of Chris Sutton as manager he was not utilised in the first team squad again, and left at the end of the season.

Connor, Paul
(2009-2010)
Forward 10 (7) Apps 0 Goals
Born 12th January 1979
1996–1999 Middlesbrough 0 (0), 1997 Gateshead (loan) 5 (3), 1998 Hartlepool United (loan) 6 (0), 1999 Stoke City (loan) 3 (2), 1999–2001 Stoke City 33 (5), 2000–2001 Cambridge United (loan) 13 (5), 2001–2004 Rochdale 94 (29), 2004–2006 Swansea City 65 (16), 2006–2007 Leyton Orient 34 (7), 2007–2009 Cheltenham Town 79 (7), 2009–2010 Imps, 2010–2011 Mansfield Town 52 (15), 2011– 2013 Gainsborough Trinity 48 (11), 2013 Shildon

Connor joined on trial in the summer of 2009 having had a decent career at Swansea, Rochdale and Orient. On paper, he looked to be on a downward trajectory though after a couple of relatively barren seasons with Cheltenham. His debut came in the 1–0 home victory over Barnet on the opening day of the season, but a thigh strain picked up in training saw him miss half of the August fixtures, then a knee injury sustained in the 3–0 home victory over Darlington a couple of days after Peter Jackson was dismissed kept him on the side-lines for almost five months. He returned to the first team squad for the game with Bradford City in January 2010 but from there on struggled to make the starting eleven. He started only five games in the remainder of the season and he departed Sincil Bank without a goal to his name in May 2010.

Cornelly, Chris
(2002-2005)
Midfielder 9 (8) Apps 0 Goals
Born 7th July 1976

1995–2000 Lower Hopton, 1999 Ossett Albion, 1999–2003 Ashton United, 2002–2003 Stockport County, 2002–2005 Imps, 2004–2005 Stamford (loan), 2005–2006 Ashton United, 2005–2006 Radcliffe Borough, 2010 Ossett Albion

Cornelly joined City initially on a part time basis, training once a week and maintaining his job as an installations manager for a CCTV company. He agreed a deal until the end of our successful first play-off season and made his Football League debut as a 61st-minute substitute for Simon Yeo in the red-card strewn 2-2 draw with Cambridge. He forced his way into the first team, and in April of 2003 found himself on the end of a red card decision as we beat York City 1-0.

The successful run in the first team saw him offered a full-time professional contract for the 2003–04 season, but his last appearance for the Imps was in our Third Division play-off final defeat by Bournemouth. Sadly, he ruptured his anterior cruciate ligaments a week before the start of the 2003-04 season. In a cruel twist of fate, he didn't make a senior appearance after signing full time, and he was released in May 2005 after a two-year battle with his injury.

Cornwall, Luke
(2003)
Forward 1 (4) Apps 0 Goals
Born 23rd July 1980
1997–2003 Fulham 4 (1), 2001 Grimsby Town (loan) 10 (4), 2003 Imps (loan), 2003–2004 Bradford City 3 (0), 2004 Woking 7 (3), 2005–2006 Dulwich Hamlet, 2006–2007 Metropolitan Police

Unremarkable striker brought in on loan in the 2002/03 season as we pushed our way up the League Two table. Only started once away at Rochdale, and was hauled off before we grabbed our 83rd minute winner in that game. Returned to Fulham and embarked on a career as unremarkable as his short spell at City.

In 2007 he quit football to become a London taxi driver, and his middle name is Clarence. There's a couple of book-worthy facts for you.

Cort, Carl
(1997)
Forward 5 (1) Apps 1 Goal
Born 1st November 1977
1996–2000 Wimbledon 73 (16), 1997 Lincoln City (loan) 6 (1), 2000–2004 Newcastle United 22 (7), 2004–2007 Wolverhampton Wanderers 94 (31), 2007–2008 Leicester City 14 (0), 2008 Marbella 7 (1), 2008–2009 Norwich City 12 (1), 2009–2011 Brentford 31 (6), 2012–2014 Tampa Bay Rowdies 18 (3)

Vastly over-rated striker who commanded transfer fees totalling £9m in his career. He cost Newcastle £1m per goal, but probably represented better value for Wolves scoring 31 times for a £2m investment.

Of course, all of this activity came after he joined us on loan from Wimbledon in 1997. He was a John Beck loan signing, a big strong target man who could get onto the end of those numerous long balls we liked to play. He scored on his Imps debut as we lost 3-1 at home to Wigan, but went on to draw a blank in the rest of his outings. He'd obviously shown something to Wimbledon though as just a month after returning there he made his league debut for them, spending 20 minutes up front in a 2-0 defeat to Aston Villa, alongside Imps legend Mick Harford. Last heard of plying his trade over in America.

He comes from a football family as the older brother of Leon Cort who troubled Lincoln playing for Southend, and the half-brother of current Chelsea starlet Ruben Loftus-Cheek.

Costello, Peter
(1991, 1992-1994)
Forward 39 (12) Apps 9 Goals
Born 31ˢᵗ October 1969
1988-1990 Bradford City 20 (2), 1990 Rochdale FC 34 (10), 1990-1992 Peterborough United 8 (0), 1991 Imps (loan), 1992-1994 Imps, 1994 Dover Athletic, 1994 Kettering Town 6 (4), 1995 Mansion FC, 1996 Instant-Dict FC, 1996-1997 Golden, 1997-1998 Kettering Town, 1998-2003 Boston United, 2003-2004 Stevenage Borough, 2004 Cambridge City

Pacey and tricky striker who signed on-loan from Peterborough for a handful of games in 1991. Steve Thompson went back for the striker in 1992 and he made a permanent move. He could operate in midfield as well and offered Steve some attacking options, but he featured mostly as the number 10. Scored some goals in the 1992/93 season including two at home in a 2-1 win over Doncaster, and two in a 3-1 away win at Darlington. Suffered an injury mid-way through the season and despite battling back only made a handful more appearance at the start of the 1993/94 campaign.

In his later years, he played around Hong Kong before returning to Lincolnshire with County rivals Boston United whom, alongside Steve Evans fraudulent dealings, he helped fire to the Football League.

Cranston, Jordan
(2015)
Defender 11 Apps 0 Goals
Born 11ᵗʰ November 1993
2013–2014 Wolverhampton Wanderers 0 (0), 2014 Nuneaton Town (loan) 7 (0), 2014 Hednesford Town 0 (0), 2014 Nuneaton Town 1 (0), 2014–2015 Notts County 9 (0), 2015 Imps (loan), 2015–2016 Gateshead 23 (1), 2016 Cheltenham Town 26 (0)

Young full back who joined on loan towards the end of the 2014/15 season as Chris Moyses successfully kept us in the National League. Impressed in his 11-game spell but was recalled by Notts County shortly after a last minute red card in our 1-1 draw with Halifax in April 2015.

The left back played for Gateshead after leaving Notts County but is currently playing league football with Cheltenham Town.

Croft, Gary
(2007-2008)
Defender 22 Apps 0 Goals
Born 17ᵗʰ February 1974
1992–1996 Grimsby Town 172 (4), 1996–1999 Blackburn Rovers 52 (1), 1999–2002 Ipswich Town 37 (1), 2002 Wigan Athletic (loan) 7 (0), 2002 Cardiff City (loan) 8 (1), 2002–2005 Cardiff City 80 (2), 2005–2007 Grimsby Town 61 (0), 2007–2008 Imps, 2015 Grimsby Borough 6 (0)

Talented left back (in his day) who once commanded a £1m transfer fee when he signed for Blackburn from Grimsby Town. By the time he made his way to Sincil Bank it was a decade later and he was well past his best. He came to replace Paul Mayo at left back in the John Schofield's second and final season in charge. He never looked fully fit and struggled with both injuries and a couple of red cards in his time.

Once Schofield moved on he still commanded a place in Peter Jackson's first team, but after just 22 outings in a full season he was never likely to be retained. Replaced by Aaron Brown ahead of the 2008/09 season and didn't play professionally again. Being an ex-Grimsby player he never really won over the Imps fans, and I guess very few were sad to see him leave.

He retained his fishy connections and joined the Compass FM commentary team as expert summariser for Grimsby matches. He also continues to be involved with a local Grimsby/Cleethorpes area estate agent that he and relatives founded around the time of his second Mariners spell.

Cropper, Dene
(2002-2004)
Forward 35 (22) Apps 3 Goals
Born 5th January 1983
2000–2001 Sheffield Wednesday 0 (0), 2001–2002 Worksop Town (loan) 20 (10), 2002–2004 Imps, 2004 Gainsborough Trinity (loan) 5 (1), 2004 Boston United 5 (1), 2004–2005 Worksop Town, 2005–2011 Matlock Town, 2011 Woolley Moor United

Dene Cropper can at best be described as a tryer. His arrival at Sincil Bank was during a time of turmoil, with administration staved off in the summer he was a cheap option striker along with Simon Yeo. However, unlike Yeo he didn't go on to be an Imps legend.

His debut was a disaster; he was dismissed for two bookable offences as we drew 1-1 with Kidderminster. Before he served his suspension, he scored one of his three Imps goals in the 2-0 home win over Rochdale.

He found goals hard to come by and for the rest of the season netted just twice, at home to Bournemouth as we lost 2-1 and away at Wrexham in a 2-0 win. He dropped in and out of the team as Keith tried many different centre forwards in an attempt to curb our apparent lack of goals.

By the end of the season he was actually a regular in the first team, starting all three play-off games including the defeat by Bournemouth in the final. The following season things didn't go well for him, he found himself unsurprisingly overlooked. He spent a majority of his time on the bench due to long layoff with injury and the performances of players such as Francis Green and Gary Taylor-Fletcher.

In February 2004, he signed on loan with Non-League club Gainsborough Trinity and after he returned to Lincoln he was subject to another loan offer, this time from Scarborough. He rejected the chance to play for Scarborough in favour of a permanent switch to local rivals Boston United. He managed to play just five times for Boston and scored once, but suffered a serious knee injury towards the end of the season which prompted his release from the club

Cropper should be remembered fondly as a member of famous 2002/03 play-off hunting side, but the harsh fact is that a goal every 30 games isn't good enough for most midfielders, let alone a centre forward. Despite trying as hard as he could he wasn't really Football League standard.

Cryan, Colin
(2005-2007)
Defender 44 (4) Apps 0 Goals
Born 23rd March 1981

1998–2004 Sheffield United 10, 2002 Scarborough (loan) 5 (1), 2003–2004 Scarborough (loan) 10 (1), 2004–2005 Scarborough 43 (5), 2005–2007 Imps, 2006–2007 Boston United 15, 2007–2011 Droylsden 106 (5)

Former Sheffield United defender who made a name for himself during Scarborough's 2004 FA Cup run in which they ended up meeting Chelsea live on television. Signed with fellow Scarborough player Scott Kerr in Keith Alexander's last season as Imps manager.

Cryan managed two seasons at Lincoln and was solid without being particularly spectacular. He made 42 appearances under Keith, but suffered an injury early in the next season and failed to regain his place. After under 18 months as a Lincoln player he joined Boston United, and later went on to make over 100 appearances for Droylsden. Once he had retired from football he went to work as a PE Teacher at Salesian College Celbridge.

Cunningham, Karl
(2011-2012)
Midfielder 2 (0) Apps 0 Goals
Born 4th November 1993
2011-2012 Imps, 2015 Ange IF 25 (16), 2016 Pitea IF 22 (6)

Former youth team player who made two appearances after Steve Tilson had been dismissed and prior to David Holdsworth coming in to replace him. It was therefore caretaker Grant Brown who showed some faith in the youngster.

He started out 3-1 away win at Alfreton, coming off in the 58th minute for Ali Fuseini. That game he kept both Jamie Taylor and Kyle Perry on the bench, and just a week later he did the same again as we drew 1-1 with Mansfield at Sincil Bank. Six days later Holdsworth joined as manager and there ended the brief run of outings for Karl Cunningham, two starts and no defeats.

Has most recently been playing in Sweden where he's enjoyed moderate success, scoring 16 goals in their fourth tier with Ange IF.

Daley - Dykes

Daley, Luke
(2012)
Midfielder 4 (1) Apps 0 Goals
Born 10th November 1989
2008–2011 Norwich City 11 (0), 2011 Stevenage (loan) 2 (0), 2011–2012 Plymouth Argyle 18 (1), 2012 Imps, 2012–2014 Braintree Town 60 (8), 2014–2015 Dartford 31 (1), 2015 Chelmsford City 47 (4)

Former Norwich winger signed by David Holdsworth in 2012 after a successful trial. He made only five appearances for City, four of them starts and a once from the bench. Like many of Holdsworth's signings he didn't really get a chance to make an impact, and with the high turnover of players it was little surprise when he left at the end of August. He spent the rest of the season at Braintree where he scored seven goals, including a brace in a 2-0 win over Grimsby. Currently doing the rounds on the non-league scene in the south of England.

Daley, Phil
(1994-1996)
Forward 30 (11) Apps 6 Goals
Born 12th April 1967
1989–1994 Wigan Athletic 161 (39), 1994–1996 Imps, 1997 Bangor City

Average striker who gained cult status without ever producing the goods. He was tall and had scored a few goals for Wigan but he could never been described as prolific. At Lincoln he ran true to form, scoring a handful of goals without ever really excelling. Scored five goals in his first season and then he suffered a cartilage injury meaning an operation in early 1995 which ruled him out for three months. After that he found it even harder to break into the side and he netted just one in his second season, although that was a winner away at Scunthorpe. Famously booked as a substitute for joining in a goal celebration.

Dali, Gomez
(2013)
Forward 1 (3) Apps 0 Goals
Born 10th January 1989
2006-2009 Nantes B, 2009-2010 Kingstonian, 2010-2011, Aylesbury, 2011-2012 Woodley, 2013 Imps, 2014 UJA Maccabi

Possibly the worst player I have ever had the misfortune to witness represent the football club I love. The total sum of his contribution to our cause under Gary Simpson was one red card, earned after just 4 minutes of our 3-0 win at Braintree for kicking out at Matt Paine. Only appeared once more for City (thankfully) before leaving to never darken our doors again. Most recently seen turning out for a French fifth tier team.

We actually paid him a wage as well. I can't get over that. Watching him play was like watching Ali Dia, the fake cousin of George Weah who conned Southampton in 1996. Only Dali was real, he wasn't anyone's cousin and he was far, far worse at football.

Davies, Tom
(2015)
Defender 0 (1) App 0 Goals
Born 18th April 1992
2011–2013 Team Northumbria, 2013–2014 F.C. United of Manchester 27 (4), 2014–2015 Fleetwood Town 0 (0), 2014 FC United of Manchester (loan) 13 (1), 2014 Alfreton Town (loan) 9 (0), 2015 Imps (loan), 2015 Southport (loan) 9 (0), 2015–2016 Accrington Stanley 32 (1), 2016 Portsmouth 7 (0)

Defender signed on loan by Chris Moyses but restricted to just one substitute appearance in his time with City as a half time replacement for Sean Newton. Booked in the game against Bristol Rovers which we lost 2-0, he didn't feature again. Has since played league football for Accrington Stanley and Portsmouth.

Davis, Darren
(1988-1990, 1996)
Defender 119 (5) Apps 7 Goals
Born 5th February 1967
1983–1988 Notts County 92 (1), 1988–1990 Imps, 1990–1992 Maidstone United 31 (2), 1992–1993 Boston United, 1993 Frickley Athletic, 1993–1995 Scarborough 48 (3), 1995 Grantham Town, 1996 Imps, 1997 VS Rugby, Hucknall Town

Davis was a tall and versatile defender who made over 100 appearances for City in the late 1980's before a move to Maidstone. He wouldn't qualify for an entry in these pages though, so to ensure I had to write about him he returned for a brief spell in 1996 after playing for Grantham Town. His form with the Gingerbreads earned him three more outings in a Lincoln shirt.

Unfortunately for Davis it wasn't a successful spell coming amidst the turmoil of managerial upheaval. He featured on the losing side three times against Rochdale (1-2), Cambridge (1-3) and Plymouth (0-3) before sloping off back into the non-league scene.

Daws, Tony
(1994-1996)
Forward 44 (10) Apps 13 Goals
Born 10th September 1966
1984–1986 Notts County 8 (1), 1986–1987 Sheffield United 11 (3), 1987–1993 Scunthorpe United 183 (63), 1993–1994 Grimsby Town 16 (1), 1994–1996 Imps, 1995–1996 Halifax Town 5 (1), 1996–1997 Scarborough 6 (0), 1996–1997 Altrincham, 1996–1997 Bradford Park Avenue

Relatively prolific striker who at one time averaged a goal every three games for Scunthorpe. He was initially brought to the club by Keith Alexander, and therefore probably earns himself the honour of being the first in a (very) long line of strikers trialled by Keith at the Bank.

He had a keen eye for goal but a back injury at Scunthorpe meant that he had already seen the best of his playing days. Nonetheless he still averaged a goal every three starts for Lincoln and played in a succession of relatively average teams.

He scored 13 times across three seasons and survived both Sam Ellis and Steve Wicks, but left the club shortly after the arrival of John Beck. His Imps career was defined by a succession of injuries that kept him out for a couple of months at a time, and although the quality was still there he just couldn't keep himself fit. Retired relatively early due to injury.

Day, Chris
(2000-2001)
Goalkeeper 18 Apps 0 Goals
Born 28th July 1975
1995–1996 Tottenham Hotspur 1 (0), 1996–1997 Crystal Palace 24 (0), 1997–2001 Watford 11 (0), 2000–2001 Imps (loan), 2001–2005 Queens Park Rangers 87 (0), 2002 Aylesbury United (loan) 7 (0), 2005 Preston North End (loan) 6 (0), 2005–2006 Oldham Athletic 30 (0), 2006–2008 Millwall 10 (0), 2008 Stevenage 288 (0)

Day signed for City under Phil Stant as the club slipped down the third division table, and he kept fellow former Spurs player Alan Marriott on the bench. Day was a decent keeper but with a weak defence in front of him he kept just three clean sheets in his 18 outings. Made three appearances for Alan Buckley before returning to Watford, and going on to have a good career with Stevenage.

Dennis, Tony
(1996-1997)
Defender 25 (7) Apps 2 Goals
Born 1st December 1963
1981–1983 Plymouth Argyle 9 (0), 1983–1984 Exeter City 4 (0), 1984–1986 Bideford, 1986–1987 Taunton Town, 1987–1988 Slough Town 76 (12), 1988–1993 Cambridge United 111 (10), 1993–1994 Chesterfield 10 (0), 1994–1995 Colchester United 65 (5), 1996–1997 Imps 1997–1998 Gainsborough Trinity 14 (0), 1998 Ilkeston Town 1 (0)

Tony Dennis is perhaps most famous for something he didn't do rather than something he did. With Terry Fleming already on a yellow card and facing a second he gave the name Tony Dennis to the referee. The ref bought it and Fleming stayed on the pitch, although he was punished retrospectively.

Away from his team mate's misdemeanour Dennis was a John Beck signing having played under him at Cambridge. He was combative and uncomplicated as a player and found it a struggle to break into the first team. He had a good run over the winter period replacing Terry Fleming for a short while and then Mark Hone. Scored early in his Imps career against his old club Cambridge, but was released at the end of the season as Beck shuffled his side around.

Diagne, Tony
(2013, 2014)
Defender 22 (4) Apps 2 Goals
Born 7th September 1990
2010–2011 Aubervilliers 0 (0), 2011–2013 Macclesfield Town 77 (4), 2013 Imps (loan), 2013–2014 Morecambe 27 (2), 2014 Imps, 2015 Macclesfield Town (loan) 30 (2)

Left sided defender who followed Gary Simpson to Sincil Bank from Macclesfield, initially on loan. He had an impressive loan spell scoring twice in a 3-0 win at Braintree. He looked to be quick and strong and it was no surprise when he ended up in League football with Morecambe.

It didn't work out well in the north-west and he joined the Imps on a permanent deal ahead of the 2014/15 season. This time he didn't have the same impact, instead of two goals against Braintree he found himself sent off. Despite this set-back he was virtually ever present until Gary Simpson left, then injuries kept him out of Chris Moyses side. He played four games in March and April of 2015, but with a year left on his contract he was allowed to join Macclesfield on a year-long loan deal. He was released on completion of his contract.

Dixon, Ben
(1992-1996)
Midfield 38 (12) Apps 0 Goals
Born 16th September 1974
1992-1996 Imps, 1993-1994 Witton Albion (loan) 4 (0), 1996-1998 Blackpool 13 (0), 1998 Woodlands Wellington, 1998-2004 Whitby Town, 2004 Gainsborough Trinity, 2004-2005 Ossett Town, 2005-2007 Lincoln United, 2007-2008 Grantham Town, 2008 Boston Town

Ben Dixon was a home grown youngster who was just 17 years 177 days old when he made his debut in early 1992. He came off the same talent production line as Matt Carbon and Darren Huckerby but with less success. Despite his talent he never settled for a period of time in the first team, but eventually left City for Blackpool in 1996. He latterly had a long spell with Witton Albion in non-league as well as a short spell in Singapore.

Dixon, Bohan
(2013-2014)
Midfielder 8 (22) Apps 3 Goals
Born 17th October 1989
2007–2008 Kingsley United, 2008–2009 Connah's Quay Nomads 8 (0), 2009–2010 Buckley Town, 2011 Hednesford Town 3 (0), 2011 Burscough, 2011–2012 McGinty's, 2012–2013 Accrington Stanley 10 (0), 2013 Marine (loan), 2013–2014 Imps, 2014–2015 Northwich Victoria, 2015 Salford City, 2015–2016 Stalybridge Celtic 29 (6), 2016 AFC Fylde 23 (5)

Bohan Dixon was one of Gary Simpson's signings arriving after a short spell at Accrington Stanley. He was used mainly as a substitute, a somewhat ungainly and unorthodox one at that. He did come off the bench to score twice against Hyde, and also chipped in with a goal in our 3-3 draw with Chester. However he wasn't able to cement a first team place and a 24th minute sending off in a tough encounter away at Grimsby didn't help his cause. He became a figure of derision for many and is often mentioned by fans as 'the worst player they've seen in a Lincoln shirt'. Those fans, it is assumed, never saw Gomez Dali.

Since leaving Lincoln he hasn't done too badly at a level that perhaps suits him better, putting in good solid seasons with Stalybridge Celtic and most recently ambitious AFC Fylde.

Dodds, Louis
(2007-2008)
Forward 40 (4) Apps 9 Goals
Born 8th October 1986
2006–2008 Leicester City 0 (0), 2006 Northwich Victoria (loan) 6 (3), 2007 Rochdale (loan) 12 (2), 2007–2008 Imps (loan), 2008–2016 Port Vale 289 (51), 2016 Shrewsbury Town 11 (2)

Young wide player signed on loan by John Schofield in the summer of 2007 from Leicester City. His arrival was understated in a summer of poor recruitment by Schofield, but Dodds turned out to perhaps be the best of the bunch. He was lively and chipped in with a couple of goals before Schofield was sacked, but he kept his place under Peter Jackson. Scored our goal of the season against Wycombe Wanderers which was his fourth in six games, but didn't score again all season.

Most fans had hoped he would move to City permanently, and he did reject a new contract offer from Leicester but opted instead to sign for Port Vale, where he resisted the temptation to score past us the following season, waiting until the 2009/10 campaign before registering a second half winner for Vale at Sincil Bank. On the final day of the 2008/09 season he netted for the Valiants against Barnet in a 2-1 win something he couldn't repeat two years later in a repeat of the fixture. A failure to score in the final game against Barnet in 2011 saw City relegated.

Dudfield, Lawrie
(2000)
Forward 2 (1) Apps 0 Goals
Born 7th May 1980
1997–1998 Kettering Town, 1998–2001 Leicester City 2 (0), 2000 Imps (loan), 2000–2001 Chesterfield (loan) 14 (5), 2001–2003 Hull City 59 (17), 2003 Northampton Town (loan) 10 (1), 2003–2004 Northampton Town 19 (7), 2004 Southend United (loan) 13 (5), 2004–2005 Southend United 36 (9), 2005 Northampton Town 6 (1), 2005–2006 Boston United 26 (7), 2006–2008 Notts County 74 (17), 2008 Cork City 12 (7), 2011 Boston United 6 (2)

Spent three games on loan at City during the reign of Phil Stant from Leicester but wasn't able to make a significant impact. He returned to his parent club and spent the rest of the season on loan at Chesterfield. The following season he scored 14 times for Hull, including one against in Lincoln. In 2005 he came on as a late substitute for Southend in the play-off final as they beat us 2-0, and the year after he popped up with a late winner at York Street for Boston against us as well. Somewhat predictably he moved on to Notts County where one of his 12 goals were against Lincoln. I was really glad when he retired from the game given his record against us.

Dudgeon, James
(2000-2001)
Defender 23 (2) Apps 3 Goals
Born 9th March 1981
1998–2003 Barnsley 0 (0), 2000–2001 Imps (loan), 2003 Scarborough 1 (0), 2003–2004 Halifax Town 10 (0), 2004–2005 Worksop Town 39 (3), 2005–2007 York City 44 (6), 2007–2008 Stalybridge Celtic 12 (0), 2007–2008 Gateshead (loan) 5 (1), 2008 Gainsborough Trinity 2008 Worksop Town (loan), 2008–2009 Newcastle Blue Star, 2009 Wakefield, 2009–2010 Ilkeston Town, 2009 Frickley Athletic (loan), 2009–2010 Goole (loan), 2010–2012 Goole

Dudgeon arrived on a season long loan from Barnsley in November 2000 initially to play under Phil Stant. He retained his first team place after Stant left under Alan Buckley which was testament to the young defender's ability. He was strong and as a youth still relatively quick, and standing at in excess of six foot certainly helped. Despite having never turned out for Barnsley he impressed Stant and Buckley, but a permanent deal was simply not on the cards due to finances.

He was a tough tackler too and he had to miss most of January after consecutive red cards in matches away at Darlington (0-3) and at home to Scunthorpe (1-1). He scored three times for City as well, significantly earning us a 1-1 draw at home to Rochdale and a vital 2-1 win over Plymouth as the season drew to a close.

He returned to Barnsley upon completion of his loan and aside from a couple of seasons at York he never achieved the potential he showed in his short Imps loan spell.

Duffy, Ayden
(2006-2009)
Goalkeeper 4 (2) Apps 0 Goals
Born 16th November 1986
2006-2009 Imps, 2008 Stamford (loan) 2009 -14 Corby

Reserve keeper who only ever got a run out if firstly Alan Marriott and latterly Rob Burch were out injured. He only kept one clean sheet for Lincoln, in a Football League Trophy game against Leicester City.

Duffy, Rob
(2012-2013)
Forward 3 (0) Apps 0 Goals
Born 2nd December 1982
2001–2005 Rushden & Diamonds 30 (1), 2005 Stamford (loan) 2 (2), 2005 Cambridge United 9 (0), 2005 Kettering Town 4 (1), 2006 Stevenage Borough 1 (0), 2006–2008 Oxford United 56 (24), 2008 Wrexham (loan) 6 (0), 2008–2009 Newport County 21 (1), 2009–2011 Mansfield Town 78 (28), 2011–2012 Grimsby Town 52 (8), 2012–2013 Imps, 2013-2014 King's Lynn Town 27 (12), 2014–2015 Ilkeston 51 (21), 2015-2016 Nuneaton Town 31 (11), 2016 Basford United 0 (0)

The signing of Rob Duffy was borderline exciting in the summer of 2012. We hadn't had much good news for a while but hearing that Duffy has signed was positive. He'd scored regularly for Oxford and Mansfield and this level and would hopefully provide some goals.

He didn't, he got injured in only his third match and was released towards the end of the season after making no more appearances. He's since scored fairly regularly for Kings Lynn, Nuneaton and Ilkeston.

Dunphy, Sean
(1990-1995)
Defender 56 (6) Apps 3 Goals
Born 5th November 1970
1989–1990 Barnsley 6 (0), 1990–1995 Imps, 1993–1994 Doncaster Rovers (loan) 1 (0), 1994–1995 Scarborough (loan) 10 (0), 1994–1995 Kettering Town 1 (0), 1994–1995 Gainsborough Trinity 4 (0), 1994–1995 Halifax Town (dual-registration) 2 (0), 1996–2000 Stocksbridge Park Steels

Dunphy arrived in early 1990, following his former manager Allan Clarke to Sincil Bank. We never got to see the player that Clarke signed, a serious knee injury in a pre-season friendly game against Leeds United meant he didn't make his debut for City until April 1992, against Maidstone United. He only made 48 starts for the Imps and five as a sub. Loan spells at Doncaster and Scarborough followed before he retired, never having given us a glimpse of what he might have been like fully fit.

Dyer, Alex
(1995)
Defender 2 (0) Apps 0 Goals
Born 14th November 1965
1983–1987 Blackpool 108 (19), 1987–1988 Hull City 60 (14), 1988–1990 Crystal Palace 17 (2), 1990–1993 Charlton Athletic 78 (13), 1993–1995 Oxford United 76 (6), 1995 Imps, 1995–1996 Barnet 35 (2), 1996–1997 F.C. Maia 0 (0), 1997–1998 Huddersfield Town 12 (1), 1998–2000 Notts County 80 (6), 2000–2001 Kingstonian 0 (0), 2001 Hayes 1 (0)

Defender signed on loan from Oxford United. Made two appearances in which City lost 2-0 (Notts County) and 3-0 (Colchester) before returning to his parent club. He was booked on his return to Sincil Bank with Notts County four years later.

Dykes, Daren
(2002-2003)
Midfielder 2 (1) Apps 0 Goals
Born 28th April 1981
2001 Newport Pagnell Town, 2000–2002 Buckingham Town, 2002–2003 Swindon Town 2 (0), 2002–2003 Imps (loan), 2003–2004 Buckingham Town, 2005–2006 Stotfold, 2006–2008 Stony Stratford Town (37), 2008–2009 Rugby Town 5 (0)

Daren Dykes is the reason this book got made. His name caught my eye in a programme and I thought he was probably the first player who I couldn't remember playing for Lincoln in matches I'd seen. I started a small blog going through an A to Z of forgotten Imps heroes. That escalated into the book you've bought (or borrowed) that you're reading now.

Daren came to us on loan from Swindon Town in Keith's first (second spell) season 2002-03. We were short on goals at the time and young Dykes was billed as an attacking midfielder who could perhaps help Yeo and Cropper put the ball in the back of the net. Coming from Swindon you'd expect he had a bit about him.

Unfortunately for Darren he joined as the club experienced a good spell of form, and despite his early inclusion he failed to make an impact. He came on as a sub in a 1-1 draw at York, but by that time we'd already scored. York's 81st minute equaliser came just two minutes after he entered the fray. Despite that set back he started in the away win at Macclesfield but came off with the game poised at 0-0. His final game was a 1-0 home win against Swansea, he was booked and came off before we scored the decisive goal. Despite two more games on the bench he didn't get on the pitch and we let him go once the month was up.

Dykes had come up from non-league after spending his youth with Spurs and his foray into league football never worked out. He played once more for Swindon before dropping back into the non-league. He never made the step back up and was last seen playing for Newport Pagnall where he'd started his career.

Maybe to honour him I should have named the book after him. The Who's who of Lincoln City (1993-2016) and Daren Dykes. It just so happens I contacted him for a brief chat about inspiring this piece of Imps history. You can read about it at the back of the book.

Eaden - Futcher

Eaden, Nicky
(2006, 2007)
Defender 34 (1) Apps 0 Goals
Born 12th December 1972
1992–2000 Barnsley 293 (10), 2000–2002 Birmingham City 74 (3), 2002 Wigan Athletic (loan) 5 (0), 2002–2005 Wigan Athletic 117 (0), 2005–2007 Nottingham Forest 28 (0), 2006 Imps (loan), 2007 Imps (loan), 2007 Halesowen Town 1 (0), 2007 Solihull Moors 1 (0), 2007–2009 Kettering Town 28 (0)

Veteran defender Eaden came on loan from Notts Forest and played in the 2006/07 season which was the last time we had an assault on the play-offs in League Two. He was an accomplished and composed left full back who lacked a bit of pace due to his advancing years, but who also always looked comfortable on the ball. His loan expired at the end of December and he re-joined for the second part of the season during which the Imps collapsed. He played both semi-finals against Bristol Rovers before departing for the non-league scene.

Elding, Anthony
(2009)
Forward 15 apps 3 Goals
Born 16th April 1982
2001–2003 Boston United 37 (6), 2001–2002 Bedford Town (loan) 4 (1), 2002–2003 Gainsborough Trinity (loan) 1 (0), 2003–2006 Stevenage Borough 109 (50), 2006 Kettering Town 15 (4), 2006–2007 Boston United 19 (5), 2007–2008 Stockport County 45 (24), 2008 Leeds United 9 (1), 2008–2010 Crewe Alexandra 26 (10), 2009 Imps (loan), 2009 Kettering Town (loan) 8 (3), 2010 Ferencváros 15 (8), 2010–2011 Rochdale 17 (3), 2011 Stockport County (loan) 21 (3), 2011–2013 Grimsby Town 59 (18), 2012–2013 Preston North End (loan) 5 (0), 2013 Sligo Rovers 24 (19), 2014 Cork City 5 (2), 2014–2015 Ballinamallard United 17 (3), 2015 Derry City 9 (2), 2015-2016 Sligo Rovers 8 (2)

Elding joined on loan from Crewe to try and pep up City's attack in the wake of the failed Magnificent Seven experiment. He looked like he might just do the job as well, netting on his debut as the 10-man Imps snatched a 2-2 draw with Brentford. Sadly, the apparent class that Elding possessed was rarely on display as he stumbled through 14 further outings scoring just twice.

The truth is that Anthony Elding was a good player and his goals at Crewe, Stockport, Grimsby and Stevenage are testament to that. It would be easy to criticise his time in a Lincoln shirt as lacking effort and desire, but he did play under Peter Jackson who fancied himself more as a Svengali-style motivator than a proper football manager with actual tactics and plans. Maybe this affected Elding, maybe he really didn't give two hoots about Lincoln, who knows. When he arrived, it was speculated we wouldn't be able to sign him permanently, but by the time his loan was up nobody was too distressed that a lack of funds might hold us back.

Ellison, Kevin
(2004)
Midfielder 13 Apps 0 Goals
Born 23rd February 1979
1996 Southport 4 (0), 1997 Chorley, 1997–1999 Conwy United 37 (7), 1999–2001 Altrincham 51 (23), 2001 Leicester City 1 (0), 2001–2004 Stockport County 48 (2), 2004 Imps (loan), 2004–2005 Chester City 24 (9), 2005–2006 Hull City 39 (2), 2006–2007 Tranmere Rovers 34 (4), 2007–2009 Chester City

75 (19), 2009–2011 Rotherham United 88 (15), 2011 Bradford City (loan) 7 (1), 2011 Morecambe 207 (57)

Kevin Ellison probably won't be remembered all that fondly by most fans. He came in on loan from Stockport County as we pushed towards our second play-off assault and turned in 13 strong and notable appearances on the left side of defence / midfield. He had an all-action and full-blooded approach to the game. As we went out to Huddersfield he had a little spat with a Terriers fan on the MCalpine pitch, and I hoped we'd see him back at Lincoln. He had an aggression and passion that could have carried us further.

Whenever we did get to see him back at Lincoln he was usually scoring or sullying any memories we had of him. There's no doubt Ellison is a talented player, but he's also a horrible bastard as well. He celebrated wildly when scoring against us for Chester, something he repeated at Rotherham for Morecambe. You get the impression Kevin Ellison would look in a mirror and start a fight with himself if he got half a chance

In two matches against Lincoln the following season he not only scored but was also booked, once in each game. Even in 2009 he was picking up bookings against us!

We should have remembered that after a £100k move to Hull he fell out of favour and Scunthorpe had a bid accepted, but sensibly he refused to move. He wasn't all bad, and if he'd signed for us in the 2004/05 season he would have been a massive asset for the club. Still playing league football at the ripe old age of 37.

Eustace, Scott
(2000)
Defender 0 (1) Apps 0 Goals
1993–1995 Leicester City 1 (0), 1995–1998 Mansfield Town 98 (6), 1998 Chesterfield 0 (0), 1999–2000 Cambridge United 51 (1), 2000 Imps, 2001–2002 Hinckley United, 2002–2003 Stevenage, 2003 Telford United

Centre half who played just one game for Lincoln after signing a deal in the summer of 2000. He suffered early in his spell with injuries, and replaced Grant Brown in the 77th minute of our 1-0 defeat at Leyton Orient on 23rd September 2000. Wasn't seen in league football again after the Imps terminated his contract for an off the field altercation. He had been given a final warning by the club in September after being handed a driving ban. His contract was terminated following a late-night disturbance outside a kebab shop which saw him put on probation for nine months.

Everington, Kegan
(2013- Current)
Midfielder 6 (15) Apps 1 Goal
Born 17th December 1985
2013- Imps 2014 Lincoln United (loan)

Young midfielder who has come through the ranks and appeared a few times in the first team. Made his debut against Grimsby in early 2014 and has been in and out of the side since. Scored in the 3-2 win away at Chester the next season. Could have a bright future with some additional game time.

Facey, Delroy
(2009-2010, 2010-2011)
Forward 36 (10) Apps 5 Goals
Born 22ⁿᵈ April 1980
1996–2002 Huddersfield Town 75 (15), 2002–2004 Bolton Wanderers 10 (1), 2002 Bradford City (loan) 6 (1), 2003 Burnley (loan) 14 (5), 2004 West Bromwich Albion 9 (0), 2004–2005 Hull City 21 (4), 2005 Huddersfield Town (loan) 4 (0), 2005 Oldham Athletic 9 (0), 2005–2006 Tranmere Rovers 37 (8), 2006–2007 Rotherham United 40 (10), 2007–2008 Gillingham 32 (3), 2008 Wycombe Wanderers (loan) 6 (1), 2008–2010 Notts County 63 (11), 2009–2010 Imps (loan), 2010–2011 Imps, 2011–2012 Hereford United 40 (6), 2013–2015 Albion Sports

Delroy Facey joined on loan initially under Chris Sutton to add some beef to the attack, and beef is one thing he had a lot of. He brought it in abundance, a big and burly centre forward who didn't get off to a great start. His first game we lost 2-1 to Port Vale at home and he missed a couple of glorious chances, although a Boxing Day winner against Chesterfield helped him get the fans on side.

He returned the following season on a permanent deal to play under Chris Sutton, and although Sutton didn't last Facey did. He formed a strong partnership with loan player Ashley Grimes and between the two of them they looked to have fired us to league safety. Unfortunately, Facey got injured in the 1-1 draw with Macclesfield and Grimes didn't score again as we went down.

After he left us Facey has done some interesting things, the main one being attempting to fix a lower league game in conjunction with Moses Swaibu. He was jailed for two and a half years after being found guilty, and is now a disgraced figure in the game.

Fagan, Chris
(2009-2010)
Forward 12 (5) Apps 3 Goals
Born 11ᵗʰ May 1989
2009 Hamilton Academicals 0 (0), 2009–2010 Imps, 2010 Jerez Industrial (loan) 12 (4), 2011 Bohemians 23 (11) 2012 St Patrick's Athletic 124 (53)

When Chris Fagan was first announced as a Lincoln player it felt a bit of a let-down. We'd been hanging on for a marquee signing, someone to bang in 20 goals a season. Although he had no proven track record he did have a bit of pedigree. He'd been snapped up as a youngster by Man Utd whilst playing for Home Farm in Ireland, and had three years with their youth set up. He wasn't offered a contract at United and made his way over to Spain to play at the Glenn Hoddle academy.

Fagan never really looked the part at Lincoln and he managed just three goals in 13 appearances. Although he had obvious talent the physicality and pace of League Two didn't suit the youngster and when Peter Jackson left the club it seemed Fagan's days were numbered He went out on loan to a Spanish Third Division side Jerez Industrial where he made a slight impact scoring four times in 12 appearances. However, it seemed inevitable that on his return he would be released, and along with Sam Clucas he was a casualty of Chris Sutton's only pre-season as Lincoln manager.

The story could have ended there for Fagan, released by a struggling fourth tier side after a series of false starts in his career. A trial at Gateshead didn't work out either and he saw in Christmas of 2010 without a club. A trial with Irish side Shamrock Rovers didn't bring a contract either, but undeterred he continued to search for a club and finally signed for Bohemians in Feb 2011.

He made only 23 appearances for the Irish side but began to find his scoring boots and netted 11 goals, including a Europa League goal against Olimpija Ljubljana. Still only in his early twenties he was finally letting his pedigree show. At the end of the 2011 season he was very much in demand and chose to sign for St Patricks Athletic going straight in as their number nine.

In five seasons playing for St Pat's he has become the player he always threatened to with an impressive ratio of 72 goals in 157 games. He has become their all-time leading European scorer with 6 goals including strikes against Legia Warsaw and Dinamo Minsk. In 2013 they won the League of Ireland, and in 2014 the FAI cup, FAI presidents cup and the Leinster senior cup. In 2014 he won the Irish golden boot and was named in team of the year and won player of the year. It's fair to say he found his feet in front of goal. The past two seasons he has hit 20 goals in 56 games despite again suffering injuries.

Chris Sutton can talk all he wants about the weak squad he inherited, but Chris Fagan scored a couple of goals and has gone on to make a half decent career out of playing football. Chris Sutton went on to make a half decent career out of not being able to manage a football club.

Fairhurst, Waide
(2013-2014)
Forward 5 (7) Apps 2 Goals
Born 7th May 1989
2008–2011 Doncaster Rovers 10 (2), 2009 Solihull Moors (loan) 4 (2), 2009–2010 Shrewsbury Town (loan) 13 (7), 2010 Southend United (loan) 3 (0), 2011 Hereford United (loan) 9 (4), 2011–2013 Macclesfield Town 37 (14), 2013–2014 Imps, 2014–2015 Macclesfield Town 32 (13), 2015–2016 Torquay United 2 (0), 2016 F.C. Halifax Town 2 (1), 2016 Boston United 5 (1)

Waide Fairhurst announced himself on the Lincoln City scene with a stunning brace on his debut against Forest Green in August of 2013. The boy clearly had a lot of talent, but after that exciting start he struggled to find a regular starting spot for Gary Simpson. When he wasn't struggling with injuries he was kept out of the side by players such as Marlon Jackson, Chris Sharp and Nick Wright. Eventually left for Macclesfield on loan before making the move permanent in the summer of 2014.

Waide has never achieved the potential he showed in a prolific spell at Shrewsbury, and despite often being amongst the goals for Macclesfield he is now plying his trade at Boston United.

Farman, Paul
(2011-2012, 2012- Current)
Goalkeeper 199 (1) Apps 0 Goals
Born 2nd November 1989
2008–2009 Blyth Spartans 0 (0), 2008 Washington (loan), 2009–2012 Gateshead 64 (0), 2011-2012 Imps (loan), 2012 Imps, 2014-2015 Boston United (loan) 4 (0)

Popular goalkeeper Paul Farman has had to do things the hard way in his career. After a trial at Newcastle didn't work out he spent some time in the non-league scene of the North-east, eventually settling at Gateshead. It was with the Heed that he first appeared at Sincil Bank in September 2011, conceding an Ali Fuseini header to help us to a 1-0 win.

He was back a few months later on loan, and he joined an Imps side in crisis. Steve Tilson had moved on and we were a side devoid of confidence and ability. After playing eight games for the club he returned to Gateshead, but he had already made himself a popular figure at Lincoln. He kept a clean sheet whilst on loan against Ebbsfleet, and again away at Forest Green. Up until that point we'd only kept two clean sheets, one of those against Farman's Gateshead!

By August of 2012 he was back at Lincoln on a permanent deal. He was virtually ever present until picking up an injury at the end of the following season against Hyde. Gary Simpson signed Nick Townsend on loan, and when he regained fitness Farman couldn't force his way into the team.

Things got much worse for him the following season. Gary Simpson signed Townsend on loan again and promised him the number one spot. Farman was relegated to the bench, and even went out to spend time on loan at Boston. It seemed the likeable Geordie's days were numbered at Sincil Bank.

He returned stronger and with the same application and devotion he had always had, and his first Imps game back was in the 3-3 draw that saw Simpson fired. Restored to the starting line-up he seized his chance, and under the watchful eye of David Preece he not only reclaimed the number one jersey, but also went on to be named the Imps Player of the Year.

In 2016/17 he is widely regarded as one of the best goalkeepers at this level, and his services have been retained by Danny and Nicky Cowley. He's already pulled off crucial saves, most recently at Chester to keep us in the game in the first half. We went on to win 5-2, but the importance of his contribution should not be under estimated. He could go on to eclipse the appearances made by Alan Marriott, recently passing the 200 mark with a clean sheet against Wrexham.

Fenn, Neale
(1999)
Forward 1 (4) Apps 0 Goals
Born 18th January 1977
1995–2001 Tottenham Hotspur 11 (0), 1998 Leyton Orient (loan) 3 (0), 1998 Norwich City (loan) 7 (1), 1998 Swindon Town (loan) 4 (0), 1999 Lincoln City (loan) 4 (0), 2001–2003 Peterborough United 50 (14), 2003 Waterford United 19 (4), 2004–2006 Cork City 84 (27), 2007–2009 Bohemians 69 (5), 2010 Dundalk 22 (4), 2010 Shamrock Rovers 9 (0)

Irish-born Fenn joined on loan from top flight Tottenham Hotspur whilst we fought in the old Second Division. After a solitary start against Mansfield in the Autoglass Windscreens Shield he dropped to the bench as we went four games without a goal against Oldham (0-2), Fulham (0-1), Stoke (0-2) and Walsall (0-1). Unsurprisingly returned to Spurs once his loan expired, and aside from one decent spell with Peterborough United he never managed to cut it in the football league. Ended up in his native Ireland with a couple of different clubs.

Finnigan, John
(1998-2002)
Midfielder 161 (5) Apps 4 Goals
Born 28th March 1976
1995–1998 Nottingham Forest 0 (0), 1998 Imps (loan), 1998–2002 Imps, 2002–2009 Cheltenham Town 220 (20), 2009–2011 Kidderminster Harriers 16 (3), 2010–2011 Bishop's Cleeve 12 (0), 2011–2012 Shortwood United

'Finns' as he was affectionately known originally joined the Imps on loan from Nottingham Forest in April of 1998 and made six appearances including the 2-1 victory at home to Brighton that sent us up into the old Division Two. Upon his release that summer by Forest he was snapped up on a free transfer.

Over the course of the next four seasons Finns set about making himself a fans favourite. He was a tireless worker in the middle of the park, always scrapping for the cause. He was never one to be amongst the goals regularly, although he did score twice in our foray out of the basement division against Stevenage in the FA Cup and Burnley at Turf Moor in the league.

As we dropped back into the bottom league his class and work ethic was quite often evident over and above some of the other journeymen we had playing for us. He was always cultured and composed, and yet also always disciplined. He was never sent off for City and ended up captaining the side through some very tough times. As we knocked through managers and careered towards administration he was the rock in the middle of the park, still fighting the cause as the ship appeared to be sinking around him.

He missed a chunk of his final season with a neck injury as we plummeted down the leagues and it became apparent that we weren't going to be able to hold on to him as money became tighter and tighter. Just two months before the end of the 2002 season he joined Cheltenham on a free transfer, more as a budgeting measure than anything else.

He had seven years at Whaddon Road and helped fire them to promotion, eventually becoming club captain. The fact he had so few clubs in his career is a testament to both his value as a player and his dedication and application. Finns should be remembered as one of Lincoln City's best midfielders despite playing throughout a time of downward trajectory.

Flash, Richard
(1997-1998)
Forward 2 (3) Apps 0 Goals
Born 8th April 1976
1995 Manchester United 0 (0), 1995–1996 Wolverhampton Wanderers 0 (0), 1996–1998 Watford 1 (0), 1997–1998 Imps (loan), 1998–1999 Plymouth Argyle 5 (0)

Richard Flash is a name you could have heard much more had it not been for injuries. He was a Manchester United youth player who once roomed with David Beckham and shared the pitch with the likes of Michael Appleton and Terry Cooke. He had an awful lot of promise but a knee injury at just 14 years old curtailed his potential. Another injury later in his United career put paid to his dreams of top flight football. He had a spell at Wolves and then Watford which is where he joined City from. He made his debut in a 0-0 draw with Cambridge but didn't have an impact and left once his loan sell concluded.

He picked up another serious injury upon returning to Watford and found himself trying to rebuild his career at Plymouth Argyle. Unfortunately, he sustained a career ending injury after 30 minutes of a trip to Cardiff in 1999 and was forced to retire aged just 23. He is now a lecturer at the UCFB.

Fleming, Terry
(1995-2000)
Midfielder 201 (9) Apps 12 Goals
Born 5th January 1973
1991–1993 Coventry City 13 (0), 1993–1994 Northampton Town 31 (1), 1994–1995 Preston North End 32 (2), 1995–2000 Imps, 2000–2001 Plymouth Argyle 17 (0), 2001–2004 Cambridge United 105

(4), 2004–2005 Grimsby Town 43 (2), 2005–2006 Kidderminster Harriers 38 (2), 2006–2007 Moor Green, 2007 Halesowen Town, 2007–2008 Grantham Town, 2008–2013, Lincoln United, 2013–2015 Sleaford Town, 2015 Boston Town

Combative. Aggressive. A little bit naughty. These are a few of the phrases that could be used to describe Terry Fleming. There's no doubt he was a key player for City after signing for John Beck shortly after Beck took over as manager. He became a key figure in the so-called ugly side that Beck assembled, picking up twice as many bookings as goals but never one to stop fighting for the team.

In the 1996/97 season, he was famously booked against Wigan, then committed a second offence just before half time. He gave the name of team mate Tony Dennis instead of his own and got away with it for a short while. However, he eventually ended up with a three-game ban and internal punishment from the club as well.

The following season was perhaps the pinnacle of Terry Fleming's Imps career. His two goals against Emley in the FA Cup earned us a replay, one of which came after six minutes of injury time. He is now officially recorded as the player who got our second goal in the penultimate match against Darlington to secure a play-off spot, and he scored in the final day win over Brighton that saw us go up automatically. He had moved away from the simple hard man reputation and cemented himself as a talented and able midfielder. He had everything the lower league player needed, and a little bit of spice as a garnish. Every team should have a Terry Fleming in it somewhere.

Despite his battling qualities we were relegated the season after, and eventually in the summer of 2000 he left on a free transfer to Plymouth Argyle. He never settled in the south, and after that he had spells at Cambridge and Grimsby. Whilst at Cambridge he was sent off at Sincil Bank in a tempestuous 2-2 draw.

As recently as 2016 he's still been helping out the Imps, arranging the use of Aston Villa's training facilities ahead of a top of the table clash with Forest Green. It would be mildly insulting if he was only remembered for the yellow card incident, however amusing it is to recount.

Mark Whiley's view

I'm going to go for Terry Fleming as my favourite player. The Imps' hard nut in midfield, or right-back, wherever he was asked to play. He was better player than people gave him credit for. Excellent set-piece delivery and a decent long throw. His style of play summed up the John Beck era perfectly.

Flitcroft, David
(1993)
Defender 2 (1) Apps 0 Goals
Born 14th January 1974
1992–1993 Preston North End 8 (2), 1993 Imps (loan), 1993–1999 Chester City 187 (18), 1999–2003 Rochdale 160 (4), 2003–2004 Macclesfield Town 15 (0), 2004–2006 Bury 122 (4), 2006–2007 Hyde United [2] 5 (0), 2007–2011 Rochdale 1 (0)

Young defender signed on loan from Preston by Keith Alexander in 1993. Played in the dramatic 4-3 reverse against Everton as well as a 4-3 win over Northampton and a 3-2 win against Wycombe. Nine goals conceded in his three games didn't give the club enough incentive to sign him, and he returned to Preston.

He latterly had a strong career in the lower leagues with Bury, Rochdale and Chester City, appearing against the Imps on several occasions.

Fofana, Mamadou
(2012-2013)
Midfielder 49 (6) Apps 1 Goal
Born 7th January 1988
2012-2013 Imps, 2015 Barrow, 2016 Oxford City

Mo Fofana was a strong but relatively ineffective central midfielder, first brought to the club by David Holdsworth during the manager's one-man quest to people traffic as many substandard foreign footballers through our books as he could.

Fofana looked like a good footballer, tall and strong and able to handle himself. Technically though it wasn't there for him, and there wasn't enough input in terms of goals for such a physically commanding player. He scored just once in the final day 5-1 victory over Hyde in 2013. The next season his input was significantly less and his last appearance was in the 2-2 draw with Woking in January of 2014. He left the club at the end of the season to pursue a career of anonymity in other non-league side's midfield.

Foley, Steve
(1994-1995)
Midfield 15 (1) Apps 0 Goals
Born 4th October 1962
1983–1984 Fulham (loan) 3 (0), 1984–1985 Grimsby Town 31 (2), 1985–1987 Sheffield United 66 (14), 1987–1992 Swindon Town 151 (23), 1992–1994 Stoke City 107 (10), 1994–1995 Imps, 1995 Bradford City 1 (0)

Veteran midfielder brought in by Sam Ellis to add some experience to his side. Foley had started out at Liverpool and had a good career at Swindon and Stoke before arriving at Sincil Bank. Sadly, we saw the shadow of the player he was as he headed towards the end of his career, and he played just 15 times for City. For those that are interested his debut was a 3-2 win over Mansfield in which he didn't score, and his final game was a 1-1 draw away at Scarborough. Played one more league game after us for Bradford before retiring a season too late.

Folkes, Peter
(2004-2006)
Defender 2 (1) Apps 0 Goals
Born 16th November 1984
2003-2004 Bradford City, 2004-2006 Imps, 2006 Tamworth

Young defender Folkes signed from Bradford as a squad player under Keith Alexander, and he fulfilled his role with gusto, rarely getting anywhere near the pitch. He made three outings for Lincoln, two in 2004/05 season against Doncaster (0-1) and from the bench against Hartlepool (0-3). He then completed the Carling Cup tie against Crewe the year after (5-1) before joining Tamworth in January 2006 when it became clear he wasn't going to develop into the player Keith hoped.

Foran, Mark
(1997)
Defender 1 (1) Apps 0 Goals
Born 30th October 1973

1990–1993 Millwall 0 (0), 1993–1996 Sheffield United 11 (1), 1994 Rotherham United (loan) 3 (0), 1995 Wycombe Wanderers (loan) 5 (0), 1996–1997 Peterborough United 25 (1), 1997 Imps (loan), 1997 Oldham Athletic (loan) 1 (0), 1997–2000 Crewe Alexandra 31 (1), 2000–2002 Bristol Rovers 43 (2), 2002–2003 Telford United 37 (5), 2003–2006 Northwich Victoria

Giant defender Foran came on loan from Peterborough in early 1997 and made just two appearances, one as a substitute. We lost both games 5-2 against Darlington and 3-1 at Wigan. John Beck was an unforgiving man and Foran was soon back at London Road. Prior to Lincoln he spent a five-game loan spell at Wycombe Wanderers, which saw Foran voted by supporters as the worst ever player to represent the club. He would have to go some way to achieve that accolade for Lincoln.

Forrester, Jamie
(2006-2008)
Forward 94 (7) Apps 37 Goals
Born 1st November 1974
1992–1995 Leeds United 9 (0), 1994 Southend United (loan) 5 (0), 1995 Grimsby Town (loan) 9 (1), 1995–1997 Grimsby Town 41 (6), 1997–1999 Scunthorpe United 101 (37), 1999–2000 Utrecht 1 (0), 1999–2000 Walsall (loan) 5 (0), 2000 Northampton Town (loan) 9 (6), 2000–2003 Northampton Town 112 (39), 2003–2004 Hull City 32 (7), 2004–2006 Bristol Rovers 52 (9), 2006 Imps (loan), 2006–2008 Imps, 2008–2009 Notts County 30 (8), 2009–2010 Lincoln United, 2010 Lincoln Moorlands Railway

I talk at many points in this book about Keith Alexander's ongoing search for a proper goal scorer. He unearthed Simon Yeo but his reign was defined by two things: the play-off appearances and his hunt for people who could score goals. I like to think that hunt ended the day he signed Jamie Forrester.

Jamie Forrester was a 'proper footballer'. Sometimes you'll talk to fans and they'll describe a player as just that, a proper footballer. A player who can dictate a game, a player who can adjust their game to suit the opposition and adjust their game to suit their own physical decline. Jamie Forrester had lost some of his pace by the time he came to Lincoln, but rather than fade into the obscurity of the non-league his footballing brain adjusted his game so he was always one step ahead. Jamie Forrester understood the game of football and what was needed to do well in it.

It took him just 16 minutes of his Imps debut to score a goal, and it was the second goal of a 5-0 win over Grimsby Town, our local rivals and his former club. Right then he wrote himself at least one paragraph in this book, even if that was the total of his contribution. It wasn't.

He ended the season on five goals having signed in March, and despite our failure to negotiate the play offs, he made his move permanent. The following year with Keith gone it was up to John Schofield to reap the rewards of some smart business.

Forrester hit four against Mansfield as we won 4-2. He hit a hat trick against Barnet in a 5-0 win, and then again against Rochdale as we won 7-1. He scored against Grimsby again as we beat them at Sincil Bank (2-0) again. He blotted his copy book slightly with a red card away at Notts County, but it was easily forgiven. Alongside Mark Stallard he looked as dangerous and as lethal as at any time throughout his career. I maintain they are the best centre forward pairing I have to write about in this book.

The following season he still managed to hit 14 goals as Schofield left and Jackson came in. He weighed in with his obligatory strike at Sincil Bank against the Cod heads (that's three in three) and won us points singlehandedly first gaining revenge for his sending off at Meadow Lane with a goal against Notts County (1-0) and then a brace as we beat Chester (2-1). Even as Stallard faded away, Jamie Forrester was still on fire.

The following season there was no room at the Inn for Forrester, he was cast aside at the same time as Alan Marriott by Peter Jackson. Whilst two of the 'Magnificent Seven' weren't scoring for us (Graham and Gall), Forrester netted eight for Notts County. Bravo Jacko, bravo.

Jamie Forrester remained in Lincoln after he retired, and is still seen at Sincil Bank every so often. Very few ex Grimsby and Scunthorpe players can commandeer the sort of respect that Jamie Forrester can with Lincoln fans.

Fortune-West, Leo
(1998)
Forward 9 (2) Apps 1 Goal
Born 9th April 1971
1988–1989 Tiptree United, 1989–1992 Bishop's Stortford, 1992–1993 Dartford, 1993–1994 Dagenham & Redbridge, 1994–1995 Stevenage Borough 17 (7), 1995–1998 Gillingham 67 (18), 1997 Leyton Orient (loan) 3 (0), 1998 Imps, 1998 Rotherham United (loan) 5 (4), 1998–1999 Brentford 11 (0), 1999–2000 Rotherham United 59 (26), 2000–2003 Cardiff City 92 (23), 2003–2006 Doncaster Rovers 90 (19), 2006–2007 Rushden & Diamonds 6 (0), 2006 Torquay United (loan) 5 (0), 2006–2007 Shrewsbury Town (loan) 19 (7), 2007–2008 Cambridge United 23 (6), 2008 York City (loan) 13 (2), 2008–2009 Alfreton Town 15 (5), 2009 North Ferriby United 2 (0), 2009–2010 Goole, 2010–2013 Armthorpe Welfare

I'd love to know what happened here, why the curse of Sincil Bank struck Leo Fortune West like it had Joe Allon. Before he came to City he had scored goals. At Lincoln, he managed just one as we got beat 4-3 by Preston, and then in a heartbeat he was gone.

Ian Atkins accused the striker of injuring one of his players in our 0-0 draw just a few weeks into the season, and although Chairman John Reames and manager Shane Westley denied he was involved it did seem to spell the end of his Imps career. When he left, he scored regular goals at Rotherham, Cardiff and Doncaster.

He should have been a superb fit for our club, he should have offered an aerial threat up front and given us someone for Tony Battersby to play off. They should have been another Forrester and Stallard. They weren't, and we got relegated. Maybe the £60,000 fee we got from Brentford was just too much of a lure.

Foster, Luke
(2005-2007, 2013-2014)
Defender 41 (8) Apps 2 Goals
2004–2005 Sheffield Wednesday 0 (0), 2004–2005 Scarborough (loan) 7 (0), 2005 Alfreton Town (loan) 18 (3). 2005–2007 Imps, 2006 York City (loan) 5 (0), 2007 Stalybridge Celtic 4 (1), 2007–2010 Oxford United 101 (3), 2010 Mansfield Town 16 (0), 2010–2011 Stevenage 24 (1), 2011–2012 Rotherham United 5 (0), 2012 Matlock Town 9 (0), 2012–2013 Preston North End 6 (0), 2013–2014 Imps, 2014–2016 Southport 64 (6), 2016 Harrogate Town 0 (0)

Foster was no more than a bit-part player and a utility man during his first spell with Lincoln. Used sparingly over a two-season period in a variety of position, he scored just once in the 5-0 thumping of Grimsby before leaving the club February 2007 for Oxford United.

He returned after a journey that took him in and out of non-league, jumping from Rotherham to Preston North End of the Championship via Matlock Town. He linked up with former assistant manager Gary Simpson for one uninspiring season both personally and as a team in 2013/14 before moving to Southport. He did score one more Lincoln goal which it is only fair to mention, we won 2-0 away at Braintree.

He did also represent his country; he was called up again to represent England C in a game against Bosnia and Herzegovina in Sarajevo in September 2008. He played the whole match as England C lost 6–2 to Bosnia, assisting a Luke Moore goal.

Walter Senkiw's view

As is the case with so many players, we Imps seem to either get promising players who never quite make it, find a few who then go on to bigger and better things and then there are those who just sign for us and then plain disappear (and we've had many of those these past few seasons !!!)

Not sure where this Mexborough born defender fits in .We never got to see him in his prime. He came to us in 2005 as a raw 19/20 year old and played only 17 times. Later he re-joined in the twilight of his career in 13/14 when we were in need of reinforcements and someone with plenty of experience to stabilise a club on its uppers. Even then, we only got to see him play 31 times, so not a full season.

I always liked Luke Foster though.

He always appeared brave. Cut from the true Yorkshire quarry where grit, determination and spirit was hewn. Technically sound and loved a tackle or a header.

For me, I would have liked to have seen him in a red and white shirt a bit more. I remember a couple of occasions where he literally bled for the cause and always appeared to give you good six or seven out of ten display. Perhaps his disadvantage was that he didn't look tall enough or mean enough for a commanding centre half and often overlooked as a result.
Maybe his head wasn't straight (he did admit that he made some "bad choices "in his younger days).

I'd like to think that Luke "Fozzie" Foster was one of those players who had promise and potential but we were never patient enough. Maybe Keith made a mistake and should have kept him on for longer but how could a young man displace the likes of the class defenders we possessed then in Morgan, McAuley, and McCombe eh?

Frecklington, Lee
(2003-2009)
Midfielder 111 (30) Apps 23 Goals
Born 8th September 1985
2003–2009 Imps, 2003–2004 Lincoln United (loan), 2005–2006 Stamford (loan) 11 (1), 2009 Peterborough United (loan) 7 (0), 2009–2013 Peterborough United 81 (8), 2012–2013 Rotherham United (loan) 13 (2), 2013 Rotherham United 114 (21)

Lee Frecklington was born in Lincoln, and to some extent born to play for Lincoln as well. He made his way through Lincoln City's Centre of Excellence and was rewarded with a scholarship place in the summer of 2002. Under John Schofield Frecklington's ability developed and was well noted and during his schooldays he undertook trials with both Norwich City and Leeds United.

He made rapid progress in Lincoln's youth set-up and in the 2003–04 season, making significant strides towards the first team. He particularly impressed in a friendly against Manchester City, and Keith Alexander gave him his full debut in the against Telford United in October 2003. He continued his progression in the final season of his scholarship and made his Football League debut as a substitute in the game at Rochdale on 12th February 2005. It was no surprise that he was handed a one-year professional contract by then manager Keith Alexander.

After a spell out on loan at Stamford he became a regular presence on the substitutes bench and in February 2006 he came off the bench to score his first league goal in the game at Stockport. His reward was his first league start the following week at home to Torquay United. Always impressing, he made 18 league appearances in the second half of the season though only three of these were starts.

Lee had a lot of ability and for a player so young was able to show it in and around the first team. Over the years we've seen lots of these 'bright young things' emerge and ultimately fail. Ollie Ryan, Gary King and even Connor Robinson were given chances that they didn't take. Lee Frecklington was different. In the 2006–07 season he featured heavily in a very pivotal role towards Lincoln's unsuccessful push for promotion to League One. John Schofield placed a lot of belief in his former protégé and he boasted a number of exceptional performances. He was named in the PFA League Two Team of the Year for the 2006–07 season, and he was only beaten to the Imps Player of the Year by Lee Beevers.

In January 2008 the Imps turned down two bids for Frecklington from Peterborough, and in his programme notes around that time Jacko remarked; "I didn't think it was the right offer or the right club for Freck, and we're now in talks to keep him at the club because he's a real asset for us. There's only one or two midfielders in the division who can do what Lee does and we've come to expect it every game despite his age."

The following season as his star continued to rise he seemed increasingly less likely to remain a Lincoln player. There was some surprise when he didn't move on in the January 2009 transfer window, and even more surprise when just six days after the window closed he finally moved to Peterborough initially on loan. Our home-grown talisman was gone, and in a master stroke of managerial genius we couldn't bring anyone in permanently to replace him. Since then he's gone on to play regularly at Championship level, whilst the manager that only a year before wanted to keep him, gave him away. Peter Jackson now runs a care home. That tells a story in itself.

Fuseini, Ali
(2011)
Midfielder 30 (5) Apps 1 Goal
7th December 1988
2006–2010 Millwall 76 (2), 2010 Lewes 1 (0), 2011 Imps, 2011 Eastleigh 1 (0), 2012–2013 Bromley 49 (6), 2013–2014 Sutton United 29 (0), 2014–2016 Bromley 85 (7), 2016 Margate 0 (0), 2016–2017 Welling United 8 (0)

Ali Fuseini had played a fair bit of football for Millwall, so it seemed safe to assume he'd know his way around a football pitch. Steve Tilson brought him in an in his first game we won 2-1 away at Bradford. Fuseini looked like he might bring a bit to the party, he had a nice touch and could spot a pass or two.

85

From there it went downhill. His brand of lightweight, often-absent midfield play wasn't really what we were looking for in the thick of a relegation battle. He featured plenty, rarely contributing anything at all. I had to check if he played in that final match against Aldershot because I can't remember him doing so. He did for the record, meaning he played a significant part in one of the worst days of my life.

The only way was up and it was perhaps ironic that the next season he should score his only Imps goal with his head. He wasn't a tall man at five feet five inches, but he managed to head the ball past Paul Farman in the Gateshead goal to give us a 1-1 draw. All that supposed talent and his only goal came off his head.

Steve Tilson was sacked, and effectively Fuseini's Lincoln career ended. He played his last game on October 18th, on October 24th David Holdsworth came in and (thankfully) we didn't have to see Fuseini in an Imps shirt again, not that you'd notice his contribution if he had kept on playing.

He wasn't a particularly wholesome character off the pitch either. Fuseini was charged with False Imprisonment and Conspiracy to Rape in 2010, and stood trial at Blackfriars Crown Court in February 2011 whilst playing for Lincoln. He was found Not Guilty.

In late 2010, Fuseini was convicted of Aggravated Vehicle Taking and disqualified from driving for 12 months. He was further arrested after leaving Lincoln in November 2011 for Disqualified Driving, and again on 5 December 2011. He was sentenced to 10 weeks' imprisonment for these offences. He was also part of the Bromley side that did the double (1-0, 2-0) over Lincoln in 2015/16 although thankfully he didn't score.

Futcher, Ben
(2002-2005)
Defender 140 (2) Apps 14 Goals
Born 20th February 1981
1999–2002 Oldham Athletic 10 (0), 2001 Stalybridge Celtic (loan) 17 (1), 2002 Stalybridge Celtic 9 (0), 2002 Doncaster Rovers 2 (0), 2002–2005 Imps, 2005–2006 Boston United 14 (0), 2006 Grimsby Town 22 (3), 2006–2007 Peterborough United 25 (3), 2007–2013 Bury 119 (3), 2010–2011 Oxford United (loan) 6 (0), 2011 Mansfield Town (loan) 13 (1), 2012 AFC Telford United (loan) 3 (0), 2012 Macclesfield Town (loan) 10 (0), 2012 FC Halifax Town (loan) 0 (0)

Futcher became one of Keith Alexander's first signings in May 2002, along with Dene Cropper. Futcher was a giant of a defender with somewhat limited ability with the ball on the deck. He was however a good, honest footballer who battled for 90 minutes. The cold truth was he just wasn't that good a footballer.

The Imps climbed the league, and despite Keith's ongoing search for a goal scorer, Futcher did better than most. He scored more goals than both Simon Yeo and Dene Cropper in the season itself, his goals giving us 1-0 wins over York, Scunthorpe, Southend, and Rochdale. He even scored in the play-off final in Cardiff. He may not have been the best footballer, but his aerial threat was plain for all to see. Futcher won "Young Player of the Season" for his efforts.

Futcher was at the heart of the Lincoln defence as we unfortunately faced two more Play-off defeats: losing out in the semi-finals to Huddersfield Town in 2003/2004. After this game Futcher decided to capitalise on his rising star, and asked for a transfer to a bigger club. No bigger clubs came forward.

We went down again at the final hurdle the following season and once again Futcher played his part. By then we had signed Jamie McCombe and Gareth McAuley, both a threat in the air but crucially both good footballers as well. It didn't seem like it would be long before the big man moved on.

When he did move on it was something of a shock. Futcher announced he would be leaving Lincoln, to sign for county rivals Boston United! He even cited footballing reasons as the motivational factor behind his move. One year after asking for a transfer to a bigger club, he moved to a side that have never finished above Lincoln, in any league. Ever. Boston had strengthened though, now boasting such ex-Premiership stars as Julian Joachim and Noel Whelan.

They struggled though, so on January 12th, just six months later he was on the move again, this time sullying any positive memories Imps fans had by signing for Grimsby Town. He played the day we beat them 5-0 and got a suitably warm reception (as you'd imagine) from the partisan home fans. He got his revenge a few weeks later. We were leading the play-off semi-final second leg against Grimsby 1-0, meaning it was 1-1 on aggregate. The next goal was crucial for either team, and in the 60th minute Futcher scored it for Grimsby. They added another in the last ten minutes giving them a 3-1 win on aggregate. Since then he's been off my Christmas card list.

Gain - Grobbelaar

Gain, Peter
(1999-2005)
Midfield 227 (36) Apps 22 Goals
Born 11th November 1976
1995–1999 Tottenham Hotspur 0 (0), 1999 Imps (loan), 1999–2005 Imps, 2005–2008 Peterborough United 71 (9), 2008–2012 Dagenham & Redbridge 149 (4)

Peter Gain joined City on loan from Spurs as we were relegated from the second division, and played just three times including a 5-0 defeat at Preston North End. John Reames however had seen enough and wisely splashed out £15,000 to bring the player to Sincil Bank.

Gain worked hard to earn a starting place; until that is Phil Stant took over and he dropped to the bench. He was considered a little light weight for the direct style of play we seemed to prefer. When Alan Buckley took over he signed his son Adam who was preferred on the left of midfield to Gainy. Eventually he forced his way in to the side scoring a goal in the superb 3-2 December 2001 win against Scunthorpe United. In a dark and desperate season, it was left up to the young player to produce the odd moment of excitement, and when Buckley left it was up to Keith Alexander to convince him to remain at Sincil Bank. He was one of the few players to survive administration and stay with the club.

Under Keith Alexander he developed into perhaps the finest player I have ever had the pleasure of witnessing in a Lincoln City shirt. He formed part of a midfield often bypassed by a long ball, but when it did land on the turf in the final third we got to see what Peter Gain was all about.

He could glide past players as if they weren't there, and he had a habit of producing exquisite goals and pieces of skill that completely betrayed the level of football he was performing at. As we surged towards the play-offs he became an integral part of everything good happening at the club, culminating in a 3-0 home win over Hartlepool in which he ran the show. He was unable to inspire us to play-off success but his trickery and ability had pushed us to within an inch of success. It was a Peter Gain pass that put Simon Yeo through to score the important equaliser on the last day against Torquay, as it had so often been a Peter Gain pass that led to the goals to keep us in the hunt.

The following season he arguably got even better. He scored seven times including spectacular strikes away at York and Carlisle. He terrorised defenders and alongside Richard Butcher formed the best midfield pairing witnessed at Lincoln in a generation. Again, we got so close to success, but again we couldn't quite get over the line.

The goals dried up in his final season and he failed to hit the heights of the previous two campaigns as we once again lost out in Cardiff, this time to Southend. Gainy was one of a few players who left in the summer of 2005 although frustratingly for Imps fans he chose Peterborough United as his destination, in the same league as City. Posh had offered him a three-year deal though and he shouldn't be chastised for chasing that financial security. Predictably he scored against the Imps in Simon Yeo's first game back at the club as we drew 1-1. Towards the end of the season he featured on the Big Ron Manager programme as a Peterborough player.

The following season he scored again at London Road against the Imps, this time City ran out 2-1 winners thanks to a brace by Ryan Amoo. Gain was criticised heavily for his celebration in that game against his old club, but as recently as 2016 he admitted that he regretted a 'moment of madness in the face of extreme provocation' (see appendices). He fell out of favour at Peterborough as

McAnthony's millions enabled them to sign more players, and in January of 2008 he signed for Dagenham, whom he helped win promotion in 2010.

Peter Gain should always be remembered as a legend of Sincil Bank, and not for a one-off celebration after he left. His skill and guile were a key component in our assault on three play-off spots, and he scored some of the most sumptuous and elegant goals I've ever seen from a Lincoln player. He had his own chant which I think sums up his talents perfectly: 'Same old Gainy, taking the piss'.

Gall, Kevin
(2008-2009)
Forward 7 (4) Apps 0 Goals
Born 4th February 1982
2001–2003 Bristol Rovers 50 (5), 2003–2006 Yeovil Town 136 (26), 2006–2009 Carlisle United 66 (9), 2008 Darlington (loan) 8 (0), 2008–2009 Imps (loan), 2009 Port Vale (loan) 7 (0), 2009 Darlington 10 (2), 2009–2010 York City 5 (1), 2010–2011 Wrexham 5 (0), 2011 FC Dallas 0 (0), 2011 Workington 4 (0), 2011 Guiseley 5 (0), 2012–2013 Stockport Sports

It actually pains me to have to write about Kevin Gall so soon after writing about Peter Gain. Gall was one of the much-heralded Magnificent Seven signed by Peter Jackson in 2008, albeit on loan from Carlisle. After leaving Lincoln he ironically played in Darlington's 1-0 Johnstone Paint Trophy win that cost Jackson his job.

Gall was crap, an affront to the shirt and devoid of any ideas or desire. He spent more time running into empty spaces away from the ball than anything. Awful, awful player whom I can't even bring myself to write about anymore.

Galloway, Mick
(1999)
Midfielder 5 Apps 0 Goals
Born 13th October 1974
1993–1997 Notts County 21 (0), 1997–1999 Gillingham 75 (5), 1999 Imps (loan), 1999–2000 Chesterfield 20 (1), 2000–2003 Carlisle United 35 (1), 2002 Gretna (loan), 2002 Hereford United (loan) 9 (0), 2003–2004 Gretna 56 (6), 2004–2005 Stirling Albion 9 (0), 2005 Workington 15 (0), 2005 Eastwood Town 10 (1), 2006 Northbank Carlisle, 2007 Penrith United 14 (0), 2007 Cowdenbeath 13 (0), 2007–2008 Workington 4 (0), 2008–2009 Hucknall Town 3 (0), 2009 Worksop Town

Midfielder signed for a two-month spell on loan from Gillingham shortly after our relegation back into the Third Division. He played in four wins and a draw in a successful loan spell, and John Reames hoped he might be able to extend the arrangement. Unfortunately, Chesterfield had £15,000 that we didn't and they were in the league above, so on completion of his loan he made a permanent move there.

Garner, Scott
(2012-2013)
Defender 13 (3) apps 0 Goals
Born 20th September 1989
2008–2009 Leicester City 0 (0), 2008 Ilkeston Town (loan), 2009–2010 Mansfield Town 51 (6), 2010–2012 Grimsby Town 31 (3), 2011 Alfreton Town (loan) 6 (0), 2012–2014 Cambridge United 5 (0),

2012–2013 Imps (loan), 2013–2014 Boston United (loan) 40 (8), 2014–2016 Boston United 85 (9), 2016 Halifax Town 12 (1)

Tall defender who came to City on loan from Cambridge to link up with David Holdsworth who had managed him at Ilkeston and Mansfield. Tough and able centre half who featured more often than most of Holdsworth's signings, but returned to Cambridge shortly after Gary Simpson took over.

Most recently had several good seasons at Boston United before moving on to Halifax Town in the summer of 2016. He also represented the England C side whilst at Mansfield.

Garratt, Martin
(2000-2001)
Midfielder 3 apps 0 Goals
Born 22nd February 1980
1998–2000 York City 45 (1), 2000 Mansfield Town 6 (0), 2000 St Patrick's Athletic 3 (0), 2000–2001 Imps, 2001 Hednesford Town (loan) 2 (0), 2002 North Ferriby United

Garratt could play at left back or left midfield and joined the Imps as we struggled in League Two. He had served his youth at York City, and had garnered a reputation as a talented footballer with a lot of promise. He was sacked from York in 2000 due to 'personal problems'. Played three games on the left of midfield for City, but didn't do enough to impress. He left at the beginning of March to play for Hednesford Town.

In 2010 Garratt was banned from various venues in York due to anti-scoial behaviour, and began to experience problems with alcoholism upon his return to his native North East. Garratt passed away at his Middlesbrough home in 2015 at the age of 34 from the effects of prescription drugs and alcohol.

Ghent, Matthew
(2000-2001)
Goalkeeper 1 (1) App 0 Goals
Born 5th September 1980
1997-2000 Aston Villa 0 (0), 2000-2001 Imps (loan), 2001Forest Green Rovers 2 (0), 2001-2003 Barnsley 8 (0), 2006 Sutton Town, 2006 Tamworth 1 (0), 2007-2008 Solihull Moors, 2009 Rushall Olympic

Former Aston Villa keeper Matthew started just one game for Lincoln City, and he played a blinder. We were struggling at home to non-league Dagenham in the FA Cup and after 89 minutes he was named man of the match. He must have been celebrating in his head as he immediately conceded a soft goal to leave us out of the cup in almost comical circumstances.

There's nothing funny about costing your team the game though and Matthew didn't play again for the club. Chris Day was immediately recalled to the side and Ghent was sent packing.

He wasn't really seen anywhere again bar FGR and a short spell with Barnsley. He drifted into the non-league game, and then in 2006 he drifted into prison for three months for kicking his pregnant girlfriend in the stomach. In 2013 he had a restraining order slapped on him after being branded a true stalker by a judge. It makes me glad he only started once for us.

Gilbert, Peter
(2012-13)
Defender 18 Apps 0 Goals
Born 31st July 1983
2002–2003 Birmingham City 0 (0), 2003–2005 Plymouth Argyle 78 (1), 2005–2006 Leicester City 5 (0), 2005–2006 Sheffield Wednesday (loan) 7 (0), 2006–2009 Sheffield Wednesday 34 (0), 2007 Doncaster Rovers (loan) 4 (0), 2009 Oldham Athletic 5 (0), 2009–2010 Northampton Town 30 (0), 2010–2012 Southend United 57 (3), 2012–2013 Imps, 2013 Dagenham & Redbridge (loan) 0 (0)

Gilbert arrived at Lincoln on a non-contract basis with a wealth of experience to draw from. He was a David Holdsworth signing who stayed for more than just a handful of games, playing 18 times for the Imps. He was a diminutive left back who had enjoyed spells at Plymouth Argyle and Northampton in his career. He was seen as an experienced professional who could help bring cohesion to the side.

He was unfortunate to play at the tail end of Holdsworth's doomed spell as manager. Gilbert was sent off away at Hereford on February 16th of 2013 and just 24 hours later Holdsworth left by mutual consent. He only played once more before joining Dagenham on loan.

Gilmour, Brian
(2009-2010)
Midfield 15 (3) Apps 2 Goals
May 8th 1987
2003–2007 Rangers 0 (0), 2007 Clyde 13 (1), 2007–2008 Queen of the South 23 (1), 2008 FC Haka 7 (0), 2009–2010 Imps, 2011Stenhousemuir 9 (0), 2011–2013KnattspyrnufélagAkureyrar 85 (21), 2013 Ayr United 76 (7)

Gilmour arrived in 2009 from FC Haka as part of Chris Sutton's failed revolution. He spent a majority of his Imps career playing in an unfamiliar left midfield position, but still registered very important goals including an equaliser in a 2-2 draw at Grimsby and the winning goal in our 2-1 January 2010 win over Bradford.

He was offered a new deal by Sutton in the close season of 2010-11 but didn't agree terms in time and had the offer withdrawn. The former Scotland U-19 and U-20 player then had a spell in Iceland before settling back in his native Scotland with Ayr.

Gilmour always looked like he had the potential to be a decent player for Lincoln, but he was in and out of the side and never really got used to the physicality of League Two football.

Gordon, Gavin
(1997-2000)
Forward 102 (13) Apps 32 Goals
Born 24th July 1979
1995–1997 Hull City 38 (9), 1997–2000 Imps, 2000–2004 Cardiff City 50 (6), 2002 Oxford United (loan) 6 (1), 2004–2006 Notts County 33 (5), 2006 Crawley Town 4 (0), 2007–2008 Histon 0 (0), 2012 Sleaford Town 7 (3)

The signing of Gavin Gordon was something of a coup back in 1997. Gordon was a promising young striker with our rivals Hull City. He was rated highly there and had found a knack of coming off the bench to score. He netted an 81st minute equaliser for Hull against Darlington in November 1997.

They lost 4-3 and by the 8th of November he was in a City shirt, exchanged for £30,000. John Beck was no mug; he knew a player when he saw one.

Gordon was a tall and strong forward who also had a great burst of pace in his locker. He was the classic Beck forward, and he immediately won the hearts of the Imps faithful by grabbing a winning goal at Colchester in just his fifth game. He spent the rest of the season drifting in and out of the side as Lincoln won automatic promotion.

Normally a centre forward who wins automatic promotion is revered for years at his club, but Gordon was a member of the most unpopular Imps side to ever win promotion. They won ugly, football wasn't the order of the day and as a big forward man Gordon, along with Lee Thorpe epitomised that ugliness. Despite his obvious talents he didn't always get the plaudits he deserved from the football world.

He couldn't keep us in the third tier the next season. His net input was five goals, six yellow cards and one sending off. His reputation as a bustling target man was being cemented, even if he wasn't scoring the goals to justify it.

After relegation, he matured as a player, it might have been the input of the original hatchet centre forward Phil Stant. Gordon added goals to his repertoire, finishing the 1999/00 season with 13. The next season he really kicked on, seemingly scoring for fun. He scored twice in games against Kidderminster (3-3), Barnet (3-4) and Cardiff (2-3) on his way to amassing 11 goals before Christmas. Those two goals against Cardiff convinced the welsh side to pay us £275,000 for his services just before the festivities, and just three games into his Cardiff career he was off the mark again.

Although he had a decent career he never caught that same form he showed in one and a half seasons at Lincoln. He found goals harder to come by at a higher level, and perhaps wasn't as suited to playing a less direct style of football. He should be remembered by Imps fondly as a player who helped us to promotion, chose to leave Hull for us and ultimately made us a significant profit that we desperately needed.

Gordon, Michael
(2009-2010)
Midfielder 4 (1) Apps 0 Goals
Born 10th November 1984
2002–2004 Wimbledon 19 (0), 2004 Swindon Town 0 (0), 2004–2005 Havant & Waterlooville 20 (0), 2005 Aldershot Town 1 (0), 2005 Crawley Town 0 (0), 2005–2006 Sutton United 16 (1), 2006–2007 AFC Wimbledon 0 (0), 2007 Harrow Borough, 2007 Hemel Hempstead Town, 2007–2009 Northwood 49 (5), 2009 Croydon Athletic, 2009 Merstham 16 (7), 2009–2010 Imps, 2011 Kingstonian, 2011–2012 Walton & Hersham, 2012 Chipstead, 2013 Walton & Hersham

Gordon was one of Chris Sutton's first signings in November 2009 just a month after he had taken over. He had never made a league appearance after moving to Swindon from AFC Wimbledon, and it showed in his Lincoln outings. We had two draws and two defeats with Gordon in the side before he dropped out of the team. He made one late season appearance as a substitute in yet another defeat before dropping back into non-league for good.

Chris Sutton rather optimistically described Gordon as; "and out and out right winger. He's direct, he runs at people and from what we've seen he'll create opportunities for others." The only opportunity he created was for another right winger to take his place.

Gowling, Josh
(2010-2013)
Defender 42 (1) Apps 0 Goals
Born 29ᵗʰ November 1983
2002–2003 West Bromwich Albion 0 (0), 2003–2005 Herfølge 30 (0), 2004–2005 Ølstykke FC (loan) 13 (0), 2005–2008 Bournemouth 83 (1), 2008 Carlisle United 4 (0), 2008–2009 Hereford United (loan) 13 (0) 2009 Gillingham (loan) 4 (0), 2009–2011 Gillingham 52 (4), 2010 Imps (loan), 2011–2012 Imps, 2012–2015 Kidderminster Harriers 106 (6), 2015 Grimsby Town (loan) 3 (1), 2015 Grimsby Town 37 (2)

Gowling took a risk dropping out of league football with Lincoln in 2011, a risk that I think many fans will have forgotten given what he has done since. Gowling is another of those players who was simply with us at the wrong time.

A strong and commanding centre back, Gowling had plied his trade a league higher with Bournemouth and Gillingham before sigiing on loan for City. Gillingham had been relegated from League One with Gowling dismissed twice, but in League Two he was virtually ever present for them. Then they lost 7-4 to Accrington, and he was allowed to join Lincoln on loan.

He signed for Steve Tilson and began to calm a leaky defence. His quality was clear and despite being on the field the night we lost 5-0 at home to Bury it was widely believed that he was someone who could have helped keep us up. As fate would have it he helped send us down, scoring in Gillingham's 4-0 win at Sincil Bank.

He opted to re-join Lincoln in the summer despite our relegation and was made club captain by Steve Tilson. Once again fate dealt a cruel blow as Tilson floundered and was eventually dismissed after a 4-0 defeat at Tamworth. He remained at Lincoln to help us avoid relegation, but left in August 2012 to sign for Kidderminster. He later turned up at Grimsby where aside from getting sent off against Lincoln he had a superb season, resulting in promotion via the play-offs and a spot in the Team of the Year.

He proved at Grimsby he had the ability to be a success at National League level, but the upheaval of a manager change really unsettled the team in our first season out of the football league. Had we had a more balanced side I firmly believe he could have had a much longer and relatively successful career at Lincoln, especially as he is now regularly playing League football again. Sadly, he had to move to our bitter rivals to achieve it.

Graham, David
(2008-2009)
Forward 2 (8) Apps 0 Goals
Born 6ᵗʰ October 1978
1995–1998 Rangers 3 (0), 1998–2001Dunfermline Athletic 39 (4), 2001Inverness Caledonian Thistle (loan) 2 (0), 2001–2004Torquay United 120 (47), 2004–2005Wigan Athletic 30 (1), 2005–2007 Sheffield Wednesday 24 (2), 2006 Huddersfield Town (loan) 16 (9), 2006–2007 Bradford City (loan) 22 (3), 2007 Torquay United (loan) 7 (0), 2007–2008 Gillingham 16 (3), 2008 Imps, 2009 Sheffield 2 (2), 2009–2010 Ilkeston Town 17 (4), 2010 Sheffield 16 (3), 2010–2011 Worksop Town 0 (0), 2011 Sheffield 22 (4)

Scottish born Graham started out at Rangers before making his name scoring 47 times in 120 games for Torquay United. His form earned him a £215,000 move to Wigan Athletic. He helped fire them to the Premier League before a £250,000 move to Sheff Weds in August of 2005.

His time at Hillsborough wasn't a happy one. He was blocked from going on a pre-season tour of the USA for a 'minor police incident' several years before. At the end of 2007 he was sent out on loan to bottom of the league Torquay after a serious breach of club discipline by manager Brian Laws, and his Wednesday career was over.

He then turned up at Gillingham for half a season looking half the player he had when first at Torquay. He scored three times for the Gills in 16 appearances before being released in January 2008.

After six months, out of the game he arrived as one of Peter Jackson's 'Magnificent Seven', signings that were meant to fire us to promotion. Rumours were rife though that his personal problems stemmed from an issue with alcohol. With the arrival of scoring sensation Adrian Patulea he found his first team appearances limited to just nine, with two starts.

His last game for Lincoln was in a 5-1 against Accrington, unfortunately for Graham he was replaced at half time by Patulea who duly scored twice. Graham was released at the end of his six-month spell.

Graham had shown glimpses of his quality when on the pitch but he just didn't get enough game time. He never looked like getting close to being fit and on match days could have been mistaken for a scruffy looking fan in the pub. Very few Imps fans mourned his departure.

After Lincoln, he drifted into non-league with Ilkeston and three separate spells with the world's oldest club Sheffield FC.

Grant, Aiden
(2015)
Goalkeeper 2 App 0 Goals
Born 27th March 1995
2014 South Shields 2014 Peterborough, 2015 Imps, 2016 Corby Town

Young goalkeeper who served his youth at Aston Villa and Newcastle. He played back up to Paul Farman for a year and a half before moving to Corby Town. Kept a clean sheet in a rare start away at Dartford. Now at Corby Town looking to establish himself in their first team.

Grant, Gareth
(2001)
Forward 4 Apps 1 Goal
Born 6th September 1980
1997–2002 Bradford City 24 (1), 1999 Halifax Town (loan) 3 (0), 2000 Bolton Wanderers (loan) 0 (0), 2001 Imps (loan), 2002 Imps, 2002 Chester City 0 (0), 2002–2005 Gainsborough Trinity, 2005 Scarborough (loan) 1 (0), 2005–2006 Harrogate Town 34 (10), 2006–2008 Farsley Celtic 20 (4), 2008 Harrogate Town 12 (1), 2009–2010 Farsley Celtic, 2010 Droylsden 2 (0), 2010 Gainsborough Trinity, 2010–2013 Farsley, 2013 Ossett Town, 2013 Pontefract Collieries

When Grant arrived on loan in February of 2001 he came billed as a quick and energetic young player with massive potential. He had featured for Bradford City in the Premier League and had scored for them in the Intertoto Cup and the League Cup.

He scored in his second match for Lincoln, a fine 4-1 win in the LDV Vans Trophy against league leaders Chesterfield. He made a four starts for City, but didn't add to his goal tally. On his return to Bradford he played twice in the Premier League, coming off the bench at the same time as Scott Kerr in a 0-0 draw with Coventry. His career never took off as it threatened to do and he ended up drifting around the non-league scene like so many ex-Imps.

Gray, Dan
(2012-2014)
Defender 44 (12) Apps, 1 Goal
Born 23rd November 1989
2008–2012 Chesterfield 45 (0), 2008 Alfreton Town (loan), 2011 Macclesfield Town (loan) 21 (1), 2011 Macclesfield Town (loan) 2 (0), 2012–2014 Imps, 2014 Alfreton Town 7 (0), 2015 Bradford Park Avenue (loan) 1 (0)

Dan Gray was an under-rated right back who played for Lincoln in times of turmoil. Aside from the Steve Tilson relegation side, David Holdsworth probably had the misfortune of assembling one of the weakest Imps teams ever witnessed. Dan Gray was a part of that side of loan players and misfits. He did possess a wicked long throw which was as potent as a corner anywhere within sight of the 18-yard area.

He spent two unspectacular years at Lincoln as we lumbered through the bad times and on into more bad times with Gary Simpson. At the end of two turbulent years at City, on and off the field, he moved on to Alfreton Town and latterly Bradford Park Avenue.

Green, Francis
(2003-2006)
Forward 87 (18) Apps 20 Goals
Born 23rd April 1980
1998–2003 Peterborough United 107 (14), 2003 Imps (loan), 2003–2006 Imps, 2005–2006 Boston United (loan) 6 (1), 2006–2007 Boston United 39 (4), 2007–2009 Macclesfield Town 65 (14), 2009–2010 Kettering Town 12 (4), 2009 Oxford United (loan) 3 (0), 2010 Oxford United 8 (1), 2010 Brackley Town 0 (0), 2011–2012 Hucknall Town (loan), 2012 Eastwood Town 10 (5), 2012 Ilkeston, 2012-2013 Spalding United, 2012-2013 Hucknall Town, 2012-2013 Corby Town 3 (1), 2013 Basford United

The signing of Francis Green heralded in a new era for Lincoln City. We had spent so long in the financial wilderness making do with cast off players and non-league hopefuls. It had seen us through to the play off final, but to kick on we needed to spend. Handing over £25k for Francis Green announced that we were back challenging for good players.

'Franny' was lightening quick and offered another dimension to an already bulging attack. He arrived not long after Gary Taylor Fletcher and between them they pushed us up into the race at the top of the table. Franny knew where the net was and a late winner against Macclesfield in October showed his potential. Another winner in January against Bury showed he could pop up with an all-important goal. Off the bench he could be devastating, if he played from the start he was livewire and always involved.

He scored eight times in his second season at Lincoln, but couldn't make a difference at the Millennium Stadium against Southend. Despite his early promise he never scored as many goals as perhaps he should have, and in his second full season he managed just five. When Keith Alexander left the club, Green followed out of the door. He moved to our close rivals Boston United and typically scored a winner for them against us at York Street.

Franny is perhaps best remembered for being the player that broke ground for us in the transfer market rather than one who made the sort of impact that earns a player legendary status. He scored a few goals and excited on occasion, but he really never achieved the potential he had shown when we first signed him.

Green, Paul
(2007-2011)
Defender 120 (9) Apps 4 Goals
Born 5th April 1987
2005 Aston Villa (youth) 2007–2011 Imps, 2011–2012 Tamworth 40 (0), 2012–2014 Forest Green Rovers 43 (2), 2013 Hereford United (loan) 7 (0), 2014 Tamworth 26 (6)

Paul Green was a dependable and cautious full back signed from Aston Villa via John Deehan's contacts. After a couple of games coming off the bench he started his first match as we went down 2-1 at home to Mansfield, in which future Imp Nathan Arnold scored the winner.

Although failure in the play-offs that year marked a start of the decline for Lincoln, Paul Green went on to prove himself worthy of praise in a succession of poor Lincoln sides. A serious hip injury prevented him from breaking into Chris Sutton's thoughts when he first took over, but once he recovered he became a stalwart of the side.

When Sutton left Tilson took over he suffered again with injuries. When he did play in the year we went down, he looked to organise the inexperienced defence. We lost three games heavily at home that season (6-1 Rotherham, 5-1 Shrewsbury, 4-0 Gillingham) and Paul Green did not play in a single one of them. When he was out, we missed him.

It is rumoured that Green was one of the players told by Steve Tilson in March of 2011 they wouldn't be retained. He then proceeded to play him in every game of that abysmal run-in than cost us our league status. At the end of the season he was released.

If that hip injury hadn't affected Paul Green than I have no doubt I'd be writing about a player who enjoyed a good career in League One or maybe higher. He had a natural ability, the instinct you need to be a fluid footballer but his fitness proved to be his short coming. He did get revenge on Steve Tilson though, he was in the Tamworth team that beat us 4-0 the year after and earned Tilson the sack.

Greenall, Colin,
(1994-1995)
Defender 55 (0) Apps 4 Goals
Born 30th December 1963
1980–1986 Blackpool 183 (9), 1986–1988 Gillingham 62 (4), 1988–1990 Oxford United 67 (2), 1990–1992 Bury 71 (5), 1992–1993 Preston North End 29 (1), 1993–1994 Chester City 42 (1), 1994–1995 Imps, 1995–2000 Wigan Athletic 193 (18)

Colin Greenall was a respected defender with over 400 league appearances when he signed for us in 1995. He was a tough veteran of fifteen years whom it seemed was approaching the end of his career. He wasn't a complete disaster, but the defences he marshalled were prone to conceding goals. When John Schofield left in October of 1994 he was appointed captain by Sam Ellis.

Ellis left in September of 1995 and Colin Greenall soon followed. A player who had arrived on a free transfer commanded a fee of £45,000, although the selling of our captain wasn't a great help. Despite appearing to be a veteran he went on to collect another 200 appearances in league and cup with Wigan, helping them lift the Football League Trophy in 1999.

Grimes, Ashley
(2010-2011)
Forward 27 (3) Apps 17 Goals
Born 9th December 1986
2006–2008 Manchester City 0 (0), 2007 Swindon Town (loan) 4 (0), 2008–2011 Millwall 21 (2), 2010–2011 Imps(loan), 2011–2013 Rochdale 74 (18), 2013–2014 Bury 15 (0), 2014–2015 Walsall 27 (2), 2015–2016 Barrow 7 (0), 2016 Southport 7 (1)

I'm going to be fair to the ex-Man City youngster. I'm going to start by highlighting how he scored 17 goals in his first four months at the club. Without those goals, we would have been relegated by Easter, and the partnership he formed with Delroy Facey looked set to push us to a respectable mid table finish. His last goal was in our 2-1 defeat at Stevenage that also proved to be the last time staying in the league looked likely. Trevor Carson left and Ashley Grimes stopped scoring.

His loss of form coincided with an injury to Delroy Facey. Ben Hutchinson wasn't up to partnering the diminutive but tricky forward and as the games wore on Grimes looked increasingly isolated up front whilst all the action happened at the other end of the pitch. He was verbally attacked as he left the pitch the day we went down. Rumours were both Tilson and Grimes would have liked a permanent deal, but relegation must have cooled his interest.

He spent those last few games epitomising everything wrong with the side that went down. He had obvious talent as 17 goals testified too, but we sank without a whimper and talented players didn't look to be trying too hard to make it happen.

Since that troubling time Grimes has climbed a league and then dropped two. He was recently sent off at Sincil Bank playing for his new club Southport after kicking out at Alex Woodyard in the first half.

Gritton, Martin
(2006-2007)
Forward 10 (18) Apps 3 Goals
Born 1st June 1978
1998–2002 Plymouth Argyle 44 (7), 2001 Yeovil Town (loan) 4 (0), 2001 Shelbourne (loan), 2002 Torquay United (loan) 5 (1), 2002–2004 Torquay United 88 (22), 2004–2006 Grimsby Town 49 (6), 2006–2007 Imps, 2007 Mansfield Town (loan) 19 (6), 2007–2009 Macclesfield Town 52 (13), 2009–2011 Chesterfield 29 (5), 2010–2011 Torquay United (loan) 12 (0), 2011 Chester 5 (1), 2011 Yeovil Town 2 (0), 2011–2012 Stockport County 11 (0), 2012 Truro City 8 (2)

For one season Martin Gritton really knew where the back of the net was. He scored 16 goals including a final day opener against Lincoln, which could have prevented us from going to the play-off semi-final matches. He then spent the rest of career trying desperately to capture that one season of great form.

It never worked out at Lincoln for him. Gritton arrived for a nominal fee from Grimsby Town having managed just six goals for them. He immediately announced his arrival at Sincil Bank by grabbing a goal in a 3-2 win at Stockport. He failed to score again that season. Keith Alexander left at the end of the year, but Gritton remained.

Early on in that season we played his old club Torquay and we were losing 1-0 into injury time. Paul Morgan got a dramatic equaliser, and then Martin Gritton got forward against his old club to notch a late, late winner. Cue delirium.

As the season progressed his chances diminished. Whilst Mark Stallard and Jamie Forrester were scoring for fun he was loaned out to Mansfield Town to get some game time. Whilst at Mansfield he played against Torquay and for the second time that season hurt his old club, this time banging in a hat trick in a 5-0 victory.

He came back and curiously made two further Lincoln appearances in the two semi-final matches against Bristol Rovers. However, that was the last we saw of him as he left Lincoln and was replaced by Steve Torpey. Cracking business.

While Torpey wasn't scoring for Lincoln, Gritton bagged nine for Paul Ince's Macclesfield side. I'm sure there is an irony there about swapping one striker still in his prime for another who couldn't score in a London tower block, but I'm afraid it's lost on me.

Grobbelaar, Bruce
(1998)
Goalkeeper 2 Apps 0 Goals
Born 16th October 1957
1973–1974 Highlanders, 1975 Chibuku Shumba, 1976 Highlands Park 0 (0), 1977–1978 Durban City, 1979–1980 Vancouver Whitecaps 24 (0), 1979–1980 Crewe Alexandra (loan) 24 (1), 1981–1994 Liverpool 440 (0), 1993 Stoke City (loan) 4 (0), 1994–1996 Southampton 32 (0), 1996–1997 Plymouth Argyle 36 (0), 1997 Oxford United 0 (0), 1997 Sheffield Wednesday 0 (0), 1997–1998 Oldham Athletic 4 (0), 1998 Chesham United 4 (0), 1998 Bury 1 (0) 1998 Imps, 1999 Northwich Victoria 1 (0), 2002 Hellenic 1 (0), 2007 Glasshoughton Welfare 1 (0)

Bruce Grobbelaar was one of the eighties most recognisable characters. The clown prince of goalkeeping was never far away from the headlines, whether it was the unsporting wobbly knee incident in a European Cup final in 1984, or the outrageous body check on Gordon McQueen in the 1983 League Cup final. With over 400 appearances for the decade's most successful club team, Liverpool he was a household name.

His career was tarnished somewhat by a match-fixing scandal and various red top tabloid stories of infidelity and bad behaviour. He eventually walked free from court and even took The Sun newspaper to court, so for that I applaud him!

He played for Lincoln, twice after signing on December 10th 1998. He kept a clean in a 0-0 draw with Macclesfield before conceding four away at Wycombe. He was released from his contract before the onset of Christmas and didn't make another league appearance for anyone. There were rumours of an argument over unpaid wages but nothing ever came of it.

Habergham – Hutchison

Habergham, Sam
(2016- Current)
Defender 18 Apps 1 Goal
Born 20th February 1992
2010-2011 Norwich City, 2011-2012 Tamworth 28 (2), 2012-2016 Braintree 168 (2), 2016 Imps

England C left back Habergham was one of the first signings Danny Cowley made upon becoming Lincoln manager. He managed Habergham at Braintree in a season that saw them finish third, and saw Sam named in the National League Team of the Year.

He's a bright and energetic full back who likes to get forward, and so far, he's registered one goal for City, a long-range cross-cum-shot against Sutton in our 3-1 defeat. He was recently named in the England C squad once again, and he looks set to enjoy a career in the Football League.

I don't think Imps fans have seen the best of Sam as yet. He was carrying an injury when he first arrived at the club, and the games come thick and fast early in the season. I expect to see him move up a gear as we get through the Christmas period, and begin to really show the sort of form that helped carry Braintree to within a whisker of the Football League.

Hamilton, Ian
(2001-2002)
Midfielder 29 Apps 1 Goal
Born 14th December 1967
1985–1988 Southampton 0 (0), 1988 Cambridge United 24 (1), 1988–1992 Scunthorpe United 145 (18), 1992–1998 West Bromwich Albion 240 (23), 1998–2000 Sheffield United 45 (3), 1999 Grimsby Town (loan) 6 (1), 2000–2001 Notts County 34 (0) 2001–2002 Imps, 2002–2003 Woking 19 (0)

Ian Hamilton had a good career predominately at Scunthorpe and West Brom, which is where he met Alan Buckley. Buckley later loaned him at Grimsby Town, and it wasn't entirely surprising when he re-joined Buckley at Sincil Bank. He was part of the team that almost dropped out of the Football League and in the main looked every inch a key component in the failure. As he neared the end of his career he came to epitomise everything that had been going wrong at Lincoln, looking lethargic and at times outright unfit and yet still claiming a wage. As we hurtled towards financial oblivion he did very little to help put bums on seats as increasingly bad results began to go against us.

He scored just one goal in our FA Cup defeat at Leyton Orient, and didn't so much as pick up a booking despite us needing battlers in the centre of the park. Keith Alexander rightly deemed him surplus to requirements before the next season kicked off, and just a couple of months in he agreed a severance package and went to play for Woking in the Conference, which was fitting reward for his efforts the previous season. Moved into IT management after football.

Mark Whiley's view

The midfielder actually had a good career with the likes of Scunny and West Brom. However, by the time he arrived at Sincil Bank those days were in the distant past. He seemed to spend most games with his right arm in the air, apologising as another misplaced pass went out of play. He summed up Alan Buckley's tenure perfectly. Rubbish!

Hand, Jamie
(2007-2008)
Midfielder 20 (6) 0 Goals
Born 7th February 1984
2001–2006 Watford 55 (0), 2004 Oxford United (loan) 11 (1), 2005 Livingston (loan) 7 (0), 2005 Peterborough United (loan) 2 (0), 2005 Peterborough United (loan) 7 (0), 2005–2006 Fisher Athletic 0 (0), 2005–2006 Northampton Town (loan) 11 (0), 2006–2007 Chester City 43 (2), 2007–2008 Imps, 2008 Oxford United (loan) 13 (0), 2008–2009 Ebbsfleet United 22 (1), 2009 Chelmsford City 17 (2), 2009–2010 Woking 6 (0), 2010 Hemel Hempstead Town, 2010–2012 Hayes & Yeading United 61 (3), 2011 Luton Town (loan) 13 (2), 2012–2013 Mansfield Town 1 (0), 2012 Eastleigh (loan) 2 (0), 2012–2013 Hayes & Yeading United (loan) 5 (0), 2013 Margate (loan) 10 (1), 2013–2014 Stockport County 0 (0), 2013–2014 Southport (loan) 0 (0), 2014–2015 Farnborough 3 (0)

Jamie Hand arrived at Sincil Bank courtesy of John Deehan, with whom he'd previously linked up at Northampton. It was the same rich vein of untapped potential that brought us Ryan Amoo (who was also awful) and Paul Green (who was actually half decent). Hand was billed as a tough tackling midfielder with a face for radio but of value to the club. It may be that he was unlucky to join a team on a steep decline; it may be that he just didn't have 'it' anymore. Whatever 'it' was his spell playing for Lincoln was nothing short of a disaster. He was a virtual passenger in midfield as Schofield and Deehan got the sack, then provided little more than yellow cards under the new manager Peter Jackson.

A suspension in January of 2008 after amassing six yellow cards spelled the end of his Imps tenure, and on March 1st he dropped down to the Conference on loan with Oxford. Come the season end they didn't want him and neither did we and his contract was terminated by mutual consent. He came back to Lincoln as a Luton player in our first season out of the league, and found himself dismissed in the 90th minute. Not a happy place for him, Sincil Bank.

Hanlon, Ritchie
(2004-2005)
Midfielder 6 (6) Apps 1 Goal
Born 26th May 1978
1996–1997, Southend United 2 (0), 1997–1998 Welling United, 1998 Rushden & Diamonds, 1998–2001 Peterborough United 47 (3), 1999 Welling United (loan), 1999 → Welling United (loan) 19 (11), 2001–2004 Rushden & Diamonds 62 (7), 2004 Stevenage Borough 18 (2), 2004 Imps (loan) 1 (0), 2004–2005 Lincoln City 11 (1), 2005 Weymouth 4 (0), 2005–2007 Cambridge United 37 (3)

Hanlon was a slick ball-playing midfielder who joined initially on loan from Stevenage after making his name at Peterborough. He made his Imps debut just before Christmas of 2004 and his deal was made permanent just days later. It was a tough Lincoln squad to come into with Richard Butcher, Peter Gain and Ciaran Toner all battling for a spot.

He scored his only Imps goal in a wonderful 2-0 win at Boston, and what a goal it was. He hit an absolute screamer from outside the area to give us a 36th minute lead. Last featured for the Imps in the 3-0 final day defeat by Yeovil. He was ruled out of all three play-off games including the 2-0 defeat by his former team Southend. He moved to Cambridge in the Conference when he wasn't retained in the summer of 2005, and as recently as 2016 he was joint manager at Hayes and Yeading.

It is widely believed that had he been fit, and had Toner and Richardson not had their little spat that all three might have been able to change our fate that warm afternoon in Cardiff. Unfortunately, football is full of 'what ifs', and Ritchie Hanlon will always be nothing more than a footnote in our play-off failures.

Harris, Jason
(1997)
Forward 0 (1) Apps 0 Goals
Born 24ᵗʰ November 1976
1994–1997 Crystal Palace 2 (0), 1995 Dover Athletic (loan), 1996–1997 Bristol Rovers (loan) 6 (2), 1997 Imps (loan), 1997–1998 Leyton Orient 40 (9), 1998–1999 Preston North End 36 (6), 1999–2001 Hull City 38 (4), 2001 Shrewsbury Town (loan) 4 (0), 2001 Southend United 5 (0), 2001–2002 Harrogate Town, 2002 Nuneaton Borough 23 (6), 2002 Harrogate Town, 2003 Goole, 2003–2004 Bridlington Town, 2004 Ossett Town

Pacey front man Harris came on loan from Crystal Palace in September 1997. He managed just 27 minutes on the pitch as a Lincoln player, replacing Colin Alcide in a 2-0 home defeat at the hands of Mansfield Town. Maybe he did something to displease then-manager John Beck, as he was soon back with Crystal Palace who had sold him to Orient by the end of September. Went on to score 11 times in two years in East London before spells with Preston and Hull.

Hartfield, Charlie
(1998)
Midfielder 3 Apps 1 Goal
Born 4ᵗʰ September 1971
1989–1991 Arsenal 0 (0), 1991–1997 Sheffield United 57 (1), 1997 Fulham (loan) 2 (0), 1997–2001 Swansea City 22 (2), 1997 Imps (loan), 1999–2000 Telford United (loan) 20 (3), 2002 Halifax Town 2 (2), 2002 Ilkeston Town

Hartfield signed on loan from Swansea for just three games in the 1998 Second Division campaign. He played in three defeats, scoring in a 2-1 loss at Wrexham in his final appearance. A permanent move was never in the offing and so he became one of those players who had nothing more than a brief flirtation with the red and white. Injury hampered his career and after Lincoln he didn't manage to sustain a league career.

After football, he served some jail time, a career long gambling addiction saw him turn to drug trafficking. He received a nine year and one month sentence for conspiring to bring amphetamines and cannabis into the UK from France.

Hawkridge, Terry
(2015-2016, 2016- Current)
Midfielder 40 (9) Apps 1 Goal
Born 23ʳᵈ February 1990
2007–2009 Carlton Town 15 (4), 2009–2010 Hucknall Town 7 (3), 2010–2012 Carlton Town 84 (21), 2012–2013 Gainsborough Trinity 37 (14), 2013–2016 Scunthorpe United 61 (2), 2015 Mansfield Town (loan) 5 (0), 2015–2016 Imps (loan), 2016 Lincoln City 23 (0)

Terry Hawkridge is a tricky and pacey winger signed on-loan from Scunthorpe by Chris Moyses. His deal was made permanent halfway through the 2015/16 season and he went on to establish himself as a first-choice wide player for Lincoln. He always looks to have a trick up his sleeve, and is capable of producing moments of brilliance on the ball. If I had a criticism of Terry it is that he often struggles to find a quality end product, be it goals or telling crosses. That said if he added that to his game he wouldn't be a Lincoln City player.

He scored his only Imps goal in the 2-0 home win against Danny Cowley's Braintree in the 2015/16 season, but has struggled to nail down a place in the first team in the 2016/17 season due in the main to the presence of Nathan Arnold and Harry Anderson. It remains to be seen if he can continue to try and play his way into the starting eleven, although he does have value as an impact player from the bench.

Hearn, Liam
(2015-2016)
Forward 13 (8) Apps 10 Goals
Born 27th August 1985
2003–2004 Hucknall Town, 2006–2007 Hucknall Town, 2007 Eastwood Town, 2007 Chasetown, 2007–2008 Quorn, 2008–2011 Alfreton Town 94 (65), 2011–2014 Grimsby Town 61 (33), 2014–2015 Mansfield Town 3 (0), 2015–2016 Imps, 2015 Barrow (loan) 1 (0), 2016 Harrogate Town (loan) 3 (1), 2016 Ilkeston 1 (0), 2016 Alfreton Town 2 (2)

Liam Hearn was a natural goal scorer, perhaps the most natural finisher I will write about in this book. He averaged a goal every two games for Grimsby and a goal every one and a half games at Alfreton. Serious injury curtailed his Grimsby career and it appeared he was finished after another injury plagued spell at Mansfield. However, manager Chris Moyses thought he could get the best out of the talented forward and gave him the chance to shine in 2015.

At first he shone bright. His eye for goal had clearly stayed with him as he hit a hat trick in an early season win over Macclesfield. With Liam Hearn on the pitch you were sure Lincoln could score a goal. By mid-November he had seven to his name as Lincoln hung onto a play-off challenge.

Unfortunately, the Barrow manager Paul Cox got in his ear and ahead of the loan deadline he suddenly requested a move to get more games under his belt. The move shocked Imps fans and surprised the manager who had to try and make do without his secret weapon. Hearn's spell at Barrow didn't go well and he ended up with just one match to his name before he was accepted back into the fold at Lincoln. Conveniently he had missed our clash with Grimsby Town, a match that had promised to be interesting for the former Cod hero.

He came back and started doing what he did best, scoring goals. He notched one away at Halifax and scored in his final appearance at Sincil Bank as we went down 3-2 to Dover. Shortly afterwards he spoke of not wanting to go out on loan and staying to help fight for our slim play-off hopes. Within days he was farmed out on loan to Harrogate Town and didn't play for the Imps again.

The story of Liam Hearn is a sad one because had he stayed I believe he could have scored the goals that would at least have given us a chance in the race for a top five finish. Despite his limited game time he always looked sharp and it appeared he was being managed really well by Chris Moyses. It seemed as if the fear of either being injured or playing against Grimsby eventually got the better of him, and ultimately cost us dearly.

Heath, Joe
(2009)
Defender 4 (1) Apps 0 Goals
Born 4th October 1988

2007–2010 Nottingham Forest 10 (0), 2009–2010 Imps (loan), 2010–2011 Exeter City 0 (0), 2010–2011 Hereford United (loan) 26 (0), 2011–2013 Hereford United 37 (0)], 2013–2014 Chester 23 (1), 2014–2015 West Kirby, 2015 Runcorn Town FC 15 (1)

Heath was a talented and lively full-back signed on loan from Nottingham Forest by Peter Jackson. Suffered with injuries whilst at City which restricted him to just four starts, which was a real shame because he had looked a very good player. He'd played a few times for Forest's first team before the move, but a hernia operation put paid not only to his Lincoln career but ultimately his Forest one as well.

Hebberd, Trevor
(1994-1995)
Midfielder 28 (5) Apps 0 Goals
Born 19th June 1958
1976–1982 Southampton 96 (8), 1978 Washington Diplomats (loan) 28 (9), 1981 Bolton Wanderers (loan) 6 (0), 1981 Leicester City (loan) 4 (1), 1982–1988 Oxford United 260 (37), 1988–1991 Derby County 81 (10), 1991 Portsmouth 4 (0), 1991–1994 Chesterfield 78 (1), 1994–1995 Imps, 1995 Grantham Town

Hebberd had been the driving force that saw Oxford rise from the Third Division to First Division, and he'd then scored the opening goal in the 1986 League Cup final which The U's won 3-0. He was named man of the match at Wembley. He later played for Derby County in the top flight as well.

Fast forward a few years and you get a shadow of the player he once was ambling about on Sincil Bank. The team Sam Ellis built was never going to be a classic side, and Hebberd was a crucial part of the inane averageness served up week in, week out. He got injured as we beat Hartlepool 3-0 in March of 1995 and left on a free transfer at the end of the season, much to the dismay of nobody at all.

Henry, Anthony
(1999-2001)
Defender 18 (3) Apps 2 Goals
Born 13th September 1979
1997-1999 West Ham, 1999–2001 Imps, 2000 Northwich Victoria (loan), 2001–2003 Folkestone Invicta, 2003–2004 Welling United, 2004–2005 East Thurrock United, 2005–2006 Dartford

Former West Ham youth team captain Henry signed for City in the summer of 1999. John Reames brought him to the club to aid our intended fight for promotion back to the Second Division. Sadly, it didn't work out that way for either party, we didn't get near promotion and Henry didn't get near establishing himself in the team.

He made his debut in a 5-2 thrashing for City at Mansfield and made his final appearance in an equally inauspicious 3-2 defeat at Sincil Bank against Leyton Orient. He did score twice in four games in the 99/00 season, once in the Autoglass Windscreens Shield against Scunthorpe and again a couple of weeks later in the league against Northampton. After the Orient defeat Phil Stant was dismissed and Henry didn't get another game for the club.

Herd, Chris
(2009-2010)
Midfielder 20 Apps 4 Goals
Born 4th April 1989

2010–2015 Aston Villa 36 (1), 2008 Port Vale (loan) 11 (2), 2008 Wycombe Wanderers (loan) 4 (0), 2009–2010 Imps (loan), 2014 Bolton Wanderers (loan) 2 (0), 2015 Wigan Athletic (loan) 3 (0), 2015– 2016 Chesterfield 23 (0), 2016 Perth Glory 0 (0), 2016 Gillingham 2 (0)

Chris Herd was a skilful former member of the Aston Villa youth set up who arrived courtesy of Chris Sutton's contacts in 2009. He came packaged with Eric Lichaj and Nathan Baker, and together the young players set about trying to keep us in the football league.

They were all very good players but the team itself never gelled with such a high turnover of new faces. Herd picked up twice as many bookings as goals and despite his obvious ability often flattered to deceive. He did have obvious ability though, and when he got a chance onn the ball it was clear for all to see. I will always recall him as a talented player in a patch work team, cobbled together from top flight youth players, a side with ability but without experience.

He returned to Villa at the end of the season and went on to represent Australia in 2014, and recently has turned out for Gillingham in League One.

Hill, David
(1993-1995)
Midfielder 66 (7) Apps, 7 Goals
Born 6th June 1966
1985-1988 Scunthorpe, 1988-1991 Ipswich, 1991 Scunthorpe (loan), 1991 Scunthorpe, 1993-1995 Imps, 1995-1996 Chesterfield, 1996 Cork City, 1997 Bohemians, 1998 Cobh Ramblers

Tough tackling midfielder who came to City with over 250 league appearances already under his belt. He could play on the right or through the centre and was known for producing the odd long range goal from nowhere. Hill put in some good performances for Keith Alexander, and he grabbed a winning goal in November 1993 at home to Torquay. He opened the scoring the evening a debutant Darren Huckerby also scored to gives us a 2-1 win against Shrewsbury.

He was ruled out of the first part of the 1994/95 season by injury, but when he got fit he cemented a place in Sam Ellis' first team. He weighed in with a few goals, most notably the only goal of the game away at Wigan on April Fool's Day. He had captained the side for a period, but failed to impress Big Sam enough. He was released in the summer as Ellis set about rebuilding the team, the same team that would see him sacked in September.

Hinds, Richard
(2011-2012)
Defender 9 Apps 1 Goal
Born 22nd August 1980
1998–2003 Tranmere Rovers 55 (0), 2003–2005 Hull City 45 (1), 2005 Scunthorpe United (loan) 7 (0), 2005–2007 Scunthorpe United 86 (8), 2007–2011 Sheffield Wednesday 67 (2), 2011–2012Imps, 2012–2013 Yeovil Town 35 (2), 2013–2014 Bury 10 (1), 2014 Llandudno 5 (0)

Experienced defender Hinds had a short spell with City after the sacking of Steve Tilson. He signed a deal until the end of the year and went on to make nine appearances in a slowly improving Imps side. Having shipped goals for fun prior to his arrival the defence began to look stronger, and in his nine matches we kept clean sheets against Ebbsfleet and Forest Green.

It was hoped he would stay on beyond Christmas but an offer from League One Yeovil proved too good to turn down and he signed for them on February 3rd, making his debut against former club Sheff Weds a day later.

Hirst, Lee
(1993-1994)
Defender 9 Apps 0 Goals
Born 26th January 1969
1990 Scarborough, 1990 Coventry City, 1993 Imps (loan), 1994 Gainsborough Trinity

Hirst was a six foot two defender signed on loan from Coventry City in 1993/94. He made nine first team appearances before returning to his parent club. He had an unremarkable stay at the club and didn't convince manager Keith Alexander to give him a deal.

Hobbs, Jack
(1999-2004)
Defender 0 (1) Apps 0 Goals
Born 18th August 1988
1999–2005 Imps, 2005–2009 Liverpool 2 (0), 2008 Scunthorpe United (loan) 9 (1), 2008–2009 Leicester City (loan) 44 (1), 2009–2011 Leicester City 70 (0), 2011 Hull City (loan) 13 (0), 2011–2014 Hull City 62 (1), 2013–2014 Nottingham Forest (loan) 25 (1), 2014 Nottingham Forest 39 (0)

Jack's actual contribution on the football pitch for Lincoln was all too brief. After impressing in the youth set up he played approximately three minutes as a late sub for Matt Bloomer against Bristol Rovers in January 2005. At 16 years and 149 days, he became the youngest ever debutant for the club.

His promise had alerted a host of other clubs and both Liverpool and Arsenal were interested in the youngster. At first it seemed Arsenal were leading the race for his signature, but Liverpool agreed a fee reported to be in the region of £750k as well as sell on clause and a friendly written into the bargain. All round it seemed a good deal for a youngster with just three minutes' league experience.

Jack made two competitive appearances for Liverpool and also returned to captain the youthful side sent to Sincil Bank for a friendly. Since then he's established himself as a solid and dependable defender with Leicester, Hull City and Nottingham Forest.

As for that lovely transfer money that should have set us up for a couple of years, if you drive down Carlton Boulevard you'll find a mothballed training ground that isn't fit for purpose. Championship 2010 turned into Blue Square 2011 and the benefits of our biggest transfer fee to date were gone in a flash. That's bad club management for you.

Hobson, Craig
(2013)
Forward 5 (7) Apps 1 Goal
Born 25th February 1988
2012-2013 Stockport County, 2013 Imps (loan), 2013-2014 Guiseley, 2014 Chester (loan), 2014-2015 Chester, 2016 Altrincham

Hobson was signed as a last throw of the dice by beleaguered manager David Holdsworth, and just two games into his short stay Holdsworth was dismissed. He stayed on loan until the end of the season, scoring once as we won 2-0 away at Alfreton but it was clear he didn't have a future at Lincoln.

The plain and simple truth was the Craig Hobson was not good enough to play for Lincoln, and his loan signing showed all the desperation that Holdsworth eventually resorted to towards the end of his reign. Scored a couple of times for Chester in a two year stay but once again failed to impress and has begun his descent down the non-league pyramid.

Hodge, Elliot
(2015- Current)
Midfielder 5 (7) Apps 0 Goals
Born 23rd December 1995
2015 Imps, 2016 Stamford (loan), 2016 Gainsborough Trinity (loan), 2016 Stafford (loan)

Hodge is the son of former Forest and England midfielder Steve, but unlike his old man he is a stocky and skilful wide player. Spent his youth at Notts County but was signed up by Chris Moyses in February 2015. He made his debut as a sub for Connor Robinson as we drew 0-0 with Dartford in April 2015.

Towards the end of Chris' tenure as manager he gave Hodge a few starts including an impressive display as we beat Chester 2-1, and a full 90 minutes on the final day of season against Woking. So far in 2016/17 he's made two appearances, and has spent a majority of his time out on loan.

Holmes, Peter
(2007)
Defender 5 Apps 0 Goals
Born 18th November 1980
1999–2000 Sheffield Wednesday 0 (0), 2000–2007 Luton Town 105 (11), 2007 Chesterfield (loan) 10 (1), 2007 Imps (loan), 2007–2009 Rotherham United 27 (2), 2008 York City (loan) 5 (1), 2009 Harrogate Town 0 (0), 2009–2010 Ebbsfleet United 28 (2), 2010–2011 Hayes & Yeading United 44 (3), 2011–2012 Dunstable Town, 2012–2013 Hemel Hempstead Town

Experienced defender who spent seven years at Luton Town before signing on loan for City in the run-in to the 2006/07 season. Made his Imps debut in front of the TV cameras as we slumped to a lunchtime defeat to Swindon Town, and went on to play in two more defeats and two draws as our automatic promotion assault faded. Wasn't kept around for the final capitulation against Bristol Rovers and spent two seasons at Rotherham before slipping into non-league football.

Holmes, Steve
(1988-1990, 1995, 1995-2002)
Defender 197 (4) Apps 32 Goals
Born 13th January 1971
1989–1990 Imps, 1989-1990 Boston F.C. (loan), 1989-1990 Gainsborough Trinity, 1994 Guisborough Town, 1993-1996 Preston North End 13 (1), 1993-1994 Bromsgrove Rovers (loan) 9 (0), 1994-1995 Hartlepool United (loan) 5 (2), 1995-1996 Imps (loan), 1995-2002 Imps, 2002-2005 Dunston Federation Brewery

Steve Holmes started his career with the Imps as a YTS trainee as far back as the 1980's. He appears briefly in the appendices of the Nannestad's 1994 book for his three unused sub appearances, and one outing in a GMVC shield game against Enfield in October 1988. We lost that game, I remember talking about it in my primary school playground in Wragby.

After a short loan spell with Boston FC, Steve moved to Gainsborough and Guisborough before Preston North End boss, and future Imps supremo John Beck spotted his potential and signed him up.

In October 1995, John Beck was appointed manager of Lincoln City and he immediately returned to Preston to sign Barry Richardson permanently for £20,000 and secure Holmes on a three-month loan deal. The pair made their debut in the 1-0 home defeat to Cardiff City the following day.

In his second spell at Sincil Bank, he held down a starting position throughout his loan period before returning to Deepdale. Although he managed to break back into the Preston first team, the signing of Paul Sparrow meant that he was able to sign for Lincoln City on a permanent basis for a fee of £30,000 in March 1996; his third debut coming in the 2-0 defeat at Leyton Orient.

Steve was a commanding presence but not an entirely inconspicuous character standing at six foot two and sporting a bright mop of ginger hair. However, once he settled into his third spell at Lincoln he never looked back.

He was ever-present in the 1997/98 season when the Imps won promotion, and was well known for his penalty taking prowess during his Sincil Bank tenure. The following season he was voted player of the year as we slipped to relegation, but Holmes' career was almost ended when he picked up a serious neck injury during the 1-0 home victory over Wrexham in May 1999. The injury kept him out of action for ten months, but he returned in spectacular style. He scored less than a minute into his comeback as the Imps defeated Carlisle United 5-0 at Sincil Bank in March 2000.

Holmes appeared in City's remaining games of the 1999/2000 season and in November 2001 he became only the 30th player since the Second World War to record 200 Football League appearances for City. In that game, he put in a man of the match performance as we slipped to a 1-0 home defeat to Kidderminster.

Holmes hobbled off just before the half-hour mark of our FA Cup 1st round replay with Bury after an accidental collision with Bury's Jason Jarrett. It was diagnosed as a strained medial ligament which was expected to keep him on the side-lines for up to two months. However, the injury became infected, causing Holmes to spend five days in hospital over the New Year period. That led to him needing an operation which would keep him out for the remainder of the season. He underwent surgery in February of 2002, but with Lincoln on the verge of administration, Holmes along with four other senior players were released by the club.

Steve moved back to his native north-east and signed for Northern League outfit Dunston Federation Brewery at the start of the 2002/03 season. He helped Dunston to a league and cup double the following season before problems stemming from the knee injury sustained back in 2001 forced him to hang up his playing boots.

He now runs a block paving company in the North East and does some coaching in his spare time.

Hone, Daniel
(2007-2012)
Defender 93 (7) Apps 4 Goals
Born 15th September 1989

2007–2012 Imps, 2010–2011 Darlington (loan) 21 (1), 2011–2012 Barrow (loan) 26 (0), 2012–2013 Gainsborough Trinity 42 (4), 2013–2016 North Ferriby United 75 (8), 2016 Halifax Town 10 (2)

Hone is a product of the centre of excellence, and made his debut in our FA Cup first round match against Nottingham Forest. The game ended as a 1–1 draw and he adequately filled in for the injured Lee Beevers. A handful of impressive outings prompted Peter Jackson to offer him a two-and-a-half-year professional contract. He scored his first Lincoln City goal in a 2–1 home victory over Rochdale in February 2008.

Hone was constantly being linked with a move up the league ladder, and it was surprising City managed to hold on to him. He went on to make 100 appearances for his hometown club and gain a reputation as a possible star of the future.

Hone was prone to the odd mistake but by and large he was a competent centre half. He played in a succession of poor Lincoln teams, starting under Jackson and getting progressively worse under Chris Sutton and Steve Tilson.

He suffered an injury which ruled him out from October 2009 to February 2010 and perhaps lost a little of the edge that had him poised for bigger things. Chris Sutton sent him out on loan to Darlington, but once he returned Steve Tilson dropped him back into the starting XI. He was sent off as we slipped to an April 2-1 defeat to Oxford and missed the crucial run in to the season that saw us relegated.

In May 2011, he was one of just three squad players to be offered a new contract after the mass clear out of players following relegation. He duly signed up for a further year, and although he played ten games early in the season he lost his place in the team after Tilson left and was loaned to Barrow in November 2011.

In May 2012, manager David Holdsworth confirmed that Hone would not be offered a new contract and he later joined Gainsborough and then ambitious North Ferriby. He moved with manager Billy Heath to Halifax Town after guiding Ferriby to the National League.

Hone, Mark
(1996-1998)
Midfielder 60 (6) Apps 4 Goals
Born 31ˢᵗ March 1968
1986–1989 Crystal Palace 8 (0), 1989–1994 Welling United 176 (13), 1994–1996 Southend United 56 (0), 1996–1998 Imps, 1998–1999 Kettering Town 31 (0), 1999–2003 Welling United 98 (2), 2003–2006 Lincoln United, 2005–2008 Spalding United, 2007–2008 Lincoln Moorlands Railway

Mark Hone was a former England semi-professional international midfield player who played for us under John Beck inbetween 1996-97. He was *ahem* combative to say the least, never one to shirk a tackle. He was sent off three times for us, all of those dismissals coming in the first half of games. The worst was his eighth minute dismissal for a horror tackle on Paul Ellender in an FA Cup tie with Gainsborough.

There was much more to Hone's game than tough tackling though, and he was an integral part of the side that won promotion in 1997/98. He temporarily spared our blushes with a 116ᵗʰ minute equaliser in the FA Cup game with Emley, but they later beat us on penalties. He played his last game for the club against Colchester at the end of the 1998 season, and wasn't retained as we got promoted. That was a shame as he added steel and grit to a midfield, doing the dirty work people often don't notice.

Since then Hone has played local non-league football and is often heard on Radio Lincolnshire giving expert opinion on Lincoln City and the local game in general. I'm sure he would want to be remembered for so much more than the man that nearly denied Paul Ellender the chance to father children.

Speaking of children his son is Danny Hone the defender you've probably just read about who made 100 appearances for the club. They are the fifth father and son team to represent the Imps, but the only pairing in this modern era.

Horrigan, Darren
(2001-2004)
Goalkeeper 0 (1) Apps 0 Goals
Born 2nd June 1983
2001–2004 Imps, 2002 Stamford Town (loan), 2003 Cambridge City (loan) 1 (0), 2003 Ilkeston Town (loan), 2004 Spennymoor United, 2004 Scarborough 1 (0), 2004–2005 Spennymoor United, 2005 Gateshead 7 (0), 2005–2006 Bishop Auckland 11 (0), 2006 Tow Law Town

Former Birmingham City youth keeper who spent four years as understudy to Alan Marriott without dislodging him from the team. Made on appearance as a sub replacing Marriott at half time as we went down 1-0 at home to Southend in March 2002.

After the Imps Horrigan drifted around the non-league circuit for a bit before working for builder's merchant Jewson as a roofing advisor.

Horsfield, Geoff
(2009)
Forward 14 (3) Apps 1 Goal
Born 1st November 1973
1992–1994 Scarborough 12 (1), 1994 Halifax Town 9 (0)., 1994–1996 Guiseley, 1996 Witton Albion, 1996–1998 Halifax Town 74 (46), 1998–2000 Fulham 59 (22), 2000–2003 Birmingham City 108 (23), 2003 Wigan Athletic 16 (7), 2003–2006 West Bromwich Albion 67 (14), 2006 Sheffield United (loan) 3 (0), 2006–2008 Sheffield United 0 (0), 2006–2007 Leeds United (loan) 14 (2), 2007 Leicester City (loan) 13 (2), 2008 Scunthorpe United (loan) 12 (0), 2009 Imps, 2009–2010 Port Vale 9 (0), 2013 Alvechurch

Veteran striker who enjoyed a fruitful career, in particular enjoying prolific spells for Halifax and Fulham. However, after nine more years and total transfer fees of £5.75m he arrived at Sincil Bank a shadow of the player he once was. He had good reason though.

On 10th October 2008, Horsfield revealed that he had been diagnosed with testicular cancer, and was advised that his playing career was finished. After receiving successful treatment, he linked up with the Imps who were managed by his former Halifax Town team-mate Peter Jackson. After an extended trial period, he signed a short-term playing contract to run from 2nd January 2009 until the end of the season.

He scored just once for Lincoln, a wonder strike as we beat Gillingham 2-1. Horsfield described it at the time as one of his 'sweetest strikes' ever. That goal soon got lonely in the 'goals scored' column

110

though, and it was destined to remain alone forever. He was released at the end of the season to join up with Port Vale.

Shortly before he joined Port Vale, Horsfield fell victim to the swine flu pandemic, and then in January 2013, he received emergency treatment for blood clots on both lungs. He's still standing as well, the old war-horse.

Hoult, Russell
(1991, 1994)
Goalkeeper 19 Apps 0 Goals
Born 22nd November 1972
1991–1995 Leicester City 10 (0), 1991 Imps (loan), 1992 Blackpool (loan) 0 (0), 1992 Cheltenham Town (loan) 3 (0), 1993 Kettering Town (loan) 7 (0), 1993–1994 Bolton Wanderers (loan) 4 (0), 1994 Imps (loan), 1995 Derby County (loan) 15 (0), 1995–2000 Derby County 108 (0), 2000 Portsmouth (loan) 10 (0), 2000–2001 Portsmouth 30 (0), 2001–2007 West Bromwich Albion 190 (0), 2005 Nottingham Forest (loan) 8 (0), 2007–2008 Stoke City 1 (0), 2008 Notts County (loan) 2 (0), 2008 Notts County (loan) 12 (0), 2008–2010 Notts County 20 (0), 2009 Darlington (loan) 6 (0), 2011–2012 Hereford United 2 (0)

Young keeper who had two spells on loan with City from Leicester, one as early as 1991 and another at the start of the 1994/95 season under Sam Ellis. Responsible for a howler to allow Torquay a 2-1 win at Sincil Bank on just his fourth match back at the club, and was sent back to Leicester once his second loan spell expired. Had a decent run as Derby keeper around the turn of the century but ended his career as a 'keeper for hire' or back up at a variety of different clubs.

Howe, Callum
(2015- Current)
Defender 28 Apps 0 Goals
Born 9th April 1994
2012-2015 Scunthorpe United, 2014 Gateshead (loan), 2015 Alfreton (loan) 13 (0), 2015 Imps, 2016 Southport (loan) 13 (1)

Highly rated defender brought in from Scunthorpe by Chris Moyses. Made his Imps debut alongside Luke Waterfall in our opening day 1-1 draw with Cheltenham but struggled to hold down a regular first team spot. Knowing chances would be limited he moved to Southport on loan in August 2016, and has been a revelation for them, earning the captaincy.

With the arrival of Sean Raggett and the form on our own captain Luke Waterfall I suspect Callum Howe will spend as much time as possible this season out on loan. That said Danny Cowley has openly stated that they like Callum so the door certainly isn't closed on his Imps career.

Howe, Rene
(2009)
Forward 17 (4) Apps, 5 Goals
Born 22nd October 1986
2003–2006 Bedford Town 81 (31), 2006–2007 Kettering Town 40 (25), 2007–2011 Peterborough United 15 (1), 2008 Rochdale (loan) 20 (9), 2008–2009 Morecambe (loan) 37 (10), 2009 Imps (loan), 2010 Gillingham (loan) 18 (2), 2010–2011 Rushden & Diamonds (loan) 19 (6), 2011 Bristol Rovers (loan) 12 (1), 2011–2013 Torquay United 81 (28), 2013–2014 Burton Albion 11 (2), 2014–2015 Newport County 29 (3), 2015 Kettering Town 26 (9)

Howe came on loan from Peterborough after struggling to break into their team having stepped up from prolific spells at Kettering and Bedford. He came with a growing reputation as a potential lower league goal poacher, but his short spell at Lincoln was tarnished by turbulence off the field. Peter Jackson brought him to the club, but early into his spell Jackson was (thankfully) dismissed. He scored a brace in the subsequent 3-0 win over Darlington, but then went 13 games scoring just twice, one a winner in Chris Sutton's second game in charge. After the 3-1 cup win over Northwich he picked up an injury and went back to Peterborough.

Howe never looked comfortable in the Lincoln side, but I think we missed a great opportunity. If he could have worked longer with a striker of Chris Sutton's calibre, he may have been able to score a few more goals. Later in his career he had a ratio of one in three at Torquay, which suggests the ability was always there. Maybe at Lincoln the desire wasn't.

Howell, Luke
(2010-2011, 2011)
Midfielder 25 (2) Apps 1 Goal
Born 5th January 1987
2005–2007 Gillingham 1 (0), 2005–2006 Welling United (loan) 7 (0), 2006–2007 Folkestone Invicta (loan) 12 (3), 2007–2011 Milton Keynes Dons 53 (1), 2010–2011 Imps (loan), 2011 Imps, 2011–2015 Dagenham & Redbridge 127 (18), 2015–2016 Boreham Wood 37 (6), 2016 Dagenham & Redbridge 7 (1)

I'm afraid I have a sincere problem with Luke Howell. He played for Steve Tilson as we fell out of the league, and despite having a bit about him I felt he was always unable to play with the sort of pride and passion that could have kept us up. I may well be unfair but his arrival just continued the cycle of bringing in loan players less concerned about the club and more concerned about their own career.

So, some of the facts. He signed on a one-month loan with the Imps after failing to break into the MK Dons first team. He made his debut in a 2–2 draw against Wycombe Wanderers. A few weeks later in a match against Morecambe he was on the end of a shocking challenge which effectively ended his loan spell at Lincoln City. Luckily (!) after four weeks out he returned and extended his loan spell until the New Year.

In January of 2011 his contract with MK Dons terminated by mutual consent and he joined City until the end of the season. He scored once for City in a 4–2 loss against Barnet. In May, he was one of just three squad players to be offered a new contract after a mass clear out of players following relegation from the Football League. He didn't accept the contract. As fate would have it he now plies his trade in the National League anyway.

Maybe I'm being unfair on Luke Howell but as a player whom Steve Tilson actually wanted at the club I would like to have seen something, anything at all in those fateful four games from April 22nd to May 7th to suggest he wanted Lincoln City to remain in the football league. I'm afraid no matter what his Wikipedia page says, I saw no passion from him at all as we surrendered meekly to Aldershot on the worst day of my Lincoln City supporting life.

Hoyte, Gavin
(2010-2011)
Defender 14 (1) Apps 0 Goals
Born 6th June 1990

2007–2012 Arsenal 1 (0), 2008–2009 Watford (loan) 7 (0), 2009–2010 Brighton & Hove Albion (loan) 18 (0), 2010–2011 Imps (loan), 2012 AFC Wimbledon (loan) 3 (0), 2012–2014 Dagenham & Redbridge 68 (0), 2014–2015 Gillingham 30 (0), 2015 Barnet 19 (1)

Another loan player brought in by Steve Tilson to little or no effect. Hoyte was clearly a decent lad but again he was a loan player unconnected to Lincoln City. He came for game time, he played as we went down 5-0 at home to Bury and 5-1 at home to Shrewsbury and once his loan spell was up he sloped back to Arsenal before enjoying a career in the lower reaches of the football league. I can't summon up enough creativity to write about anymore bloody Steve Tilson loan signings at the moment, thank god I've got a home-grown hero coming up next in Darren Huckerby.

Huckerby, Darren
(1993-1995)
Forward 23 (8) Apps 7 Goals
Born 23rd April 1976
1993–1995 Imps), 1995–1996 Newcastle United 1 (0), 1996 Millwall (loan) 6 (3), 1996–1999 Coventry City 94 (28), 1999–2000 Leeds United 40 (2), 2000–2003 Manchester City 69 (22), 2003 Nottingham Forest (loan) 9 (5), 2003 Norwich City (loan) 16 (5), 2003–2008 Norwich City 174 (36), 2008–2009 San Jose Earthquakes 28 (9)

I'm not sure we've ever had a home-grown talent who has gone on to have such a solid career in the top flight of English football. Hucks broke through under the watchful eyes of Keith Alexander in the youth set up, and scored within six minutes of his debut away at Shrewsbury.

His Lincoln career may have looked unremarkable judging by the stats, but as a youth player he was exciting to watch. His pace was terrifying and he played with an arrogance and confidence that suggested he might go on to greater things. He survived three managers, Keith, Sam Ellis and Steve Wicks before the infamous John Beck cashed in on his prized asset. £500,000 and a lucrative friendly later Mr Beck had the means to finance an ultimately successful promotion bid. It is widely believed the Huckerby money financed the move for Gareth Ainsworth although the two players actually played three times together for Lincoln, winning two and drawing one. Hucks scored on his last Imps outing, a 1-1 draw at home to Hartlepool.

That lucrative friendly turned out to be far more than we could ever have imagined thanks to the generosity of Kevin Keegan. He promised a full strength side would perform in front of a packed Sincil Bank, and when he signed Alan Shearer for a world record fee a short time before it was assumed Shearer wouldn't play. He did and for a few days in the summer of 1996 the world's attention turned onto Lincoln City. Shearer got his debut goal, Newcastle got a 2-0 win and within two years City had got promoted.

Huckerby went on to move around for transfer fees totalling just under £10m and featured for such giants as Leeds United and Manchester City. He is perhaps most revered by fans of Norwich City where he put in over 170 appearances in a five-year spell. Not bad for a humble boy from the Lincoln YTS set-up, not bad at all.

Hughes, Jeff
(2005-2007)
Midfielder 60 (8) Apps 12 Goals
Born 29th May 1985
2003–2005 Larne 47 (1), 2005–2007 Imps, 2007–2008 Crystal Palace 10 (0), 2007–2008 Peterborough United (loan) 7 (1), 2008 Bristol Rovers (loan) 0 (0), 2008–2011 Bristol Rovers 129 (28), 2011–2013

Notts County 89 (20), 2013–2015 Fleetwood Town 47 (4), 2015–2016 Cambridge United 9 (0), 2016 Tranmere Rovers (loan) 18 (1), 2016 Tranmere Rovers

Jeff Hughes came from the same Irish conveyor belt of talent that brought Gareth McAuley to Sincil Bank, and almost brought James McClean as well. Spotted by Keith Alexander playing for Larne he impressed enough to earn a two-year deal in 2005. He made his debut against Bristol Rovers, a team he would end up playing for.

Hughes was a tricky winger with a good turn of pace, but at times looked too lightweight in his first season. He had a tendency to drift out of games despite showing obvious potential. His second season was more successful as he moved to cement a first team spot. Under John Schofield he flourished and began to find his eye for goal. A brace in the 7-1 win over Rochdale caught the eye, and winners in successive games against Boston (2-1) and Wycombe (1-0) at Christmas of 2006.
As the team faded towards the end of the season Hughes kept his performance levels high. Three of Lincoln's four play-off goals against Bristol Rovers came from his boot, and his final Imps performance was the second leg tie where he scored twice. Our failure to get promoted meant Hughes would inevitably move to a bigger club, and it was Crystal Palace where he moved on a free transfer.

Bristol Rovers didn't forget him though and within eighteen months he was playing for them, amassing well over 125 appearances in his spell there. He is still going strong only recently dropping into the National League, albeit with Tranmere Rovers who are arguably as big as they come on the non-league scene.

Hughton, Cian
(2009-2011)
Defender 64 (5) Apps 5 Goals
Born 25th January 1989
2008–2009 Tottenham Hotspur 0 (0), 2009–2011 Imps, 2012 Birmingham City 0 (0)

Famous for being the son of Chris Hughton and not a great amount else. I can't say Cian was a bad player, that would be unfair. I think physically he struggled to adjust to our league and Jackson, Sutton and Tilson didn't entirely recognise it and continued to play him. He was an average player in a terrible team and that combination will never bring greatness.

Signed by Jackson after a short trial from Spurs, he played just seven times before Jacko was fired. Opened the scoring for Lincoln in crucial wins over Chesterfield (2-1) and Barnet (2-1) either side of the 4-0 FA Cup defeat by Bolton. If anything, he had his best spell playing for Chris Sutton, he ended the season by scoring in-between a Davide Somma brace against Torquay (3-2) before grabbing a consolation against Macclesfield (1-2).

The relegation season he just didn't seem to have the physicality for a fight and he played in the drubbing against Bury although he missed the thrashings against Gillingham, Shrewsbury and Rotherham at home. However, he was on the pitch the day we went down and that unforgivable performance can, well, never be forgiven. Hence 'unforgivable'.

Hulme, Kevin
(1995)
Midfielder 6 (2) Apps 0 Goals
Born 2nd December 1967

1988–1993 Bury 110 (21), 1990 Chester City (loan) 4 (0), 1993–1994 Doncaster Rovers 34 (8), 1994–1996 Bury 29 (0), 1996 Imps (allegedly), 1996–1997 Macclesfield Town, 1997–2000 Halifax Town 33 (4), 2000–2001 York City 38 (7)

Workman-like journeyman midfielder who was swapped for Dean West in a shockingly bad judgement call by Steve Wicks in 1995. Played a handful of matches according to the statistics although anyone at the games probably wouldn't find enough to mention. Outlasted Wicks but not John Beck and he was soon on his way with a flea in his ear. Ineffective and now works as a roofer.

Hunt, Stephen
(2011)
Defender 14 Apps 2 Goals
Born 11th November 1984
2003–2004 Southampton 0 (0), 2004–2006 Colchester United 22 (1), 2006–2012 Notts County 116 (4), 2011 Imps (loan)

Defender who came on loan from Notts County in our futile bid to stay in the Football League. He scored on only his second appearance as we won away at Cheltenham, and then played in a superb run of form that saw us needing just three points to secure our safety. He even scored the goal that should have secured our football league status away at Macclesfield, only for Ben Hutchinson to be sent off and Macc to equalise in injury time.

Played his last match as we slipped to a 2-1 defeat at Stevenage and left before that fateful run in that saw us miserably surrender our league status. Could he have helped keep us up if he'd stayed? Almost undoubtedly. Hunt had appeared over 100 times for Notts County and offered an assured and calm head in a team that lacked direction and leadership. It's no coincidence our collapse came after he left.

Hutchinson, Andrew
(2009-2012)
Forward 5 (17) Apps 1 Goal
Born 10th March 1992
2009-2011 Imps, 2009 Hinckley United (loan) 3 (0), 2011 Harrogate Town (loan) 3 (1), 2011 Lewes (loan) 18 (1), 2012 Lincoln United 5 (2), 2013 Eastwood Town 6 (2), 2013 Lincoln United

Lincoln born Hutchinson was drafted into the Imps squad during the 2008-2009 season by Peter Jackson, after serving his time as a scholar with us. He made four appearances in total in his first season, scoring his first and only goal in a 1-1 away draw with Bradford City.

In 2009 he spent a month on loan with Conference North side Hinckley United. At the end of his scholarship, Hutchinson alongside fellow scholars Kern Miller and Nathan Adams agreed a six-month professional contract with the club.

In May 2011, he was one of just three squad players to be offered a new contract by Lincoln after a mass clear out of players following relegation from the Football League. Hutchinson, however was to miss the entire 2011-12 season due to injury and was released at the end of May. Despite scoring just once in 22 outings he still has a better goal to games ratio than Dene Cropper.

Hutchinson, Ben
(2010-2011)
Forward 29 (11) Apps 4 Goals
Born 27th November 1987
2005–2008 Middlesbrough 8 (1), 2006–2007 Billingham Synthonia (loan) 14 (7), 2008–2011 Celtic 5 (0), 2009–2010 Swindon Town (loan) 10 (1), 2010 Dundee (loan) 9 (1), 2010–2011 Imps (loan), 2012 Kilmarnock 4 (0), 2012–2014 Mansfield Town 38 (7), 2014 Nuneaton Town 11 (0), 2015 Basford United 11 (2)

Some facts: He signed for Chris Sutton through his Celtic contacts. Played for almost all of the disastrous 2010-11 season and had little to no effect given his billing as a 'big name'. He had apparently cost Celtic £1m when he signed from Middlesbrough, although I suspect that was heavily performance related, which meant the total would probably be closer to no pounds.

Sutton left and Steve Tilson kept faith with the forward, but on a cold Tuesday night in October it all began to go very wrong. Early in the second half, with City trailing 1-0 Hutchinson approached the fans and called us 'the worst fans in the world' for getting on his back. Steve Tilson didn't defend his striker in the Echo a couple of days later either:

"I was not aware of what is supposed to have happened, but I think that's a little bit of naivety if it did. You are out on the pitch, and it does not matter what level, you are an icon to a lot of people. As much as you might be receiving some stick, you have to be on your best behaviour."

In the weeks afterwards Imps fans took to singing 'we're the worst fans, in the world, we're the worst fans, in the world' (repeat) much to Hutchinson's dismay. He scored once more for the club after this event and went 23 games without looking like hitting a goal.

Not only did he have that incident staining his reputation but later in the season he got himself needlessly sent off in a game against Macclesfield which, had we won, we would have stayed up. He was sent off with the score at 1-0 to City, but the eleven men hit a last-minute equaliser to cost us two vital points. I reiterate, those two points would have kept us up. Could he have helped prevent the goal? Football is full of speculation, but there's absolutely no doubt had he scored the goals he was brought in to score we would still be a Football League club.

Aside from maybe two decent performances Hutchinson ambled about the pitch almost half-heartedly as we slipped out of the football league, and didn't look in the slightest bit bothered as we lost 3-0 to Aldershot on the final day.

I'm going to be blunt here, Ben Hutchinson was a waste of space in a City shirt, he was possibly the worst player Chris Sutton brought to the squad, and that is including Drewe Broughton. He is one of the principle factors in our relegation and he is an affront to my good surname. I refuse to write anymore about him, where he's been and what he's done since because no self-respecting Lincoln City fan should care.

Hutchison, Graham
(2012-2013)
Defender 7 Apps 0 Goals
Born 17th January 1993
2011 Imps, 2012-2013 Birmingham, 2012-2013 Imps (loan), 2014-2015 Worcester City, 2015 FC Halifax, 2015-2016 Telford (loan), 2016 Worcester City

Young defender who had initially been on City's books as a youth but earned himself a move to Birmingham City before he turned pro. Returned to take his place in the Imps defence at the beginning of the 2012/13 season under David Holdsworth.

Played seven games at the heart of our defence but only ended up on the winning side once as we beat Hyde 3-2. City failed to keep a clean sheet and eventually he not only returned to Birmingham but drifted back down to non-league football with Worcester, Halifax and Telford before settling back at Worcester City for the 2016 season.

Ipoua - Kovacs

Ipoua, Guy
(2005)
Forward 0 (6) Apps 0 Goals
Born 14th January 1976
1992 AS Nancy 0 (0), 1993–1994 Torino 0 (0), 1994–1995 Atlético Madrid 0 (0), 1995–1996 Novelda, 1996–1997 Sevilla, 1998–1998 Alicante, 1998–1999 Bristol Rovers 24 (3), 1999–2001 Scunthorpe United 65 (23), 2001–2003 Gillingham 82 (13), 2003–2004 Livingston 1 (0), 2004–2005 Doncaster Rovers 9 (0), 2004 Mansfield Town (loan) 5 (0), 2005 Imps (loan), 2005–2006 Hereford United 19 (7), 2006 Forest Green Rovers 7 (0), 2007 Oryx Douala

Before coming to England Ipoua's list of clubs is very impressive. Nancy (a French club, not just Sid Vicious' wife), Torino (currently employing Joe Hart), Atletico Madrid (I'm sure you know who they are) and Sevilla. He came to England in 1998, and after a failed trial at Crystal Palace he signed for Bristol Rovers. However, it was at Scunthorpe where he made his name for scoring goals, including one against Lincoln at Sincil Bank on Boxing Day 2000.

Eventually he made his way up to Gillingham and then back down the leagues to end up as another striker Keith Alexander hoped might fill the void left by Marcus Richardson, after he was loaned out for belting Ciaran Toner. Ipoua wasn't the answer and before long he was playing non-league football for Hereford.

Jackson, Marlon
(2013)
Forward 6 Apps 0 Goals
Born 6th December 1990
2009–2012 Bristol City 5 (0), 2009 Hereford United (loan) 5 (0), 2009–2010 Aldershot Town (loan) 24 (1), 2010 Aldershot Town (loan) 9 (0), 2011 Northampton Town (loan) 6 (1), 2011 Cheltenham Town (loan) 1 (0), 2012 AFC Telford United (loan) 8 (1), 2012–2013 Hereford United 25 (7), 2013–2014 Bury 8 (1), 2013 Imps (loan), 2014 Halifax Town 14 (0), 2014–2015 Oxford City 24 (5), 2015 Tranmere Rovers 11 (0), 2015-2016 Oxford City 8 (7), 2016 Newport County 2 (0)

Young striker-cum-winger loaned from Bury under Gary Simpson. Struggled to make any impact at all as City slumped to four defeats and an FA Cup draw with Plymouth whilst he was at the club. Since then has found his way into league football with Newport County.

Jarrett, Albert
(2010-2011)
Midfielder 23 (3) Apps 1 Goals
Born 23rd October 1984
2003–2004 Wimbledon 9 (0), 2004–2006 Brighton & Hove Albion 23 (1), 2005 Stevenage Borough (loan) 4 (0), 2006 Swindon Town (loan) 6 (0), 2006–2007 Watford 1 (0), 2007 Boston United (loan) 5 (2), 2007 Milton Keynes Dons (loan) 5 (0), 2008–2009 Gillingham 16 (0), 2009–2010 Barnet 45 (2), 2010–2011 Imps, 2011 Aldershot Town (loan) 2 (0), 2011–2012 Lewes 14 (0), 2012–2014 Bromley 30 (0), 2014 Sutton United 1 (0), 2014–2016 Dulwich Hamlet 31 (1)

Albert Jarrett probably won't be remembered very fondly by fans of the club. He arrived along with Mustapha Carayol in the summer of 2010 and at face value looked a really good signing. He could

118

score a couple of goals but also had pace and trickery that Chris Sutton hoped would unlock League Two defences.

He played a majority of both Chris Sutton's tenure and the first half of Steve Tilson's spell in charge. He often lacked consistency and composure but he weighed in with a winning goal against Nuneaton in the cup that set up a second-round tie with Hereford that we ultimately lost. He was also responsible for earning us our first point of the season at Crewe.

He rapidly fell out of favour with Tilson and after three appearances from the bench was loaned out to Aldershot. Once he returned to Lincoln his contract was cancelled by mutual consent amidst rumours of high wages. Steve Tilson went on to use that saving to bring in uncreative kids from average teams to ensure a nice and easy slide down to the National League.

Could Jarrett have helped keep us up? He never appeared to have the stomach for a battle, but he did have a little bit of skill and creativity, and perhaps in those final ten games he might have brought just a single goal or chance. Who knows?

John-Lewis, Lennell
(2006-2010)
Forward 48 (33) Apps 9 Goals
Born 17th May 1989
2006 Grantham Town 4 (0), 2006–2010 Imps, 2010–2013 Bury 83 (9), 2013–2015 Grimsby Town 92 (23), 2015 Newport County 28 (3)

Young player given his debut by John Schofield in the 2-1 FA Cup defeat by Port Vale in 2006. John-Lewis always threatened to turn into a good player for us, but he never managed to play under a settled manager. His best spells probably came under Peter Jackson who gave him a run in the team shortly after coming to the club in 2007. He scored as a late sub after coming on against Stockport in just his fourth outing for the club, and ended the 07/08 season with three goals to his name.

The following season he became a regular fixture in and around the first team without ever truly excelling. His solitary goal at Bournemouth earned us a 1-0 win, but other goals he scored simply came as consolation efforts in poor defeats. He equalised in our FA Cup replay with Kettering, only for them to score again and win the tie in injury time.

He scored just once in his final season with Lincoln, a late winner away at Barnet. Despite featuring prominently in Chris Sutton's sides, he once again never scored or threatened as much as a pacey and powerful striker should. There was no surprise when he was released in May 2010.

The main surprise was that instead of drifting into the non-league scene he forged a career in the Football League with Bury. Latterly he played for Grimsby, firstly being sent off in our 1-1 draw in 2013/14, and then giving Grimsby a second minute lead in 2014/15 play-off final only for Bristol Rovers to win on penalties. However, his goal scoring exploits earned him another crack at league football with Newport County.

Johnson, Alan
(1994-1996)
Defender 64 (7) Apps 1 Goal
Born 19th February 1971

1989–1994 Wigan Athletic 180 (13), 1994–1996 Imps, 1995–1996 Preston North End (loan) 2 (0), 1996–2000 Rochdale 59 (4)

Tough and able defender signed by Keith Alexander in 1994 from Wigan Athletic. Was a fan favourite for his committed displays despite the upheaval during his tenure, but when John Beck came in his days were sadly numbered. He suffered from injuries that kept him out of the team for spells, and ahead of his first full season as manager, Beck moved Johnson on to Rochdale.

There were rumours of an extra fee payable to Wigan if Johnson made 65 starts for City, and conspiracy theorists everywhere believed that is why he was sold on after impressing fans. I love a good conspiracy theory.

Johnson, David
(1993-1996)
Forward 94 (15) Apps 23 Goals
Born 29th October 1970
1991–1993 Sheffield Wednesday 6 (0), 1991 Hartlepool United (loan) 7 (2), 1992 Hartlepool United (loan) 3 (0), 1993–1996 Imps, 1996 Altrincham

'Magic' Johnson arrived from Sheffield Wednesday in 1993 and instantly became a fans favourite. He had been highly thought of at Sheffield Wednesday, and they turned a £100k bid down for him from Hartlepool the season prior to him signing for us. Wednesday had also accepted a £40k offer from Scunthorpe United, which Johnson turned down, making him even more of a fans favourite! Eventually the tribunal set his fee at £32k which was brilliant news for City.

He was a right sided forward with a touch of flair, and initially it seemed he would play out wide. He drifted into the centre and ended up as our leading scorer in the 1993/94 season with 13 goals, including our only strike against Bolton in the FA Cup defeat that Sky televised live.

His next two seasons were disrupted by injury and management changes. He scored seven times in 1994/95 including a famous winner against Premiership giants Crystal Palace at Sincil Bank, and a winner at home to Huddersfield in the FA Cup. The following season was blighted by injury as well, and he only managed seven starts under John Beck before leaving the club at the end of the season.

Despite a relatively low goal haul for three full seasons Magic Johnson will always be remembered fondly by Imps fans for popping up with those goals in cup ties. My personal highlight has to be the winner against a strong Palace side, and what should have been the winner over two legs had referee Gary Willard not found seven minutes of injury time in the return leg at Selhurst Park.

Jones, Gary
(1993)
Forward 0 (5) Apps 2 Goals
Born 6th April 1969
1988–1990 Doncaster Rovers 20 (2), 1991–1993 Boston United, 1993–1996 Southend United 70 (16), 1993–1994 Imps (loan), 1995–1999 Notts County 117 (38), 1996–1997 Scunthorpe United (loan) 11 (5), 1998–2000 Hartlepool United 45 (7), 1999–2000 Halifax Town (loan) 8 (1), 2000–2002 Halifax Town 68 (9), 2002–2003 Nuneaton Borough, 2002–2003 Hucknall Town, 2002–2003 Gainsborough Trinity, 2003–2007 Armthorpe Welfare, 2006–2008 Selby Town, 2007–2009 Armthorpe Welfare, 2009–2010 Winterton Rangers

Jones was a centre forward signed on loan by Keith Alexander in his first spell as Imps manager, proving even then he was on his striker search! Jones scored twice in five appearances from the bench before returning to Southend. He had registered goals in a 2-2 draw with Bury, and one in our 4-3 win over Northampton.

It wasn't a case of not proving himself, Jones was a popular and lively striker who went on to have a decent career scoring every three or four games wherever he went. However at the time a certain Barry Fry was holding the purse strings at Southend and he wouldn't let his prize asset go on the cheap. Lincoln were simply priced out of a move. When he finally left Roots Hall for Notts County it cost the Meadow Lane based side £140,000 which was significantly more than we had floating around Sincil Bank at the time. Or ever.

Jones, Jake
(2013)
Midfielder 7 (6) Apps 0 Goals
Born 6th April 1993
2011–2013 Walsall 3 (0), 2011–2012 Redditch United (loan), 2013 Imps (loan), 2013–2014 Tamworth 5 (1), 2014-2015 King's Lynn Town, 2015 Halesowen Town, 2015 King's Lynn Town, 2015 Leamington

Jones played 13 games for City after initially signing on loan from Walsall for David Holdsworth. Gary Simpson liked what he saw from the winger and decided to offer him terms for the following season. Jones verbally accepted and it seemed the Imps had bagged their first signing of the summer.

Just days later he signed for Tamworth leaving the Imps hierarchy fuming. He had been the subject of a Twitter 'love in', with fans asking him to stay and him reciprocating. Maybe after that he decided he couldn't live up to the expectations? Maybe Tamworth just offered more money.

Fate dealt him a bad hand in the Midlands and after just a handful of games for Tamworth he cancelled his own contract for 'personal reasons' and disappeared down the non-league pyramid. Bad decision Jake, and as you snubbed us in 2013 I'm snubbing you by not bothering to write any more or even research you particularly deeply. Gutted, eh?

Jordan, Todd
(2013-2015)
Defender 41 (6) Apps 1 Goal
Born 4th December 1991
2013-2015 Imps, 2014-2015 Stalybridge Celtic (loan), 2015 Alfreton

Limited utility man often employed in the middle of the park by Gary Simpson. Most fans appreciated Jordan's committed approach to the game, but few could forget how out of his depth he actually was. Todd was a nice lad, but so is Alan Long, and you don't see Alan Long getting a run out every week.

He did score a 12th minute goal for City early in his Imps career that ultimately gave us a 3-2 win over Telford, and in fairness I think we should remember that contribution, and not the next season and a half of bland under achieving.

Just as a barometer of Gary Simpson's selection habits circa 2014, Todd Jordan often started in the midfield ahead of Jon Nolan, the same Jon Nolan that (despite being a bit of a tool) fired Grimsby to the football league and now plays for Chesterfield. Just goes to show commitment will only get you so far, eventually you need to show a little bit of raw talent too.

121

Kabba, Sahr
(2014-2015)
Forward 0 (3) Apps 0 Goals
Born 13th April 1989
2013-2014 Havant and Waterlooville, 2014-2015 Imps, 2015 Gloucester, 2015 Welling

Signed for Gary Simpson in the summer of 2014 but never got a decent run in the first team to showcase his talents. Played a total of 22 minutes for the club, all three appearances coming as a substitute and all coming in defeats for City. Joined Gloucester in the 2015 January transfer window as he didn't fit in with new manager Chris Moyses plans. That decision has proven to be right as Kabba has remained a level below City.

Kanyucka, Patrick
(2011)
Defender 2 (4) Apps 0 Goals
Born 19th July 1987
2004–2008 Queens Park Rangers 24 (0), 2008–2009 Swindon Town 20 (1), 2009–2010 Northampton Town 3 (0), 2010–2011 CFR Cluj 10 (0), 2010Unirea Alba Iulia (loan) 13 (0), 2011 Imps, 2011–2012Tamworth 13 (0), 2012 Staines Town 6 (0), 2012–2013 Maidenhead United 7 (0), 2013–2014Roi Et United 21 (9), 2015 Limerick 18 (0), 2016 Shan United 10 (0)

I'm sure Pat Kanyucka was a decent player. He would have to be right? He played for QPR and Swindon amongst others so somebody must have seen something in him. Steve Tilson certainly did and he signed on a short-term contract ahead of our relegation battle in 2011. His first game was a 2-1 win away at Bradford, but Kanyucka only lasted 45 minutes before being substituted and blamed for the first goal.

After that auspicious start he struggled to break into the first team, although he did appear in the 5-1 home defeat against Shrewsbury as a second half substitute. He was on the pitch when we drew 1-1 with Macclesfield in a match that had we won, we would have stayed up. Unfortunately Kanyucka couldn't prevent Sam Wedgebury scoring in the 90th minute of that clash.

He started the next game, a home clash with Rotherham. He didn't finish it though, he was sent off after 62 minutes with the Imps trailing 4-0. They scored the resulting penalty on their way to a 6-0 win. Unsurprisingly he never played for Lincoln again. There was some poetic justice though as he appeared for Tamworth the following season in a 4-0 win for the hosts that resulted in Steve Tilson losing his job. Every cloud and all that.

Keane, Jordan
(2015)
Defender 7 Apps 0 Goals
Born 19th September 1993
2012-2014 Stoke City, 2013-2014 Tamworth (loan), 2014-2015 Alfreton, 2015 Imps (loan), 2016 Nuneaton

Defender brought in by Chris Moyses to help out a few months after he took over from Gary Simpson. He made his Lincoln debut in a 2-1 home defeat by Forest Green and was only on the winning side once in his short Imps career. Played his last game and kept his only clan sheet against Dartford in April 2015 before returning to Alfreton. Some of the more cynical observers see this as our lowest point, having to loan players from Alfreton and then putting them straight in the first team. There's no doubt that we haven't looked back since Chris signed his own players in the summer of 2015. That said Jordan Keane wasn't that bad, it was just what he represented that was a problem.

Keates, Dean
(2006-2007)
Midfielder 22 (2) Apps, 4 Goals
Born 14th June 1988
1995–2002 Walsall 156 (12), 2002–2004Hull City 50 (4), 2004–2005Kidderminster Harriers 49 (7), 2005–2006 Imps, 2006–2007 Walsall 53 (15), 2007–2009 Peterborough United 84 (12), 2010 Wycombe Wanderers 13 (1), 2010–2015 Wrexham 153 (13), 2015–2016, Rhyl 22 (1), 2016 Rushall Olympic 0 (0)

Keates arrived at Sincil Bank after our play-off defeat by Southend as we looked to kick on and win automatic promotion the season after. We had seen plenty of him from his time at Hull and Kidderminster where he'd always shown himself to be a cultured and combative midfielder despite his 5'5 stature. In a Lincoln shirt, he didn't disappoint showing his dead ball ability and his tigerish devotion to proper tackling. In his 21 starts he became a firm fan favourite always amongst the goals or the bookings. Two red cards in November and December kept him out of a couple of games, and he made his last Imps appearance in a 4-1 win at Sincil Bank against Barnet in January of 2007.

His reluctance to relocate to Lincolnshire got the better of him and he moved to Walsall much closer to his family in the transfer window. Fans were gutted that such a talent couldn't be persuaded to stay at Sincil Bank. He moved to struggling Walsall who suffered relegation at the end of the season, and re-appeared at Lincoln as a visitor with the Saddlers a few months later.

Less than a year afterwards his decision to relocate for 'personal reasons' took a bit of a hit as he moved to Peterborough United, not that much closer to home than Lincoln. I suppose pay cheques have a bearing on where you play as well. Currently managing Wrexham in the National League, where his first job was to get rid of Sean Newton to York. He may not have had sound judgement to stay with City, but his judge of character is spot on.

Kell, Richard
(2007)
Defender (0) 1 App 0 Goals
Born 15th September 1979
1998–2001 Middlesbrough 0 (0), 2001 Torquay United (loan) 4 (1), 2001 Torquay United 11 (2), 2001–2005 Scunthorpe United 83 (8), 2005–2006 Barnsley 2 (0), 2006 Scarborough (loan) 2 (0), 2006–2007 Imps

The former Scunthorpe defender played just once for Lincoln, as a late substitute in a 2-2 draw at Accrington. He replaced Ryan Amoo. That's literally all I can really tell you about Richard Kell. Possibly the most obscure player included in the book. 10 minutes of football, that means I've written more words than he spent minutes on the pitch. Let's move on shall we?

Kelly, Julian
(2011)
Defender 21 Apps 0 Goals
Born 6th September 1989
2008–2011 Reading 7 (0), 2010 Wycombe Wanderers (loan) 9 (1), 2011 Lincoln City (loan) 21 (0), 2011–2013 Notts County 54 (4), 2014 Spalding United, 2014 Carlton Town, 2014 Grantham Town

On paper Julian Kelly looked a good prospect. He'd been with Arsenal up until he was 16, then switched over to Reading to turn pro before dropping down to Wycombe Wanderers on loan. He had a reputation as a quick and lively full back who could play on the wing. He joined us on loan (as most unwanted Football League reserve players did under Tilson) in January 2011. His debut saw us lose to his old club Wycombe.

His next five games saw the Imps take maximum points and steer themselves away from the threat of relegation. Five wins in five was unheard of in that awful season and Kelly looked every part the rampaging full back we needed. However, a 5-1 home defeat by Shrewsbury halted that run of form, and from there on we looked a ragged side. Kelly's last home game for City was another drubbing, 4-0 by Gillingham. He featured in a surprise away point at Gresty Road before leaving the club.

Steve Tilson blamed his loan players leaving as a reason for the continued struggles; "I'm not one for making excuses but finding a consistent level of performance has been difficult due to players returning to their parent clubs and that's a position we find ourselves in again with Julian Kelly returning to Reading. He was arguably our most consistent performer in recent months and he will be missed." Maybe he should have tried negotiating longer deals, or even more out of leftfield using the players at his disposal?

Kelly turned up next at Notts County and had reasonable success there scoring 4 times in over 50 appearances. At the end of the 2013 season his contract wasn't renewed and he drifted into non-league football despite a trial at Grimsby. He was last seen turning out for Grantham Town, and despite being a decent player with over twenty Imps appearances for me he will always be remembered as part of the worst defence I've ever seen at Sincil Bank. Losing 6-0. To Rotherham. At home.

Keltie, Clark
(2010-2011)
Midfielder 27 (4) Apps 0 Goals
Born 31st August 1983
2001–2008 Darlington 181 (11), 2008–2009 Rochdale 34 (1), 2009 Chester City (loan) 0 (0), 2009 Gateshead (loan) 3 (0), 2010–2011 Imps, 2011–2012 Þór Akureyri 13 (1), 2012 Cork City 0 (0), 2012 Darlington 15 (0), 2012 Víkingur Ólafsvík 13 (0), 2012 Darlington 1883 3 (0), 2013 Perth SC

Keltie came to play for Chris Sutton and was still around once Steve Tilson took over. He never excelled in a Lincoln shirt, but then towards the end of his spell he didn't feature. Keltie wasn't a bad player but he played for bad managers in a bad side. It's pretty hard to do yourself any justice under those conditions.

In November 2011 he faced criminal prosecution after crashing his car into a telephone box in Newcastle. Keltie was also found to have a string of past motor related offences, a spokeswoman for Northumbria Police mentioned "Clark Keltie, 28, of Denton Burn, Newcastle, has been charged with careless driving, failing to stop after an accident and failing to report an accident. Given the exploits of Moses Swaibu, Ali Fuseini and Delroy Facey it seems the relegated team were cursed!

Kerley, Adam
(2004)
Forward 0 (2) Apps, 0 Goals
Born 2nd February 1985

2004 Imps, 2005 Lincoln United (loan), 2005, Spalding (loan), 2006 Gainsborough Trinity, 2007 Eastwood Town

Kerley was a prolific scorer for City's reserves during the early part of his Imps career, but only made two substitute appearances for the first team, one in the LDV Vans Trophy against Doncaster and one in the League versus Kidderminster. He never broke into the first team though and he spent time out on loan before moving to Gainsborough Trinity.

Kerr, Scott
(2005-2011)
Midfielder 234 (15) Apps 9 Goals
Born 11ᵗʰ December 1981
1999–2001 Bradford City 1 (0), 2001–2003 Hull City 0 (0), 2002 Frickley Athletic (loan) 5 (1), 2003–2005 Scarborough 84 (1), 2005–2011 Imps, 2011–2013 York City 78 (0), 2013–2014 Grimsby Town 37 (1), 2014 Bradford Park Avenue 11 (2), 2014 Hyde (loan) 5 (0), 2014–2015 Stalybridge Celtic 8 (0), 2015–2016 Spennymoor Town, 2016 Ossett Albion

Scott Kerr will divide opinion amongst Imps fans, and you're either going to love or hate the next few paragraphs. For me Scott Kerr was the perfect example of a committed and resilient player who always showed the right attitude and application when performing for the Imps.

He started out at Bradford but after making just one appearance he wound up at Scarborough via a couple of clubs. His performances there, particularly in their 2005 cup run brought him to the attention of several clubs. He expressed his desire to leave Scarborough in June 2005 to return to the Football League and held talks with Barnet, managed by his England C manager Paul Fairclough and Lincoln managed by the late, great Keith Alexander. He opted to sign for us on a two-year deal and was one of several arrivals that summer.

He enjoyed an impressive debut season with The Imps as we made the play-offs for a fourth and final time under Big Keith. In the 2006–07 season, under new head coach John Schofield, now-captain Kerr was able to flourish as the ball spent much more time on the deck in the middle of the park. He formed a solid partnership with Lee Frecklington in midfield and helped us push into the end of season lottery for a fifth (and final) successive season.

In the next season Kerr continued to captain the side and be dominant and battling presence some fans will remember him as. He had to win over the affections of new manager Peter Jackson, something that came to be a running theme in his time at Lincoln. Following the sale of Frecklington to Peterborough in January 2009, Kerr found himself playing with many midfield partners as Peter Jackson experimented to find the best combination, after trying to play alongside Shane Clarke, the 'magnificent' Stefan Oakes and eventually Michael O'Connor on loan from Crewe Alexandra.

Kerr started to flourish due to the freedom O'Connor gave him and he scored his first two goals of the season in Lincoln's 2–0 win at Accrington Stanley in April. He was unsurprisingly named as Lincoln's Player of the Year for the 2008–09 season.

The following season it started all over again as Jackson left and Chris Sutton came in. Once again Scott found himself having to prove his worth all over again, but an impressive outing in the cup against Northwich Victoria helped convince Sutton that he was of value to the squad. He had been set to join York City on loan in November 2010 after being out of the team at Lincoln, but after re-establishing himself the move no longer appealed to him. Within 12 months it was Steve Tilson he had to win over, and that battle was far more difficult.

Kerr was released from his Lincoln contract to sign for York on a one-and-a-half-year contract on 31st January 2011, somewhat ironically around the time of a complete collapse on the field, a lack of direction and organisation from the players and ultimately relegation. There are an awful lot of ifs and buts about that terrible spell in early 2011, but I am 100% certain had Scotty Kerr been in our midfield we'd still be a Football League club now.

Chris Gooding's view

In the early Summer of 2005 walking to local newsagents to pick up the Lincolnshire Echo, I was desperate to read of some transfer news regarding players joining the mighty Imps for the forthcoming season. On approaching the shop I could see the billboard outside telling me what I wanted to know, Lincoln had made their move in the market.

Once the news had sunk in, the name of Scott Kerr was a name that took my interest because I'd remembered him from the season before in a live game I had watched in his Scarborough days versus Chelsea. Once I had put the jigsaw together, the conclusion was a good signing.

Scott Kerr made 221 league appearances for Lincoln and anybody who makes that number you would assume would go down as a club favourite. Amazingly this is not the case because even to this day, the career of Scott causes much debate.

Recently I read the term "Pub Player" and this label I can't understand for many reasons. It is very important that we all remember his entire time at Lincoln was in the football league and for the most he was the captain.

Whether we liked them or not, Managers such as Keith Alexander, John Schofield, Peter Jackson and Chris Sutton, all saw that Scott was good enough to get in the side and I would guess that if we asked Lee Frecklington, he would be very complimentary.

It was a duo that worked and caused teams many a problem, especially in the Schofield reign. I suppose if I had some criticism I would say he held on to the ball a second too long and certainly didn't score enough goals but in the present day that fashionable term 'holding midfielder' would describe him perfectly so I could understand and was happy what he brought to the team.

The day that Steve Tilson walked through the doors of Sincil Bank was the beginning of the end of his time at Lincoln. He was replaced as captain by Delroy Facey and by the end of January found himself in a York City shirt. A decision that left the player to this day hurt. At the time he said; "The club was a big part of my life; I played under some great Managers like Keith Alexander. I reached two play offs and I understood what the club meant to the fans".

Now of course this could be just a throwaway comment but for me I believe him. He had spent the majority of his career with us, been involved in good sides with good players, why wouldn't he care for the club? It makes Steve Tilson's decision even more baffling. You would think he would need a trusted member, a link between manager and players and you would most defiantly need a leader on the pitch.

A point that was not lost on the previous managers which I suppose was why they were all considerably better. I fully accept that people's opinion will still vary on our former captain. Personally I would like to compliment Scott as a person and as a player at his time at Lincoln.

I'll leave you with this thought..."If Scott Kerr had not left when he did, could relegation have been avoided?"

Key, Lance
(1995)
Goalkeeper 5 Apps 0 Goals
Born 13th May 1968
1990–1996 Sheffield Wednesday 0 (0), 1993 Oldham Athletic (loan) 2 (0), 1995 Oxford United (loan) 6 (0), 1995 Imps (loan), 1995 Hartlepool United (loan) 1 (0), 1996 Rochdale (loan) 14 (0), 1996–1997 Dundee United 3 (0), 1997 Sheffield United 0 (0), 1997–1999 Rochdale 19 (0), 1998–2001 Northwich Victoria 51 (0), 2000 Altrincham (loan) 15 (0), 2001–2004 Kingstonian 136 (0), 2004–2008 Histon 124 (0), 2008 Wivenhoe Town, 2010–2011 Rushden & Diamonds

Lance Key made just five appearances for the Imps on loan from Sheffield Wednesday at the start of the tumultuous 1995/96 season. His debut saw us beat Preston North End 2-1, but then he conceded 11 in just four further games before being replaced by John Vaughan. He struggled to find regular first team football anywhere in the Football League but appeared regularly for Northwich Victoria and latterly was a member of the Histon team that reached the Second Round of The FA Cup in 2005/06.

Kilbey, Tom
(2011)
Midfielder 6 (1) Apps 0 Goals
Born 19th October 1990
2007 Millwall 0 (0), 2007–2011 Portsmouth 2 (0), 2009 Dagenham & Redbridge (loan) 0 (0), 2011 Imps (loan)

Kilbey was loaned to Lincoln in March 2011, hardly a prestigious time to be a Lincoln City player. He made his debut against Rotherham at home in a game I mention far too much in this book as we went down 6-0. Perhaps that should have been an omen. We conceded 18 goals in his seven-game stay and picked up just a single point. I don't need to tell you how the season ended.

Kilbey also featured in three series of the crass, scripted 'reality' show The Only Way Is Essex, in which his sister Cara 'starred'. I can't comment on the programme as I've never watched it, but if Kilbey's football skills were anything to go by, it was a very poor TV show.

King, Gary
(2008-2009)
Forward 5 (7) Apps 1 Goal
Born 27th January 1990
2008–2009 Imps, 2009 Boston United (loan) 11 (3), 2009–2010 Accrington Stanley 8 (1), 2010 Hinckley United 14 (4), 2010 Louth Town 2 (1), 2010 Stamford 0 (0), 2010 Harrogate Town 17 (2), 2011 Stamford, 2011–2012 Worksop Town, 2012 Grantham Town, 2012 Stamford, 2012 Corby Town 2012 Grantham Town, 2012 Stamford, 2012–2013 Spalding United, 2013 Corby Town, 2013 Brigg Town, 2013 Grantham Town, 2013-14 Coalville Town, 2014 Grantham Town, 2014 Deeping Rangers, 2014-2015 Holbeach United, 2015 Lincoln United

Gary King had been with City since under-9's level, and signed his first professional contract on 19th April 2008. Later that day, he made his first start for Lincoln and scored against Brentford in the 39th minute of the game. Lincoln later went on to win this match 3–1. It was to be his only goal for Lincoln, and despite a short spell with Accrington Stanley he didn't go on to make the grade as a league footballer. He did go on to play for almost every Lincolnshire non-league side he possibly could, most recently Lincoln United.

Kovacs, Janos
(2008-2010)
Defender 66 Apps 4 Goals
Born 11th September 1985
2003–2005 MTK 1 (0), 2004–2005 Bodajk (loan), 2005–2008 Chesterfield 57 (2), 2007 York City (loan) 8 (1), 2008–2010 Imps, 2010 Luton Town 17 (1), 2010–2012 Hereford United 25 (2), 2011–2012 Luton Town (loan) 17 (2), 2012–2013 Luton Town 40 (5), 2013 Budapest Honvéd

Giant Hungarian Kovacs became a cult figure at Sincil Bank with a series of committed if not convincing displays at centre half. He had been offered a new contract at Chesterfield, but the likelihood of him signing decreased significantly after former Imps defender Kevin Austin joined the Spireites. Peter Jackson eventually picked him up as part of his Magnificent Seven, the players he hoped would fire us to League Two success. They didn't, but Kovacs wasn't too bad. He scored in his first home appearance for the team with a headed equaliser in a pre-season friendly against Premier League side Aston Villa which City won 3-1. Eventually the tribunal set a fee of £17,500 for Kovács along with a sell on clause should he move for more money.

In his first season, he managed three goals, all of them in City wins with one coming against his old club Chesterfield. He scored on the opening day of the following season to give us hope of a good campaign, but couldn't save Peter Jackson's job just a few weeks later. Chris Sutton came in and Kovacs' days were numbered. His last start came in the cup away at Northwich Victoria. He then missed all of December before being transfer listed and then almost immediately had his contract terminated by mutual consent to join Luton Town.

Larkin - Lucas

Larkin, Colin
(2012-2013)
Forward 15 (20) Apps 8 Goals
Born 27th April 1982

2001–2002 Wolverhampton Wanderers 3 (0), 2001–2002 Kidderminster Harriers (loan) 33 (6), 2002–2005 Mansfield Town 95 (25), 2005–2007 Chesterfield 80 (11), 2007–2009 Northampton Town 54 (3), 2009–2012 Hartlepool United 54 (4), 2012–2013 Imps, 2013 Harrogate Town 13 (1), 2013–2014 Gateshead 31 (9), 2014 Harrogate Town 1 (0), 2014-2015 West Auckland Town, 2015 Sunderland RCA

Lively striker who had a decent season at Mansfield Town which set him up for a career of floating around the lower leagues. Came to Lincoln under David Holdsworth and enjoyed a goal every three and a half games which, unlike most of Holdsworth's signings, was a good contribution.

At the time Holdsworth said: "We do require goals and Colin's come for all the right reasons. He's fit and ready to go, which is a really important factor. He's a very good addition to our squad. It's nice to be able to bring in a guy who's 30 years old but very quick and very able. As a manager, it's nice for me to be able to attract that type of player."

He netted eight times for Lincoln before leaving the club in 2013 to be closer to his North-East home. It mustn't be forgotten he was on penalty duties for City which helped his goal tally.

Laurent, Francis
(2011-2012)
Forward 5 (9) Apps 1 Goal
Born 2nd January 1986

2005–2006 FC Sochaux-Montbéliard B 12 (0), 2006–2007 SV Eintracht Trier 05 14 (4), 2007–2008 1. FSV Mainz 05 II 25 (7), 2007–2008 1. FSV Mainz 05 6 (0), 2008–2010 Southend United 56 (9), 2010–2011, AFC Compiègne 3 (0), 2011 Northampton Town 6 (0), 2011–2012 Imps, 2012 K.V.K. Tienen 15 (0), 2013–2014 FC Chambly 29 (5)

Laurent had been a powerful and pacey forward who played under Steve Tilson for Southend. A serious injury had hampered his career and his came to Sincil Bank just after we dropped out of the league, with the potential to be a top player for us.

At the time of his signing Steve Tilson said: "He is 6ft 2ins, a right winger with loads of pace, great with the ball at his feet. He has got to get a bit more consistency into his game but I'd like to think his pace will cause problems."

As it was he never got to play for Steve Tilson as he was sacked before Laurent could regain fitness. David Holdsworth gave him ample chances, but he scored just once in a 2-0 away win at Forest Green. His last game in a City shirt was the 5-0 win against Darlington as an 82nd minute substitute for Jamie Taylor. He latterly signed for KVK Tienen along with former Imps Jean-Francois Christophe and Jean Arnuad.

Leaning, Andy
(1994-1996)
Goalkeeper 51 Apps 0 Goals
Born 18th May 1963

1985 Rowntree Mackintosh, 1985–1987 York City 69 (0), 1987–1988 Sheffield United 21 (0), 1988–1994 Bristol City 75 (0), 1994–1996 Imps, 1996 Dundee 0 (0), 1996–2000 Chesterfield 22 (0)

Leaning signed for us in 1994 to challenge Mike Pollitt for the number one jersey, which he immediately did. He made his debut in a 2–1 defeat to Crewe Alexandra on 26 March and missed just one game through injury until the end of the season.

The following season Russell Hoult signed on loan and kept Leaning out of the side again, but he regained his starting XI place once Hoult departed. He briefly lost it again to Steve Sherwood before playing in the last two games of the season.

Once again the following season he was displaced, this time by Lance Key. He regained it once again as Sam Ellis departed, but once John Beck arrived at the club he brought Barry Richardson and the popular Leaning once again deputised, appearing in cup competitions only. He left at the end of the season for Dundee.

He was part of the Chesterfield team that almost reached the 1996/97 FA Cup final, agonisingly losing out to Middlesbrough

Ledsham, Karl
(2014)
Midfielder 0 (4) Apps 0 Goals
Born 17ᵗʰ November 1987
2008-2009 St Helens Town, 2009-2010 Skelmersdale United, 2010-2015 Southport, 2013-2014 Cambridge United (loan), 2014-2015 Imps, 2014 Telford (loan), 2015 Barrow, 2015 Stockport

Ledsham had put in several good performances against City whilst playing for Southport, including scoring in their 4-2 win over us in 2013. Therefore, many fans were delighted when the powerful midfielder turned up at Sincil Bank in 2014. He had goal in him having scored ten in one season for Southport. However, his spell didn't turn out as expected as injury restricted him to just four appearances from the bench. He went out on loan to Telford before joining Barrow at the end of the season.

Lennon, Stephen
(2010)
Midfielder 15 (4) Apps 3 Goals
Born 20ᵗʰ January 1988
2006–2010 Rangers 3 (0), 2008–2009 Partick Thistle (loan) 9 (0), 2010 Imps (loan), 2010 Dundalk 9 (0), 2011 Newport County 9 (2), 2011–2013 Fram 43 (17), 2013–2014 Sandnes Ulf 28 (3), 2014 FH 35 (20)

Lennon came from Scottish Premier League side Rangers on loan in February 2010. He was another of Chris Sutton's loan players that had clear talent, but didn't look comfortable with the rigours of lower league football (see Gilmour, Brian). He started well with two goals in his first four games as we beat Accrington (2-1) and lost to Rotherham (2-1). He failed to keep that momentum going and grabbed just one more goal from fifteen further outings, although he was used as a striker and a midfielder at various times.

Lennon was allegedly offered a permanent deal at the end of the season was quoted as saying he would be delighted to sign for the Imps on a permanent basis. As negotiations drew on he complained that he couldn't find anywhere to live in the City and subsequently missed Sutton's deadline. The offer was withdrawn and Lennon returned to Rangers, where he was released at the end of his contract. He's spent the last few years kicking around the Icelandic football scene.

Lescott, Aaron
(2000)
Defender 3(2) Apps 0 Goals
Born 2nd December 1978
1995–2000 Aston Villa 0 (0), 2000 Imps (loan), 2000–2001 Sheffield Wednesday 37 (0), 2001–2004 Stockport County 72 (1), 2004 Bristol Rovers (loan) 8 (0), 2004–2010 Bristol Rovers 199 (5), 2010 Cheltenham Town (loan) 8 (0), 2010–2011 Walsall 34 (1), 2011–2013 Halesowen Town 5 (0)

Perhaps not quite as successful as his brother Joleen, he nonetheless has a far manlier name. He came on loan from Aston Villa in the year 2000 and made just three starts with two further outings from the bench. Didn't have a great time either as City won just one of his five games with the club, but later signed for Sheffield Wednesday for £100k.

He was a member of the Bristol Rovers squad that beat us in the 2007 play-off semi-finals, but he missed both matches due to a red card in their 1-1 draw with Barnet a few weeks earlier.

Lewis, Graham
(1999-2001)
Forward 3 (5) Apps 0 Goals
Born 15th February 1982
1999–2001 Imps, 2000–2001 Northwich Victoria 12 (2), 2000–2001 Frickley Athletic (loan), 2001– 2003 Frickley Athletic, 2002–2003 Belper Town (loan), 2002–2003 Lincoln United, 2003–2004 Goole, 2003–2004 Brigg Town, 2003–2004 Ilkeston Town, 2003–2004 Gedling Town, 2004–2005 Lincoln Moorlands, 2005–2006 Reading Town, 2006–2008 Bracknell Town, 2007–2008 Burnham, 2008–2010 Reading Town 32 (22), 2010–2011 Thatcham Town, 2010–2011 Abingdon United, 2011–2012 Reading Town, 2012 Marlow

Former YTS player who simply didn't make the grade as a professional player. Lewis was a pacey forward; he would go on to make five appearances in total during the second year of his youth contract. He was offered a three-month professional contract for the 2000–2001 season by Phil Stant and went on to make two further league appearances before being released. Since then he's plied his trade with a broad range of non-league sides.

Liburd, Richard
(2003-2004)
Defender 22 (5) Apps 0 Goals
Born 26th September 1973
1992–1993 Eastwood Town, 1993–1994 Middlesbrough 41 (1), 1994–1998 Bradford City 79 (3), 1998 Carlisle United 10 (0), 1998–2003 Notts County 154 (9), 2003–2004 Imps, 2004 Eastwood Town, 2006 Boots Athletic, 2007 Basford United, 2008 Hucknall Town 0 (0)

Full back with higher league experience brought in after our first play-off appearance to strengthen the squad. He could operate at full back or further up in the midfield and his short spell at City saw him play in both positions. He suffered ankle ligament damage after being ever present for the first 14 games of the campaign, and following that he struggled to get back into the side, leaving the club at the end of the season after only a handful more starts.

Lichaj, Eric
(2009)
Midfielder 6 Apps 0 Goals
Born 17th November 1988
2006 Chicago Fire Premier 4 (0), 2008–2013 Aston Villa 32 (1), 2009 Imps (loan), 2010 Leyton Orient (loan) 9 (1), 2011 Leeds United (loan) 16 (0), 2013 Nottingham Forest 120 (2)

Talented American-born midfielder who came via Chris Sutton's contacts to help us avoid relegation in the 2009/10 season. He didn't make the best of starts as he was sent off in only his second appearance, a 3-1 defeat at Morecambe.

He came back into the side and played four more times, although he didn't feature in a Lincoln win. He obviously had talent but he couldn't seem to adjust to League Two football and he returned to Villa after his two months were complete.

He's gone on to make over 100 appearances for Nottingham Forest in the Championship which is where he currently plays his football. He's also represented his country eleven times since 2010.

Littlejohn, Adrian
(2004-2005)
Forward 1 (8) Apps 0 Goals
Born 26th September 1970
1989–1991 Walsall 44 (1), 1991–1995 Sheffield United 69 (12), 1995–1998 Plymouth Argyle 110 (29), 1998 Oldham Athletic 21 (5), 1998–2001 Bury 99 (14), 2001–2003 Sheffield United 3 (0), 2003–2004 Port Vale 49 (10), 2004–2005 Imps, 2005 Rushden & Diamonds 15 (0), 2005–2006 Mansfield Town 7 (0), 2006 Leek Town 4 (0), 2007–2008 Retford United

Another journeyman striker who came in to fill that goal scoring void Keith Alexander always felt he had, and another who failed miserably. He spent six months at Lincoln but started just one game, a 1-0 defeat away at Swansea. It wasn't easy for him to break through though, Gary Taylor Fletcher, Marcus Richardson, Martin Carruthers, Franny Green and Simon Yeo were also all in or around the squad. He was released from his contract after failing to score in nine outings.

Towards the end of his playing days Littlejohn began working at the Sheffield United academy. He ventured into physiotherapy and in 2014 took up a position as academy physio at Rotherham United.

Lloyd-McGoldrick, Danny
(2012)
Midfielder 3 (9) Apps 3 Goals
Born 3rd December 1991
2010-2011 Southport, 2012 Imps, 2013 Tamworth, 2014-2016 AFC Fylde, 2016 Stockport, 2016 Tamworth

Danny Lloyd as he was known was yet another of David Holdsworth's short term signings, and one of the few to impress. Indeed, many fans were bemused that he started so few games as he always seemed to have the ability to make an impact when he played.

In his four-month spell, he scored three times including two in the 5-0 home win over Darlington, and a consolation as we slumped to relegated Bath City, 2-1. At the end of his spell there were strong rumours of him moving to City, but he opted for Tamworth instead. Still terrorising full backs in the division below us, and potentially still has the ability to play in the National League.

Logan, Richard A
(2003)
Forward 16 (3) Apps 1 Goal
Born 24th May 1969
1989–1990 Belper Town, 1990–1994 Gainsborough Trinity, 1993–1996 Huddersfield Town 45 (1), 1995–1998 Plymouth Argyle 86 (12), 1998–2000 Scunthorpe United 80 (7), 2000–2003 Imps 2002 Gainsborough Trinity (loan)

Logan agreed a three-year contract to join in July 2000 after being released by Scunthorpe. He appeared without a goal in Lincoln's first five games of the 2000–01 season, but picked up an ankle injury away at Hull. Logan made a return as a substitute in the 2–0 home defeat to Mansfield Town in September 2000 before suffering a prolapsed disc in his back. The injury required surgery and would keep Logan out of the first team picture for fourteen months.

He returned to the substitutes' bench for the 2–1 home victory against Hull City in November 2001 but it was not until the 2–1 away defeat to Oxford United three months later that he made a first-team appearance. It was his first outing in a nightmare 16 months.

He wrote himself a little piece of history by grabbing his only Imps goal on the opening day of the 2002/03 season, scoring after 11 minutes against Kidderminster. However, a calf strain in the 0–0 draw at Torquay United in September once again ruled him out. In a bid to regain fitness Logan was loaned to former club Gainsborough who managed by none other than Phil Stant. Once again he suffered a prolapsed disc in his back which required surgery and side-lined him for the remainder of the season. He agreed to a deal to terminate his contract two months early in April 2003. As of 2009, Logan is a builder and is still living in his native Barnsley, although given his health history I hope he's not indulging in any heavy lifting.

Logan, Richard J
(2005)
Forward 8 Apps 2 Goals
Born 4th January 1982
1998–2003 Ipswich Town 3 (0), 2001 Cambridge United (loan) 5 (1), 2001–2002 Torquay United (loan) 16 (4), 2002–2003 Boston United (loan) 8 (6), 2003 Boston United 27 (4), 2003 Peterborough United (loan) 11 (1), 2003–2006 Peterborough United 72 (13), 2004 Shrewsbury Town (loan) 5 (1), 2005–2006 Imps (loan), 2006–2007 Weymouth 23 (5), 2007–2012 Exeter City 193 (47), 2012 Wycombe Wanderers 8 (0), 2012–2013 Dorchester Town 6 (0)

Another Keith Alexander striker solution, and one that could have done a job judging by his modest return at Exeter City after his Lincoln spell. He signed on a one month loan and ended that with a goal against Chester in a 3-1 win. His loan was extended ahead of the Oxford fixture in which he scored for us in a 1-1 draw. He didn't score again and his loan wasn't extended.

Logan was a decent forward who perhaps would have signed permanently but for the controversial suspension of Keith in January of the New Year. It wasn't to be and he later had a good spell in Devon over a five-year period.

Lormor, Tony
(1990-1994)
Forward 101 (12) Apps 34 Goals
Born 29th October 1970

1987–1990 Newcastle United 8 (3), 1988–1989 Norwich City (loan) 0 (0), 1990–1994 Imps, 1994 Halifax Town (loan) 7 (1), 1994 Peterborough United 5 (0), 1994–1997 Chesterfield 113 (35), 1997–1998 Preston North End 12 (3), 1998 Notts County (loan) 7 (0), 1998–2000 Mansfield Town 74 (20), 2000–2002 Hartlepool United 48 (9), 2002 Shrewsbury Town (loan) 7 (2), 2002–2003 Telford United 4 (0), 2003–2005 Sutton Town, 2005–2006 Heanor Town

Lormor joined the Imps from Newcastle United for a fee of £25,000, and went on to amass over 100 appearances. He netted on his League debut for City in a 1-0 win over Wrexham, and impressed immediately after his arrival at Sincil Bank, finishing top scorer in two of his first three seasons at the club, and only missing out to Gordon Hobson by one in his first season.

In his pomp Lormor was an excellent centre forward with a quick footballing brain and an instinct for being in the right place at the right time. He was this writers' favourite player alongside David Puttnam for his ability to make things happen when City really needed it.

His highlights were four goals as we thrashed Carlisle 6-2 in 1991, and a hat trick the following season as we despatched county rivals Scunthorpe 4-2 at Sincil Bank. Unfortunately, Tony suffered a cruciate knee ligament injury which forced him to miss the whole of the 1992/93 season, and after 18 months on the side-lines he struggled to recover his previous form. He was released on a free transfer after making just 10 appearances the following season.

He was described by one fan in a copy of Deranged Ferret thus; "The biggest compliment I can pay him is that if he wasn't a player I'm sure he'd be a supporter. In these days when players move from club to club at the drop of a hat and seem commited to only picking up wages it was nice to see someone who actually enjoyed playing football."

He did regain his old form with Chesterfield, banging in 36 goals from 114 appearances for the Spireites, before a £15,000 move to Mansfield Town, and then a £30,000 transfer to Hartlepool United. Later in his career he took up refereeing, and still living close to Lincoln he was a regular in the middle in the Lincoln Sunday League. He also served as Commercial Manager for Mansfield in 2007/08 having held a similar position at Chesterfield the season before.

Loughlan, Tony
(1993-1994)
Midfielder 8 (9) Apps 4 Goals
Born 19ᵗʰ January 1970
1988–1989 Leicester United, 1989–1993 Nottingham Forest 2 (1), 1993–1994 Kettering Town 5 (1), 1993–1994 Imps, 1994–1995 Dundalk 11 (0), 1995–1996 Hinckley Town, 1996–1998 Corby Town

Loughlan signed for City in October 1993, making a return to the football league after spending time with Forest earlier in his career. He marked his debut on 30th October 1993 with the only goal as City defeated Rochdale at Spotland for the first time in 26 years. He netted three more goals under Keith Alexander, once in the league against Chesterfield (2-2) and again in the Autoglass Windscreens Shield against the same opposition (2-1), as well as a goal against Darlington in the next round. However, he struggled with injury and despite being a popular figure on the terraces he left Lincoln at the end of the season, firstly on trial at Birmingham and latterly back to his native Ireland with Dundalk.

In August 1989, Loughlan and team-mate Neil Lyne had been signed by Nottingham Forest from Leicester United; the transfer would later be highlighted in the 1997 Premier League report of Rick

Parry and Steve Coppell on bung culture in football. Brian Clough and Ron Fenton would later be charged with misconduct by the FA over the affair though the charges against Clough were later dropped.

Louis, Jefferson
(2012)
Forward 14 Apps 6 Goals
Born 22nd February 1979
1999–1999 Risborough Rangers, 2000–2002 Thame United, 2002–2004 Oxford United 55 (7), 2003 Woking (loan) 8 (0), 2004 Gravesend & Northfleet (loan) 5 (2), 2004 Forest Green Rovers 8 (1), 2004– 2005 Woking 23 (3), 2005 Bristol Rovers 9 (0), 2005 Hemel Hempstead Town 1 (1), 2005 Lewes 2 (0), 2005 Worthing 6 (2), 2005–2006 Stevenage Borough 18 (6), 2006 Eastleigh 6 (1), 2006–2007 Yeading 8 (4), 2007 Havant & Waterlooville 20 (5), 2007–2008 Weymouth 21 (7), 2008 Maidenhead United 3 (0), 2008 Mansfield Town 18 (4), 2008–2009 Wrexham 42 (15), 2009–2010 Crawley Town 18 (5), 2009–2010 Rushden & Diamonds (loan) 26 (7), 2010–2011 Gainsborough Trinity 9 (1), 2010–2011 Darlington (loan) 6 (0), 2011 Weymouth 1 (0), 2011 Hayes & Yeading United 10 (1), 2011 Maidenhead United 12 (3), 2011–2012 Brackley Town 8 (13), 2012 Imps 2012 Newport County 17 (2), 2012 Whitehawk (loan) 6 (4), 2013 Brackley Town 24 (7), 2013–2014 Hendon 25 (22), 2014 Margate 17 (9), 2014 Lowestoft Town 15 (3), 2014–2016 Wealdstone 57 (18), 2016 Staines Town 10 (3), 2016 Oxford City 2 (1)

In 1979, a centre forward was born to score goals for those who needed him. This man promptly escaped from a maximum-security stockade to the Los Angeles underground. Today, still wanted by the government he survives as a soldier of fortune. If you have a goal scoring problem, if no one else can help, and if you can find him....maybe you can hire Jefferson Louis.

Okay so that's a mixture of the opening monologue from the A Team and some bits about Louis, but like a footballing soldier of fortune he floats from club to club scoring goals and leaving a mark. There are a lot of players who play for numerous clubs, but with Louis it's a bit different. Jefferson Louis isn't a bad footballer at all.

A look at his stats above will show you that wherever he (briefly) plays football, he scores goals. Thirteen in eight matches for Brackley. If you think that was a level too low to take a proper reading of his skills, what about one in three at places like Rushden or Wrexham?

Along with his cousin and 'BA Baracus' Richard Pacquette he rocks up and makes a difference at teams before promptly disappearing again. For Lincoln, it was a couple of months at the end of the 2011/12 season. We weren't scoring goals, Steve Tilson had left and the squad was low on confidence. David Holdsworth knew where to find him, and in he came. He scored in the first minute of his Imps career as we drew 3-3 with Braintree and then again a few days later as we drew 1-1 with Kidderminster. He helped us to a 2-1 win over Hayes and Yeading with a goal, and scored against Fleetwood as Jamie Vardy hit a double for them in a 2-2 draw. He came and served his purpose, scoring six in 14 games to keep up that impressive goals to game ratio. Then he was off to fight another goal drought in another part of the country.

Jefferson Louis. The man. The legend. He's still out there today just waiting for the call from an ailing non-league club. If your team is struggling for goals, maybe you can find him too.

Lucas, Richard
(1994)
Defender 6 Apps 0 Goals
Born 22nd September 1970
1989-1992 Sheffield United, 1992-1995 Preston North End, 1994-1995 Imps (loan), 1995-1997 Scarborough, 1997-1998, Hartlepool, 1998-2000, Halifax Town, 2000-2001 Boston United, 2001-2005 Hednesford Town

Joined up with the squad under Sam Ellis on a loan from Preston. Played six games, including wins over Scarborough (2-0) and Hereford (3-0). Also, played as we beat Hull City in the Autoglass Windscreens Shield 1-0 at Sincil Bank, but returned to Preston shortly after. Went on to feature against the Imps in a career that saw him play for Scarborough, Halifax and Hartlepool.

Mardenborough - Musselwhite

Mardenborough, Steve
(1993-94)
Forward 16 (9) Apps 2 Goals
Born 11th September 1964

1982–1983 Coventry City 0 (0), 1983–1984 Wolverhampton Wanderers 9 (1), 1984 Cambridge United (loan) 6 (0), 1984–1985 Swansea City 36 (7), 1985–1987 Newport County 64 (11), 1987–1988 Cardiff City 32 (1), 1988–1989 Hereford United 27 (0), 1989–1990 IFK Östersund, 1990 Cheltenham Town 15 (4), 1990–1993 Darlington 106 (18), 1993–1994 Imps, 1994 Scarborough 1 (0), 1995 Stafford Rangers 22 (4), 1995 Colchester United 12 (2), 1995 Swansea City 1 (0), 1995–1996 Newport County 5 (0), 1996 Cwmbran Town 1 (0), 1997–1999 Inter Cardiff 68 (16), 1999–2001 Aberystwyth Town 51 (15), 2001–2002 Rhayader Town 21 (7), 2002 Haverfordwest County 6 (1), 2002Port Talbot Town 5 (1), 2002–2003 Llanelli 15 (1), 2003 Carmarthen Town 7 (1), 2003 Barry Town 1 (0)

Steve had five minutes of fame as a Wolves player in the early 80's, scoring the winner against the then mighty Liverpool at Anfield. Following that he scored 11 in two seasons for a poor Newport County side before a switch to Darlington. He always seemed to perform against us and his signing for Lincoln was met with a positive reaction.

The early 90's was no classic period for Lincoln and in his 21 games he managed just two goals, one in an away draw with Chester and one at home in a 2-0 win over Colchester. He was seen as an exciting pacey forward, but just a few games before he scored his only home goal a young man by the name of Darren Huckerby made his debut. Steve didn't look quite so quick then, and soon he was on his way. It was harsh on the veteran forward who I always remembered as a quick and committed player.

He had a spell at Colchester and again at Newport but soon found his way into the Welsh leagues when he had probably the best spell of his career first with Inter Cardiff and then with Aberystwyth. He last played for Barry Town in a one game spell in 2003.

Margetts, Jonny
(2016)
Forward 5 (2) Apps 5 Goals
Born 28th September 1993

2014–2015 Hull City 0 (0), 2014 Gainsborough Trinity (loan) 13 (10), 2014 Harrogate Town (loan) 6 (2), 2014 Gainsborough Trinity (loan) 7 (2), 2015 Cambridge United (loan) 1 (0), 2015–2016 Tranmere Rovers 10 (2), 2015–2016 Stockport County (loan) 6 (4), 2016 Altrincham (loan) 6 (2), 2016 Southport (loan) 3 (2), 2016 Imps, 2016 Scunthorpe United

Not many players leave a club with a goal ratio of one per start, but that's exactly what Jonny Margetts did just before the transfer window shut in autumn 2016. He had been on a successful trial with the club and impressed Danny Cowley sufficiently to earn himself a deal. Once he got on the pitch he proved to be a natural goal scorer, bagging four in one game against Southport. The future looked very rosy for Lincoln and Jonny Margetts.

Our 'friends' from up the A15 had other ideas though and out of the blue on deadline day in August 2016 they paid a rumoured transfer fee of £55,000 to land his services. It was an offer neither club nor player could say no to, and before he'd completed three months as an Imps player he was on his way. It could have been so beautiful, but thanks to money we'll never know. He has been linked with a loan move back to City, but only time will tell.

Maris, George
(2016)
Forward 6 (7) Apps 2 Goals
Born 6th March 1996
2014–2016 Barnsley 3 (0), 2015 Nuneaton Town (loan) 9 (0), 2015 Guiseley (loan) 7 (0), 2016 Imps (loan), 2016 Cambridge United

Maris signed on loan from Barnsley until the end of the 2015/16 season, and had Chris Moyses remained in charge he might have been brought back permanently. He was energetic and pacey in an Imps shirt and chipped in with a couple of goals, including an 81st minute winner at home to Chester.

Despite his promise a change of management meant he was unlikely to head back to Lincoln, and in June 2016 he signed a one year deal with League Two side Cambridge United, where so far he has found it tough to get regular first team football.

Marriott, Adam
(2016- Current)
Forward 6 (5) Apps 3 Goals
Born 14th April 1991
2009–2012 Cambridge United 56 (10), 2012 Cambridge City (loan) 5 (4), 2012 Bishop's Stortford (loan) 6 (2), 2012–2014 Cambridge City 69 (57), 2014–2016 Stevenage 19 (3), 2016 Imps

Lively striker who would be playing further up the Football League if it hadn't been for a serious injury. Scored goals for fun whilst at Cambridge City and earned himself a move to Stevenage. However, he was restricted to just 19 appearances and 3 goals before being released.

Scored three times for City early in the 2016/17 season including a lovely volley away at Macclesfield and another just a couple of days later against Gateshead.

He suffered a dislocated elbow in a behind closed doors friendly with Peterborough which has also stunted his Imps career, but if he retains full fitness then much is expected of Marriott. On the few outings, he has had in 2016/17 he's shown himself to be energetic and a natural goal scorer, similar in many respects to Jamie Taylor.

Marriott, Alan
(1999-2008)
Goalkeeper 395 Apps 0 Goals
Born 3rd September 1978
1997–1999 Tottenham Hotspur 0 (0), 1999–2008 Imps, 2008–2009 Rushden & Diamonds 12 (0), 2009–2014 Mansfield Town 201 (1)

A lot of players I've written about for this book need introduction, or I've had to dig deep to find the information about them. For a select few I hardly need to write anything, and that is the case with Alan Marriott.

His Imps history speaks for itself. Signed from Tottenham Hotspur around the same time as Peter Gain, young Mazza went on to amass a record number of appearances for a goal keeper. He appeared in two domestic finals for Lincoln and helped us to a record five play-off appearances. At his best he was a brick wall in the sticks, some matches he was simply unbeatable.

He was always a firm favourite amongst the City supporters, and a clean sheet against Torquay. February 2007 saw him break a long-standing Club record, it being his 100th for City in League and cup competitions.

His appearance against Swindon Town the following month was his 310th League game, and that saw him break Dan McPhail's all-time Club goalkeeping appearance record that had stood for over 70 years. Alan Marriott nroke recordsa and made friends.

If anything he was held back by that lack of height and maybe he could have commanded his box a little more. However, for nine years he was the first name on the team sheet, a keeper held in high repute by opponents and team mates alike. A testimonial and a chance to see his days out at Lincoln City seemed inevitable.

Peter Jackson didn't agree and at the end of the 2007/08 season the popular keeper was released one year short of his testimonial requirements. He was replaced by a decent keeper, Rob Burch, but somehow it seemed a harsh ending to a superb career. He went to Rushden first before turning in another solid 200 outings for Mansfield Town, ironically ending his career as a league player as we languished in the National League.

Mazza is a true Imps legend and a keeper who will always be held in the very highest esteem by Lincoln City fans. I can't do him justice with a few paragraphs amongst a collection of loan players and other people rejects. He was sorely missed up until the arrival of Paul Farman.

Marsden, John
(2015)
Forward 2 (4) Apps 0 Goals
Born 9th December 1992
2011 Aberystwyth Town 2 (0), 2012–2013 Stockport Sports 31 (21), 2013 Stoke City 0 (0), 2013–2014 Shrewsbury Town 3 (0), 2014–2015 Southport 28 (5), 2015 Imps (loan), 2015 Macclesfield Town 2 (0), 2015 Colwyn Bay, 2016 Stockport County 7 (3)

Thoroughly non-descript striker signed on loan from Southport after scoring a late equaliser against Lincoln earlier in the season. Only ended up on the winning side once in his six matches and showed nothing to suggest he would be worth a second look. Played a couple of times for Macclesfield before dropping down a league with Colwyn Bay.

Marshall, Marcus
(2014)
Midfielder 25 (8) Apps 2 Goals
Born 7th October 1989
2008–2010 Blackburn Rovers 0 (0), 2010 Rotherham United (loan) 23 (0), 2010–2012 Rotherham United 51 (4), 2012 Macclesfield Town (loan) 14 (1), 2012–2013 Bury 9 (0), 2012–2013 Grimsby Town (loan) 14 (2), 2013 Grimsby Town (loan) 11 (0), 2013–2015 Morecambe 15 (0), 2014 Imps (loan), 2015–2016 Grimsby Town 16 (0), 2016 Boston United 1 (0)

Joined City under Gary Simpson on a season long loan having previously spent time at Rotherham and Grimsby. Marshall undoubtedly had talent, and we saw it in glimpses here and there. He had the ability to change a game, but all too often went into hiding when games turned into a proper fight.

He did score a couple for Lincoln, the most notable in our excellent 3-1 win at Blundell Park to secure our first league double over Grimsby in thirty years. He had scored a late winner just three days earlier against Alfreton to cap a wonderful Christmas. He simply didn't show enough consistency to earn a full-time deal, and once he left the club he was released by Morecambe and ended up first at Grimsby and most recently Boston United.

Martin, Jae
(1996-1998)
Forward 35 (13) Apps 6 Goals
Born 5th February 1976
1993–1995 Southend United 8 (0), 1994 Leyton Orient (loan) 4 (0), 1995–1996 Birmingham City 7 (0), 1996 Imps (loan), 1996–1998 Imps, 1998–2000 Peterborough United 18 (1), 1999 Grantham Town (loan), 2000 Welling United (loan), 2000–2001 Woking, 2000–2005 Moor Green, 2004–2005 Bromsgrove Rovers (loan), 2005–2006 Evesham United, 2005–2006 Solihull Borough, 2005–2006 Barnt Green Spartak, 2005–2006 Stourport Swifts, 2006–2007 Bedworth United, 2007–2008 Stratford Town, 2007–2008 Woodford United, 2007–2008 Evesham United, 2007–2008 Atherstone Town, 2008–2009 Sutton Coldfield Town, 2008–2009 Coleshill Town, 2008 Woodford United

Striker-cum-winger who originally came on loan from Birmingham City at the beginning of John Beck's first full season in charge, He had an impressive loan spell which at one point prompted Beck to hold him aloft on his shoulders after a 1-0 win against Barnet (in which Martin scored the only goal) in a 'sign him up' gesture to the board. He scored one more during his loan spell as we beat Colchester 3-2 at Sincil Bank. Eventually the board agreed to put £1 on the admission prices to fund the transfer, and he came in for the princely sum of £30k.

He faded almost as soon as he came on board permanently, and after scoring twice in his loan spell added just two more all season, including our consolation goal in the 7-1 hammering away at Colchester. The following season he faded even more with a combination of injuries and poor form contributing to him making just seven appearances, scoring once at home against Doncaster. He was released as we achieved promotion and unfortunately didn't represent the same value for money as Beck's other 'sign him up' player, Kevin Austin.

Matthews, Neil
(1992-1995)
Forward 80 (16) Apps 22 Goals
Born 19th September 1966
1984–1987 Grimsby Town 11 (1), 1985 Scunthorpe United (loan) 1 (0), 1986 Halifax Town (loan) 9 (2), 1987 Bolton Wanderers (loan) 1 (0), 1987–1990 Halifax Town 105 (29), 1990–1992 Stockport County 33 (15), 1991 Halifax Town (loan) 3 (0), 1992 Imps (loan), 1992–1995 Imps, 1994 Bury (loan) 3 (1), Dagenham & Redbridge 3 (2), Gainsborough Trinity, 1997–1998 Guiseley, 1998–2001 Leigh RMI 13 (2), 2001 Chorley

Skilful centre forward who initially joined on-loan from Stockport County in 1992. He scored in his first three consecutive Imps outings and this prompted manager Steve Thompson to part with £20k for his services on a permanent basis. Ended his first season with eleven goals and looked to have an impressive future ahead of him with The Imps.

The 1993/94 season saw Keith Alexander take over as manager and despite playing number 9 for a majority of the season Matthews found goals harder to come by. He did hit a brace at home to Hereford which took his tally to four in two games at Sincil Bank against them. He also netted in the

4-3 reverse against Everton in 1993 that saw 9153 fans pack into Sincil Bank. He appeared sporadically under Sam Ellis the following season, scoring just twice. One was (of course) in the home tie with Hereford followed by a consolation for us a week later against Barnet. His contract wasn't renewed after a series of minor injuries and he left ahead of the 1995/96 season.

Eventually a back problem caused his retirement from football in 2001, after which he joined the staff of Huddersfield Town's youth academy.

May, Rory
(2003)
Forward 2 (7) Apps 0 Goals
Born 25th November 1984
2003–2004 Imps, 2003–2004 Halifax Town (loan) 3 (0), 2004–2005 Tamworth 7 (1), 2004–2005 Moor Green (loan), 2004–2005 Redditch United (loan), 2004–2005 Redditch United, 2005–2006 Sutton Coldfield Town, 2005–2006 Stourport Swifts, 2005–2006 Redditch United, 2006–2007 Solihull Borough, 2006–2007 Brackley, 2006–2007 Solihull Borough, 2007–2008 Stratford Town 21 (14), 2007–2008 Hednesford Town 9 (3), 2007–2008 Worcester City (loan), 2008–2009 Willenhall Town

Keith Alexander signed May after he'd served his youth at Coventry City, and hoped he would bring the goals that he was eternally searching for. He wasn't even remotely close. Gary Taylor-Fletcher and Francis Green arrived, and Rory May was sent on his way.

Mayo, Paul
(1999-2004, 2005-2007)
Defender 168 (27) Apps 14 Goals
Born 13th October 1981
1999–2004 Imps, 2002–2003 Dagenham & Redbridge (loan) 3 (1), 2004–2005 Watford 25 (0), 2005–2007 Imps, 2007–2009 Notts County 41 (0), 2008 Darlington (loan) 7 (1), 2009 Mansfield Town 12 (1), 2009–2010 Corby Town, 2010–2011 Gainsborough Trinity, 2011–2012 Corby Town, 2012–2013 Stamford, 2013 Boston United, 2013–2014 Lincoln United

Home-grown left back who came through the ranks to feature in the most important period in Imps history. Mayo was a steady left back with a wicked left foot and an ability to get forward. He made his debut as early as 2000 just before John Reames stepped down as manager. Once he'd broken through he immediately got a run of games and ended up making 19 appearances in his first season, and a solid 34 the next.

Injury and a loss of form kept him out of the side under Alan Buckley and he was restricted to just 16 appearances ahead of our administration battle. He was one of the players retained by Keith Alexander, and the following season he was a mainstay of the play-off team. He suffered an injury mid-term and went on loan to Dagenham to gain some match fitness, but when he came back he looked as sharp as a ghurka's blade. His goal against Scunthorpe in the play-off semi-final really showed his passion as he leapt in the air with a fist pump after his 18th minute strike gave us a 2-0 lead.

The following season he began to attract scouts, and three goal in six games didn't do his reputation any harm. Watford, then of the second tier, came in with a £65,000 bid and he stepped up two divisions. He played the remainder of the season for them and started in the side the next season. He was dropped in October and only played twice more for the club. New Watford boss Aidy Boothroyd deemed him surplus to requirements

He was soon back at Lincoln on a free transfer representing good business by Keith Alexander. He took great delight in scoring in the 5-0 rout of Grimsby Town in March, but tasted play-off disappointment yet again as we went out in the semi-finals to our fishy foes. The same exercise was repeated the next season and Mayo decided enough was enough. He turned down a new deal and moved to Notts County, bringing to an end his second term at the club.

Many Imps fans were surprised he attracted the attention of Watford as he was often maligned and criticised. Internet forums used to joke 'I Blame Paul Mayo' whenever we lost. However, his dedication to the club shouldn't be criticised at all, and he did feature in some of the happiest times of the last twenty years.

McCallum, Gavin
(2010-2012)
Forward 43 (13) Apps 6 Goals
Born 24th August 1987
2005–2007 Yeovil Town 1 (0), 2006 Tamworth (loan) 13 (0), 2006–2007 Crawley Town (loan) 2 (0), 2007 Dorchester Town (loan) 15 (5), 2007–2008 Weymouth 24 (6), 2008 Havant & Waterlooville 12 (2), 2008–2009 Sutton United 41 (14), 2009–2010 Hereford United 27 (8), 2010–2012 Imps, 2011–2012 Barnet (loan) 2 (0), 2012–2013 Woking 49 (5), 2013–2014 Sutton United 22 (5), 2013–2014 Tonbridge Angels (loan) 4 (1), 2014 Eastbourne Borough 92 (14)

Canadian International McCallum was another one of those players who had talent, but never seemed to be willing enough or fit enough to put it to good use. Chris Sutton brought him in ahead of the 2010/11 season from Hereford on a two-year deal. He'd scored twice against us in a 2-0 win the previous season and that had convinced the manager he was worth an investment.

As he was under 24 a fee had to be agreed between the Imps and Hereford, eventually being agreed but 'undisclosed'. He made his debut for City in a 2-0 loss to Torquay United in August 2010. McCallum scored his first goal for Lincoln in January 2011, as we lost 2–1 at home to Wycombe Wanderers. He then scored the winning goal in a tight match versus Bradford City in February. The game ended in a 2–1 away win at the Valley Parade, with McCallum paying tribute to his father after scoring the winning goal in the 79th minute.

Despite this moderate success there were times when McCallum looked unbeatable, and there were times when he was completely anonymous. If he had found some consistency and a degree of application, he might just have had enough in his locker to pull us away from relegation. As it transpired, he didn't. He made 37 appearances as we surrendered our league position, and all too often he had no impact at all.

He was transfer listed on relegation but nonetheless started our Blue Square Premier campaign in the starting XI. He found the net three times, twice in three games after Steve Tilson left the club. He remained on the transfer list and eventually joined Barnet on loan in January. After two games for the Londoners his contract with Lincoln was cancelled as David Holdsworth started to put his faith in hundreds of different loan players.

McCammon, Mark
(2012, 2012)
Forward 3 (5) Apps 2 Goals
Born 7th August 1978

1997–1999 Cambridge United 4 (0), 1999–2000 Charlton Athletic 4 (0), 2000 Swindon Town (loan) 4 (0), 2000–2003 Brentford 74 (10), 2003–2005 Millwall 21 (2), 2004–2005 Brighton & Hove Albion (loan) 7 (0), 2005–2006 Brighton & Hove Albion 18 (3), 2006 Bristol City (loan) 11 (4), 2006–2008 Doncaster Rovers 54 (6), 2008–2011 Gillingham 52 (5), 2010-2011 Bradford City (loan) 4 (0), 2011-2012 Braintree Town 5 (1), 2012 Sheffield FC 0 (0), 2012 Imps (loan), 2012 Imps

McCammon was a journeyman striker who hadn't ever been prolific. He arrived as a short-term fix for David Holdsworth on the back of a racial tribunal case against his old club Gillingham. He scored on his debut as we lost 2-1 to Mansfield, and he notched another on his first start for the club against Newport County as we won 2-0. Things looked promising.

After that, nothing. He signed on a permanent deal for the season after but left after just two outings. During his spell, he kept Jamie Taylor out of the side, and Taylor went on to score just ten less goals for City in two seasons than McCammon had in his entire career. Welcome to the genius management of David Holdsworth.

Onto that discrimination case. In February 2012, McCammon began action against Gillingham at an employment tribunal alleging racial discrimination. He claimed Andy Hessenthaler was "racially intolerant" and that the club had tried to "frustrate him out". The Tribunal found that he had indeed been a victim of racial discrimination. Ironically he had initially joined Gillingham as a replacement for another former Imp, Delroy Facey.

He also made eight appearances for Barbados in-between 2006 and 2008, and his hat trick in a 7-1 with over Anguilla gave his nation their biggest ever victory.

McCauley, Gareth
(2004-2006)
Defender 77 (7) Apps 8 Goals
Born 5th December 1979
1996–2000 Linfield 40 (4), 1999–2000 Ballyclare Comrades (loan) 7 (0), 2000–2002 Crusaders 90 (6), 2002–2004 Coleraine 65 (4), 2004–2006 Imps, 2006–2008 Leicester City 74 (5), 2008–2011 Ipswich Town 115 (7), 2011 West Bromwich Albion 163 (10)

Gareth McAuley was a cut above almost all the defenders that have ever played for Lincoln City, and that is some claim given the quality of defender Keith Alexnder signed. He came from Ireland via the same contacts that brought us Jeff Hughes and could have brought us James McClean. He cost us the princely sum of £10k, the only time in his career he has commanded a transfer fee. Obviously, Keith used him upfront a bit at first as he struggled to get into a side boasting the meanest defence in the division. For one season we had McAuley, McCombe, Futcher and Morgan to choose from at centre half. That's a frightening array of central defenders, and McAuley struggled to get into the side.

Eventually Paul Morgan became side-lined with an injury, which gave McAuley his chance to partner Ben Futcher at the back. He immediately drew the plaudits for his excellent performances, which included a man of the match display against Derby County. After that he battled for a starting centre back role with fellow giant Jamie McCombe for much of the season.

His also displayed a degree of versatility, earning a starting role as the right full-back, replacing the perpetually out of form Matt Bloomer. He continued to play in this position for the rest of the season, helping Lincoln to the play-off final. He wasn't just renowned for his defensive prowess either, he also chipped in with 5 goals, including both in the 2–1 aggregate victory over Macclesfield in the play-off semi-final.

In 2005 he received his first full Northern Ireland cap whilst still a Lincoln player, appearing from the bench as they went down 4-1 to Germany. His cap was a real boost for The Imps and vindicated Keith's extensive use of his Ireland contacts.

During the next season, he cemented a spot in the centre of the Imps defence. He replaced the departing Ben Futcher and enjoyed a fantastic season. Despite our own failings in the play-offs he was named in the League Two Team of the Year, which meant he caught the attention of a number of bigger clubs. The lure of playing at a higher level saw McAuley reject City's offer of a new contract in the summer of 2006, and he moved on a free transfer to Leicester.

Latterly he has played regular Premier League football for West Brom and represented Northern Ireland as they qualified for Euro 16, their first major tournament appearance in twenty years. He's still one of our own.

McCombe, Jamie
(2004-2006, 2016- Current)
Defender 103 (8) Apps 10 Goals
Born 1st January 1983
2001–2004 Scunthorpe United 63 (2), 2003–2004 Halifax Town (loan) 7 (1), 2004–2006 Imps, 2006–2010, Bristol City 119 (9), 2010–2012 Huddersfield Town 54 (8), 2011–2012 Preston North End (loan) 6 (0), 2012–2015 Doncaster Rovers 53 (2), 2015–2016 Stevenage 14 (0), 2016 Imps

City first picked up Jamie McCombe from Scunthorpe United in a transfer that ignited controversy between the two sides, close rivals for a couple of seasons in the mid 2000's. He was a key component in the side that Keith built, making significant impact in the 2004/05 season in particular. He was Imps' Player of the Season in 2004/05, but his ambition out-stripped that of the club.

His last City appearance of his first spell came in the 2005/06 League 2 play-offs when he was captain of the side against Grimsby. That match was also the last match of Keith Alexander as an era came to an end.

He went on to enjoy good career, his best spell coming in four seasons at Bristol City where he was often amongst the goals as well as the clean sheets. He had a successful spell at Huddersfield as well, playing his football at Championship level in the main.

The towering centre-back returned to the Club in January 2016, Chris Moyses surprisingly bringing him back on a deal that would run until the end of 2016/17. He has made just six appearances since his return, firstly being ruled out by injury and latterly kept out of the side by Raggett and Waterfall.

In October 2016, he agreed a deal to become the Imps player coach a move designed to allow him to pass on his vast league experience, and to give him a route into coaching for the future. It's unlikely we'll see much more of McCombe on the pitch, especially with Callum Howe waiting in the wings.

McDaid, Robbie
(2016)
Forward 3 (13) Apps 4 Goals
Born 23rd October 1996
2015 Leeds, 2016 Imps (loan), 2016 York City

McDaid was a confident and able striker who came from Leeds United to try and push Chris Moyses' side on toward the top five. He wasn't given enough starts to gain any real consistency but he did notch four goals. Signed for York City in November of 2016 as they fight to stay in the National League. If I were a betting man I'd say he'll weigh in with a few goals.

McNamara, Niall
(2003-2005)
Forward 5 (10) Apps 0 Goals
Born 26th January 1982
2000-2001 Notts Forest, 2001-2002 Notts County (0) (0), 2002-2003 Belper Town, 2003-2005 Imps, 2004-2005 Eastwood Town

Niall is very much the forgotten man of an unforgettable team. He was often a late or unused sub in Keith's team charge to a play-off semi-final, and he failed to register a goal for the club. He earned a one year deal over the summer of 2004, but only played once more for Lincoln as we opened the next season with a 1-0 win at Gay Meadow. Niall had the occasional opportunity to impress but never looked like making the grade.

Medley, Luke
(2011-2012)
Forward 0 (6) Apps 0 Goals
Born 21st June 1989
2007–2008 Bradford City 9 (2), 2008 Cambridge City (loan) 5 (0), 2008–2010 Barnet 19 (1) 2009 Havant & Waterlooville (loan) 8 (2), 2009–2010 Woking (loan) 17 (2), 2010 Havant & Waterlooville (loan) 13 (0), 2010–2011 Mansfield Town 16 (5), 2011 Aldershot Town (loan) 4 (0), 2011–2012 Kidderminster Harriers 13 (0), 2011–2012 Imps (loan) 2012 Woking (loan) 0 (0), 2012 Bromley 3 (0), 2013 Hayes & Yeading United 4 (0), 2013 Goole 6 (0), 2013 Crawley Down Gatwick, 2014 Margate 1 (0), 2014–2016 Walton Casuals 65 (22), 2016 Chatham Town

Medley was one of David Holdsworth's many loan signings, a phrase I'm almost getting tired of typing. He came in having scored six times at our level the season before with Mansfield, but ominously it was Kidderminster Harriers, also of our league who were happy to let him join. David Holdsworth was delighted with his arrival, quoted in the matchday programme as saying; "Luke Medley is another young man with an understanding of this league and my methods as he worked with me at Mansfield Town. He will prove he's a very good cameo player, but he's also a young man ager to start games."

He made six of the much lauded cameo appearances without proving to be as exciting as he sounded. He returned to Kidderminster only to have his contract terminated by mutual consent on Valentines Day.

Megson, Gary
(1995)
Midfielder 4 (0) Apps 0 Goals
Born 2nd May 1959
1977–1979 Plymouth Argyle 78 (10), 1979–1981 Everton 22 (2), 1981–1984 Sheffield Wednesday 123 (13), 1984 Nottingham Forest 0 (0), 1984–1985 Newcastle United 24 (1), 1985–1989 Sheffield Wednesday 110 (12), 1989–1992 Manchester City 82 (2), 1992–1995 Norwich City 46 (1), 1995 Imps, 1995 Shrewsbury Town 2 (0)

Veteran midfielder who played four times for the Imps in a short spell, twice in the League Cup against Notts County and twice in the league against Preston North End and Gillingham. After three straight defeats, he left to play a couple of times for Shrewsbury.

Had a very good career other than that playing mostly in the top flight for the likes of Sheffield Wednesday and Manchester City. Upon retiring as a player, he forged a decent career as a manager most significantly with West Brom.

Mendes, Junior
(2007)
Forward 4 (6) Apps 0 Goals
Born 15th September 1976
1995–1996 Chelsea 0 (0), 1996–2000 St Mirren 120 (21), 1998, Carlisle United (loan) 6 (1), 2000–2002 Dunfermline Athletic 13 (0), 2002–2003 St Mirren 17 (6), 2003–2004 Mansfield Town 57 (12), 2004–2006 Huddersfield Town 30 (5), 2005–2006 Northampton Town (loan) 12 (2), 2006 Grimsby Town (loan) 15 (0), 2006–2007 Notts County 37 (5), 2007 Imps (loan), 2008–2009 Aldershot Town 12 (1), 2009 Stevenage Borough (loan) 6 (1), 2009 Ilkeston Town 1 (0), 2009–2010 Ayr United 21 (0), 2012–2013 Nairn County 0 (0), 2014 Clydebank 0 (0)

While Martin Gritton was out on loan scoring goals, Junior Mendes was brought into the fold and didn't score at all. He'd had a decent career with plenty of appearances in the Scottish top flight as well as a good spell at Mansfield Town. He was unable to help the Imps in any way as we strode to our highest league placing since 1998 and he ended up earning his corn in the conference for a while before moving to Scotland.

Mendes was capped by the Caribbean island of Montserrat nine times, scoring once for them. To put that into context, in 2002 Montserrat lost a friendly to Bhutan to 'win' the title of worst team in the world on FIFA Rankings.

Mendy, Arnaud
(2014-2015)
Midfielder 34 (4) Apps 1 Goal
Born 10th February 1990
2007–2008 FC Rouen 11 (3), 2008–2011 Derby County 1 (0), 2009 Grimsby Town (loan) 1 (0), 2010 Tranmere Rovers (loan) 12 (1), 2011–2013 Macclesfield Town 42 (4), 2012–2013 Luton Town (loan) 8 (0), 2013 Luton Town 10 (0), 2014-2015 Imps, 2015-2016 Whitehawk 13 (1), 2016 Hemel Hempstead

Mendy was a towering if not altogether skilful midfielder signed by Gary Simpson in February 2014. He retained his place in the side after Simpson left although he wasn't then retained for the next season. Mendy was a workman-like midfielder who never seemed able to find the next gear. His one goal against Aldershot was a poor return for a six-foot three midfielder and it is no surprise to see him drop down the divisions.

Mettam, Leon
(2005-2007)
Forward 5 (4) 1 Goals
Born 9th December 1986
2005–2007 Imps, 2007–2008 Stamford, 2008–2009 Corby Town 35 (23), 2010–2012 Gainsborough Trinity, 2012–2014 Worksop Town 80 (66), 2014–2016 Tamworth 18 (5), 2015 King's Lynn Town (loan) 5 (3), 2016 King's Lynn Town

Mettam was a product of the Lincoln youth set up and his emergence in 2005 gave fans cause to think there might be a new home-grown star in our midst. After a January 2006 debut, he had to wait ten months to force his way into contention, and when he did he seized the advantage with a goal as we ran out 5-0 winners at Barnet. A young Mettam could have been forgiven for letting things go to his head. In truth it probably did.

After a run in the team he had to wait until early 2007 for another chance. On 20th February 2007, he came on as a 69th minute sub in a match we went on to lose 4-1. On 79 minutes he was shown a straight red card and he departed, never to be seen on the Lincoln City turf again.

Mike, Adie
(2002-2003)
Forward 5 (14) Apps, 3 Goals
Born 16th November 1973
1992–1995 Manchester City 16 (2), 1993 Bury (loan) 7 (1), 1994 Linköping (loan), 1995–1997 Stockport County 9 (0), 1996 Hartlepool United (loan) 7 (1), 1997 Doncaster Rovers (loan) 5 (1), 1997–1998 Doncaster Rovers 44 (4), 1998–1999 Leek Town, 1999 Hednesford Town 18 (3), 1999–2000 Southport 15 (1), 2000–2002 Northwich Victoria 54 (13), 2002 Stalybridge Celtic 7 (0), 2002–2003 Imps, 2002–2003 Gainsborough Trinity (loan), 2003 Cliftonville, 2003 Droylsden 2003 Mossley 6 (3), 2003–2004 Leek Town

Former Premier League striker Mike was entering the final stages of his career when he signed for Keith Alexander. They knew each other from Mike's time at Northwich Victoria and as we were always short on goal scorers he came on a short-term deal. Upon joining Keith remarked; "Adie's a very good player and did very well for me at Northwich. If we get him fit I'm sure he'll push our other strikers for a place in the starting team."

Three goals in his first seven games suggested we might have found a new hero, but then nothing through until New Year sullied those hopes. He played his last game as he had his first against Boston.

His goals did bring us three points, a 68th minute strike at Shrewsbury was added to by Ben Sedgemore to bring home a 2-1 win.

Mike had built a reputation as a quick and powerful striker, but as his pace faded and the goals didn't come he looked increasingly frustrated. However even if his entire Lincoln career is nothing more than a goal in a 2-1 win then so be it, that 2-1 contributed to our first ever day out at a national stadium. Adie Mike played his part in that, no matter how small (see also Shayne Bradley).

Miles, Taylor
(2016- Current)
Midfielder 0 (1) Apps 0 Goals
Born 11th July 1995
2014-2015 Concord Rangers, 2015-2016 Braintree, 2016 Imps, 2016 Boston Utd (loan)

Taylor Miles is a former West Ham youth who has followed Danny and Nicky Cowley from Concord Rangers to Braintree and now from Braintree to Lincoln. We've not see enough of him as yet to make a proper judgement, but he is billed as a ball playing midfielder with a wicked set-piece. In a conversation with Danny Cowley I was told that a free kick on the edge of the area is like having a penalty with Taylor Miles in your side.

He picked up a broken ankle on the opening day of the 2016/17 season against Woking and as of 31st October had just recovered full fitness. He's currently at Boston United on loan to pick up match fitness.

Miller, Kern
(2009-2011)
Defender 0 (1) Apps 0 Goals
Born 9th September 1991
2009–2011 Imps, 2011–2012 Barnsley 0 (0), 2011 Accrington Stanley (loan) 2 (0), 2012 Hereford United (loan) 0 (0), 2012 Hereford United 0 (0), 2012 Gainsborough Trinity 1 (0), 2012 Worksop Town (loan) 8 (0), 2012 Boston United 6 (0), 2012–2013 Worksop Town, 2013–2014 Grantham Town, 2015 King's Lynn Town 36 (0), 2016 Stamford

Young defender who only made one appearance for City, as an 83rd minute sub for Janos Kovacs. Much was hoped for the youngster but before he broke into the first team he was snapped up by Barnsley. Never made the grade and was last seen playing for Stamford Town where he headed a goal in a recent 3-2 FA Cup 4th Qualifying replay win over National League side Wrexham.

Miller, Paul
(1997-2001)
Midfielder 106 (25) Apps 12 Goals
Born 31st January 1968
1986-1987 Yeovil Town, 1987 Bristol Rovers (loan), 1987-1994 Wimbledon 80 (10), 1987 Newport County 6 (2), 1990 Bristol City (loan) 3 (0), 1994-1997 Bristol Rovers 105 (22), 1997-2001 Imps, 2001-2005 Lincoln United

Experienced midfielder signed by John Beck, which in itself is unusual as Beck didn't really bother with a midfield. He scored just three games into his Lincoln career to give us a 1-0 win at Shrewsbury in late 1997, but the goals never flowed regularly enough for him to be remembered as an Imps great.

Once the chips were down and we slipped back in the basement league Miller often went missing when the need for real fight emerged. He wasn't the worst player from that time by any means, but he was one of a long line who simply didn't contribute regularly enough. Deranged Ferret once described Miller as "Always has his moments and even weighs in with some goals. The trouble is he doesn't have the spirit for the third division."

Played his last game in an Imps shirt in the final day 0-0 draw at Exeter City before dropping down to represent Lincoln United for a few years, where he earned a reputation as a committed and influential ex-pro.

Miller, Tom
(2012-2015)
Defender 116 (2) Apps 11 Goals
Born 29th June 1990
2008–2010 Rangers 0 (0), 2009–2010 Brechin City (loan) 0 (0), 2010–2011 Dundalk   2011–2012 Newport County 37 (1), 2012 Imps (loan), 2012–2015 Imps, 2015 Carlisle United 27 (5)

David Holdsworth had a habit of signing relatively poor players from other non-league clubs during his reign as manager, but one exception to this was Tom Miller. Miller initially arrived as a centre back with a devastating long throw, and upon completion of his loan spell the management had seen enough to want him back at the Bank. He duly signed from Newport on a permanent deal, and went on to reveal he was so much more than a big throw.

Miller did always have promise, as a youngster he was signed by Glasgow Rangers after serving as a youth at Norwich City. Only a cruciate ligament injury and then a broken foot halted his progress with the Scottish giants.

Miller eventually settled at right back for City and through turbulent times emerged as a consistent and talented player who was fully committed to the red and white of Lincoln. He produced his best football once Holdsworth departed and was voted Player of the Year for the 2013/14 season. Once Gary Simpson left he continued adding value to the side and even earned Chris Moyses six points early into his reign with goals at home against Dartford and Southport to give us back to back 1-0 wins.

The more he played the better he got and it came as no surprise at all when he opted to join League Two side Carlisle United upon completion of his contract. Nobody could fault Tom's efforts during a tough era in Lincoln City history, and no fans begrudged him his move up to the Football League. He's still at Carlisle, and he's almost always been a first team regular for them.

Mills, Gary
(2012-2013)
Midfielder 23 (1) Apps 0 Goals
Born 20th May 1981
1998–2006 Rushden & Diamonds 124 (0), 2006–2007 Crawley Town 21 (0), 2007 Rushden & Diamonds 17 (0), 2007 Tamworth, 2007–2008 Kettering Town 27 (2), 2008–2009 Stevenage Borough 32 (0), 2009–2011 Mansfield Town 44 (1), 2010 Forest Green Rovers (loan) 2 (0), 2011 Rushden & Diamonds 20 (0), 2011 Bath City 4 (0), 2011–2012 Nuneaton Town, 2012–2013 Imps, 2013–2014 Boston United 0 (0), 2013–2014 King's Lynn Town (loan) 20 (0), 2016 King's Lynn Town

(Yet) Another David Holdsworth signing that didn't end particularly well, Mills arrived from Nuneaton having played for Holdsworth at Mansfield Town. He was immediately named club captain and given a first team spot. No initially cause for alarm.

He had won a few honours in his time as well playing for Rushden and Diamonds. In over 125 outings for them he had earned promotion from the Conference and then again from League Two. On paper it all looked very positive.

Mills was billed as the type of player that does the unseen work, the harassing and pressuring of opponents, the simple distribution of the ball and the constant breaking up of play. If this was the case he was really good at it, because it was completely unseen in his 24 outing for Lincoln. What we did see was a lot of pointing and shouting, which is good for a captain, but a lack of actual touches tarnishes that somewhat. He became a figure of derision and didn't do himself any favours with his often abrasive and confrontational style on social media.

He played his last game for City in December 2012 before having his contract terminated by mutual consent when Gary Simpson arrived at the club. Nobody really mourned his departure and he ended up at Boston and latterly Kings Lynn.

He came, he saw, he pointed, he shouted and he went.

Minett, Jason
(1995-1997)
Defender 48 (10) Apps 5 Goals
Born 12th August 1971
1990-1993 Norwich City 3 (0), 1992-1995 Exeter City 88 (3), 1995-1997 Imps, 1996-1998 Exeter City 19 (0), Doncaster Rovers 58 (4), 1998-2000 Boston United 9 (1), 2000-2001 King's Lynn 23 (1), 2001-2002 Stocksbridge Park Steels (loan), 2001-2002 Grantham Town 58 (2), 2001-2004 Lincoln United, 2004-2007 Grantham Town 30 (2)

Popular right back signed after three seasons at Exeter City in 1995. He only missed four games of the 1995/96 season which saw us changed managers twice in just a few short weeks. He even weighed in with a few goals during that tough campaign, scoring in back to back league matches against Doncaster (1-1) and Hereford (2-1). Later bagged a brace in the reverse fixture against Doncaster (4-0) and another in the penultimate match away at Northampton (1-1).

He found his chances severely limited the next season although he was often on the bench in our Coca Cola Cup run, coming on against Man City at Maine Road. By January 1997 it became clear he had no future at Sincil Bank and he re-joined Exeter City on January 17th.

Molango, Maheta
(2005)
Forward 7 (7) Apps 1 Goal
Born 24th July 1982
2003–2004 Atlético Madrid, SV Wacker Burghausen 5 (0), 2004–2007 Brighton & Hove Albion 6 (1), 2005–2006 Imps (loan)), 2006 UB Conquense (loan) 8 (0), 2006 Oldham Athletic (loan) 5 (1), 2006 Wrexham (loan) 3 (0), 2007 Grays Athletic 2 (0), UB Conquense, 2009–2010 FC Villanueva del Pardillo, 2010 AD Unión Adarve Barrio del Pilar

Another of 'the strikers of Keith Alexander', drafted in on loan from Brighton ahead of the 2005/06 season to add a bit of bite to our depleted forward line. Gary Taylor-Fletcher had left, Simon Yeo had left and we needed goals. Molango looked quick and powerful and it was hoped he could score regularly at our level. He couldn't.

He did net once as we beat Crewe 5-1, but fellow new strikers Gary Birch and Marvin Robinson also scored taking the shine off his efforts. In all of his 14 outings he managed just the one goal and returned to the south coast once his loan spell was up.

The story of the goal-shy striker born in Switzerland doesn't end there. Having obtained a LL.B and B.A. Political Science from Charles III University of Madrid, he joined the employment law department of the Madrid office of Baker & McKenzie in 2007, and in 2008 he moved to the United States to study for the LL.M program in International Legal Studies at the American University Washington College of Law. He graduated in 2009 whilst also being the recipient of the college's Rubin Scholarship.

Bright fella this Molango. He just struggled to hit a cow's arse with a banjo.

Morgan, David
(2012-2013)
Midfielder 7 (3) Apps 0 Goals
Born 4th July 1994

2012–2014 Nottingham Forest 0 (0), 2012 Imps (loan) 2013 Dundee (loan) 1 (0), 2013–2014 Tamworth (loan) 9 (1), 2014–2015 Ilkeston 40 (2), 2015 Nuneaton Town 29 (1)

Midfielder signed on a short-term loan to feature in an ever-changing side built by David Holdsworth. He looked a decent midfielder but in a side that changed more often than I change my pants it was hard to settle and make any real impact. He returned to Forest after we drew 1-1 with Gateshead, and his next professional game was for Dundee as they lost 5-0 to Celtic at Celtic Park. That was unsurprisingly his only outing for Dundee and most recently he's been turning out for Nuneaton.

Morgan, Paul
(2001-2007)
Defender 227 (11) Apps 2 Goals
Born 23rd October 1978
1997–2001 Preston North End 0 (0), 1997–1998 Sligo Rovers (loan) 0 (0), 2001–2007 Imps, 2007–2009 Bury 20 (0), 2008–2009 Macclesfield Town (loan) 39 (0), 2009–2012 Macclesfield Town 67 (0)

Paul Morgan is, in my humble opinion, the best centre half I am writing about in this book, and that includes Gareth McAuley. Had he stood at six foot four or five I have no doubt at all he would have represented his country and played Premier League football.

Irishman Morgan came through the youth ranks at Preston North End and despite his obvious potential, he made only one senior appearance during his four years there. He joined City on a free transfer in 2001.

Once he found regular first team football he developed into one of the most talented defenders in the lower leagues. He did receive his call-up into the full Northern Ireland squad, but it was cruelly taken away after he picked up an injury just four months after his arrival at Sincil Bank.

Keith Alexander made Morgan his captain at the start of ground breaking 2002/03 campaign, and he led an unfancied side all the way to the play-off final, earning himself the nickname 'Ireland's Bobby Moore' from City fans. He made the decision to sign a new two-year contract at the end of March 2003 ahead of the match against Bournemouth, much to the delight of fans who held him in such high esteem. There were few surprises when he was named Player of the Year for that historic season, the seconf central defender in as many years to win it after Grant Brown.

It wasn't hard to pinpoint what Paul Morgan did for the team. As well as organise and encourage the defence he was a match for any centre forward when it came to pace, and often found a clever and fair tackle in situations where only a foul looked possible. He led fiercely and unflinchingly with a commitment to the cause that truly epitomised everything Keith was trying to achieve.

The following season he was named 2004 BBC East Midlands 'Footballer of the Year' ahead of the likes of Nottingham Forest's Andy Reid and Leicester City's Ian Walker, a real honour for a Lincoln City footballer. Once again we challenged at the right end of the table and once again Captain Morgan was at the heart of our success.

He signed another new deal, this time for three years in 2005, and it looked very much like our inspirational captain was around for the long haul. Against Macclesfield Town on New Year's Day, meanwhile, he made his 200th Football League appearance for the Imps.

Sadly, with Keith leaving the club his captain also felt he needed to move on. Shortly after our fifth play-off defeat at the hands of Bristol Rovers he informed Head Coach John Schofield that he wished to leave the Club, and he left by mutual consent in June 2007. Twenty-four hours later he re-joined his former boss Keith Alexander at Bury before following him to Macclesfield on a season-long loan a year later, although in fairness to Paul it did coincide with his wife being relocated to Manchester with the police force.

Paul Morgan was one of only a couple of players to feature in each and every single one of our play-off appearances, and his departure did leave a hole in our defence that hasn't really looked like being filled until as recently as the 2016/17 season. His organisation and leadership qualities helped players like Jamie McCombe, Lee Beevers and Gareth McAuley to flourish and go on to have really good careers in the higher leagues. He was consistently linked to sides much higher up the Football League and was widely regarded as one of the best defenders in the lower leagues. There's no doubt Paul Morgan deserved to progress in the same manner as our other successful defenders, and perhaps that injury just four months in to his Imps career robbed him of the opportunity to show the football world what he could do on the international stage.

Moses, Adie
(2006-2008)
Defender 46 (8) Apps 1 Goal
Born 4th May 1975
1993–2001 Barnsley 151 (3), 2001–2003 Huddersfield Town 69 (1), 2003–2006 Crewe Alexandra 57 (0), 2006–2008 Imps, 2008–2009 Mansfield Town 38 (0), 2009 Gainsborough Trinity 15 (0)

Experienced defender brought in to counteract the departure of Gareth McAuley to Ipswich at the end of the 2005/06 season. Moses had a good football pedigree but appeared at Lincoln towards the end of his career. He scored on his Imps debut in a 1-1 draw against Notts County, but from there it all went downhill. He was a member of the squad beaten by Bristol Rovers in the 2006/07 play-off semi-finals, but once John Schofield left he found chances very limited under Peter Jackson, exasperated by injury concerns. He eventually left for Mansfield Town but retired from the game in 2009 because of injury.

In 2008, Moses graduated from Staffordshire University with a degree in Professional Sports Writing and Broadcasting. He now works as a financial consultant for Paul Kerr Associates offering financial advice to professional footballers.

Mudd, Paul
(1995-1996)
Defender 3 (4) Apps 0 Goals
Born 13th November 1970
1989-1990 Hull City, 1990-1993 Scarborough, 1993-1995 Scunthorpe United, 1995-1996 Imps, 1996-1996 Halifax (loan)

Mudd come in as Sam Ellis desperately tried (and immediately failed) to build a side for the 1995/96 season. He started just two games all season, ironically both against Colchester as we lost 3-0 under Ellis and drew 0-0 under John Beck. In between he had a spell on loan at Halifax, but to be blunt he just didn't bring anything to the table and was released in the glorious summer of 1996.

Muldoon, Jack
(2015- Current)
Forward 52 (8) Apps 12 Goals
Born 19th May 1989

2008 Brigg Town, 2008–2009 Sheffield 22 (3), 2009–2010 Glapwell, 2010 Alfreton Town, 2010–2012 Stocksbridge Park Steels, 2012 Brigg Town, 2012–2013 North Ferriby United 22 (2), 2012–2013 Sheffield (loan) 21 (9), 2013–2014 Worksop Town, 2014–2015 Rochdale 6 (0), 2015 Halifax Town (loan) 12 (2), 2015 Imps

Popular forward Jack Muldoon came to City via a short stay at Rochdale, but he has become an instant fan favourite with his committed and energetic displays. The arrival of James Caton at the end of the 2015/16 season saw Muldoon move into a central position to play off Matt Rhead, and in the main it was a very successful experiment.

He made his Imps debut against Cheltenham in our 1-1 draw and scored his first goal two matches later as we drew 1-1 at Eastleigh. He went on to score nine goals that season, five coming after his switch to centre forward.

He scored against Crewe in the pre-season of 2016/17 but then picked up an injury in the season opener against Woking which eventually led to a spell on the side-lines. He came back as hungry as ever and netted a superb late goal in the 3-0 win over Braintree. He added to his tally as we ran riot at Chester in October, a smart one-two with Matt Rhead giving us an unassailable advantage.

Muldoon also suffers from diabetes and gave an insightful interview to the Echo at the tail end of the 2015/16 season. He is a likeable character and his non-stop running and commitment to the cause is cherished by manager and fans alike. He trains as if it's a first team game and his performance levels ensure he remains a favourite on the terraces.

Mullarkey, Sam
(2008-2009)
Forward 7 (11) Apps 1 Goal
Born 24th September 1987
2006–2007 Lincoln United 3 (0), 2007–2008 Grantham Town 53 (19), 2008–2009 Imps, 2009-2010 Lincoln United, 2011 Stamford, 2015 Lincoln United

Mullarkey joined the Imps, the team he supported as a boy in 2008. He was offered a 1-year contract by Peter Jackson, becoming Jackson's 8th signing of the summer. He made his league debut coming on as substitute for the awful Kevin Gall in the home draw with Grimsby Town.

He scored his first goal in the 1-1 draw with Notts County, a wonderful strike that cancelled out future Imp Delroy Facey's opener. Mullarkey strangely rejected a fresh contract after the club had hoped to sign him up for the 2009-2010 season. He is still playing in the City, firing Lincoln United to the FA Cup 4th qualifying round in 2016.

Musselwhite, Paul
(2009-2011)
Goalkeeper 0 (1) apps 0 Goals
Born 22nd December 1968
1986–1988 Portsmouth 0 (0), 1988–1992 Scunthorpe United 132 (0), 1992–2000 Port Vale 312 (0, 2000 Sheffield Wednesday 0 (0), 2000–2004 Hull City 95 (0), 2004–2006 Scunthorpe United 74 (0), 2006 Eastleigh 8 (0), 2006–2007 Kettering Town 2 (0), 2007 Port Vale 0 (0), 2007–2008 Harrogate Town 8 (0), 2008–2009 Gateshead 57 (0), 2009–2011 Imps, 2011–2013 York City 3 (0)

Musselwhite signed as player-goalkeeping coach for Peter Jackson and survived both him and Chris Sutton. He became assistant-caretaker manager to Scott Lindsey following Chris Sutton's resignation, but played just once at 41-years old a 1–0 defeat at Southend United, following an injury to Joe Anyon.

Musselwhite was a cult figure at Lincoln and had his own terrace song 'we all dream of a team of Musselwhites'. However, after relegation a new contract offer from Lincoln was entirely dependent on Joe Anyon leaving the club, so Musselwhite opted to sign for Conference Premier club York City, again as a player-goalkeeping coach.

Nelson - Onwere

Nelson, Mitchell
(2011)
Defender 9 (1) Apps 0 Goals
Born 31st August 1989
2007-2009 Tooting and Mitcham, 2010-2011 Bournemouth, 2010-2011 Eastbourne (loan), 2011 Imps, 2013-2016 Sutton United, 2016 Welling

Nelson joined the Imps after a spell at Bournemouth and featured for Steve Tilson as we plummeted down the National League table. He'd served his youth at Colchester before leaving without a pro deal, then after a failed trial at Brentford he ended up with Tooting and Mitcham.

He had a relatively uninspired time being kept out of the City defence by Josh Gowling and Adam Watts. He was sent off in just his third outing for two bookable offences at Luton. He survived until mid-November before David Holdsworth decided he was surplus to requirements.

Newton, Sean
(2013-2015)
Defender 80 Apps 6 Goals
Born 23rd September 1988
2007–2008 Chester City 2 (0), 2007 Southport (loan) 13 (1), 2008 Droylsden (loan) 15 (1), 2008–2009 Droylsden, 2009 Barrow 4 (0), 2009–2012 AFC Telford United 110 (4), 2012 Stockport County (loan) 7 (1), 2012–2013 Stockport County 43 (6), 2013–2015 Imps, 2015 Notts County (loan) 8 (0), 2015 Wrexham 60 (8)

Newton had two good seasons at Lincoln, but won't be remembered fondly for the manner of his exit and his overall attitude. Such a shame as his delivery into the box was second to none outside the top flight, and if he could defend and had a half decent right foot he could have gone much further.

Newton was in the headlines before signing for City in 2008, the day after he played in an FA Cup Second Round FA Cup replay against Chesterfield. Newton scored twice for Droylsden in a 2–1 victory to secure a third-round tie against Ipswich Town. However, it emerged after the game that Newton was due to serve a one-game suspension after picking up his fifth yellow card of the season. Droylsden had been informed of the suspension by the Football Association on 10th December, but Newton played anyway. The FA investigated and the club were expelled from the competition, after being found guilty of fielding an ineligible player. Newton joined Stockport shortly after.

At Lincoln he formed part of the Gary Simpson squad that looked to have enough quality to challenge for the play-offs. His delivery and attacking prowess was superb, and with Tom Miller he gave our flanks a real potency not seen since Bailey and Bimson had prowled them a decade earlier.

He could pop up with a crucial goal such as a last-minute equaliser away at Alfreton that earned us a point. The season after he bagged one in the passionate 3-2 derby win at Sincil Bank over Grimsby, and he went on to have a good season for the Imps as Simpson was dismissed and Chris Moyses came in. After Gary left Newton didn't find the net again, and rumours of a bad attitude began to spread like wildfire. Towards the end of the season, believing he was going to get a football league opportunity he pressed for a loan move to Notts County, which he got. He didn't impress there at all.

He left on a free transfer at the end of the season and immediately signed for Wrexham, also of the National League. Since then he has shown nothing but vitriol to Lincoln, and convinced his close friend Jon Nolan to join him there for a short time. Karma remembers though and as soon as former Imps Dean Keates took over at Wrexham he got rid of Newton to York City.

N'Guessan, Dany
(2007-2009)
Forward 76 (23) Apps, 16 Goals
Born 11ᵗʰ August 1987
2003–2005 Auxerre 0 (0), 2005–2007 Rangers 0 (0), 2006–2007 Boston United (loan) 23 (5), 2007–2009 Imps, 2009–2011 Leicester City 31 (3), 2010 Scunthorpe United (loan) 3 (1), 2011 Southampton (loan) 6 (0), 2011 Millwall (loan) 1 (0), 2011–2013 Millwall 29 (2), 2012 Charlton Athletic (loan) 7 (4), 2013–2014 Swindon Town 24 (8), 2014–2015 Port Vale 11 (2), 2015 AE Limassol 10 (1), 2015 Doncaster Rovers 8 (0)

When I think of my 'ideal' footballer I think of a strong and powerful winger, equally as comfortable playing through the middle. They'll have the raw physique to get them through, but they'll have a splash of flair and trickery about them too. Crucially they would be a goal threat and always show an exemplary attitude and complete commitment to the cause. Dany N'Guessan was almost that footballer. Almost.

When Steve Evans said in the press he felt John Schofield had been an 'armchair scout' when signing Dany, I understood his point. We first witnessed the young Frenchman playing for Evans on loan from Rangers and I'm not sure John Deehan's contacts extended as far as Auxerre or Glasgow. However, once we'd seen him we decided, like Lee Beevers before him, that he was going to be ours.

I was excited to see Dany play for Lincoln; I couldn't understand what the catch was. He had it all, and as he settled in I was hoping that we'd see what he could do on a consistent basis. Unfortunately, with Dany that was where he lacked.

He struggled to settle at all in the first few months and didn't show the sort of form that had made him popular at York Street. It soon appeared that when he was good, he was very good. When he was bad he may as well not have been there.

He had a stop start Lincoln career in terms of contribution. Throughout the transfer window of early 2009 he suddenly found form scoring 6 in 10 games right up until early March. Then like on so many occasions he went missing for the latter part of the season. Leicester City agreed with my view that there was a quality player in there, and at the end of the season he left.

Since then he's made a good living from threatening quality only to fail to deliver on a regular basis. It's a crying shame that a player I firmly believe could have played Premiership football seemed unable to apply himself enough to showcase his talents.

Nicholson, Shane
(1988-1992, 2006-2007)
Defender 193 (16) Apps 10 Goals
Born 3ʳᵈ June 1970
1986–1992 Imps, 1992–1996 Derby County 74 (1), 1996–1998 West Bromwich Albion 52 (0), 1998–1999 Chesterfield 24 (1), 1999–2001 Stockport County 77 (3), 2001–2002 Sheffield United 25 (3), 2002–2004 Tranmere Rovers 54 (6), 2004–2007 Chesterfield 68 (12), 2006–2007 Imps (loan), 2007 Boston United (loan) 6 (0)

Home-grown defender Nicholson made his debut for the club on 22nd November 1986 in a match against Burnley, at the time becoming the youngest ever Lincoln City player to play in the Football League, at the age of 16 years and 172 days. He went on to play in seven league games during the 1986–87 season, a campaign which ended in relegation. He was also a part of the successful 1988 GMVC winning side. After the club's promotion to the Division Four, Nicholson became a first team regular, playing 126 league games in four seasons, scoring six goals.

Once established as a first team regular at such a young age other clubs were bound to pay an interest and he ended up moving to second division side Derby County. He flirted with the first team without ever becoming established and a move to West Brom followed.

In his third season with West Brom he was suspended after failing a drugs test, testing positive for traces of amphetamines. He was sacked by the club, a decision against which he unsuccessfully appealed. From there he had a good career and put his troubles behind him, gaining a reputation as a good honest footballer. He returned to City, albeit briefly on loan to help out John Schofield 20 years after first appearing for the club. He played eight final times for the club, including great wins over Peterborough away (2-1) and Boston (2-1) and Grimsby (2-0) at the Bank.

Nicolau, Nicky
(2011-2013)
Defender 35 (16) Apps 4 Goals
Born 12th October 1983
2002–2004 Arsenal 0 (0), 2004 Southend United (loan) 9 (1), 2004–2005 Southend United 22 (1), 2005–2006 Swindon Town 5 (0), 2006 Hereford United (loan) 10 (1), 2006–2009 Barnet 81 (4), 2009– 2010 Woking 21 (1), 2010 Dover Athletic 11 (1), 2010–2011 Boreham Wood 15 (3), 2011–2013 Imps, 2013–2014 Chelmsford City 29 (0), 2014 Welling United 0 (0), 2014–2015 Chelmsford City 14 (2), 2015 Bishops Stortford 0 (0)

Nicolau linked up with his former Southend manager Steve Tilson when he arrived in that sad summer of 2011. He was a full back who could operate further up-field if needed and in truth he wasn't a bad player. A bit of the zest that made him a Barnet regular seemed to be lacking, but he always put in an honest shift under difficult conditions.

Injuries meant he didn't manage to get an enforced spell in the team whilst Tilson was in charge, but the following season he managed a run in the team, scoring four times. He was unable to prevent David Holdsworth from losing his job, and in the summer Nicolau was released.

Nolan, Jon
(2013-2016)
Midfielder 64 (11) Apps 6 Goals
Born 22nd April 1992
2011–2013 Stockport County 62 (3), 2013–2016 Imps, 2015–2016 Wrexham (loan) 6 (0), 2016 Grimsby Town 18 (4), 2016 Chesterfield

Jon Nolan is a good footballer. When appearing in red and white he often drifted in and out of games, but his talent is undeniable. He is what your dad would call 'a proper footballer', with a good touch and a degree of vision. There was no doubt in my mind Nolan would end up playing league football, once he sorted out that consistency.

He is also prone to making bad decisions, and requesting to go out on loan to Wrexham when the Imps were in the middle of a gruelling season was one of those decisions. It was no doubt influenced by his good friend and Wrexham player Sean Newton. Whatever he had achieved (in short spells) on the pitch was soon forgotten when he hightailed across the country.

His game time was limited when he returned and he wound up at Grimsby after we terminated his contract. Needless to say, he went on to score the goals that helped then to achieve Football League status again. Then he turned his back on them and moved up a division to Chesterfield. There's no denying his talent, but he wouldn't be warmly welcomed back at Sincil Bank, which is a shame.

Nutter, John
(2011-2012)
Defender 58 (1) Apps 3 Goals
Born 13th June 1982
2001 Wycombe Wanderers 1 (0), 2001–2004 Aldershot Town 58 (5), 2002St Albans City (loan) 7 (0), 2002 Gravesend &Northfleet (loan) 4 (0), 2004–2006Grays Athletic 77 (1), 2006–2008 Stevenage Borough 60 (8), 2007–2008 Gillingham (loan) 3 (0), 2008–2011 Gillingham 135 (3), 2011–2013 Imps, 2012–2013Woking (loan) 5 (0), 2013–2015Woking 64 (1)

Nutter had a forged a good reputation as a strong full back before he came to City. After good performances in the non-league with Aldershot and Stevenage he ended up at League One Gillingham where he made 135 league appearances in a three-year spell.

He arrived at Lincoln as part of Steve Tilson's attempt to get back into the football league at first stab. He had a reputation as an attacking full back who had dropped down a level too far. Even by his own admission he felt he'd dropped down further than he needed to, and it seemed he might be our Trevor Matthewson, the 1988 GMVC winning captain who swapped second tier football for non-league Sincil Bank.

Nutter was ever present in our first appalling season scoring a couple of goals. He never had a chance to shine in such a poor City side but he also never let the team down. He suffered from inconsistency brought on by the upheaval in management as Tilson was sacked and David Holdsworth came in. He scored in a crucial 2-0 home win against Newport after a fans demonstration that sparked a run of three wins to help us towards safety.

In his second season, he was named as captain but began to struggle with travelling as he had a young family. His last goal for Lincoln was in a 3-3 draw with Stockport, and his final appearance was in the 3-2 AET win at Walsall in the FA Cup. Shortly afterwards due to family commitments he moved initially on a two-month loan down to Woking. In just his second game for Woking he was on the end of a 7-0 defeat at the hands of Hyde, but they still made his move permanent and he went on to make 70 appearances for the Cards spanning almost two seasons. His last professional game was as a last-minute sub in a 1-0 over Forest Green.

After football John settled in the south and has recently been working as a PE Teacher at a prep school.

Oakes, Stefan
(2008-2010)
Midfielder 35 (12) Apps 1 Goal
Born 6th September 1978

1998–2003 Leicester City 64 (2), 2002 Crewe Alexandra (loan) 7 (0), 2003 Walsall 5 (0), 2003–2005 Notts County 45 (5), 2005–2008 Wycombe Wanderers 110 (5), 2008–2010 Imps, 2010 Tamworth 10 (0), 2010 F.C. New York, 2011 Tamworth 1 (0), 2013 Oadby Town 9 (0)

There's no doubting the talent Stefan Oakes had early in his career. A league cup winner medal with Leicester City and over 100 appearances for Wycombe Wanderers proved that at one point he had talent, and a lot of it. He came from a footballing family, his brother Scott Oakes turned out regularly for Luton Town amongst others.

Signed by Peter Jackson as one of the 'Magnificent Seven' that were going to fire us up the league, Oakes' Lincoln career never really got off the ground. He was billed as a man who could peel a carrot with his left foot, but 25% of his appearances starting with him peeling an orange on the bench while the others did the hard work. When he made it onto the pitch he was often found letting others do the hard work once again.

Injury and general decline proved to be the undoing of Stefan. When he wanted to he showed glimpses of what he was capable of, the odd sumptuous cross or dangerous free kick. However, for many his Lincoln outings he ambled around the pitch looking lost and out of his depth.

Once Peter Jackson left the club he hung around Chris Sutton's squad for a few months before leaving the club at the end of the 2009/10 season. He didn't find his way back into league football and he drifted from Tamworth to Oadby Town before retiring.

Oscar Chamberlain's view

If I ever make a list of all the people who have disappointed me in my life, the first name I put on it will be Stefan Oakes.

When he signed for the Imps in June 2008, I genuinely thought he was going to be the man to lead the Imps into League One. Maybe I was blinded by his CV which included Premier League experience and a League Cup triumph with Leicester or perhaps it was Peter Jackson's claim that Oakes could peel carrots with his left foot. Either way, I was excited.

I had seen him play for Wycombe a couple of times which only strengthened my belief that he was destined to become the best signing the Imps had made in the six years that I had been following them.

Maybe my expectations were unrealistic. Perhaps his performances weren't as bad as I remember but I put so much faith in him and I felt that he had let me down. He certainly isn't the worst player I've seen at Lincoln and he wasn't even the worst player signed by the club that summer (David Graham, anyone?) but for me he was the biggest disappointment.

There were glimpses of his undoubted ability. Every now and then he would produce a magnificent, effortless 60-yard pass but I think those flashes of genius just made me angrier. I always felt that with a little more effort and desire he could have achieved something special at Lincoln.

He did have several injury problems so my assessment of him is probably a little bit unfair and maybe I'm just annoyed at myself for having so much belief in him.

Nevertheless, the hatred I have for Stefan Oakes, no matter how irrational, is still there after all these years and as far as I'm concerned he belongs in the same category as my ex-girlfriend and my high school English teacher.

I also no longer like carrots.

Oatway, Charlie
(1998)
Midfielder 3 Apps 0 Goals
Born 28th November 1973
1993–1994 Yeading, 1994–1995 Cardiff City 32 (0), 1995–1997 Torquay United 67 (1), 1997–1999 Brentford 57 (0), 1998 Imps (loan), 1999–2007 Brighton & Hove Albion 224 (8), 2007–2009 Havant & Waterlooville 6 (0)

Oatway joined on loan for a month during our foray into the third tier and started three matches, all of them 2-1 defeats against Gillingham, Stoke and Walsall. At the time Brentford were in the league below us and had he impressed the opportunity for a permanent move may have arisen. He didn't impress sufficiently to remain at the club, but he did go on to make almost 250 competitive appearances for Brighton and Hove Albion.

O'Connor, Michael
(2009)
Midfielder 9 (1) Apps 1 Goal
Born 6th October 1987
2005–2009 Crewe Alexandra 77 (3), 2009 Imps (loan), 2009–2012 Scunthorpe United 97 (12), 2012–2014 Rotherham United 64 (7), 2014–2016 Port Vale 70 (10), 2016 Notts County 0 (0)

O'Connor came in on loan for the final couple of months of the 2008/09 season which was Peter Jackson's only full season in charge. He came on as a sub in the 5-1 mauling we suffered at Grimsby for his debut, and despite us conceding four goal when he was on the pitch he earned a starting spot and didn't let it go.

O'Connor was a real class act, a battler with a smart touch and a trick or two up his sleeve. It was apparent from his performances that our chances of signing him permanently were virtually zero, especially as he was rated highly at Crewe. He only arrived on loan by virtue of a 'breach of discipline' that made him unpopular with Crewe manager Gudjon Pordarson.

His arrived as a short-term replacement for the departing Lee Frecklington, and had our business with Peterborough been a little more fruitful for Lincoln we might have had an opportunity of signing O'Connor permanently. He certainly warranted it as he was already a Northern Ireland international.

He scored in our 3-2 defeat at Barnet and was ever present until injury forced him out of the final fixture of the season. On conclusion of his time at Lincoln he earned another Northern Ireland call up, lasting 62 minutes of a 3-0 friendly defeat by Italy.

Upon completion of his loan he was released by Crewe and snapped up by high flying Scunthorpe United. He has since enjoyed a fruitful career amassing 300 league appearances at various clubs, and being capped by his country 11 times.

O'Keefe, Josh
(2010-2012)
Midfielder 40 (10) Apps 5 Goals
Born 22nd December 1988
2007–2009 Blackburn Rovers 0 (0), 2009–2010 Walsall 13 (0), 2010–2012 Imps, 2012 Southport 7 (0), 2012–2014 Hereford United 51 (15), 2014–2015 Kidderminster Harriers 20 (0), 2014 Telford United (loan) 5 (0), 2014–2015 Chester (loan) 3 (0), 2015–2016 Altrincham 27 (1), 2016 Chorley 10 (1)

O'Keefe is a player who will be defined more by the squad he was a member of than anything else. He played 40 games the season we were relegated from the Football League, and despite showing promise and netting a few goals he will always be remembered as a part of the worst Imps squad in living memory. The former Blackburn trainee was signed by Chris Sutton and retained his place under Steve Tilson. There was no doubting he had some ability, perhaps more suited to non-league than league football though.

He was tall and often looked ungainly on the ball and despite his experience he couldn't force his way into our National League squad on a permanent basis. After Steve Tilson departed he played a couple of games before leaving by mutual consent on Boxing Day of 2011. At the time Imps fanzine, Deranged Ferret regarded it as 'a late Christmas present', as O'Keefe had come to represent everything that had been wrong with the club.

He ended up having a fairly prolific time at Hereford where he scored 15 times in 50 outings in the National League, although never against Lincoln. Latterly featured for Kidderminster Harriers where he was also well regarded.

Oliver, Vadaine
(2012-2013)
Forward 22 (19) Apps 13 Goals
Born 21st October 1991
2010–2012 Sheffield Wednesday 0 (0), 2012–2013 Imps, 2013–2015 Crewe Alexandra 34 (3), 2014–2015 Mansfield Town (loan) 30 (7), 2015 York City 37 (7), 2016 Notts County (loan)

Vadaine signed for David Holdsworth and arrived with less fanfare than other signings, and found early in his Imps career that Colin Larkin, Rob Duffy and even Luke Daley were keeping him out of the team. The youngster was always committed and often looked dangerous, but his outings were reserved to ten or fifteen minutes at the end of games.

On his first start he scored against Telford to earn us a 1-1 draw and a week later in his second start he scored an 88th minute winner against Hyde at Sincil Bank. The powerful striker had finally broken through. Two late goals in the FA Cup win at Walsall ensured that people started taking note of his scoring prowess.

He scored 13 goals in all including a last day hat-trick away at hapless Hyde. There was never any question of him staying in the summer, not once league clubs were alerted to him. He left for Crewe and latterly appeared at Mansfield and York, who curiously have loaned him to League Two side Notts County.

Onwere, Udo
(1994-1996)
Midfielder 50 (3) Apps 5 Goals
Born 9th November 1971

1990–1994 Fulham 85 (7), 1994–1996 Imps, 1996 Dover Athletic, 1996–1997 Blackpool 9 (0), 1997–1999 Barnet 36 (2), 1999 Aylesbury United, 1999–2000 Hayes 3 (0), 2000 Maidenhead United

Udo Onwere was a tough tackling Londoner who signed for Lincoln under the reign of Sam Ellis. His first game was blighted by a red card, one of only two City players to be sent off on his debut. The rest of the season was blighted by injury and he was restricted to just a handful of first team outings. He had an operation on damaged cartilage in late 1994.

However, in a turbulent 1995/96 season he was one constant. As Sam Ellis, Steve Wicks and finally John Beck occupied the manager's office, Onwere missed only a handful of games. He popped up with a couple of goals too in draws at home to Bury (2-2) and Scunthorpe (2-2). As the season progressed stability was returned to the football club and Onwere faded, playing his last game in the 2-1 win over Mansfield in April 1996.

Onwere became a cult hero in his time at Sincil Bank spawning a chant to the tune of The Outhere Brothers song 'Boom, Boom', which basically just went 'Boom, boom, boom, let me here you say Udo. Onwere'. It was catchier in real life than it is on paper.

After football he entered the legal profession, which is where he still works today in London.

Pacquette - Puttnam

Pacquette, Richard
(2012)
Forward 9 (4) Apps 3 Goals
Born 28th January 1983
2000–2004 Queens Park Rangers 31 (6), 2002–2003 Stevenage Borough (loan) 7 (2), 2003–2004 Dagenham & Redbridge (loan) 3 (1), 2004 Mansfield Town (loan) 5 (1), 2004 Milton Keynes Dons 5 (0), 2004 Fisher Athletic, 2004 Brentford 1 (0), 2004–2005, Farnborough Town 5 (1), 2005 Stevenage Borough 1 (0), 2005 St Albans City 1 (0), 2005 Hemel Hempstead Town 2 (0), 2005 Hampton & Richmond Borough 6 (0), 2005–2006 Worthing 30 (17), 2006 Thurrock (loan) 4 (0), 2006–2008 Havant & Waterlooville 66 (22), 2008 Maidenhead United (loan) 5 (3), 2008–2009 Maidenhead United 32 (20), 2009 Histon (loan) 3 (0), 2009–2010 York City 13 (1), 2010–2011 Eastbourne Borough 33 (10), 2011 Hayes & Yeading United 18 (4), 2011 Maidenhead United 3 (3), 2012 Imps, 2012 Bromley 13 (5), 2012–2013 Eastleigh 2 (1), 2013 Sutton United 7 (1), 2013–2014 Maidenhead United 44 (15), 2014–2015 Eastbourne Borough 35 (8), 2015–2016 Hampton & Richmond Borough 11 (2), 2015 Lewes (loan) 6 (0), 2016 Walton & Hersham 5 (3), 2016 Hampton & Richmond Borough 0 (0), 2016 Metropolitan Police 4 (1)

Richard Pacquette has played for an awful lot of clubs, and wherever he plays he manage to knock in a goal or two. We signed him in early 2012 to help the team Tilson built stay in the Football Conference. He came packaged with his cousin Jefferson Louis, and between them they did what was required. Like Hannibal and BA they came in our time of need, and the plan came together, although I'm not sure if he had to be sedated when travelling to Lincoln. Fools.

I felt with Pacquette and Louis on we might always pinch a goal. Pacquette got three in an Imps shirt, two against Gateshead away (3-3) and one against Southport (2-0) at the Bank.

I guess it was inevitable that he wouldn't stay after his short spell ended. Like a football gun-for-hire he strode off to his next club, and then the next, and probably then a couple more.

Parish, Elliot
(2011)
Goalkeeper 9 Apps 0 Goals
Born 20th May 1990
2009–2012 Aston Villa 0 (0), 2011 Imps (loan), 2011 Cardiff City (loan) 0 (0), 2012–2013 Cardiff City 0 (0), 2012 Wycombe Wanderers (loan) 2 (0), 2013–2014 Bristol City 19 (0), 2014 Newport County (loan) 7 (0), 2014–2015 Blackpool 13 (0), 2015–2016 Colchester United 25 (0), 2016 Accrington Stanley 2 (0)

When Steve Bruce recalled Trevor Carson after our 2-1 defeat by Stevenage towards the end of 2010/11 season it caused then-manager Steve Tilson all sorts of problems. He'd already told many senior players they weren't going to be retained and he couldn't swallow his pride and bring talented Joe Anyon back into the side. He thought he'd solve the problem as he solved all his problems, and that was to borrow someone else's player.

The issue was that in mid-March most clubs have settled squads, young players are out on loan and they're not looking to do business. One exception to this rule was Aston Villa, who were willing to loan twentieth-choice youth keeper Elliot Parish. Tilson assumed (wrongly) that Parish would be better than Anyon so he snapped him up.

Now I'm not blaming Parish for us going down, but I will state firmly that had Carson remained with the club we would have stayed up. Had Anyon been chosen in goal we would have stayed up. If we'd put an outfield player in goal and hoped for the best, we might have stood a chance. Instead we exposed young Parish to what I assume is the worst couple of months of his life.

The kid was out of his depth and he wasn't protected by defence that was weaker than a house built of straw. In nine outings, he conceded 23 goals including six against Rotherham, four against Gillingham and three in that final day defeat by Aldershot. It may be history clouding my memory but I can't recall him making a single save. He was out of his depth, and as he drowned he took our club down with him.

Since Parish has gone on to make a decent league career, and with game experience has come a degree of consistency. However irrespective of what he achieves between now and the day he retires he will always be the keeper who seemed to lube up his gloves before taking to the field.

Parkinson, Steve
(1991-1994)
Forward 2 (4) Apps 0 Goals
Born 27 August 1974
1991 Horncastle Town, 1991-1994 Imps, 1993 Witton Albion (loan), 1994 Kings Lynn (loan)

Horncastle lad Parkinson signed first as a YTS and latterly as a pro for City, but always found his chances limited. Made his full debut in 2-1 defeat against Halifax and went on to make six appearances for City without scoring a goal. Played his last game against Gillingham in 1994 before being released.

Patulea, Adrian
(2008-2009)
Forward 19 (14) Apps 11 Goals
Born 10th November 1984
2004–2005 FCM Târgoviște 10 (3), 2005–2008 Petrolul Ploiești 23 (5), 2006–2007 Astra Ploiești (loan) 12 (0), 2007–2008, Al Hamriya (loan) 0 (0), 2008–2009 Imps, 2009–2011, Leyton Orient 22 (1), 2010 Hayes & Yeading United (loan) 8 (3), 2011 Hereford United 6 (0), 2011–2012 Farul Constanța 27 (15), 2012–2013 CSMS Iași 29 (6), 2013–2014 Vaslui 23 (1), 2014–2015 Academica Argeș 14 (7), 2015–2016 Farul Constanța 29 (22), 2016 Pafos FC 0 (0)

Patulea had arrived at Lincoln to request a trial with Peter Jackson which the typically bullish Jackson had refused. Patulea took to running around the training pitch with his wife on his back in order to try and create an impression, and he was granted a chance. He spent six weeks training with the first team squad and finally convinced Jackson to sign him in addition to his Magnificent Seven. Unfortunately, his arrival turned them into the Hateful Eight.

He scored a second-half hat-trick against Lincoln United in a friendly to announce himself on the Sincil Bank stage and the internet was alight with his name. He instantly seemed to have won the hearts of Lincoln supporters who clamoured for him to sign. It eventually became apparent that Patulea's former club, Petrolul Ploiești, still held his playing registration and that had scuppered a move to non-league Burgess Hill a few weeks before.

City eventually managed to negotiate a deal for him and he signed for the club on 29th August 2008. His international clearance documents did not come through in time for him to play in the derby with Grimsby Town, but he scored his first League goal on his debut for Lincoln City, coming off the bench to score a goal in the Imps' 2–0 win over Barnet.

He started his first game of the season away at Brentford, taking just 30 minutes to notch his second goal in a City shirt. He went on to score eleven times from just 19 starts for Lincoln. His all action displays won him many fans, but there always seemed to be an under current between him and Jackson. The media loved them both, but Jackson perhaps felt only one of them should love the media back, and Peter Jackson did love the media.

The season unsurprisingly ended with a manager versus player argument. Adrian Patulea couldn't get a run in the first team despite being the only player looking capable of scoring goals. He claimed he hadn't been offered a new deal and Jackson claimed he had. As the season drew to a close there was no middle ground and the popular striker left for Leyton Orient. Jackson only last a few months more before being dismissed himself.

Peacock, Richard
(1999-2001)
Midfielder 49 (27) apps 7 Goals
Born 29th October 1972
1992-1993 Sheffield FC, 1993-1999 Hull City 174 (21), 1999-2001 Imps, 2001-2002 Stalybridge Celtic 30 (5), 2002 Chester City 7 (0), 2002-2004 Worksop Town, 2004-2005 Buxton, 2005-2006 Lincoln United

Half decent midfielder who suffered from playing in an increasingly bad Lincoln team. Had two seasons with us, both of which we spent fighting against relegation from the Football League. We finished 15th and 18th with Peacock in the side, and despite him grabbing a few goals he wasn't able to have a significant enough impact to really carry the team forward.

He made his City debut in a strong opening day win over Rotherham, but then played eight games before experiencing another win as we suffered a stop/start season under John Reames. He later played under Phil Stant, but when Alan Buckley took over his days were numbered. Left at the end of the 2000/01 to drop down to the non-league scene with Stalybridge Celtic.

Pearce, Allan
(2002-2004)
Forward 9 (12) Apps 1 Goal
Born 7th April 1983
2002 Barnsley 0 (0), 2002 Worksop Town (loan), 2002–2004 Imps, 2004 Bradford Park Avenue, 2004–2005 Waitakere United (6), 2006 Worksop Town, 2006 Waitakere United 83 (42)

Young forward who was one of Keith Alexander's lesser known signings. Pearce was a future New Zealand international, but his time at Lincoln was defined by endless appearances from the subs bench, and whenever he did get a chance he often seemed to be out of his depth.

He scored once for Lincoln as we ran out 3-0 winners at home to Hartlepool in 2003, and he was an unused sub as we went down 5-2 in the play-off final. Despite a friendly goal against Kevin Keegan's Man City he wasn't able to secure a first team spot and he left at the end of the 2003/04 season.

Pearce, Ian
(2009-2010)
Defender 8 (7) Apps 0 Goals
Born 7th May 1974
1990–1993 Chelsea 4 (0), 1993–1997 Blackburn Rovers 63 (2), 1997–2004 West Ham United 142 (9), 2004–2008 Fulham 57 (1), 2008 Southampton (loan) 1 (0), 2008–2009 Oxted & District, 2009 Kingstonian, 2009–2010 Imps, 2011–2012 Kingstonian 2 (0), 2012 Lingfield

Pearce had a good career playing in the top flight of the English game, featuring for West Ham and Blackburn, which is where he met Chris Sutton. He came to Lincoln at the very tail end of his career as Sutton's assistant, but he also registered as a player to help our survival fight.

He was certainly willing to fight for the cause after being sent off as an unused sub during a mass brawl on the touchline of our November 2009 clash with Cheltenham Town. Alongside Sutton he helped keep us in League Two, but left when Sutton did shortly after the next season started.

Pearson, Greg
(2004)
Forward 1 (2) Apps 1 Goal
Born 3rd April 1985
2004–2005 West Ham United 0 (0), 2004 Barnet (loan) 10 (1), 2004 Imps (loan), 2004–2005 Canvey Island (loan) 5 (2), 2005–2006 Rushden & Diamonds 29 (1), 2006 Hucknall Town (loan) 4 (2), 2006–2008 Bishops Stortford 66 (42), 2008–2012 Burton Albion 128 (37), 2011–2012 Aldershot Town (loan) 5 (0), 2012 Crewe Alexandra (loan) 9 (3), 2012–2013 Grimsby Town 12 (2), 2013 Kidderminster Harriers (loan) 6 (1), 2013–2014 Nuneaton Town 13 (0), 2013 Hednesford Town (loan) 7 (2), 2014–2015 Brackley Town 9 (1), 2015 Bishop's Stortford 7 (3), 2015 Halesowen Town, 2015 Hinckley AFC 3 (3)

Forward signed on a short-term loan by Keith Alexander in 2004. Started his first game for Lincoln, a 3-2 defeat at Scunthorpe but then dropped to the bench. Came on to score a last-minute consolation as we went down 2-1 at home to Notts County, and then got 8 minutes away at Bristol Rovers before returning to West Ham.

Had a couple of prolific seasons at Bishop Stortford and averaged one in four for Burton Albion, and was rumoured to be linked with the Imps later in his career, but never added to his tally of one start and one goal in a City shirt.

Pearson, Matthew
(2012)
Midfielder 2 (0) Apps 0 Goals
Born 3rd August 1993
2011–2012 Blackburn Rovers 0 (0), 2012 Imps (loan), 2012–2013 Rochdale 9 (0), 2013 FC Halifax Town (loan) 17 (0), 2013–2015 FC Halifax Town 84 (5), 2015 Accrington Stanley 61 (4)

Midfielder who played just two matches for City, both of them in the FA Trophy as we drew 0-0 with Carshalton at home and then went down 3-1 away. He was recalled by his parent club immediately after the Carshalton match.

He had a couple of good seasons at Halifax once he left Blackburn, earning an England C call up in 2013. He was a member of the Halifax team that humiliated Lincoln 5-1 in the 2013/14 season. Eventually earned a deal with Accrington in League Two, and in 2016/17 his 120th minute goal knocked Premier League side Burnley out of the League Cup.

Peat, Nathan
(2004-2004)
Defender 8 (5) Apps 0 Goals
Born 19th September 1982
1999–2005 Hull City 2 (0), 2003–2004 Cambridge United (loan) 6 (0), 2004–2005 Imps (loan), 2005–2007 York City 48 (2), 2007–2009 Harrogate Town 59 (7), 2009–2011 Gainsborough Trinity, 2011–2015 North Ferriby United 128 (1), 2015 Scarborough Athletic 0 (0)

No nonsense full back brought in on loan from Hull City in 2004. Made his debut from the bench in the fine 3-1 Carling Cup win against Derby County, but never managed to break into the first team. Despite being a left back he was often utilised as a left sided midfielder, and he made his final City appearance as an 81st minute sub for Gary Taylor Fletcher in the December 2004 bore draw with Cheltenham. Latterly featured heavily for North Ferriby after spells at Harrogate Town and York City.

Pembleton, Martin
(2008-2009)
Midfielder 4 (2) Apps 0 Goals
Born 1st June 1990
2008–2009 Imps, 2009 Lincoln United, 2009–2010 Winterton Rangers, 2010–2011 Bottesford Town, 2011–2012, Buxton, 2012–2013 Goole, 2013 Bottesford Town

Slightly-built Pembleton joined the Centre of Excellence at Lincoln City as a nine-year-old and progressed through the system. He started a two-year apprenticeship at the beginning of the 2006-2007 season, and eventually made his first team debut on 24th March 2008, at home to Hereford United in the 2–1 win.

Iffy Onuora was a fan of the young midfielder, speaking after the youngster's first start he said; "He's got a good attitude, a good engine and is confident in his ability, and he didn't look out of place. It's easy to see we have some excellent prospects here at the club but at the moment they are very much in their early stages of learning."

In April 2008 Pembleton, alongside Gary King, was offered a one-year professional contract. He failed to make a first team appearance as a professional being restricted to just six appearances as an unused substitute and in March 2009 he joined Lincoln United on loan. He was released at the end of the season.

Perkins, Chris
(2001)
Midfielder 11 (1) Apps 1 Goals
Born 9th January 1974
1992–1994 Mansfield Town 8 (0), 1994–1999 Chesterfield 147 (3), 1999–2000 Hartlepool United 8 (0), 1999 Chesterfield (loan) 8 (0), 1999–2000 Chesterfield (loan) 23 (0), 2000–2001 Chesterfield 8 (0), 2001 Imps, 2002 Stalybridge Celtic, 2003 Lancaster City, 2004 Rossendale United, 2005 Chorley

Midfielder who signed short term deal under Phil Stant. Retained his place after Stant was dismissed and played in Alan Buckley's first two games in charge, wins at Mansfield (3-2) and Kidderminster (2-1). Scored once for City, a 90th minute consolation as we went down 3-2 at home to Orient. Left at the end of the season and drifted onto the non-league scene.

Perry, Jason
(1998)
Defender 13 (2) Apps 0 Goals
Born 2nd April 1970
1987–1997 Cardiff City 281 (5), 1997–1998 Bristol Rovers 25 (0), 1998 Imps, 1998–2001 Hull City 15 (0), 2001–2003 Newport County 30 (0), 2003–2005 Cwmbran Town 55 (3)

Former Welsh international who played most of his football for Cardiff City. Joined City in the summer of 1998 and played 15 times in Division Two for us before dropping down to Division Three with Hull City. Never made his mark and was past his best when he came to Sincil Bank.

Perry is now a Lecturer and the director of football at Bridgend College. He also works for the BBC as both a columnist and commentator covering Cardiff City and the Wales national team

Perry, Kyle
(2011-2012)
Forward 14 (12) Apps 3 Goals
Born 5th March 1986
2004–2006 AFC Telford United 68 (32), 2005 Sutton Coldfield Town (loan) 4 (2), 2007 Hednesford Town 1 (0), 2007 Willenhall Town (26), 2007–2008 Chasetown 11 (6), 2008–2009 Port Vale 31 (0), 2009 Northwich Victoria (loan) 7 (2), 2009–2010 Mansfield Town 40 (9), 2010–2011 Tamworth 40 (17), 2011–2012 Imps, 2012 AFC Telford United (loan) 19 (1), 2012–2013 Nuneaton Town 12 (0), 2012 Hereford United (loan) 8 (0), 2013 Tamworth (loan) 12 (0), 2013–2015 Altrincham 84 (18), 2015–2016 Hednesford Town 28 (7), 2016 Worcester City 8 (1), 2016 Stafford Rangers

Kyle Perry was a (very) poor man's Matt Rhead, big and burly but without the minimum requirement of application. His Imps career started well enough with a debut goal away at Southport, but after that he simply never got going. Scored just twice more, both of them coming in a match at his old club Telford. Never made an impact up until Steve Tilson left and was used sparingly as a sub after that by David Holdsworth.

Eventually he was allowed to join Telford on loan, and ludicrously nobody thought to put a clause in the deal to stop him playing against Lincoln. He scored in the return match at Sincil Bank and subsequently never played for Lincoln again.

Perry was a typical non-league centre forward who had nothing much to offer other than a physical presence, and even that he struggled to use to his advantage.

Pettinger, Paul
(2001-2003)
Goalkeeper 5 Apps 0 Goals
Born 1st October 1975

1992–1996 Leeds United 0 (0), 1994 Kettering Town (loan), 1994–1995 Torquay United (loan) 3 (0), 1995 Halifax Town (loan) 7 (0), 1995 Rotherham United (loan) 1 (0), 1996 Gillingham 0 (0), 1996– 1997 Carlisle United 0 (0), 1997–2001 Rotherham United 16 (0), 2001–2003 Imps, 2002 Kettering Town (loan) 12 (0), 2002–03 Telford United (loan) 3 (0), 2003 Gainsborough Trinity[3] 14 (0), 2003– 2004 Kettering Town[4] 26 (0), 2004 Hucknall Town[4] 16 (0), 2004–2005 Harrogate Town[5] 41 (0), 2005–2007 Stalybridge Celtic 68 (0), 2007 Worksop Town 11 (0), 2007–2008 Ilkeston Town 27 (0), 2008 Frickley Athletic 0 (0), 2008 Belper Town, 2008–2009 Matlock Town 7 (0), 2010 Sheffield F.C. 1 (0)

Signed to provide competition for Alan Marriott ahead of the 2001 season and managed three outings at the beginning of the year before being dislodged by Mazza. Spent the next two years not playing, appearing just twice more in the Football League Trophy before leaving to tour the non-league scene.

Phillips, David
(1999-2000)
Midfielder 16 (3) Apps 0 Goals
Born 29th July 1963
1981–1984 Plymouth Argyle 73 (15), 1984–1986 Manchester City 81 (13), 1986–1989 Coventry City 100 (8), 1989–1993 Norwich City 152 (18), 1993–1997 Nottingham Forest 126 (5), 1997–1999 Huddersfield Town 52 (3), 1999–2000 Imps, 2000–2001 Stevenage Borough 19 (1)

Former Welsh international who had a strong career in the top flight. Dropped down to play for City at the tail end of his career and it showed. Played just a handful of times in a season blighted by injury and never showed anything of the ability he'd clearly had at one time in his career. After City he continued the downward trajectory.

In 2000 Deranged Ferret probably summed up Dave Phillips much more succinctly than I have the inclination to try and do; "At least we have a yardstick to measure how poor (I've changed that from an expletive) player he is. He supported Bridgend Rugby Football Club as a boy and this may explain why does nothing but kick the ball into touch or over the crossbar. It doesn't explain his inability to tackle though".

Philpott, Lee
(1998-2000)
Midfield 36 (21) Apps 3 Goals
Born 21st February 1970
1986–1989 Peterborough United 7 (0), 1989–1992 Cambridge United 178 (23), 1992–1996 Leicester City 91 (3), 1996–1998 Blackpool 82 (6), 1998–2000 Imps, 2000–2003 Hull City 60 (2), 2003–2004 Weymouth 75 (5), 2004–2007 Harrogate Town 82 (2), 2007–2008 Hinckley United 10 (1)

Skilful and one-time pacey wide man who spent two years at Lincoln around the turn of the century. Played for most of our only season in Division Two without finding the net, but managed three the following season as we finished mid table in the bottom tier.

Philpott had clearly had the best of his football early in his career at Cambridge and Leicester, but nonetheless he was a talented wide man who struggled to impose himself in the third tier, but did markedly better the year after. Upon completion of his contract he defected to Hull City.

Lee founded LPM Football Agents Limited in May 2008 and heads a team of agents based across the UK.

Pinkney, Grant
(2000-2002)
Midfielder 0 (1) Apps 0 Goals
Born 31st January 1983
2000-2002 Imps, 2002 Evesham

Former trainee who made just one brief appearance for City in the 4-0 FA Cup 1st round match with Bracknell Town in 2001. That equates to just four minutes of football, or half the time it took me to research and write this entry. I've now spent more time writing about Grant Pinkney's Lincoln City playing career than he spent actually playing in it.

Platnaeur, Nicky
(1994-1996)
Defender 30 (1) Apps 0 Goals
Born 10th June 1961
1982–1983 Bristol Rovers 24 (7), 1983–1984 Coventry City 46 (6), 1984–1986 Birmingham City 28 (2), 1986 Reading (loan) 7 (0), 1986–1989 Cardiff City 115 (6), 1989–1991 Notts County 57 (1), 1991 Port Vale (loan) 14 (0), 1991–1993 Leicester City 35 (0), 1993 Scunthorpe United 14 (2), 1993–1994 Mansfield Town 25 (0), 1994–1996 Imps, 1997–1998 Hinckley United 51 (2)

Another ageing veteran who rocked up at Sincil Bank in the twilight of his career (see Dave Phillips, Steve Foley, Trevor Hebberd, Ian Hamilton) but unlike most Platnaeur wasn't actually that bad. Signed by Keith Alexander in 1993/94 he settled in at left back after overcoming an injury early in his City career. He was injured again in a 1-1 draw at Sincil Bank with Carlisle under Sam Ellis, and never fought his way back into the side. Made one more appearance on the opening day of the 1995/96 season against Preston.

Platt, Conal
(2011-2013)
Forward 17 (1) Apps 2 Goals
Born 14th October 1986
2004–2005 Liverpool 0 (0), 2006–2007 Bournemouth 0 (0), 2006 Morecambe (loan) 3 (0), 2007 Weymouth (loan) 11 (0), 2007–2008 Weymouth 20 (2), 2008 Rushden & Diamonds (loan) 10 (0), 2008–2010 Forest Green Rovers 80 (10), 2010–2012 Cambridge United 33 (2), 2011 AFC Telford United (loan) 3 (0), 2011 Imps (loan), 2012–2013 Imps, 2013 Gainsborough Trinity 9 (0), 2013–2014 Stalybridge Celtic 22 (3)

Lively forward who signed permanently from Cambridge United after a successful loan spell under David Holdsworth. Was unlucky to break his leg in February 2012 in a behind closed doors friendly with Doncaster Rovers. By the time he had recovered he was playing under Gary Simpson, and despite one more outing against Southport he was released, Simpson claiming that as the club were in a relegation battle he couldn't accommodate Platt's recovery.

Pollitt, Mike
(1992, 1992-1994)
Goalkeeper 68 Apps 0 Goals
Born 29th February 1972

1990–1991 Manchester United 0 (0), 1990 Oldham Athletic (loan) 0 (0), 1991 Macclesfield Town (loan) 1 (0), 1991–1992 Bury 0 (0), 1992 Imps (loan), 1992 Altrincham (loan) 5 (0), 1992–1994 Imps, 1994–1995 Darlington 55 (0), 1995–1998 Notts County 10 (0), 1997 Oldham Athletic (loan) 16 (0), 1997–1998 Gillingham (loan) 6 (0), 1998 Brentford (loan) 5 (0), 1998 Sunderland (loan) 0 (0), 1998 Sunderland 0 (0), 1998–2000 Rotherham United 94 (0), 2000–2001 Chesterfield 46 (0), 2001–2005 Rotherham United 175 (0), 2005–2014 Wigan Athletic 36 (0), 2006 Ipswich Town (loan) 1 (0), 2007 Burnley (loan) 4 (0), 2013 Barnsley (loan) 2 (0)

Keeper who only just scrapes into the book after leaving at the start of the 1994/95 season. Featured regularly under both Steve Thompson and Keith Alexander, but was never what could be regarded as a 'safe' pair of hands. Famed for having a punch up outside Ritzy in October of 1992 and playing against Barnet with a black eye.

He was transfer listed by Sam Ellis and quickly moved to Darlington before spending the rest of career hopping from club to club. Established himself as Rotherham's number one in two spells and surprisingly eventually kept goal in the Premier League for Wigan Athletic.

Poppleton, David
(1999-1999)
Midfielder 5 (2) Apps 0 Goals
Born 19th December 1979
1998-1999 Everton, 1999 Imps (loan)

Young midfielder signed on loan from Everton in time for our League Cup game against Barnsley at Sincil Bank. He played seven times for City but never ended up on the winning side and returned to Everton after his loan spell. Never cracked professional football, and after a spell away from the game he joined Armthorpe Welfare as a coach.

Injury robbed him of any chance of gaining a permanent contract, which was unfortunate given that his competition for places was with the likes of Dave Phillips and Richard Peacock In his short spell at City he turned in some excellent performances. He now runs a property management company and is a Sheffield Wednesday season ticket holder.

Power, Alan
(2011- Current)
Midfielder 187 (23) Apps 28 Goals
Born 23rd January 1988
2006–2008 Nottingham Forest 0 (0), 2007–2008 Grays Athletic (loan) 6 (2), 2008–2010 Hartlepool United 6 (0), 2010–2011 Rushden & Diamonds 41 (3), 2011 Imps

200 plus appearances, a bulk of them as club captain. One constant during perpetual times of upheaval and instability. A cultured and dedicated footballer consigned to showcase his talents to an unappreciative crowd. These are the things that stand out for me when talking about Alan Power.

The 2016/17 season hasn't been kind on our club captain. He joined from Rushden and Diamonds in our first season out of the Football League, and he's been here ever since. He's had to battle away in teams that featured players like Gomez Dali or Todd Jordan. He's had to fight alongside players lacking heart such as Sean Newton or Jon Nolan. He's become frustrated at times, and isn't averse to turning in a bad performance or two. It would be a crying shame if the Lincoln City spell of this composed footballer is defined by the weakness of the players that have played alongside him.

After so many seasons as one of the first names on the team sheet Power has found himself fighting for his life in 2016/17. He was not only dropped and restricted to the last five minutes of some matches, but our recruitment policy looked directed towards finding his replacement. Luke Waterfall took his armband, and Elliott Whitehouse seemingly came in to take his first team spot. Alan Power looked to be finished.

135 minutes of football later and those doubting him have a clear indication of the work ethic and resilience of this great servant to the club. Despite being frozen out he remained sharp and ready, and Lee Beevers awful injury gave him a chance to shine against Boreham Wood. He came on and had a superb game, followed up by another good outing at Chester. Is it enough to convince the managers of his worth? Or is he destined to be remember in the same vein as Scott Kerr, just a workman-like midfielder who got so many games due to the awfulness of his team mates? Only history will tell us.

Preece, David
(2012-2013, 2013-2016)
Goalkeeper 8 (1) Apps 1 Goal
1994–1997 Sunderland 0 (0), 1997–1999 Darlington 106 (0), 1999–2005 Aberdeen 83 (0), 2005–2008 Silkeborg IF 74 (0), 2008–2009 OB 0 (0), 2009–2012 Barnsley 7 (0), 2012–2013 Imps, 2013 Keflavík (loan) 0 (0), 2013 Keflavík 9 (0), 2013–2016 Imps

Experienced keeper Preece could have had a strong career had injury not dogged his time at Sunderland. He went on to perform well for Darlington and Aberdeen before signing for Lincoln as a back up to Paul Farman under David Holdsworth.

He played a handful of times for City and proved himself as an influential and experienced voice during a time of turmoil. He joined Keflavik to gain fitness for the English season, and returned to Lincoln firstly as a player and latterly as a key member of Chris Moyses coaching staff. Paul Farman credits him with helping to improve his game significantly.

When Moyses moved on Preece threw his hat into the ring for the manager's role, but the board let him go ahead of appointing Danny Cowley. Recently he's been earning a reputation as a respected writer having a column in the Non-League paper amongst others.

Pulis, Anthony
(2009-2010)
Midfielder 8 (0) Apps 0 Goals
Born 21st July 1984
2002–2004 Portsmouth 0 (0), 2004–2008 Stoke City 2 (0), 2004–2005 Torquay United (loan) 3 (0), 2006 Plymouth Argyle (loan) 5 (0), 2006–2007 Grimsby Town (loan) 9 (0), 2008 Bristol Rovers (loan) 1 (0), 2008–2011 Southampton 0 (0), 2009–2010 Imps (loan), 2010–2011 Stockport County (loan) 10 (1), 2011 Barnet (loan) 4 (0), 2011–2012 Aldershot Town 5 (0), 2012–2014 Orlando City 44 (4)

Another failed Chris Sutton loan signing, Anthony is the son of West Brom manager Tony Pulis. He signed on loan from Southampton to try and add steel in the midfield which he didn't do.

He started out at Portsmouth before a move to Stoke City. He never broke into the first team but spent a lot of time out on loan at the likes of Torquay, Grimsby and Plymouth. After four fruitless years at Stoke he moved to Southampton which is where he signed from when he arrived at Sincil Bank.

He never looked comfortable or able to fully adjust to the tempo of League Two football. He dropped straight into the Imps first team without making any major contribution, and it was felt perhaps he'd come for game time to get over injury. As he worked his way back to fitness he did start to look better, but there were no tears when he returned to his parent club.

After playing for us he spent time on loan at Aldershot and Stockport but never made regular first team appearances for Southampton. Upon completion of his Southampton contract he was released.

Later in his career he found regular first team football with Orlando City making 44 appearances before retiring to move into coaching which is where he is today.

Puttnam, David
(1990-1995)
Midfielder 185 (19) Apps 22 Goals
Born 3rd February 1967
1988-1989 Leicester United, 1989-1990 Leicester City, 1990 Imps (loan) 1990-1995 Imps, 1995-1997 Gillingham, 1997 Swansea, 1997 Yeovil

The year after City regained their Football League status three players joined the Club on loan from Leicester City. One was midfielder Paul Groves who went on to achieve success at Grimsby. Defender Grant Brown also signed, and he went on to establish legendary status at Sincil Bank by becoming City's record appearance holder. The final and arguably the most skilful of the trio was winger Dave Puttnam.

Dave had started his professional career with home town team Leicester City after he was spotted playing for Leicester United but had been unable to break into the first team. After a successful loan period with the Imps he signed a permanent deal a fee of £35,000. He scored away at Scunthorpe in only his second game for City and went on to play in every remaining league game of the 1989/90 season.

Due to his trickery and ability to beat players he was always favourite amongst the fans, and was named "Player of the Season" in 1992/93. However, the next two seasons were disrupted by a succession of injuries and he wasn't able to achieve his full potential. In his last full season (1994-95) he made just 11 league and cup starts, but still managed to score four goals.

He scored on the opening day of the turbulent 1995/96 season as City ran out 2-1 winners at Preston North End, but by the end of September he had been allowed to leave by Steve Wicks, moving to Gillingham.

I was personally gutted when Puttnam left. As a young fan he was exciting and brought an element of flair and skill to the Lincoln team. He scored the odd spectacular goal as well, and had it not been for injuries there's no doubt he would have made well over 250 appearances and scored more goals as well. In 2007 he was voted 54th in the Imps centenary 'legends' poll, which backs up my argument that he was (to put it simply) ace.

Raggett - Ryan

Raggett, Sean
(2016- Current)
Defender 16 Apps 2 Goals
Born 17th April 1993
2010-2016 Dover Athletic, 2016 Imps

Raggett is an extremely talented defender with real aerial ability that we snatched from Dover and (if rumour is to be believed) from under the noses of Barrow. His fee had to be settled by tribunal because (shockingly) we couldn't reach an agreement with Dover Athletic. However much we've had to pay, it isn't enough.

Sean Raggett is raw. He carries the ball a bit far at times and he's made the odd naïve mistake. However over and above all he is a very good footballer, a defender who can tackle, head and even play a little bit. I can't ignore the fact that he is here on a pit-stop, learning a bit more of the trade before he continues to make his way up to the Football League, and maybe beyond. Rumours suggest he'd been watched by Everton at the tail end of last season, and as well as Barrow there was interest from Tranmere too. Whatever the truth is, the England C international is hot property.

For now, the quietly spoken monster of a defender is an Imp, and with him in the side we look less likely to concede goals and more likely to grab one from a set piece. Whilst writing this book a Raggett goal got us back in the game against Chester (5-2) and he snatched an emotional winner away at leaders Forest Green (3-2). He can defend and attack. Double bubble.

Rayner, Simon
(2004-2007)
Goalkeeper 6 (1) apps 0 Goals
Born 8th July 1983
2001–2002 Bournemouth 0 (0), 2001–2002 Bournemouth Poppies (loan) (0), 2001 Salisbury City (loan) 1 (0), 2002–2003 Barry Town 21 (0), 2003–2004 Port Talbot Town 25 (0), 2004–2007 Imps, 2006 Alfreton Town (loan) 20 (0), 2007 Torquay United (loan) 10 (0), 2007–2008 Torquay United 13 (0), 2008–2010 Crawley Town 81 (0), 2011 Three Bridges 0 (0)

Canadian-born Rayner came to City as understudy for Alan Marriott, and stayed as his understudy without ever threatening to dislodge him from the first team.

He made his debut in a 1-1 draw with Chester in September 2004 and appeared again in the Football League Trophy a few days later. He then waited a year before another run of three games, ending with a 1-0 home defeat by Cheltenham. It was then another 12 months before he featured again, this time in a Carling Cup defeat to Scunthorpe, and again as a sub in a trophy game against Grimsby. However, the lack of first team chances resulted in him going out on loan to Torquay, before the move was made permanent at the end of the season.

Regis, Dave
(1997)
Forward 0 (1) Apps 0 Goals
Born 3rd March 1964

1990 Barnet, 1990–1991 Notts County 46 (15), 1991–1992 Plymouth Argyle 31 (4), 1992 Bournemouth (loan) 6 (2), 1992–1994 Stoke City 63 (15), 1994 Birmingham City 6 (2), 1994–1996 Southend United 38 (9), 1996–1997 Barnsley 16 (1), 1996 Peterborough United (loan) 7 (1), 1997 Notts County (loan) 10 (2), 1997 Scunthorpe United (loan) 5 (0), 1997 Leyton Orient 4 (0), 1997 Imps, 1998 Scunthorpe United 4 (2), 1998 Wivenhoe Town

London born Dave Regis is both the younger brother of Cyrille Regis and the uncle of Jason Roberts. He appeared for 11 different clubs in the Football League, making a total of 180 starts. His City career was as brief as it could be with one substitute appearance in our 5-1 defeat at Peterborough United in 1997.

Reid, Craig
(2015-2016)
Forward 2 (0), 0 Goals
17ᵗʰ December 1985

2004–2006 Coventry City 0 (0), 2006 Tamworth (loan) 2 (0), 2007–2008 Cheltenham Town 14 (0), 2008 Grays Athletic 3 (0), 2008 Newport County (loan) 10 (4), 2008–2011 Newport County 96 (58), 2011–2012 Stevenage 49 (8), 2012–2013 Aldershot Town 39 (11), 2013–2014 Southend United 6 (0), 2014 Stevenage 4 (0) 2014–2015 Kidderminster Harriers 35 (4), 2015 Brentwood Town 3 (0), 2015–2016 Imps, 2016 Gainsborough Trinity 12 (3), 2016 Gloucester City 2 (0)

Craig Read came in as emergency for cover for the departed Liam Hearn, but it was clear he wasn't the answer very quickly. He played twice, once in a 2-2 draw with Barrow which Liam Hearn was forced to sit out and again in the miserable Boxing Day defeat to Halifax. He scored a couple of times for Gainsborough Trinity after leaving Lincoln.

Remy, Ellis
(2003)
Forward 0 (2) Apps 0 Goals
Born 13th February 1984

2002–2003 Hastings United, 2003 Imps, 2003 Kettering Town (loan) 2 (1), 2003–2005 Grays Athletic 16 (2), 2004 Redbridge (loan), 2004 Redbridge, 2004–2005 Braintree Town, 2005 East Thurrock United, 2005–2006 Margate 12 (3), 2006 Bromley 9 (3), 2006 Staines Town 8 (0), 2006 Harrow Borough 1 (0), 2006 East Thurrock United, 2006–2007 Folkestone Invicta, 2007–2008 Welling United 13 (1), 2008 Heybridge Swifts 4 (0), 2008–2009 Enfield Town, 2009–2010 Bishop's Stortford, 2009–2010 Potters Bar Town (loan) 13 (8), 2010–2011 Brentwood Town, 2011 Maldon & Tiptree, 2011–2012 Aveley 19 (2), 2012 Hemel Hempstead Town 4 (1), 2012–2013 Eastbourne Borough 20 (3), 2013 Hitchin Town 7 (1), 2014 Haringey Borough 5 (0), 2014 Histon 0 (0), 2014–2015 Tilbury 3 (0)

Arrived along with Rory May as the answer to our goal scoring problems in 2003 but managed just 32 minutes on the park in a Lincoln shirt. Came on for the last 25 minutes of our 1-0 opening day defeat by Oxford that season and then came on against Stockport with seven minutes to go with the game poised 0-0. We conceded and he didn't play again. Gary Taylor Fletcher arrived a week later, Rory May dropped to the bench and Ellis Remy began his quest to play for every non-league club in the south of England.

Rhead, Matt
(2015- Current)
Forward 58 (2) Apps 32 Goals
Born 31ˢᵗ May 1984

2004 Norton United, 2004–2007 Kidsgrove Athletic, 2007–2009 Eastwood Town, 2008 Kidsgrove Athletic (loan), 2009–2010 Nantwich Town, 2009–2010 Congleton Town 20 (19), 2010–2011 Eastwood Town 37 (13), 2011–2012 Corby Town 22 (8), 2012–2015 Mansfield Town 120 (15), 2015 Imps

If opposition fans hate your centre forward, then you know he has got something about him. You don't even need opposition fans to tell you that if he averages a goal every two games either.

Matt Rhead is a monster of a centre forward. He's built like a hod-carrier and strolls around the pitch like a doorman spoiling for a fight. Teams have to double up on him, and even when he's sandwiched between two non-league defenders he's still adjudged to have fouled them. He can play a classic hold-up role, nodding and chesting the ball left and right as he sees fit.

There's got to be a catch and with Rheady it has to be fitness. It's not that he's particular unfit, but there's only ever going to be one pace a man of his size can operate at, and that is 'steady'. In 2016/17 he has upped his fitness a gear though and he resumed as he started off the last season. On fire.

The thing you don't always see immediately with Matt Rhead is that he is actually incredibly talented. He has a habit of scoring outrageous goals, from an overhead kick outside of the area to a sublime 30-yard chip on the spin. Just as recently as October 2016 he lobbed a deft and delicate effort over a packed defence and into the top corner against Chester.

He doesn't just score goals either, but he creates them. In 2015/16 there was a tendency to just 'hit the big man' and hope for the best, and whilst he had Liam Hearn at the side of him that tactic worked well. He looked isolated for large parts of the season, but still came out with 23 goals in all competitions. Would he be a one trick pony?

Imps fans might not have been able to find out. Rhead handed in a transfer request with a view to cutting down his commute from Stoke. It seemed he was destined for Barrow, but Danny Cowley waxed lyrical in the media about him, and he reciprocated. A bro-mance blossomed and before the season kicked off we got the news that was better than a new signing: Rhead was an Imp for another season.

He came back leaner, meaner but no less able to create and score goals, and every bit as keen to get into opposition faces and rile them up. He's scored three braces in wins over Woking (3-1), North Ferriby (6-1) and Torquay (2-1), and were it not for Theo Robinson's dubious goals claim he might have claimed two against Chester as well. There's no doubt the big man is on fire again, and if he keeps performing at this rate the secret of success will be finding a partner for him.

He's so good I'm going to forgive the last-minute equaliser he scored for Mansfield Town in the 2012 FA Cup that cost us a home tie with Liverpool.

Richardson, Barry
(1995-2000)
Goalkeeper 150 Apps 0 Goals
Born 5th August 1969
1988–1989 Sunderland 0 (0), 1988–1989 Seaham Red Star (loan), 1989–1991 Scarborough 30 (0), 1991 Stockport County 0 (0), 1991–1994 Northampton Town 140 (0), 1994–1995 Preston North End 34 (0), 1995–2000 Imps, 1999 Mansfield Town (loan) 8 (0), 2000 Sheffield Wednesday (loan) 0 (0), 2000–2001 Doncaster Rovers 62 (0), 2001–2003 Halifax Town 24 (0), 2003–2004 Gainsborough

Trinity, 2004–2008 Doncaster Rovers 2 (0), 2008–2009 Nottingham Forest 0 (0), 2009–2010 Cheltenham Town 0 (0), 2010–2013 Peterborough United 0 (0), 2014 Wycombe Wanderers 1 (0)

Barry Richardson became John Beck's first signing as City manager, and he made his debut alongside fellow new boy Steve Holmes in a 1-0 home defeat to Cardiff City in October 1995. He went on to play in every game for the rest of the season.

Barry was a character in the sticks, immensely popular with Imps fans but at times bordering on eccentric. With his long hair and constant antics, he often attracted both banter and abuse from away fans. The most striking possibly being Manchester City fans in the Stacey West the night we beat them 4-1 in the Coca Cola Cup. Barry, with his long hair, had to endure chants of 'where's your caravan', which he seemed to revel in. He played his part in the Club's promotion season of 1997/98, keeping 12 clean sheets from his 26 League appearances.

Barry was never far from controversy either and he will probably be remembered for his part in the infamous battle of Moss Rose in April of 1998. Barry was sent off for his part in mass 22-man brawl along with Ben Sedgemore (who later joined the Imps). The Macclesfield mascot was also escorted from the pitch amidst violent scenes. Richardson, Jason Barnett and Lee Thorpe later received misconduct charges from the FA.

Richardson would famously try and rile opposition fans as much as possible, if memory serves me correctly he had travelling Exeter fans baying for blood in 1999 with his antics and behaviour that would now be described as 'top bantz', by idiots.

He fought for the number one shirt with John Vaughan in the late 1990's, and returned from a loan spell at Mansfield to regain his jersey. However, the emergence of Alan Marriott eventually usurped them both and he joined Conference side Doncaster Rovers on a free transfer.

In 2009 he returned with Cheltenham Town to face off against Chris Sutton's Imps side, and once again showed his potential as an MMA fighter. Aaron Brown was sent off for a challenge in front of the dugouts which sparked a mass brawl, the main protagonists being City's assistant boss Ian Pearce and Richardson. Both were sent off once the ugly scenes had calmed down. Despite this many Imps fans still regard Richardson as a cult hero for both his eccentricity and his overly committed approach to scuffling.

Adam Barlow's view

Barry Richardson arrived at Lincoln City in October 1995 with the club rock bottom of the football league, on its third manager of the season, and in total disarray. Lincoln City had been leaking goals left right and centre and Richardson was John Beck's first signing; replacing the previous season's player of the year Andy Leaning. It didn't take long for Richardson to win over the fans however, as the Imps climbed away from the relegation zone as the season progressed.

The Imps at the time were very much an in your face, scrap for everything, kind of team not averse to winding up the opposition to gain an advantage and Richardson epitomised that. He wasn't the tallest of keepers yet he was 100% committed to coming off his line and dominating the box. Lincoln were also developing a crazy gang mentality with Richardson at the core of it. He was prone to the odd rush of blood and bad decision but he won Lincoln far more games than he lost.

For the next few seasons he had to battle John Vaughan for the number one position and was out of the side for periods of time. Vaughan was the polar opposite of Richardson and never seemed to command the backline or be as fired up as Barry. The Imps were losing their way a little in the promotion season of 97/98 but when Richardson returned to the side the team picked up around February and March. It was also during this season that the infamous "Battle of Macclesfield" happened when Richardson was shown a straight red (Along with future Imp Ben Sedgemore of Macclesfield) for his part in a ruckus that lead to a 22 man brawl.

The following season saw perhaps the lowest point of his Imps career as he and the side struggled for form early on; a mistake at Bristol Rovers standing out in the memory. Around Xmas with the side bottom of the league, the club brought in Bruce Grobbelaar much to the confusion of fans and anger of Richardson and Vaughan. However after two games including a humiliating 4-1 away defeat at Wycombe he was on his way and sense returned to Sincil Bank.

99-00 was Barry's last season at the club as Alan Marriot became the number one. The highpoint of the season was Barry winding up the handful of Exeter fans behind the goal as he saved a penalty in one of his final games for the club. He left the club at the end of the season and went on to play for the likes of Mansfield and Halifax before becoming a very respected goal keeping coach. As his coaching career progressed he lost none of his fire as we saw when he returned with Cheltenham town and was sent to the stands for his part in a touchline scrap with Imps assistant coach Ian Pearce during Chris Sutton's time in the hot seat. I for one hope that one day he returns to the club as goalkeeper coach. Life would never be dull.

Richardson, Marcus
(2003, 2003, 2004-2005)
Forward 45 (12) Apps 14 Goals
Born 31ˢᵗ August 1977
1999–2000 Slough Town, 2000–2001 Harrow Borough, 2001 Cambridge United 16 (2), 2001–2002 Torquay United 39 (8), 2002–2004 Hartlepool United 27 (5), 2003 Imps (loan), 2003 Imps (loan), 2004–2005 Imps, 2005 Rochdale 2 (0), 2005 Yeovil Town 4 (0), 2005–2006 Chester City 34 (4), 2006 Macclesfield Town 8 (3), 2006 Weymouth 0 (0), 2006–2007 Cambridge United 20 (3), 2007 Crawley Town 18 (2), 2007 Bury 1 (0), 2007–2009 Farnborough 88 (32), 2009 Henley Town, 2009–2010 Windsor & Eton, 2010–2012 Reading Town, 2012–2014 Marlow, 2014 Highmoor Ibis

Richardson was a powerful and ungainly striker who initially came in on loan from Hartlepool as an intended solution to the eternal goal scoring problem Keith Alexander always felt he was suffering from. Unlike most of the experiments though, Richardson was a decent player. He was unorthodox at times, often looking to be all arms and legs and no composure, but one thing he did do was score goals.

It took him a few matches to get going, but before the conclusion of his first loan spell he'd hit five goals in eight games, including three in consecutive matches. Hartlepool recalled him at the end of October, and Keith desperately searched for a way to bring him back in. He re-joined on loan in December before making the move permanent in January of 2004. He scored another five goals before the end of the season to give him a total of ten from 41 games.

The following season he found goals a little harder to come by, but he still offered a threat when he got a chance. A red card just ten minutes after coming on as a sub against Chester didn't help him establish a starting role, but just three games later he scored a dramatic last minute winner against Northampton which kicked off a spell of four in four games including two in a 3-1 over Yeovil.

Unfortunately, February 2005 saw him involved in a training ground incident with Ciaran Toner which immediately cost both him and Toner their places at Lincoln. The 'incident' certainly consisted of a fight, that much we do know. There was allegedly damage done to Gary Simpson's car as well, if rumours are to be believed because of Toner being knocked out across the bonnet. Whatever happened neither played for the Imps again. It was a crying shame as well because a few months later against Southend in the play-off final we desperately needed another option from the bench, but in Richardson's absence we had to settle with bringing Matt Bloomer on as we slumped to a 2-0 defeat.

In December 2005, he returned to Sincil Bank with Chester and predictably scored their consolation goal as we ran out 3-1 winners. It would be a shame if he were only remembered for that training ground bust up, but the potential cost to our promotion bid was immense.

Ridings, David
(1994)
Forward 10 Apps 0 Goals
Born 27th February 1970
1990–1993 Curzon Ashton, 1990–1991 Macclesfield Town 1 (0), 1993–1994 Halifax Town 21 (4), 1994 Imps, 1994–1995 Ashton United, 1995–1996 Crewe Alexandra 1 (0), 1995–1996 Hednesford Town (loan), 1996–2002 Leigh RMI, 2002–2003 Stalybridge Celtic, 2002–2003 Curzon Ashton

Former Halifax player who was named the Conference Player of the Month shortly before signing for £10,000 under Keith Alexander in 1994. He was brought with the intention of providing a route to goal, being both a midfield provider but also able to chip in with goals himself. Sadly he didn't produce anything like that in a Lincoln shirt, and despite his billing as one for the future he never hit any form for Lincoln at all. Made just ten appearances for the club before dropping down to play for Curzon Ashton, a level of football more suited to his ability.

Ridley, Lee
(2008)
Defender 15 Apps 0 Goals
Born 5th December 1981
2000–2007 Scunthorpe United 100 (3), 2007–2010 Cheltenham Town 61 (1), 2007–2008 Darlington (loan) 6 (0), 2008 Imps (loan), 2010–2011 Grimsby Town 39 (0), 2011–2013 Gainsborough Trinity 9 (0), 2012–2013 Worksop Town (loan) 13 (0), 2013 Grantham Town (loan) 2 (0), 2013–2014 Grantham Town 9 (0), 2014 Bottesford Town

Ridley was a full back who made his name playing for Scunthorpe over a seven-year period. Moved on to Cheltenham and it was from there Peter Jackson picked him up on loan in 2008. He had appeared for Darlington on loan as they trounced us 4-0 at home over Christmas 2007, and he impressed enough to convince Jacko he'd be worth a go in our side.

Ironically he played for Darlington against Rochdale on January 1st, then four days later was back at Spotland in a Lincoln kit playing left back as we ran out 2-1 winners. He went on to make 15 solid appearances for City, always looking composed and assured in the defence. His initial one month loan lasted until April, and he played his last game as we ran out 2-1 winners at Chester City. Latterly played for Grimsby after their relegation from the Football League.

Robertson, Jon
(1995-1998)
Defender 42 (2) Apps 1 Goal
Born 8th January 1974
1991–1995 Wigan Athletic 112 (4), 1995–1998 Imps, 1998-2002 Southport, 2002 Stalybridge Celtic, 2002–2003 Leigh RMI, 2003–2004 Lancaster City, Runcorn

Chunky defender brought to Lincoln by John Beck for £15,000 after four good years playing for Wigan Athletic. He only missed three games all season after signing and formed a good partnership with Grant Brown in the back four. However, the following season after starting the first five games he picked up an injury, and that allowed Grant in to partner new signing Kevin Austin. Robertson never really regained his place in the side. He did feature at centre half with Grant when we travelled to Colchester in November 1996 with Austin slipping in to left back. We lost 7-1 and Robertson didn't start another game until Grant picked up an injury in March 1997. He was eventually released after we gained promotion having only played three matches during that successful season.

Described by the Deranged Ferret as; "Always struggled to break into the first team given the number of central defenders at the club. When he had a brief run in the team he looked an assured player who didn't do much wrong."

Robinson, Connor
(2012-2016)
Forward 28 (45) Apps 8 Goals
Born 11th October 1994
2012-2016 Imps, 2016 North Ferriby

Former youth team player of which much was expected, but sadly it never materialised. He was given his debut by David Holdsworth in 2012 in a 1-0 home defeat by Hayes and Yeading.

Granted he played under difficult times at Lincoln, surviving Holdsworth and Gary Simpson. He looked to have some composure and pace, but often also looked lightweight and uncombative. He grabbed his first goal in August of 2012, snatching a late equaliser as we drew 1-1 away at Gateshead. He had perhaps his best season in front of goal from there scoring three more times, once a last-minute equaliser against Ebbsfleet (1-1) and another in the reverse fixture against Gateshead (1-1). Many Imps fans felt he was developing into a player who could one day be worth something to the team.

The following season he scored just once, a now-trademark last minute equaliser against Chester City. He was in and out of the team on a regular basis and never found the consistency to nail down even a permanent place on the bench. Eventually after not scoring all season in 2015/16 he was released by Danny Cowley and signed for North Ferriby, but he has since left there to pursue a career outside of the game. Conner is a likeable lad who will make a significant impact on the local non-league scene if he so desires..

Robinson, Marvin
(2005-2006)
Forward 25 (15) Apps 11 Goals
Born 11th April 1980
1998–2003 Derby County 12 (1), 2000 Stoke City (loan) 3 (1), 2002–2003 Tranmere Rovers (loan) 6 (1), 2003–2004 Chesterfield 32 (6), 2004 Notts County 2 (0), 2004 Rushden & Diamonds 2 (0), 2004–2005 Walsall 10 (4), 2005 Stockport County 3 (0), 2005–2006 Imps, 2006 Macclesfield Town 5 (0),

2006–2008 Oxford United 30 (3), 2007 Cambridge United (loan) 4 (1), 2008–2009 Kettering Town, 2008–2009 Redditch United, 2009–2010 Nantwich Town 19 (7), 2010–2012 Hednesford Town, 2012–2013 Brackley Town 35 (4), 2013 Leamington (loan), 2013 Oxford City 7 (1), 2014 Hednesford Town 55 (11)

So-called journeyman striker who I think actually did better than he is often credited for in a Lincoln shirt. He came to the club on a six-month deal amidst the exodus that followed the play-off defeat by Southend and therefore always had big boots to fill in Gary Taylor-Fletcher and Simon Yeo. He scored in just his second outing as we beat Crewe 5-1 in the Carling Cup and then notched again in the next round as we went down 5-4 to Fulham.

He had to wait until October for his first league goal, but once he'd struck he scored in three consecutive games Wycombe (1-2), Rochdale (2-1) and finally MK Dons (1-1). In January his contract was extended, and he ended the season with 11 goals from 40 matches, including a goal of the season contender away at Boston United. As Keith left the club Robinson wasn't retained and he carried on his nomadic wandering of lower league and non-league clubs.

Robinson, Steve
(2005-2006)
Midfielder 11 (1) Apps 0 Goals
Born 17th January 1975
1993–2001 Birmingham City 81 (0), 1995 Kidderminster Harriers (loan), 1996 Peterborough United (loan) 5 (0), 2001–2005 Swindon Town 161 (5), 2005–2006 Imps, 2005–2006 Worksop Town (loan), 2006–2009 Worksop Town, 2008–2009 Grantham Town (loan) 4 (0)

Midfielder nicknamed 'Turbo' by the Swindon fans for his all action displays for them. Sadly, never eclipsed that at Sincil Bank after sustaining a foot injury during his only pre-season at the club. He turned out to be more 1.2 petrol hybrid than anything slightly turbo. By the time he battled back the side looked settled and he made just eleven mediocre starts after a loan spell at Worksop. His contract wasn't renewed in the summer of 2006 and he later joined Worksop permanently.

Robinson, Theo
(2016)
Forward 4 (2) Apps 3 Goals
Born 22nd January 1989
2006–2009 Watford 2 (0), 2007 Wealdstone (loan), 2007–2008 Hereford United (loan) 43 (13), 2009 Southend United (loan) 21 (7), 2009–2011 Huddersfield Town 45 (16), 2010 Millwall (loan) 7 (2), 2011 Millwall 4 (1), 2011 Derby County (loan) 13 (2), 2011–2013 Derby County 67 (18), 2013 Huddersfield Town (loan) 6 (0), 2013–2015 Doncaster Rovers 63 (9), 2015 Scunthorpe United (loan) 8 (3), 2015–2016 Motherwell 10 (0), 2016 Port Vale 14 (2), 2016 Imps

Robinson is a well-travelled striker who should just be hitting a peak in his career, but instead finds himself playing at the lowest level he's ever played at. He has a reputation built on pace and direct, attacking football, and his short-term deal came as a surprise to many who couldn't understand why the one-time Jamaican international has to stoop as low as the National League for a deal.

He's scored a couple since he's been with us and his all-round play looks good. His first touch has been poor at times, but he compensates for that with his non-stop running and harassing of opposition defenders. He hasn't perhaps looked as sharp as you'd expect a 27-year old former Championship forward to be, and he's been guilty of spuring a couple of really good chances.

I'm sure he's here to stake a claim for a deal with a league club, and if he is best of luck to him. He has the work rate and the pace to be a handful even if he doesn't regain the killer touch. The best we can hope for is he starts scoring goals (not claiming everyone else's) and helps us win a few points before he departs.

Robson, Paul
(2012)
Defender 28 (2) Apps 0 Goals
Born 4th August 1983
2001–2003 Charlton Athletic 0 (0), 2004–2005 Bridlington Town 3 (1), 2005–2007 Long Island Rough Riders 46 (1), 2008–2011 Crystal Palace Baltimore 63 (1), 2011 Newport County 7 (0), 2012 Imps, 2012-2013 North Ferriby United 51 (1), 2013-2014 Scarborough Athletic F.C. 71 (1)

I've said before good players can suffer from playing in poor teams, but Paul Robson's list of former clubs doesn't suggest he was overly talented. His performances in a weak City side weren't always strong and committed either. He signed for David Holdsworth and made his debut in the 0-0 home draw with Carshalton Athletic in the FA Trophy. Over the course of the next six months he did sufficiently well to earn a new deal, but (like with most players of that era) he fell out of favour the following season.

He suffered an injury in mid-September which kept him out for a while, and eventually he left the club after our 4-2 defeat by his former side Newport. David Holdsworth left soon after, and nowadays Robson turns out for Scarborough Athletic.

In a recent debate on the internet forum Lincoln City Banter a couple of fans had Robson down as their worst ever player. I assume they never saw Drewe Broughton play, but it does give you a firm idea of the impact Robson had.

Rocastle, Craig
(2004)
Midfield 0 (2) Apps 0 Goals
Born 17th August 1981
2001–2003 Kingstonian 28 (0), 2003–2005 Chelsea 0 (0), 2004 Barnsley (loan) 5 (0), 2004 Imps, 2004–2005 Hibernian (loan) 13 (0), 2005–2006 Sheffield Wednesday 28 (1), 2006 Yeovil Town (loan) 8 (0), 2006–2007 Oldham Athletic 35 (2), 2007–2008 Port Vale 23 (1), 2008 Gillingham (loan) 2 (0), 2008–2009 Thrasyvoulos 14 (0), 2009 Welling United 2 (0), 2009 Dover Athletic 2 (0), 2009–2010 Forest Green Rovers 15 (0), 2010–2011 Sporting Kansas City 29 (0), 2012 Thrasyvoulos 15 (0), 2012 Missouri Comets (indoor) 7 (0)

Craig Rocastle was a cousin of the late David Rocastle and he signed to bolster our push for a play-off spot in late 2004. His opportunities were limited to two substitute appearances in a 1-1 home draw with Kidderminster and a 3-0 win at Spotland, Rochdale. Upon expiry of his loan he returned to Chelsea and ended up spending the next season in the Scottish top flight with Hibernian. We never got to see what he could do but he had a decent career as a cultured, ball-winning midfielder.

Rodney, Nialle
(2012)
Forward 2 (4) Apps 0 Goals
Born 28th February 1991

2009–2011 Nottingham Forest 3 (0), 2010 Ilkeston (loan) 9 (1), 2011 Burton Albion (loan) 3 (0), 2011–2012 Bradford City 5 (0), 2011 Darlington (loan) 1 (0), 2011 Mansfield Town (loan) 2 (0), 2012 Imps, 2013 AFC Telford United 3 (0), 2013–2014 Hartlepool United 12 (0)

Unremarkable forward brought in by David Holdsworth on loan to little or no effect at all. Never looked like making an impact in a poor Lincoln side an unsurprisingly released once his short-term deal expired. Turned up briefly at Hartlepool before drifting out of football. He now plays Sunday League football in Grantham and is the founder, head designer and co-owner of clothing company ENOS

Rowe, Danny
(2013-2014)
Forward 15 (8) Apps 3 Goals
Born 29th January 1990
2010-2013 Fleetwood, 2012 Stockport (loan), 2012-2013 Stockport (loan), 2013-2014 Imps, 2014 AFC Fylde

Danny Rowe was undoubtedly a man who had the talent to succeed, but he just never settled at Lincoln. He had spells out of the team both injured and through a loss of form, and despite showing glimpses of real quality he never performed on a consistent level. One thing he never lacked was confidence and self-assurance though, and he was one of a new breed of prolific Twitter users.

He was a Gary Simpson signing in June of 2013 and came to the club billed as a skilful forward who could also drop back into midfield. He scored on his Imps debut as we beat Macclesfield 1-0, but an injury a few weeks later picked up against Luton Town ruled him out for a couple of months. Upon his return, he struggled to break into the side, and notched just two more goals in a City shirt, a last-minute winner against Salisbury away (2-1) and a 31st minute winner away at Wrexham (1-0). He wasn't retained and later joined AFC Fylde where he is currently scoring for fun, bagging five hat tricks so far in the 2016/17 season.

Russell, Simon
(2011-2012)
Midfielder 20 (10) Apps 1 Goal
Born 19th March 1985
2002–2004 Hull City 1 (0), 2004–2008 Kidderminster Harriers 134 (14), 2008–2010 York City 24 (0), 2009 Tamworth (loan) 11 (0), 2010 Cambridge United (loan) 15 (0), 2010–2011 Cambridge United 31 (6), 2011–2012 Imps, 2012–2013 Alfreton Town 15 (0), 2013–2016 Gainsborough Trinity 125 (26), 2016 North Ferriby United 1 (0)

Russell was a wide player brought in by Steve Tilson for our first year in the Blue Square Premier league. He'd been player of the season for Cambridge the year before as well as having several solid seasons at Kidderminster Harriers. Initially he looked lively, impressing in a pre-season Lincolnshire Cup match against Scunthorpe United.

He scored just one goal for Lincoln in a 3-0 win over Ebbsfleet shortly after David Holdsworth took over as manager. However, he never showed the form that had caused Cambridge fans to vote him as their player of the year and he made his last appearance in March 2012 as we slipped to a 2-1 defeat at Mansfield Town. After a spell at Gainsborough he's back in our league in the 2016/17 season with struggling North Ferriby.

Ryan, Ollie
(2004-2008)
Forward 10 (29) Apps 0 Goals
Born 26th September 1985
2004–2008 Imps, 2004–2005 Spalding United (loan), 2005–2006 Ilkeston Town (loan) 5 (0), 2007–2008 Hucknall Town 4 (1), 2007–2008 Bourne Town 1 (1), 2008–2009 Boston United, 2009–2010 Harrogate Town, 2010 Belper Town (loan), 2010–2011 Northwich Victoria, 2011–2012 Frickley Athletic, 2012 Scarborough Athletic, 2013 Staveley Miners Welfare

Ollie Ryan impressed then-manager Keith Alexander whilst serving his scholarship, and at the end of his second year he was named Lincoln's Young Player of the Season. He made his debut, as a substitute, in the 3–0 FA Cup defeat at Hartlepool United in November of 2004. His Football league debut came just a week later in the 3–0 away victory over Darlington. By the end of his scholarship, Ryan had made six league appearances for the Imps, all from the substitutes bench.

Much was expected of the Boston born forward, and like Connor Robinson a few years later it seemed only a matter of time before his endeavour was rewarded with goals and a prolonged run in the first team.

His first season as a professional saw him make intermittent appearances without finding the net, a pattern repeated during his second professional season. Despite scoring regular goals for the reserve team he could not find a goal for the first-team. He was, however, given a final opportunity to impress when he agreed a new six-month contract in May 2007.

He continued to struggle to find not only a starting position but also an elusive goal in his third professional season despite scoring 119 goals in 125 appearances for the reserves. On 2nd October 2007, he made his first league start for almost two years in the 1–1 away draw with Bury. He kept his starting role for the next three league and cup games culminating in the 4–0 away defeat to MK Dons which saw Lincoln's manager John Schofield sacked. During that time he kept Jamie Forrester, Mark Stallard and Ben Wright out of the side. Ahead of the 1-1 draw with Morecambe, Schofield's penultimate game, it was a partnership of Ryan and Torpey that started with the other three strikers sat watching.

He was offered a chance to impress new manager Peter Jackson when he was handed a starting role in the game at Wycombe Wanderers in November 2008. Disastrously he was sent-off after just 27 minutes for an awful tackle on Will Antwi. From there Jackson, who to his credit did put faith in youth, seemed to prefer Lenny John-Lewis as his young up-and-coming starlet. It seemed Ryan had finally run out of chances and after four years and no senior goals it was no surprise when, in March 2008, he agreed to cancel his contract with City and join up with Hucknall Town. He scored for Hucknall on his debut. That, Alanis Morissette, *is* ironic.

Sam-Yorke - Swaibu

Sam-Yorke, Delano
(2014, 2014-2015, 2015)
Forward 34 (10) Apps 9 Goals
Born 20th January 1989
2008–2010 Woking 40 (3), 2009 Cray Wanderers (loan) 6 (1), 2010–2011 AFC Wimbledon 0 (0), 2010–2011 Basingstoke Town (loan) 24 (10), 2011–2013 Basingstoke Town 77 (30), 2013–2015 Cambridge United 33 (7), 2014 Imps (loan), 2014–2015 Imps (loan), 2015 Imps, 2015–2016 Forest Green Rovers 16 (0), 2016 Boreham Wood (loan) 16 (1), 2016 Woking 10 (3)

Like Jae Martin before him, Delano Sam-Yorke was a player who impressed immensely during a loan spell, but then faltered once he signed a permanent deal. His arrival on-loan from Cambridge was seen as a bit of a coup, and in his first spell he hit three goas in nine games. His all-round play looked very good as well, and the club were eager to see him make a return.

He went back to Cambridge and scored twice in a 2-1 aggregate win over Halifax to secure a play-off place. He then played in the final as they regained their league status. With promotion came a lack of opportunities and he re-joined City on loan the following season after playing three times for Cambridge.

He scored just twice in eleven games, the second goal coming in the 3-3 draw with Forest Green that cost Gary Simpson his job. A further three goals (and a red card) in four games prompted new manager Chris Moyses to make his loan move permanent as we chased a possible play-off place. Unfortunately, with the comfort of a full-time deal came a spell of indifference, and just one goal followed through to the end of the season, as well as another red card. Chris Moyses had seen enough and he was allowed to join Forest Green at the end of the season. Since then he's struggled for goals and fitness both there, and at his latest club, Woking.

Sandwith, Kevin
(2004-2005)
Defender 40 (5) Apps 2 Goals
Born 30th April 1978
1995–1999 Carlisle United 3 (0), 1999–2001 Telford United 38 (1), 2001–2002 Doncaster Rovers 12 (0), 2002–2004 Halifax Town 51 (2), 2004–2005 Imps, 2005–2006 Macclesfield Town 35 (3), 2006–2008 Chester City 54 (3), 2008–2009 Weymouth 30 (0), 2009–2010 Oxford United 32 (3), 2010–2011 Mansfield Town 24 (1), 2011–2012 Gainsborough Trinity 25 (1), 2012– 2013 Buxton 0 (0), 2014 AFC Wulfrunians 1 (0)

Sandwith joined City in March 2004 for the sum of £10,000. He'd previously scored for Halifax as the non-league side knocked us out of the LDV Vans Trophy. A series of impressive displays over the next few months convinced Keith Alexander he could be the answer to our left back issue.

For a season, he was the answer. Sandwith looked assured and competent at full back and made the step up to the Football League with relative ease. He played just three times after his move, with loan player Kevin Ellison being preferred at left back. Once Ellison left the club, Sandwith made the shirt his own.

He made 42 appearances that season including both legs of the play-off semi-final and the final itself. He didn't always offer the same level of attacking option as perhaps Ellison had, and he wasn't quite as combative as Stuart Bimson but he was a good solid full back who seemed to improve as the season wore on. He scored twice, once as we went down 3-2 to Wycombe at Sincil Bank and once in a 3-0 win over Kidderminster.

Surprisingly at the end of the season he opted to join Macclesfield Town instead of remain with the Imps, a move which ensured he would be roundly booed whenever he returned to Sincil Bank. Went on to play for both Chester City and Oxford United, getting booed for both.

In January of 2016 Sandwith, now operating as a Sports Coach was the subject of a bankruptcy order in Telford County Court.

Saunders, Matthew
(2010) 18 (1) Apps 3 Goals
Midfielder
Born 21th September 1989
2009–2011 Fulham 0 (0), 2010 Imps (loan), 2012–2014Dagenham & Redbridge 41 (4), 2014Whitehawk 1 (0), 2014 Dover Athletic 1 (0), 2014–2015 Hemel Hempstead Town 10 (0), 2015 Aldershot Town 8 (0), 2016 Hemel Hempstead Town 1 (0)

Matthew Saunders was a midfielder signed on loan at the same time as the lacklustre Michael Uwezu and the much-maligned Joe Anderson from Fulham. Of the three Saunders was undoubtedly the pick of the bunch.

He made his debut in the 4-0 FA Cup defeat against Bolton and then made two more first team appearances before returning to Fulham. However, Chris Sutton had seen enough to convince him the cultured midfielder had something to offer and he brought him back for the remainder of the season. It was a good call, and one of the few decisions Sutton made that I agreed with.

His second loan spell was far more productive bringing three goals from 18 outings. I liked Saunders as he had a lovely dead ball strike and unlike some of the other loan players he worked really hard for the club. It was hoped we'd bag him on a free transfer once the season ended like we did with Adam Watts and Joe Anderson.

He returned to Fulham where he was apparently highly rated, although not highly enough to earn another deal and he found himself released as we slipped out of the Football League. With Sutton long gone he didn't feature on Steve Tilson's radar and ended up signing for Dagenham and Redbridge.

Just 18 days in to his Dagenham spell, his goal was the decider in a match against Bradford causing manager John Still to enthuse on his ability and potential. That potential was never realised after suffering an ankle injury and in 2014 he left Dagenham by mutual consent to move to Whitehawk of Brighton. Remember them? I prefer not to.

Since then he's done the rounds of southern non-league clubs such as Dover and Aldershot as well as having a spell out in India. Curiously his first game for Aldershot was a 3-0 thumping at Sincil Bank in a game remembered for another Charlee Adams strike.

It's widely thought that his injury curtailed what could have been a promising career and he currently plays for Hemel Hempstead Town.

Schofield, John
(1988-1994, 2000-2001)
Midfielder 273 (20) Apps 16 Goals
Born 16th May 1965
1988 Gainsborough Trinity, 1988–1994 Imps, 1994–1997 Doncaster Rovers 110 (12), 1997–1999
Mansfield Town 86 (0), 1999–2000 Hull City 25 (0) 2000–2001 Imps

John Schofield plied his trade in the non-League scene before joining City from Gainsborough Trinity in November 1988. It was Colin Murphy who brought John to Sincil Bank shortly after promotion from the GMVC for a fee of £10,000. He enjoyed a superb debut as the Imps defeated Burnley 4-1 at Turf Moor, who at the time were top of the league.

He was always a hardworking and combative midfielder, and became a regular feature in City's first team. He was appointed club captain in the 1993/94 season and was later 'Player of the Season' by the Imps' supporters. Schofield earned himself 47th spot in the Imps official 'all-time top 100 legends' in 2007.

After 231 committed League appearances, he departed Sincil Bank in November 1994 for Doncaster Rovers. Moves to Mansfield Town (86 apps) and Hull City (19 apps) followed before a return to Sincil Bank in June 2000 when he was appointed as the Club's new Head of Youth Development.

John was a born leader both on and off the pitch, and as well as playing a further 24 games for the Imps he also concentrated on the Club's youth development programme. He is a UEFA 'A' licence holder, and was appointed as first team coach prior to the start of the 2005/06 season. In 2006/07 he took over as head coach alongside John Deehan, and the club finished fifth, their highest League position for eight years.

Having signed a new contract to officially become Team Manager, he suffered a poor start to the 2007/08 season. He was sacked in October 2007 after a miserable capitulation on TV at MK Dons.

Sedgemore, Ben
(2001-2004)
Midfielder 92 (26) Apps 6 Goals
Born 5th August 1975
1994 Northampton Town (loan) 1 (0), 1995-1996 Mansfield Town 9 (0), 1996 Peterborough United 17 (0), 1996-1998 Mansfield Town 62 (6), 1998-2001 Macclesfield Town 100 (6), 2001-2004 Imps, 2004-2006 Canvey Island 72 (4), 2006-2007 Cambridge United 4 (1), 2006-2007 Rushden & Diamonds 1 (0), 2006-2007 Havant & Waterlooville 23 (0), 2007-2008 Chelmsford City, 2007-2009 King's Lynn 12 (0), 2009 Boston United, 2009-2011 Stamford

Ben Sedgemore was well known to Imps fans having played a key part in the Battle of Moss Rose when playing for Macclesfield. He was sent off along with Barry Richardson for a mass brawl that broke out in the April 1998 clash between the two sides.

He joined up with Lincoln as we battled against relegation in early 2001, and he remained as we fought administration. He was one of a handful of players retained by Keith Alexander for the 2002/03 season.

Sedgemore ended up playing a crucial role as the Imps achieved a play-off spot against all odds. He was a combative and committed midfielder, not the most skilful but never found wanting desire and application. His programme articles 'Sedges Sermon' were always witty and well written as well, and he gained a reputation for being an educated man as well as a key component of the squad.

He was unfortunate that in both seasons under Keith Alexander he failed to feature in any of the play-off games due to injury. His 2002/03 season was ended in a 2-0 defeat at Bury in March, and he played his last game on the final day of the 2003/04 season against Yeovil.

He is currently on the Management Committee of the Professional Footballers' Association. Alongside his footballing career Ben also has a Degree in Psychology and Law and a Masters in Finance, Marketing and Management from Loughborough University. Like I said, an educated man.

Semple, Ryan
(2006-2008)
Forward 0 (4) Apps 0 Goals
Born 4th July 1985
2002–2006 Peterborough United 41 (3), 2003–2004 Farnborough Town (loan) 9 (2), 2006–2008 Imps, 2006–2007 Chester City (loan) 3 (0), 2007–2008 Rushden & Diamonds (loan) 4 (0), 2007–2008 Oxford United 1 (0), 2008 Brackley Town, 2008–2009 Deeping Rangers 36 (30), 2009–2010 Gainsborough Trinity, 2010–2012 Boston United 87 (9), 2012–2013 Corby Town, 2013 Bury Town, 2014 Boston United

Semple had been highly rated at Peterborough and arrived in an unofficial exchange for Simon Yeo in the summer of 2006. However, injury dogged his time at City and he was restricted to just four appearances from the bench. Played his last game in November 2006 as we went down 3-1 to Darlington. He was still around the squad when Peter Jackson took over a year later, and his contract was finally terminated in January 2008.

Sharp, Chris
(2013)
Forward 3 (0) Apps 1 Goal
Born 19th June 1986
2010-2011 TNS, 2011-2013 Telford Utd, 2013-2014 Hereford United, 2013 Imps (loan), 2014-2015 Stockport County, 2015 Colwyn Bay, 2015-2016 Salford City, 2016 Bradford Park Avenue

Sharp joined on loan from Hereford under Gary Simpson and made three starts. He scored just once as we whimpered to a 4-1 defeat at Forest Green. He kept Waide Fairhurst out of the side whilst on-loan, but went back to Hereford once his spell was finished. Failed to score at all for Hereford on his return and ultimately, as many of the short-term players we have had during our National League spell, he drifted further down the leagues towards obscurity.

Sheridan, Jake
(2011-2014)
Midfielder 47 (21) Apps 1 Goals
Born 8th July 1986
2005–2007 Notts County 30 (1), 2007–2011 Tamworth, 2011–2012 Eastwood Town, 2011–2012 Imps (loan), 2012–2014 Imps, 2013–2015 Alfreton Town 9 (0), 2015 Boston United (loan)

Sheridan was a good, honest and hardworking midfielder who built his career on effort and tenacity rather than flair and ability. He initially joined on loan from Eastwood Town and put in whole hearted, battling displays in a variety of positions as David Holdsworth looked to halt the club's slide towards relegation. The manager described him at the time as "a campaigner, although a young man with a bright future hopefully for this football club." His effort and desire won him many fans on the terraces, but similarly his limited ability often led to him being a scapegoat amongst other sections of the support. He was basically marmite, but on the wing for City.

He ended up with more red cards for Lincoln than he did goals, sent off in the Boxing Day 2013 clash with Grimsby having previously been dismissed in February 2013 against Dartford. His only Imps goal arrived as we won away at Braintree in 2014 after the departure of Holdsworth.

Recently been playing at Alfreton and suffered an horrendous leg break in October 2016 which looks to have put paid to his career.

Sherwood, Steve
(1995)
Goalkeeper 6 (1) Apps 0 Goals
Born 10th December 1953
1971–1976 Chelsea 16 (0), 1973 Millwall (loan) 1 (0), 1974 Brentford (loan) 16 (0), 1974–1975 Brentford (loan) 46 (0), 1976 Hartford Bicentennials (loan) 13 (0), 1976–1987 Watford 211 (1), 1987–1992 Grimsby Town 183 (0), 1993 Northampton Town 16 (0), 1994–1995 Imps, 1995–1997 Gateshead 64 (0), 1997–1998 Gainsborough Trinity

Well-travelled keeper best known for his spell at Watford in the mid-eighties when he made a League Cup final appearance for them. Joined City under Sam Ellis as cover for Andy Leaning and ended up making seven appearances keeping three clean sheets. His City debut came when he replaced the injured Leaning midway through a game at Wigan, it was the first time a City goalkeeper had been replaced by another goalkeeper in a Football League match.

On his arrival at Sincil Bank, manager Sam Ellis said; "Steve Sherwood has done well for us since he joined as cover for Andy Leaning on deadline day. Steve would not have expected to be thrust into the first team so quickly, but he has performed admirably in goal for us over the last couple of games."

Managed to squeeze another couple of seasons out of his career with Gateshead after leaving City in the summer of 1995.

Simmons, Alex
(2013- Current)
Forward 6 (21) Apps 2 Goals
Born 13th March 1996
2013 Imps, 2015 Boston Utd (loan), 2015-2016 Boston Utd (loan), 2016 Halifax (loan)

Simmons is a youth team player who hasn't managed to successfully hold down a spot in the side since emerging from the youth set up. He's scored twice for City, two minutes after coming on as a sub in our 3-1 defeat at Forest Green in 2015, and a last-minute goal in our 3-1 win over Boreham Wood a couple of weeks later.

He is rated by the current managers though, and the start of the 2016/17 season has been particularly fruitful for him. A spell out on loan at Halifax has yielded a glut of goals, and playing just one level below the National League will no doubt have given him valuable experience to come back to the Imps and continue his development.

I'm still waiting for another Lee Frecklington to come through the ranks, and at present Alex Simmons is the closest we have. Whether he succeeds or whether he becomes another Ollie Ryan or Connor Robinson remains to be seen.

Sinclair, Frank
(2008-2009)
Defender 22 (2) Apps 0 Goals
Born 3rd December 1971
1990–1998 Chelsea 169 (7), 1991–1992 West Bromwich Albion (loan) 6 (1), 1998–2004 Leicester City 164 (3), 2004–2007 Burnley 92 (1), 2007 Huddersfield Town (loan) 13 (0), 2007–2008 Huddersfield Town 29 (0), 2008–2009 Imps, 2009 Wycombe Wanderers (loan) 9 (0), 2009–2010 Wrexham (loan) 17 (0), 2010–2011 Wrexham 39 (0), 2011 Hendon 10 (0), 2012–2015 Colwyn Bay 66 (8), 2015 Brackley Town 13 (0)

Frank Sinclair was a vastly experienced defender who had top flight experience with Leicester and Chelsea and had even played in the 1998 World Cup for Jamaica. He came to Sincil Bank heralded as one of the 'Magnificent Seven', a claim which really came back to haunt manager Peter Jackson, and if it doesn't haunt him it bloody well should.

Sinclair wasn't magnificent for Lincoln at all, in fact he was quite the opposite. He struggled for fitness at first and then struggled for form throughout the season. He didn't last the whole campaign, joining Wycombe Wanderers on loan where he typically helped them to achieve promotion from our division. He was released upon expiry of his contract, an expensive folly and a shadow of his former self.

Sinclair, Tony
(2010-2011)
Defender 26 (1) Apps 0 Goals
Born 5th March 1985
2004–2006 Beckenham Town, 2006–2007 Maidstone United, 2006–2007 Beckenham Town, 2006–2007 Fisher Athletic, 2007–2009 Welling United, 2009–2010 Woking 42 (0), 2010–2011 Gillingham 20 (0), 2011–2012 Imps, 2012-2013 Carshalton Athletic, 2012–2013 Dulwich Hamlet, 2013-2014 Greenwich Borough, 2013-2015 Carshalton Athletic

Ineffective full-back brought in by Steve Tilson as we approached our first season out of the Football League. He could operate equally as inefficiently at centre half as well, and he made 27 absolutely un-noteworthy appearances in our inaugural season in the Blue Square Premier.

Sinclair was sent off in Steve Tilson's last match in charge, a horrific 4-0 defeat away at Tamworth. He was sent off in the 60th minute as we trailed 1-0, and if his red cad contributed to our former manager getting the boot then at least he did do something positive for the team.

David Holdsworth didn't fancy Sinclair though, he had his own ideas about trialling every useless non-league player he could think of, and as such he Sinclair didn't play for the club after our 2-0 defeat at home to York on January 7th 2012. Dark times.

Smith, Adam
(2008, 2012-2013)
Midfielder 26 (15) Apps 2 Goals
Born 20th February 1985
2001–2008 Chesterfield 66 (3), 2008 Imps (loan), 2008–2009 Gainsborough Trinity 13 (2), 2008–2009 York City (loan) 7 (2), 2009–2010 York City 37 (2), 2010–2012 Mansfield Town 43 (8), 2011 Aldershot Town (loan) 6 (0), 2011–2012 Aldershot Town (loan) 6 (0), 2012–2013 Imps, 2013–2015 FC Halifax Town 80 (4), 2015–2016 Wrexham 12 (1), 2015–2016 Guiseley (loan) 8 (0), 2016 Guiseley 8 (0), 2016 Alfreton Town 1 (2)

Smith first joined on loan in 2008 and made his debut against Rochdale helping set up the first goal in a 2–0 victory. He made a total of four appearances all as a substitute. After his debut manager Peter Jackson enthused about his new loan signing; "The majority of Lincoln fans won't have heard of him as he's played most of his football in Chesterfield's reserves but he's a big handful with a good turn of pace and he probably changed the game for us when he came on." Note the use of the word 'probably'.

He didn't continue to have that affect, and it was decided not to extend his loan upon expiry. He left the club at the same time as Ryan Semple, a similar player who had a similar effect. Very little.

Smith resurfaced in 2012 as David Holdsworth brought him back to the club on a one-year deal after managing him at Mansfield Town a year or so before. He made 34 further appearances for City scoring twice, in defeats against Forest Green (1-2) and in the FA Cup against Mansfield (1-2). He was also sent off just minutes after coming on in our 1-1 festive draw with local rivals Grimsby Town.

Smith struggled to impress and once Holdsworth left the club he played just six more games before Gary Simpson released him. Since then he's plied his trade in the National League, most recently with struggling Guiseley.

Smith, Ben
(2007-2008)
Goalkeeper 9 Apps 0 Goals
Born 5th September 1986
2006 Stockport County 0 (0), 2006–2010 Doncaster Rovers 15 (0), 2007–2008 Imps (loan) 9 (0), 2009 Morecambe (loan) 3 (0), 2010–2012 Shrewsbury Town 36 (0), 2012–2013 Rochdale 0 (0), 2013 Southport 2 (0)

Goalkeeper needlessly signed by Peter Jackson in 2007 on loan from Doncaster. Was brought in to replace fan favourite Alan Marriott and immediately went into the first team. His arrival didn't stem the flow of goals as we lost 1-0 in his opening game. Further thrashings against Darlington (4-0) and Hereford (3-1) followed as well as defeats by Bradford (2-1) and Grimsby (1-0). Once it dawned on our manager that perhaps Marriott wasn't to blame Smith was returned to Doncaster.

Ben is now a successful businessman, owning several businesses in Shrewsbury with his wife, having settled there during a playing spell.

Smith, Khano
(2009-2010)
Forward (apparently) 5 (1) Apps 0 Goals
Born 10th January 1981

2003 Carolina Dynamo 12 (4), 2003–2005 Dandy Town Hornets 28 (15), 2005–2008 New England Revolution 85 (8), 2009 New York Red Bulls 8 (0), 2009–2010 Imps, 2010 New England Revolution 15 (0), 2011 Bermuda Hogges 5 (2), 2014 Real Boston Rams 1 (0)

When the Imps signed Khano Smith from New York Red Bulls in October 2009. He came on a short-term deal having impressed the hopeless Chris Sutton during a ten-day trial. He appeared to have all the qualities the Imps were looking for. He'd played international football (for Bermuda) and had scored 15 goals in 28 games for the oddly named Dandy Town Hornets before stepping up to the MLS. In retrospect I'm wondering if the Dandy Town Hornets were a kids team he had gatecrashed.

Standing at six feet and three inches and weighing about four stone wet through he didn't look like a League Two footballer, and from the outset it was apparent he wasn't. In his five outings for Lincoln he was consistently the worst player on the pitch by a mile. The FA Cup tie with Northwich Victoria stood out as Smith wasn't just ineffective, he may as well not even have turned up. Bear in mind we won that game 3-1, essentially with ten men.

He was unsurprisingly released once his three-month trial expired and he sloped back off to America to play first for New England Revolution then the Bermuda Hogges. He never really got his career back on track after his dismal outing in England and the last we heard of him was assistant manager of Orlando Pride Women's Team.

Smith, Mark
(1993-1994)
Defender 26 (0) Apps, 1 Goal
Born 21ˢᵗ March 1960
1977–1987 Sheffield Wednesday 282 (16), 1987–1990 Plymouth Argyle 82 (6), 1990–1992 Barnsley 104 (10), 1992–1993 Notts County 5 (0), 1992 Port Vale (loan) 6 (0), 1993 Huddersfield Town (loan) 5 (0), 1993 Chesterfield (loan) 6 (1), 1993–1994 Imps

Smith was a veteran defender brought to the club by Keith Alexander for one season in 1993. He scored a crucial equaliser in a 3-3 draw with Carlisle, but found himself drifting in and out of the side. In March 1993, he was appointed player coach as Keith didn't have an assistant, and the year after he stayed on as youth team coach for manager Sam Ellis. After two years at Lincoln he moved to Notts County where he served as caretaker manager after the sacking of Colin Murphy and prior to the appointment of Sam Allardyce.

Smith, Paul Anthony
(1997-2003)
Forward 146 (38) Apps 21 Goals
Born 25ᵗʰ January 1976
1993-1997 Nottingham Forest 0 (0), 1997-2003 Imps, 2004-2006 Ilkeston Town, 2006-2007 Sheffield 1 (0)

Former Forest trainee Paul Smith was one of just a handful of players to survive the administration-led cull in 2001 and go on to enjoy play-off success of sorts under Keith Alexander. Smith would have made far more appearances for Lincoln had he not suffered from a string of injuries.

Smith was never prolific in the box and his lack of goals perhaps does a disservice to his overall contribution during some tough years. Had we not entered administration I think it would be unlikely he would have been kept on but as one of the 'cheaper options' he was retained to help balance the books. He played his part in the run up to the final against Bournemouth, scoring in the first leg at Sincil Bank. However, the 5-2 defeat in Cardiff was the last action he saw in a Lincoln shirt and he dropped down to play for Ilkeston Town.

I found it hard to write about Smith because he always frustrated me as a player. Some matches he looked every inch the limited lower league footballer, but on occasion there were glimpses of quality that were all-too rare. Perhaps it was the injuries, we'll never know but I always felt the was more to come from Paul Smith.

Smith, Paul Michael
(1987-1995)
Forward / Defender 290 (15) Apps 40 Goals
Born 9th November 1964
1982–1986 Sheffield United 36 (1), 1985–1986 Stockport County (loan) 7 (5), 1986–1987 Port Vale 44 (7), 1987–1995 Imps, 1995 Halifax Town

Without a doubt one of my all-time favourite Lincoln City players. Smith joined just after the start of our GM Vauxhall Conference season, signing for £40,000 to help push us back towards league football. Initially he arrived as a pacey wide man and striker and four goals in his first five games suggested he might just be able to do that. Eventually the goal scoring exploits were taken over by John McGinlay and Phil Brown, but aside from five games injured towards the end of March, he played every game he was eligible for as we returned to the Football League.

In 1988/89 he had another injury hit season, but once again was amongst the goals. He scored five in five games around Christmas after returning from a spell out, then wasn't seen again until mid-February. When he did return to the team he found goals harder to come by although a brace at home to York in a2-1 win proved he still knew where the back of the net was.

The following season he began appearing at full back, and that is where he eventually settled to feature under Colin Murphy, Allan Clarke, Steve Thompson, Keith Alexander, and Sam Ellis. In over 300 outings for City he proved to be a faithful and dedicated servant of the club.

It was Sam Ellis that eventually let Smith go after eight years of solid service. He had a short spell at Halifax Town, but years of struggling with injuries had taken its toll. After playing football he was rumoured to have joined the police force.

Smith, Sam
(2011-2012)
Forward 22 (7) Apps 9 Goals
Born 20th May 1990
2007-2011 Rushden & Diamonds, 2011-2012 Imps, 2012-2014 Cambridge Utd, 2013-2014 Hereford Utd (loan), 2014-2015 Telford Utd, 2015 Brackley, 2016 Woking (loan)

Smith was a part of Steve Tilson's failed revolution, heralded as the next bright young thing on his arrival. He had been highly rated at Rushden as a youth and his move to City fuelled speculation we might be in for an immediate return to the Football League. 29 minutes into his debut he scored his first Imps goal, and the future looked very rosy.

He scored just twice more in thirteen games as the Imps plummeted down the league. Steve Tilson was sacked and the very next game Smith hit a brace for caretaker Grant Brown to bring back a 3-1 victory from Alfreton Town.

Injury meant he missed the latter part of the season and therefore missed a chance to play himself into David Holdsworth's long term plans. He signed for Cambridge United but failed to really get going for them. The following season he was loaned out to Hereford, making just one appearance on his return to the U's as they lost a play-off semi-final to Halifax. Without Smith they won the other leg and the final to regain league status, and he was released. Most recently seen keeping warm in a nice coat on the bench at Bishop Stortford.

Somma, Davide
(2010)
Forward 14 Apps 9 Goals
Born 26th March 1985
2004–2005 Perugia 0 (0), 2005–2007 Pro Vasto 39 (2), 2007–2008 Olbia 15 (1), 2008–2009 San Jose Earthquakes 4 (0), 2009–2013 Leeds United 33 (12), 2009–2010 Chesterfield (loan) 3 (0), 2010 Imps

There are two types of loan players, those who don't make a difference which equates to 85% of players brought in on loan. There are then those that do, those that get remembered fondly with foggy eyed nostalgia. Davide Somma made a significant difference.

He signed on loan from Leeds and immediately earned the Imps a point against Crewe with a debut goal. After a couple of games, he really began to fire earning a draw at Dagenham (1-1) and scoring twice to earn a win away at Torquay (3-2). In effect his goals were the difference between staying up or going down.

Sutton was quick to enthuse about his new striker in his March programme notes for a clash with Northampton; "Since Davide has come in he's not just scored goals he's offering us so much more in terms of his link up play and awareness. He offers a genuine goal threat. The one thing he can do is finish but there's still parts of his game, by his own admission, he can work on and I'm confident I can help him with his game."

From the cold February through to his final day sending off against Macclesfield it really felt like 'Somma time' at Sincil Bank. Unsurprisingly fans were clamouring for him to be signed full time and despite Chris Sutton signalling his interest in the player it seemed like Leeds rated him highly and he didn't return to Sincil Bank. Their intuition was right as he scored 12 Championship goals for them the following season, but after that his progress was blighted by injury.

Somma was a player who should never have found himself playing in the basement division, he had an air of poise and class that simply wasn't at home amongst the hatchet-men and has-beens. Shortly after the World Cup of 2010 he was called up to the South Africa side for three games, scoring once.

Sparrow, Matt
(2015-2016)
Midfielder 23 (5) Apps 0 Goals
Born 3rd October 1981
1999–2010 Scunthorpe United 336 (36), 2010–2013 Brighton & Hove Albion 47 (6), 2013 Crawley Town 17 (3), 2013–2015 Scunthorpe United 35 (4), 2015 Cheltenham Town (loan) 11 (1), 2015–2016 Imps, 2016 Gainsborough Trinity 1 (0)

197

Vastly experienced midfielder brought in by Chris Moyses to be a leader on the field in the 2015/16 season. Spent the best of his years at Scunthorpe United featuring in our play-off duels of 2003 and eventually playing Championship football with them and with Brighton.

He looked a shadow of his former self at Lincoln and never imposed himself on the team. His time was punctuated by numerous bookings, eight in total from 23 starts. It was no surprising when he wasn't retained after Chris left the club, and he spent a short spell at Gainsborough before moving out to Australia as a coach.

Spencer, Scott
(2011)
Forward 2 (8) Apps 0 Goals
Born 1ˢᵗ January 1989
2006–2009 Everton 0 (0), 2008 Yeovil Town (loan) 0 (0), 2008 Macclesfield Town (loan) 3 (0), 2009 Rochdale 4 (0), 2010–2011 Southend United 17 (4), 2011 Imps, 2011–2014 Hyde 102 (50), 2014 Halifax Town (loan) 3 (2), 2014–2015 Stockport County 24 (6), 2015–2016 Hyde 2016 Stockport County

Scott Spencer was signed by Steve Tilson after being released by Southend which should tell you everything you need to know about his time at Lincoln. Despite coming through the ranks at Everton there was no indication that Spencer had what it took to score goals for Lincoln, and even when a chance was gift wrapped and placed at his feet just a few yards from goal against his old team, he still failed to capitalise. He was released as we slipped out of the league.

He managed to score a goal on his return to Sincil Bank with Hyde Utd, although he ended up losing that game 3-2. He found his level with the side from the North West and averaged a goal every two games before joining Stockport County.

Scott has found his time at Lincoln led to his career being tainted a little. He was handed a three-month suspension in February of 2016 for failing to report "an approach by a third party related to seeking to influence the outcome or conduct of a match or competition", in relation to the conviction of former Imps Delroy Facey and Moses Swaibu.

It is It is important to note Spencer was not involved in any attempt to fix matches and did not accept monies or gifts in order to do so.

Stallard, Mark
(2006-2008)
Forward 59 (13) Apps 21 Goals
Born 24ᵗʰ October 1974
1991–1996 Derby County 27 (2), 1994 Fulham (loan) 4 (3), 1996 Bradford City (loan) 1 (0), 1996–1997 Bradford City 42 (10), 1997 Preston North End (loan) 4 (1), 1997–1999 Wycombe Wanderers 73 (23), 1999–2004 Notts County 185 (66), 2004–2005 Barnsley 15 (1), 2004–2005 Chesterfield (loan) 9 (2), 2005 Notts County (loan) 16 (3), 2005–2006 Shrewsbury Town 37 (6), 2006–2008 Imps, 2008–2009 Mansfield Town 27 (8), 2009 Corby Town 0 (0)

Wherever Mark Stallard played, fans loved him. He is revered as a hero in Bradford after just 42 games and 10 goals. He was loved at Notts County after five good years and he was loved in

Wycombe for a two-year spell amongst the goals. The scene was set for him to arrive at Lincoln and fail to produce.

He didn't, he produced the goods from his very first kick. He was a typical robust, all action centre forward, possessing neat flashes of skill and an uncompromising approach to winning and keeping the ball. He was 'big and hard' as the song went, but he made sure he brought goals to the party too.

Hereford (2-1), Accrington (3-1) and former club Wycombe (3-1) all felt the force of Mark Stallard as he collected a brace in each game. He bagged two more in the 7-1 destruction of Rochdale and ended that unsuccessful play-off season with 17 in all competitions in a terrifying strike force alongside Jamie Forrester.

In his next season, he struggled to find the same form after being kept out of the first team by Steve Torpey and at one point even Ollie Ryan. Once Schofield was sacked and Peter Jackson came in he found his chances decreasing even more, often seeing Louis Dodds or Lenny John-Lewis preferred up top. A red card away at Rotherham signalled the end of Stallard's Imps career and upon completion of his contract he dropped down the Blue Square Premier with Mansfield, where it will come as no surprise to find he scored goals.

Stanley, Craig
(2015-2016)
Midfielder 26 (3) Apps 2 Goals
Born 3rd March 1983
2002–2004 Walsall 0 (0), 2003–2004 Raith Rovers (loan) 19 (1), 2004 AFC Telford United 12 (1), 2004–2006 Hereford United 81 (4), 2006–2011 Morecambe 174 (15), 2011 Torquay United (loan) 19 (1), 2011–2012 Bristol Rovers 34 (1), 2012–2014 Aldershot Town 51 (2), 2014–2015 Eastleigh 32 (5), 2015 Imps, 2016 Southport (loan) 5 (0)

Craig Stanley was a holding midfielder brought in to compliment Matt Sparrow as an experienced head in the middle of the park. He had helped Morecambe and Eastleigh to top five finishes in the National League and was seen as a cool head and a commanding voice who would help organise the side.

His Imps career was blighted by an injury sustained after the 1-0 win over Guiseley in January, and despite triggering a second years deal in the summer of 2016 it soon became apparent that Stanley wasn't fancied by the new management duo of Danny and Nicky Cowley. He was sent out on loan to Southport along with Callum Howe, but returned after Andy Bishop was sacked. His contract was terminated by agreement in September of 2016 without him featuring once for the new managers.

Stant, Phil
(1990-1991, 1996-2001)
Forward 51 (30) Apps 22 Goals
Born 13th October 1962
1982–1983 Reading 4 (2), 1986–1989 Hereford United 89 (38), 1989–1991 Notts County 22 (6), 1990 Blackpool (loan) 12 (5), 1990 Imps (loan), 1991 Huddersfield Town (loan) 5 (1), 1991 Fulham 19 (5), 1991–1993 Mansfield Town 57 (32), 1993–1995 Cardiff City 79 (34), 1993 Mansfield Town (loan) 4 (1), 1995–1997 Bury 62 (23), 1996 Northampton Town (loan) 5 (2), 1997–2001 Imps, 2001 Brighton & Hove Albion 7 (1), 2001–2002 Worcester City 15 (7), 2002 Dover Athletic 4 (0), 2002 Hayes 3 (0), 2002 Hinckley United 7 (2), 2002–2003 Gainsborough Trinity 28 (13), 2003–2004 Ilkeston Town 10 (1)

Phil Stant was as tough as a bag of nine inch nails, and he was just as likely to cause damage as well. He had a distinguished lower league career scoring goals more or less anywhere he played his football. He served in the Falklands and wrote an engaging and honest book called 'Ooh Aah Stantona' about his life as a journeyman lower league player and all round tough nut.

Initially he disappointed in a Lincoln shirt, signing in 1990 with a reputation for grabbing goals already firmly earned, yet he failed to hit the target once in seven outings. He was written off as a victim of the curse of the well-known striker at Lincoln (see Leo Fortune West & Joe Allon).

However, his work with Lincoln City wasn't done and in 1996 John Beck snapped him up to provide some ferocity and aggression to the Imps forward line. He made his second Imps debut away at Hull on Boxing Day of 1996, and scored. He scored in his next four games, including two as we beat Doncaster 3-1 in late January. Whatever 'curse' had stuck in 1990 was firmly restricted to a single month.

He wasn't just scoring robust headers and close range scrambles either. His neat little flick against Swansea at Sincil Bank was voted Goal of the Season by DF, and a stunning strike against Scunthorpe came in third.

Stant's arrival signalled the end for giant Dutchman Gijsbert Bos and the ageing target man went on to make over 80 appearances for City averaging a goal every four games, although a majority of those came in that first fruitful season. He moved behind the scenes and appeared sporadically as a substitute as we got promoted, and then relegated. When John Reames relinquished the manager's role in 2000 Phil Stant took over as manager. 30 matches later he was fired along with assistant George Foster.

Stephens, David
(2010)
Defender 3 Apps 0 Goals
Born 8th October 1991
2009–2010 Norwich City 0 (0), 2010 Lincoln City (loan) 3 (0), 2010–2012 Hibernian 23 (0), 2012–2015 Barnet 130 (2), 2015 Boreham Wood 18 (1)

Signed by Chris Sutton to shore up a leaky defence, Stephens was a product of the Norwich youth system. He made one appearance for the Canaries before coming to Sincil Bank on loan. He made just three appearances for us, two of them clean sheets against Macclesfield and Bury. Upon completion of his loan his moved to the Scottish Premier League with Hibernian, then made over 130 appearances for Barnet. Most recently seen playing for Boreham Wood in the National League.

Stergiopoulos, Marcus
(2000)
Midfielder 3 (6) Apps 1 Goal
Born 12th June 1974
1992-1995 Morwell Falcons 31 (0), 1995 Brunei, 1995-1996 Morwell Falcons 22 (1), 1996 Fawkner Blues 10 (0), 1996-1997 Morwell Falcons 24 (1), 1997-1999 Carlton Blues 53 (2), 1999-2000 Football Kingz 28 (1), 2000-2001 Imps, 2000-2001 Morwell/Gippsland Falcons 12 (0), 2001-2002 Sydney United 9 (0), 2001-2002 Northern Spirit FC 7 (0), 2002-2003 A.P.I.A. Leichhardt Tigers 25 (3), 2003-

2004 South Melbourne FC 19 (0), 2004-2005 Altona Magic 41 (5), 2006 Kingston City FC 26 (3), 2007 Oakleigh Cannons 28 (0), 2008-2010 Dandenong Thunder 44 (8), 2011 Fawkner Blues

Nine games and one goal, but what a goal it was. He had trials at Wimbledon and Notts County before coming to Lincoln, and scored a great goal in a friendly against Rotherham. The Australian midfielder of Greek descent joined City at the start of the 2000/01 season and instantly became a recognisable figure with his surfer boy haircut and his exotic sounding name. His performances didn't warrant the attention though and until the evening of September 5th 2000 he didn't look likely to make a mark on the home fans.

We'd already been beaten comprehensively in the first leg of the League Cup by Sheffield Utd by 6-1. Sterg was a 75th minute sub, but two games later he broke into the first team as we registered a 3-0 home win with Southend. Bring on the second leg against Sheff Utd, and a damage limitation exercise.

In the 58th minute of that game Sterg scored a stunning free kick to silence Blades fans travelling to Lincoln. We held out for a credible 1-0 win, and although we were out 6-2 on aggregate there were positives to take. The performance of our Australian midfielder was one.

However, he struggled to hold down a first team place and his last Imps appearance came just a month later as a late sub in a 2-1 win at home against York. He sat on the bench for the final match of his Imps career, a day that saw us lose 4-3 to Barnett after being 3-0 up inside half an hour. I assume he saw enough that day to convince him he wanted to get back over to Oz.

He forged a good playing career in his home country, retiring in 2010 and taking over as manager of Croydon City in 2013. He's now a sales and marketing manager for a sportswear firm in Australia.

Sterling, Worrell
(1996-1997)
Forward 18 (9) Apps 0 Goals
Born 8th June 1965
1983 – 1989 Watford 94 (14), 1989 – 1993 Peterborough United 193 (29), 1993 – 1996 Bristol Rovers 119 (6), 1996 – 1997 Imps

Sterling was signed by John Beck at the tail end of a good career at Watford, Peterborough and Bristol Rovers. Unfortunately, by the time he rocked up at Sincil Bank it became clear his best days were behind him. He made his debut as we slipped to a 2-1 defeat against Torquay United on the opening day of the season and he went on to be a bit part player through niggling injuries and a loss of form. He made his last appearance in a 4-0 home win over Swansea during which he was replaced by a debutant Craig Stones. After football, he went in to teaching and he presently lectures at Peterborough Regional College in Sport Studies.

Stirling, Jude
(2006)
Defender 0 (6) Apps 0 Goals
Born 29th June 1982
1999–2002 Luton Town 10 (0), 2002 Stevenage Borough (loan) 3 (0), 2002–2003 Stevenage Borough 17 (1), 2003 St Albans City (loan) 3 (0), 2003 Boreham Wood (loan) 16 (1), 2003–2004 Hornchurch 13 (1), 2004 Boreham Wood, 2004–2005 Dover Athletic 9 (1), 2005 Tamworth 5 (0), 2005 Grays Athletic

4 (1), 2005–2006 Kingsbury Town 18 (0), 2006 Oxford United 6 (0), 2006–2007 Imps, 2007 Peterborough United 16 (1), 2007–2011 Milton Keynes Dons 81 (4), 2010 Milton Keynes Dons 4 (0), 2011 Grimsby Town (loan) 6 (0), 2011 Barnet (loan) 8 (0), 2011–2012 Notts County 1 (0), 2014 Billericay Town 0 (0), 2015 Brimsdown

Unorthodox defender with a giant throw that spent just six games on loan at City in 2006. Despite his relatively short time at the club he became something of a fan favourite for his ungainly style and that long throw. His actual contribution was minimal although he only ended up on the losing side once in a Lincoln shirt.

He had a successful spell at MK Dons after leaving Lincoln as well as spending time on loan at Barnet and Grimsby. Imps fans of a certain age will remember chanting 'Juuuuuuuude' for those few minutes he did actually get on the pitch.

Stones, Craig
(1996-2000)
Midfielder 13 (13) Apps 0 Goals
Born 31st May 1980
1996–2000 Imps, 1999–2000 Grantham Town (loan), 2000–2001 Spalding United, 2000–2003 Brigg Town, 2002–2003 Gainsborough Trinity, 2002–2007 Brigg Town, 2006–2009 Sleaford Town, 2009–2010 Bottesford Town, 2010 Sleaford Town

Former youth team player who never really made the step up into the first team. He appeared sporadically over a four-year period. He made his debut as a 72nd minute substitute for Worrell Sterling as we ran out 4-0 winners over Swansea at Sincil Bank. Managed 18 outings the following season as we hunted automatic promotion, which was his most consistent spell in and around the first team. Once we went up to the next tier he found his chances limited, making just three appearances as we were relegated back to division three, and then three more the following season before being released.

Storey, Brett
(1995-1996)
Midfielder 0 (2) Apps 1 Goal
Born 7th July 1977
1995–1996 Sheffield United 0 (0), 1995–1996 Imps, 1997-1998 Matlock Town, 1998 Stalybridge Celtic, 1998 Matlock Town, 1998 Alfreton Town, 1998 Leigh RMI, 1998 Alfreton Town, 2000 Shatin SA, 2010 Staveley Miners Welfare

Midfielder who was nothing more than a squad player in the turbulent 1995-96 season. He made just two appearances in a City shirt, one a 2-1 win over Mansfield at Sincil Bank and the other a goal scoring cameo as we beat Torquay 5-0.

He disappeared from the professional game after that, but at least he'll always be able to claim he did more for Lincoln than Drewe Broughton and Kevin Gall put together. Mind you I suspect by just reading about him you've done more for Lincoln than those two.

During the latter stages of his career he spent a period of time in Hong Kong playing for Shatin SA, based in the Sha Tin district.

Swaibu, Moses
(2008-2011)
Defender 58 (5) Apps 3 Goals
Born 9th May 1989
2007–2008 Crystal Palace 0 (0), 2007–2008 Weymouth (loan) 1 (0), 2008 Bromley 15 (0), 2008–2011 Imps, 2011 Kettering Town 6 (0), 2011–2013 Bromley 59 (1), 2013 Sutton United 2 (0), 2013 Whitehawk 4 (0),

It is hard to remember Moses Swaibu the half decent defender, given his later conduct. He arrived on trial under Peter Jackson and did enough to earn himself a full-term contract, making his debut in a 1-1 draw away at Morecambe in February of 2009.

He was a tall and athletic defender who was perhaps guilty of naivety at times. He had pace though as well, and many fans had high hopes that he might turn into a gem for the club. He scored his first goal for the club on 9th February 2010 during the 2–1 defeat away at Chesterfield, with an audacious chip from 20 yards.

Having made 10 appearances that season, Swaibu was awarded the Young Player of the Year Award. The club rejected transfer bids from Birmingham and Aston Villa, and he signed a new two-year deal under Peter Jackson. He eventually left Lincoln in January 2011 by mutual consent after we were relegated from the Football League.

Whilst at Lincoln he courted controversy, firstly he was arrested on December 20th, 2010 after allegedly stealing a cooked chicken from Tesco on Wragby Road, but police did not pursue that allegation. He was then charged with stealing a newspaper from the same store just a month later.

Things didn't get better for him after he left Lincoln. In January 2014, Swaibu was charged with conspiracy to defraud, arising from an investigation into match fixing and an alleged betting syndicate. It was part of the same investigation that included former Imps Delroy Facey and Scott Spencer.

On 29 April 2015, he was found guilty at Birmingham Crown Court of conspiracy to commit bribery and jailed for sixteen months. I don't think he'll be appearing in a Lincoln City 'Hall of Legends' anytime in the near or distant future.

Taylor - Turner

Taylor, Jamie
(2011-2013)
Forward 52 (22) Apps 23 Goals
Born 16th December 1982
2000–2001 Broadbridge Heath 35 (25), 2001–2002 Horsham 39 (32), 2002–2004 Aldershot Town 32 (5), 2003 Horsham (loan) 7 (4), 2003 Carshalton Athletic (loan) 7 (1), 2004 AFC Wimbledon 25 (10), 2004–2006 Horsham 96 (73), 2006–2007 Woking 11 (1), 2007–2008 Dagenham & Redbridge 15 (2), 2008 Grays Athletic (loan) 16 (9), 2008–2009 Athletic 18 (3), 2009–2011 Eastbourne Borough 104 (35), 2011–2013 Imps, 2013–2014 Sutton United 39 (15), 2013–2014 Eastbourne Borough (loan) 5 (4), 2014–2016 Margate 34 (8) 2016 Eastbourne Borough (loan) 7 (3), 2016 Eastbourne Borough 10 (2)

Jamie Taylor came on board just after we dropped out of the Football League in 2011. The previous year he'd done well at Eastbourne, and it was supposed he would be the 'little man' to Kyle Perry or Sam Smith.

He didn't have the best of starts at the club, scoring just once before April 2012. Injuries didn't help, nor did Steve Tilson leaving and David Holdsworth joining the club. By the time we lost 4-0 to Stockport on the 7th of April he'd sat out games in favour of Jefferson Louis, Richard Pacquette, Mark McAmmon and Francis Laurent. He was thrown on for the next match against Darlington, we won 5-0 and he scored. He did the same in the next two games against Fleetwood (2-2) and Ebbsfleet (3-2).

The next season the tricky forward really came into his own, scoring on the opening day against Kidderminster and not looking back. He terrorised opposition defences, at one point scoring eight times in just ten games. He thrived playing alongside Vadaine Oliver in particular, and together they looked a decent partnership, enough to carry some of the other misfits of the time. He still suffered from the odd niggling injury, but ended the season as top scorer with 15 goals from 45 matches, a respectable goal every three games.

At the end of his contract he opted to move back down south closer to his family, signing for Sutton and more recently having a good spell back at Eastbourne.

Taylor, John
(1996)
Forward 5 Apps 2 Goals
Born 24th October 1964
1982 Colchester United 0 (0), 1982–1988 Sudbury Town, 1988–1992 Cambridge United 160 (46), 1992–1994 Bristol Rovers 95 (44), 1994–1995 Bradford City 36 (11), 1995–1997 Luton Town 37 (3), 1996 Imps (loan), 1996 Colchester United (loan) 8 (5), 1997–2004 Cambridge United 172 (40), 2004 Northampton Town 8 (1), 2004–2005 Dagenham & Redbridge 5 (1)

John Beck brought the striker in on loan and he truly fitted the Beck mould. He'd played under the controversial manager at Cambridge United and enjoyed notable success, plus he was a big lump. Beck wanted to land big balls on the big strikers' head.

He scored on his Imps debut as we ran out 2-0 winners at Cardiff, replacing Gjisbert Bos in the team. He retained his place, when fit, for the duration of his loan spell. He scored once more as we drew 1-

1 with Scarborough before he went back to Luton Town. He joined Colchester United where just a month later he scored twice as they hammered us 7-1 at Layer Road. Cheers John.

Taylor-Fletcher, Gary
(2003-2005)
Forward 89 (4) Apps 31 Goals
Born 4th June 1981
1999–2001 Northwich Victoria 43 (11), 2001 Hull City (loan) 5 (0), 2001–2003 Leyton Orient 21 (1), 2001–2002 Grays Athletic (loan) 4 (3), 2002 Dagenham & Redbridge (loan) 3 (1), 2002–2003 Dagenham & Redbridge (loan) 5 (0), 2003–2005 Imps, 2005–2007 Huddersfield Town 82 (21), 2007–2013 Blackpool 215 (36), 2013–2015 Leicester City 21 (3), 2014 Sheffield Wednesday (loan) 4 (0), 2015 Millwall (loan) 10 (0), 2015–2016 Tranmere Rovers 21 (2), 2016 Accrington Stanley

Every so often a player comes along who can be described as a 'real footballer', someone who stands out from his peers in possession of a natural ability. One such player was Gary Taylor-Fletcher.

GTF came from Leyton Orient early in Keith Alexanders second reign as manager. There was little doubt his arrival was funded by our 2003 play-off final appearance, but even so he'd experienced a stuttering career. Keith knew him from his time at Northwich, but a move to Leyton Orient which followed had turned sour. After trialling Ellis Remy and Rory May it became clear that we needed a better option up front, and in August 2003 we got the striker we always craved. We didn't know it at the time of course, at the time it was just another potential solution to the striking problem.

It took him just three games to register his first goal as we went down 2-1 at Gigg Lane, but it became apparent very quickly that this wasn't just another ten-game wonder rocking up at the Bank. He was quick but had a footballing brain that often belied his status as a League Two player. Anyone who watched him play in the first season would have predicted he go on to play top flight football. We went to Leyton Orient and in a virtuoso display he scored a superb brace to give us a 2-1 win. As we romped to the play-off semi-finals against Huddersfield he hit 19 goals, and in truth I think that 2004/05 team was the finest I've ever seen in Lincoln City shirts.

The following season he started with a bang, netting in the first five consecutive games which equalled a club record. Injuries curtailed that run and he eventually went on to score a handful more through the season as we looked like genuine title contenders. His performances culminated in a 2-0 March win on Sky TV against Scunthorpe which really put us into the automatic promotion frame. However, a further six league games without a goal, and the semi-final and final goal-less as well cost us our best chance of promotion under Keith Alexander, and rumours in Cardiff suggested he'd already agreed a pre-contract with Huddersfield. Either way his contract wasn't renewed and sure enough he moved to West Yorkshire.

He's gone on to have a good career at Huddersfield and particularly Blackpool whom he helped fire to Premier League football. He appeared for future champions Leicester as well as they first marched onto the Premier League scene, but since then his fall has been dramatic, in 2014/15 playing top flight football and in 2015/16 playing fifth tier. He's now at Accrington Stanley in League Two.

Many people will argue that in terms of technical ability and flair GTF is the best player we've seen since 1993/94 which is the period of time this book covers. I'll always put forward an argument for Peter Gain, but GTF came with a real goal threat. For me at times he seemed to lack a bit of fight, for a player of his talents to go seven or eight games without a goal in League Two was criminal, and he wasn't carrying the side by any means, we had a great team in the period he played for us. His later career is testament to his skill, but I'll always feel we could have seen more of him on the biggest stage we played at, those play-off semi-finals and final.

Tempest, Greg
(2015-2016)
Midfielder 17 (4) Apps 0 Goals
Born 28th December 1993
2012–2015 Notts County 16 (0), 2012 Ilkeston (loan) 5 (0), 2014–2015 Boston United (loan) 14 (1), 2015–2016 Imps, 2016 Nuneaton Town

Honest and hard-working midfielder brought in by Chris Moyses after a spell at Boston United. It took him a while to break into the team but when he did he always managed to put in committed if not limited displays. Became a cult hero because of his unkempt curly hair, prompting all his team mates to wear comedy wigs for the team photoshoot.

He broke into the side and as the season progressed he looked better and better. However once Danny Cowley took over as manager Tempest's days were numbered, and he dropped down to Nuneaton in the National League North which is where he currently plies his trade.

Thomas, Jordan
(2011-2014)
Midfielder 0 (2) Apps 0 Goals
Born 8th August 1995
2011-2014 Imps

Youngster who only made two substitute appearances for City, both in our first season in the National League. Grant Brown gave him five minutes of a 1-1 draw with Mansfield shortly after Tilson was sacked, and then David Holdsworth sent him on as we drew 0-0 with Carshalton in the FA Trophy. Didn't feature again and left at the end of the 2013-2014 season.

Thompson, Curtis
(2011-2012)
Midfielder 0 (1) Apps 0 Goals
Born 2nd September 1993
2011 Notts County 56 (2), 2011–2012 Imps (loan), 2012–2013 Ilkeston (loan) 6 (0)

Thompson played just two minutes of our 2-0 defeat away at Cambridge United in October of 2011. He was drafted in by caretaker manager Grant Brown, but David Holdsworth opted to terminate his loan almost immediately on his arrival as manager. Has gone on to make over 50 appearances for Notts County, which is an awful lot more league football than most of David Holdsworth's own loan players have made.

Thompson, Tyrone
(2002, 2011-2012)
Midfielder 31 (1) Apps 1 Goal
Born 8th May 1982

2000–2003 Sheffield United 1 (0), 2002 Imps (loan), 2003 Doncaster Rovers (loan) 1 (0), 2003–2004 Huddersfield Town 2 (0), 2004–2005 Scarborough 43 (2), 2005–2007 Halifax Town 79 (1), 2007–2008 Crawley Town 44 (4),2008–2010 Torquay United 47 (1), 2010–2011 Mansfield Town 18 (1), 2011 Grimsby Town 3 (1), 2011 FC Halifax Town 3 (0), 2011–2012 Imps, 2012–2013 Sheffield 7 (0), 2013 Gainsborough Trinity 10 (0), 2014 Goole AFC

Thompson made his Sheffield United debut in a 6-1 over the Imps in 2000, and it was with City he played his next competitive games. He joined on loan in 2002 in Keith's first season back in charge. He had three starts including the 4-3 LDV Vans win over York City. His loan wasn't extended and that could have been it for his Imps career.

His travels took him to Mansfield in 2010 and it was there he crossed paths with David Holdsworth, so when Holdsworth came to Lincoln it was almost inevitable he sign players he knew from his 'little black contact book'. Like Adam Smith he contacted Thompson and brought him in to assist our battle for survival. Holdsworth said of Thompson; "He was formerly with me at Mansfield and is certainly an able man with a very good pedigree at this level and a higher standard."

He played for us for six months from January 2012 to the end of the season. It wasn't a great time to be a Lincoln fan, but I thought Thompson brought some steel and organisation to a midfield often left in disarray due to the high turnover of average players. Six months was probably the longest we ever hoped to keep a player for in that time and Thompson at least brought some consistency to the starting eleven. He chipped in with a goal too as we drew 3-3 with Braintree at Sincil Bank.

He left at the end of the season to follow Curtis Woodhouse to Sheffield FC, and then later followed him to Goole as well.

Thompson, Reece
(2012)
Forward 0 (1) Apps 0 Goals
Born 11th November 1993
2012 Imps, 2012–2014 Retford United, 2014–2015 Frickley Athletic 26 (9), 2015–2016 York City 14 (3), 2016 North Ferriby United

Reece Thompson was a former YTS player for City given his one and only chance by Tinkerman Holdsworth as we slipped out of the FA Trophy to Carshalton. He left for Retford eventually climbing into league football with York City via Frickley Athletic. His single goal away at Gateshead in September 2016 earned North Ferriby their third win of the season.

Thomson, Jake
(2012)
Midfielder 3 Apps 0 Goals
Born 12th May 1989
2008–2010 Southampton 14 (0), 2009 Bournemouth (loan) 6 (1), 2009–2010 Torquay United (loan) 15 (1), 2010–2011 Exeter City 16 (0), 2011 Cheltenham Town (loan) 5 (1), 2011 Kettering Town (loan) 4 (0), 2011–2012 Forest Green Rovers 28 (0), 2012–2013 Newport County 22 (0), 2012 Imps (loan), 2013 Salisbury City 6 (0), 2014 A.F.C. Portchester 0 (0)

You'd be forgiven for thinking you can't quite place Jake Thomson. He joined on loan from Newport, played in two defeats and a draw before going back to Wales. I couldn't remember him either, but he played in the same starting XI with such heavyweights as Paul Turnbull, Scott Garner and Jake Sheridan. If you ever need a barometer of how far we've come, I urge you to try and remember who Jake Thomson is.

Thorpe, Lee
(1997-2002)
Forward 211 (11) Apps 67 Goals
14th December 1975
1994–1997 Blackpool 12 (0), 1995 Bangor (loan) 3 (1), 1997–2002 Imps, 2002–2004 Leyton Orient 55 (12), 2004 Grimsby Town (loan) 6 (0), 2004–2005 Bristol Rovers 35 (4), 2005–2006 Swansea City 18 (3), 2005 Peterborough United (loan) 6 (0), 2006 Torquay United (loan) 10 (3), 2006–2007 Torquay United 41 (8), 2007–2008 Brentford 19 (4), 2008–2009 Rochdale 32 (6), 2009–2010 Darlington 8 (0), 2010–2011 Fleetwood Town 28 (3), 2011 AFC Fylde 13 (7)

Robust striker Lee Thorpe joined the Imps just prior to the start of the 1997/98 season. He was a classic 'John Beck' centre forward, strong and never one to shy away from a fight. He went on to become a semi-prolific player for City. He was the Imps top scorer in all competitions in each of his five seasons at Sincil Bank.

Thorpe had a unique style that combined good old fashioned centre forward play with outright thuggery. He was definitely a player you wanted on your side rather than up against you, and all-too often he found himself at the centre of confrontations. However, mixed in with that aggression was a decent centre forward, and in May 2000 he was named the first Player of the Year of the new millennium.

Whatever people thought about Thorpe, he did score crucial goals. In his first season he netted 14, not only in the final game to seal automatic promotion, but also goals that gave us victories over Cardiff (1-0), Brighton (1-0) and Exeter City (2-1). The following season he scored twice at Meadow Lane to give us a 3-2 win over Notts County, and then found his shooting boots with just a handful of games to go. He scored six in five games to give us a fighting chance at survival, although we were ultimately relegated. In 2000 there was a famous 90th minute equaliser against Peterborough which helped carve his name into Imps folklore. If you needed a crucial goal he had the capability to get it, but if you wanted a scrap then he could provide hat as well.

He may have been amongst the goals for City, but he was often amongst the cards as well. He was sent off four times during his Lincoln career, two of these dismissals came in successive games in October 2001 leading to a seven-match suspension.

Despite his poor disciplinary record, he was still one of the key members of the City squad during our brief foray into the third tier, and in the seasons afterwards. Our dire financial situation in May 2002 meant cut-backs, and it saw Thorpe move to Leyton Orient on a free transfer to save costs, on the same day that the Club went into administration. Keith Alexander stated eighteen months later that he would have loved to have kept Thorpe at the club for the first play-off season, but it was purely a financial decision.

Not only did Thorpe do well scoring goals for City, but he also enjoyed scoring against us. He netted against the Imps whilst playing for Leyton Orient, Bristol Rovers and Darlington. It was his goal that prompted the sacking of Peter Jackson in September 2009, so even seven years after leaving the club he was still doing us a service.

Tomlinson, Ben
(2013-2015)
Forward 80 (7) Apps 32 Goals
Born 11th October 1989
2008–2011 Worksop Town, 2011–2012 Macclesfield Town 25 (6), 2012–2013 Alfreton Town 39 (11), 2013–2015 Imps, 2015 Barnet 4 (0), 2015 Grimsby Town (loan) 7 (0), 2015–2016 Tranmere Rovers (loan) 10 (0), 2016 Barrow (loan) 14 (4)

From one robust and often over-committed striker to another. Tomlinson signed for Gary Simpson after a fruitful spell at Alfreton Town, and whatever people may say about him he always gave his all in a City shirt. He signed for an 'undisclosed four figure fee' which rumours say was close to £9000. It represented good business for the club as Tomlinson proved to be quite adept at scoring goals.

He scored 18 in his first full season for Lincoln, and like Lee Thorpe also managed to pick up a red card. He often seemed in competition with himself to get more cards than goals, but thankfully for City the goals won out, although 13 yellows and a red made it close!

Manager Gary Simpson always recognised that Tomlinson was going to attract attention from the men in black; "Tomo will pick up bookings due to the way he plays and you can't take that away from him – at the end of the day you can't change him and I don't want to change him."

The following season he hit another 14 goals as Gary Simpson got the sack and Chris Moyses took over. Tomlinson began to represent (for many fan) everything that had been wrong with the Simpson reign. He was often accused of being arrogant and hard to work with. I don't agree, even when forced to play out on the left I thought he was committed to the cause. That said, I didn't have to work with him.

He left at the end of the season to pursue a career in league football, but sadly it hasn't worked out as well as he might have hoped. Loan spells with Tranmere, Barrow and (much to the ire of Imps fans) Grimsby followed. He was unable to convince any of them he was worth a shout permanently, and so far, in the 2016/17 season he has five Barnet appearances to his name, and the obligatory yellow card.

Toner, Ciaran
(2004-2005)
Midfielder 11 (6) Apps 2 Goals
Born 30th June 1981
2000–2002 Tottenham Hotspur 0 (0), 2001–2002 Peterborough United (loan) 6 (0), 2002 Bristol Rovers (loan) 6 (0), 2002–2004 Leyton Orient 52 (2), 2004–2005 Lincoln City 15 (2), 2005 Cambridge United (loan) 8 (0), 2005–2008 Grimsby Town 94 (14), 2008–2010 Rochdale 50 (1), 2010–2011 Harrogate Town 32 (2), 2011–2012 Guiseley 44 (6), 2013–2015 Gainsborough Trinity 52 (9)

Toner was an accomplished and composed midfielder who added real value to the squad when he signed in August 2004. It took him some time to settle in, but goals against Grimsby in a 4-2 win and then a week later against Mansfield in a 2-0 win certainly helped. It appeared at that stage he would go on the cement a place in the first team, especially as he gave a solid performance in his next outing against Oxford in which we won 3-0.

Unfortunately for all connected with the club he was involved in a training ground incident with giant striker Marcus Richardson that allegedly resulted in a Ciaran Toner shaped dent in the bonnet of Gary

Simpson's car. Both players were immediately made available for transfer, and Toner spent the rest of the season on loan at relegated Cambridge United.

Torpey, Steve
(2007-2008)
Forward 8 (6) Apps 0 Goals
Born 8th December 1970
1989–1990 Millwall 7 (0), 1990–1993 Bradford City 96 (22), 1993–1997 Swansea City 162 (44), 1997–2000 Bristol City 70 (13), 1998 Notts County (loan) 6 (1), 2000–2007 Scunthorpe United 239 (61), 2007–2008 Imps, 2007–2008 Farsley Celtic (loan) 6 (1), 2008 Farsley Celtic 18 (2), 2008 North Ferriby United 15 (2), 2009 York City 2 (0), 2010–2011 York City 0 (0)

There was a time Steve Torpey scored goals. That time was not at Sincil Bank, and Torpey will only ever be remembered as a symbol of 'when it all started to go wrong'.

After five failed play-off attempts trust was placed in Steve Torpey to come in and score the goals to push us towards a sixth. Not only did he fail to score, he failed to ever look like scoring. In fact, he did absolutely nothing at all in a Lincoln shirt.

When the board and manager should have been strengthening as Keith did in 2004, they faltered and we got the cheap option, a man who had once been a goal scorer, but by the time he 'graced' our pitch he didn't even look like a footballer.

John Schofield got the sack and after just two more starts his Imps career was over. Peter Jackson didn't fancy the aging striker and he was replaced by Ben Wright. He went on for another few years which in my opinion was flogging a dead horse. He's now coaching at York City.

Torres, Sergio
(2009-2010)
Midfielder 8 (1) Apps 2 Goals
Born 8th November 1993
2002–2004 Club Atletico Banfield 14 (1), 2004 Molesey, 2004–2005 Basingstoke Town 69 (10), 2005–2008 Wycombe Wanderers 86 (6), 2008–2010 Peterborough United 24 (1), 2009–2010 Imps (loan), 2010–2014 Crawley Town 122 (7), 2014 Whitehawk 84 (4)

Talented and tricky midfielder of Argentine descent brought in on loan immediately after the dismissal of Peter Jackson. He could have a claim on being the only South American player to represent City, but he actually holds an Italian passport courtesy of his grandmother. Whatever.

He made an immediate impact for Chris Sutton, scoring as we beat Aldershot 1-0. His signing was immensely popular with the fans who felt a player of his skill would be a great addition to the side, and if we could afford him permanently it would be a signal of our intent.

He scored again as we beat Telford in the FA Cup but returned to Peterborough once his time was up. He was rumoured to be a target in the 2010-11 close season but he opted to move to Crawley in the Blue Square Premier. His choice was vindicated as he scored six times and they were promoted as champions that season as we slipped out of the Football League.

Townsend, Nick
(2014, 2014-2015)
Goalkeeper 31 Apps 0 Goals
Born 1st November 1994
2013–2015 Birmingham City 0 (0), 2013 Oxford City (loan) 9 (0), 2014 Imps (loan), 2014–Imps (loan), 2015 Barnsley (loan) 0 (0), 2015 Barnsley

Townsend was a popular keeper who arrived on loan as cover for the injured Paul Farman in 2014. He was initially recommended by fellow Birmingham youngster Charlee Adams who was enjoying a loan spell with us. He went straight into the starting eleven for the home match against Kidderminster Harriers and kept a clean sheet. In his second performance, a 1–1 draw with Chester, he earned himself a spot in the Non-League Paper's Team of the Week. When Paul Farman returned from fitness he couldn't get back in the team. At the end of the season he returned to Birmingham.

The following season he was contracted to Birmingham, but still had a trial with Mansfield Town that came to nothing. Townsend reportedly told Birmingham that if he had to play at Conference level again, he would prefer to return to City, a move which made him very popular with the fans.

He signed a season-long loan with City, and according to Gary Simpson was being brought in as first choice keeper. He dropped straight into the team, and kept his place for the first 17 matches of the season. However, Townsend was cup tied, and City had to recall Farman from his exodus at Boston United to play. Farman came back and had a blinder, and Townsend found himself on the bench. By January 2015, he had made no more appearances, so Birmingham recalled him.

Turnbull, Paul
(2013)
Midfielder 14 (1) Apps 0 Goals
Born 23rd January 1989
2005–2011 Stockport County 128 (7), 2008 Altrincham (loan) 6 (0), 2011–2013 Northampton Town 14 (0), 2012 Stockport County (loan) 26 (2), 2013 Imps (loan), 2013–2016 Macclesfield Town 94 (11), 2016 Barrow

Experienced midfielder who spent four months on loan at Sincil Bank at the end of the 2012/13 season. Initially came to the club under David Holdsworth, but played much of his football for Gary Simpson as we battled to find a way out of the relegation battle.

Helped push us up the table and played his last game in the 5-1 final day victory at Hyde which secured our National League status. Has since played his football at the same level for Macclesfield and most recently Barrow joining up with former manager Gary Simpson.

Turner, Sam
(2010-2011)
Midfield 0 (2) Apps 0 Goals
Born 30th August 1993
2010–2011 Imps, 2011–2013 Lincoln Moorlands Railway, 2013 Ånge IF

Lincoln born former youth player Turner made just two appearances for City, both from the subs bench. He replaced Albert Jarrett in the 89th minute of a 2-1 win against Macclesfield, and then Mustapha Carayol in the 86th minute of a 2-0 defeat at Shrewsbury. There ended to Lincoln City career of Sam Turner. He still probably contributed more that season than Drewe Broughton.

Uwezu - Yussuf

Uwezu, Michael
(2010)
Forward 0 (3) Apps 0 Goals
Born 12th December 1990
2009–2010 Fulham 0 (0), 2010 Lincoln City (loan) 2 (0), 2010–2011 Northampton Town 4 (1), 2011–
2012 Forest Green Rovers 25 (2), 2014 Thamesmead Town, 2016 FC Linköping City 10 (7)

Nigerian-born Uwezu started his career with Arsenal's academy but switched early on to West London side Fulham, where he earned his first professional contract.

On January 1st 2010 he signed on a month's loan with City along with Matt Saunders. His first appearance came in the 4-0 FA Cup defeat at Premiership side Bolton as a substitute for Lenny John-Lewis, an odd choice given his lack of football prior to that. It seemed especially harsh on Jamie Clarke whose goals had fired us to the third round as he was omitted from the squad.

Uwezu made two further appearances from the bench before returning to his parent club Fulham having made no impact at Sincil Bank. Uwezu suffered from being one of the many experiments Chris Sutton conducted with our club. He didn't have time to adjust to the rigours of lower league football and a month on loan from a Premiership academy simply wasn't enough to adjust to the hustle and bustle of League Two football. He played consistently for Fulham reserves but didn't make a senior appearance, and upon release a trial at Carlisle came to nothing.

Uwezu did feature for Forest Green in 2011/12 making 25 appearances and scoring just twice. After a brief spell at Thamesmead in the lower reaches of non-league he earned himself a move to Swedish second division side FC Linkoping City, which he chose (according to made up rumours) because of its close spelling to Lincoln City.

Vaughan, John
(1996-1999)
Goalkeeper 77 Apps 0 Goals
Born 26th June 1964
1982–1986 West Ham United 0 (0), 1985 Charlton Athletic 6 (0), 1985 Bristol Rovers 6 (0), 1985
Wrexham 4 (0), 1986 Bristol City 2 (0), 1986–1988 Fulham 44 (0), 1988 Bristol City 3 (0), 1988–1993
Cambridge United 178 (0), 1993–1994 Charlton Athletic 6 (0), 1994–1996 Preston North End 66 (0),
1996 Imps, 2000 Colchester United 5 (0), 1997 Colchester United 6 (0), 1999 Chesterfield 3 (0)

A John Beck favourite who followed the controversial manager from Cambridge to Preston and then from Preston to City. Outlasted his mentor at City and appeared in goal for virtually all of our Second Division season, and again as we sunk into the third. Never disgraced himself and proved to be an able and experienced head. Eventually replaced after Torquay hit us for five at Plainmoor in September 1999, stepping back up to the Second Division with Colchester.

Waite, Tyrell
(2014-2015)
Forward 2 (4) Apps 0 Goals
Born 1st July 1994

2011–2012 Ilkeston, 2012–2015 Notts County 9 (1), 2012–2013 Nuneaton Town (loan) 4 (0), 2013–2014 Ilkeston (loan), 2014–2015 Nuneaton Town (loan) 3 (0), 2014–2015 Ilkeston (loan), 2014–2015 Imps (loan), 2015 Imps, 2015 Skellefteå 15 (9), 2016 Nuneaton Town, 2016 Kidderminster

Waite arrived in November 2014 when he joined on a youth loan from Notts County. He returned to County, and the club agreed to cancel his contract so that he was able to join Lincoln City on a permanent basis. He agreed a contract until the end of the 2014-15 season. However, after a total of just six first team appearances during his two spells with the club, he was released from his contract in March 2015.

Walker, Justin
(2000-2002)
Midfielder 77 (12) Apps 5 Goals
Born 6th September 1975
1992-1997 Nottingham Forest 0 (0), 1997-2000 Scunthorpe United 132 (2), 2000-2002 Imps, 2002-2003, Exeter City 39 (5), 2003-2005 Cambridge United 59 (2), 2004 York City (loan) 9 (0), 2005-2006 Chester City 21 (0), 2006-2008 Ilkeston Town 34 (1), 2008 F.C. Halifax Town 8 (0)

Justin Walker was a talented and cultured midfielder who played for City in times of turmoil. Had he arrived a year or two later he may well have been a vital component of our play off push, but instead he'll always be remembered as one of the guys who left as we entered administration.

Walker made his name at Scunthorpe United and it was surprising when Phil Stant managed to secure his signature in the summer of 2000. He didn't fit the mould of a Stant and Foster player, he was far more composed than the sort of brutish bully-boy they preferred. He featured in almost every game in his first season, but began to come into his own when Stant left and Alan Buckley took over and tried to play football the right way. A crucial late goal away at leaders Chesterfield in April of 2001 confirmed Third Division football after a season battling against relegation. For his endeavours Walker was named Player of the Year

The following season Walker again turned in good performances amid a backdrop of financial insecurity and uncertainty about the future. A vital last minute winner at Bristol Rovers gave us the edge over our relegation rivals, and further goals against Carlisle (3-1) and Hartlepool (1-1) helped secure the points we needed to be assured league football for 2002/03. However, there was nothing that could be done on the pitch to ensure financial survival and Walker was one of the players who was released at the end of the season as a cost cutting exercise.

Wallace, Kieran
(2015)
Midfield 6 (0) Apps 0 Goals
Born 26th January 1995
2013-2014 Nottingham Forest, 2014 Sheffield United, 2015 Imps (loan), 2016 Fleetwood (loan)

Young midfielder brought in by Chris Moyses to strengthen the squad for the 2014/15 season run in. Played six games but ended up on the losing side four times, and returned to Sheffield once his loan spell was completed. Recently signed on loan for Fleetwood after failing to break into the first team at Bramall Lane.

He represented England at under 17 level and I suspect he'll probably go on to have a decent career in the lower leagues, even if we didn't see evidence of that in a Lincoln shirt.

Walling, Dean
(1997-1999)
Defender
Born 17th April 1969
1987–1990 Rochdale 65 (8), 1990 Kitchener Spirit, 1991 Franklin Grizzlies, 1991 Guiseley 2 (2), 1991–1997 Carlisle United 236 (22), 1997–1999 Imps, 1999–2001 Doncaster Rovers 42 (0), 2001 Northwich Victoria 14 (0), 2001–2002 Cambridge United 20 (0), 2002 Gainsborough Trinity, 2002–2003 Nuneaton Borough 1 (1)

Defender signed from Carlisle for a club-record fee of £75,000 in 1997. Formed part of a formidable defence along with Steve Holmes, Jason Barnett and Kevin Austin as the Imps steamed to automatic promotion. Scored eight goals in his first season including winners against Leyton Orient (1-0), Scunthorpe (1-0) and Hull City (1-0). Grabbed the equalising goal in the FA Cup 1st round against Gainsborough, then scored a brace in the replay to give us a 3-2 win.

In that first season Walling epitomised everything good about a John Beck team. He was strong, tough and absolutely 100% committed to the cause. He got forward to cause trouble from set pieces but wasn't found wanting at the back either. He was called up to represent St Kitts and Nevis due to his performances for Lincoln, and it's fair to say we got our money's worth in that first season.

Injury kept Walling out for all but three games of the following season, and he returned just in time to see us relegated back into the fourth tier. He featured in the final day defeat against Wycombe Wanderers before sealing a £15k move to Doncaster Rovers.

He now runs a soccer club in Lincoln, coaching young players and can be found writing for the local paper about all-things Imps related. He should always be commended for playing for a side called 'Franklin Grizzlies' as well. It sounds more like a burger bar than a football team!

Wanless, Paul
(1995-1996)
Midfielder 9 (1) Apps 0 Goals
Born 14th December 1973
1991–1995 Oxford United 32 (0), 1995–1996 Imps, 1996 Woking (loan), 1996–2003 Cambridge United 285 (50), 2003–2005 Oxford United 65 (10), 2005–2007 Forest Green Rovers 38 (0), 2007–2009 Llanelli 7 (0), 2010 Oxford City

Another case of decent player who came to the club at the wrong time. Signed by Sam Ellis but given first team football by Steve Wicks, Wanless never pressed a case for a permanent starting role. City lost six and drew two of the league games he played in, with two victories coming in the Autoglass Windscreens Shield. It was no surprise when John Beck took over an immediately sent Wanless out on loan to Woking. His contract wasn't renewed at the end of the season, but he went on to have a good career at Cambridge United, eventually becoming their club captain. Returned to Sincil Bank with an equalising goal in the 2-2 draw that saw both Terry Fleming and Scott Willis sent off.

Ward, Chris
(2002-2003)
Forward 6 (2) Apps 2 Goals
Born 28th April 1981
1999–2001 Lancaster City, 2001–2002 Birmingham City 0 (0), 2001–2002 Forest Green Rovers (loan) 5 (1), 2001–2002 Southport (loan) 3 (0), 2002–2003 Barrow 8 (3), 2002–2003 Leigh RMI 5 (1), 2002–

2003 Imps, 2003–2004 Northwich Victoria, 2004–2005 Bamber Bridge 37 (14), 2005–2007 Kendal Town, 2006–2007 Mossley, 2006–2009 Clitheroe, 2008–2009 Chorley, 2009 Lancaster City 5 (2)

Tall striker signed by Keith Alexander to try and complete his ongoing search for a goal scorer. Scored twice in eight outings, once as we ran out 4-1 winners at Carlisle and once to earn us a vital draw away at Darlington. He couldn't nail down a first team place though and Keith didn't feel he offered the goal threat that his signing was intended to do. He was released after the play-off final defeat by Bournemouth.

Warlow, Owain
(2005-2009)
Midfielder 8 (19) Apps 0 Goals
Born 25ᵗʰ October 1987
2005–2009 Imps, 2008 Kettering Town (loan) 4 (0), 2009–2011 Llanelli 42 (3), 2011 Gainsborough Trinity, 2011 Worksop Town (loan), 2011–2013 Worksop Town, 2014 Merthyr Town, 2015 Tamworth 0 (0)

Former youth team midfielder first given his chance by John Schofield in early 2007. Made his debut against Torquay in a 1-0 win for City and went on to make five appearances in his first season. His second season saw him start a handful of games, including the 5-2 defeat in the Football League Trophy against Hartlepool that turned out to be Schofield's penultimate game. He also came on as a sub in the 4-0 defeat by MK Dons that earned Schoey the sack.

Played a handful of times under Peter Jackson before being loaned out to Kettering Town in the 2008/09 season, and was released in the summer of 2009 after which he returned to his native Wales with Llanelli.

Waterfall, Luke
(2015- Current)
Defender 53 (1) Apps 9 Goals
Born 30ᵗʰ July 1990
2008–2009 Tranmere Rovers 0 (0), 2008 Altrincham (loan) 1 (0), 2009–2010 Ilkeston Town 35 (2), 2010–2013 Gainsborough Trinity 104 (8), 2013–2015 Scunthorpe United 9 (1), 2014 Macclesfield Town (loan) 17 (2), 2014–2015 Mansfield Town (loan) 5 (0), 2015 Wrexham 9 (1), 2015 Imps

Luke Waterfall is a remnant of Chris Moyses' squad, one of the players perceived as good enough to remain and operate under the regime of Danny and Nicky Cowley. Along with Lee Beevers he has probably been the single most improved player as well. Alongside Callum Howe and Chris Bush he looked an edgy defender prone to lapses in concentration, but since the new manager took over he has grown in stature and composure.

His threat from set pieces speaks for itself, ten goals from under sixty outings is better than a lot of strikers we've had (Ben Hutchinson I'm looking at you). Since he's been elevated to captain he has got better and better, still young enough to be quick and energetic but experienced enough to read the game properly and take up good positions.

Many thought Raggett would be partnered by Jamie McCombe in the 2016/17 season, and the emergence of Luke Waterfall has been a real blessing. Not since the days of Morgan, McAuley and a younger McCombe have we had a centre back pairing that felt as safe as Waterfall and Raggett. Has the potential to play league football with us for many years to come.

As this book was going to press Waterfall netted a crucial last minute equaliser as we beat leaders Forest Green 3-2 at The New Lawn. He's going the right way about writing himself into the Imps history books.

Watson, Karlton
(2012)
Defender 5 (2) Apps 0 Goals
Born 30th April 1992
2011 Nottingham Forest, 2012 Imps, 2013-2014 Telford

Young defender who signed on a short-term deal during David Holdsworth's reign as manager. Only ended up on the winning side once in his seven-game spell, and that was as a last-minute sub as we beat Ebbsfleet 3-2. Wasn't retained at the end of the season and most recently has played for Telford.

Watt Phil
(2006-2008)
Defender 1 (1) Apps 0 Goals
Born 10th January 1988
2006-2008 Imps

Former youth defender who emerged on the first team scene under John Schofield. Had a disaster on his debut as City were soundly thrashed 4-0 at home by Shrewsbury, and only played once more as a sub for the injured Adie Moses as we went down 3-1 in the FA Cup to Forest at the City Ground.

Wattley, Dave
(2003-2004)
Defender 1 (3) App 0 Goals
Born 5th September 1983
2002-2003 QPR, 2003-2004 Imps

Wattley started just one game for Lincoln and made three other appearances as a sub. He signed at a time we had Morgan, Weaver and Futcher as first choice centre halves, and found his chances limited by injury as well. He left the game after his Lincoln spell. Interestingly of the four games he played we won three and scored 11 goals.

Watts, Adam
(2009, 2010-2011)
Defender 77 Apps 1 Goal
Born 4th March 1988
2007–2010 Fulham 0 (0), 2007 Milton Keynes Dons (loan) 2 (0), 2009 Northampton Town (loan) 5 (0), 2009 Imps (loan), 2010–2011 Imps, 2012 Gainsborough Trinity 8 (0), 2012–2015 Eastbourne Borough 93 (5)

Adam Watts signed on loan from Fulham via Chris Sutton's contacts, and at first glance he was just what we needed. He was a tall and commanding centre back who could organise his defence. He was Sutton's first signing and he went straight into the team against Aldershot for his first match.

After two clean sheets in his first two games his loan was extended until January 2010, and ahead of that deadline it was announced he was signing permanently. The signing was widely regarded as a bit of a coup as Watts could clearly handle himself more than adequately at our level.

Devastatingly he suffered a fracture of the left fibula in our February 2010 clash with Grimsby Town. On his return, it was clear he wasn't the same player as he had been prior to injury, and he was made available for free transfer in May 2011 as we slipped out of the league. Despite this snub from Tilson he still outlasted the manager, even making a handful of appearances the following season. His last game for City was our FA Cup 4th qualifying round replay defeat to Alfreton.

Most recently he's been turning out for Eastbourne Borough. The story of Adam Watts is another story of what might have been, because before his injury he looked a class act for the club.

Watts, Julian
(1998-1999)
Defender 3 Apps 0 Goals
Born 17th March 1971
1990–1992 Rotherham United 20 (1), 1992–1996 Sheffield Wednesday 18 (1), 1992 Shrewsbury Town (loan) 9 (0), 1996–1998 Leicester City 38 (1), 1997 Crewe Alexandra (loan) 5 (0), 1998 Huddersfield Town (loan) 8 (0), 1998–1999 Bristol City 17 (1), 1998–1999 Imps (loan), 1999 Blackpool (loan) 9 (0) 1999 Luton Town (loan) 6 (0), 1999–2001 Luton Town 67 (8), 2001–2004 Northern Spirit 66 (2)

6'3" centre half Watts had a three-match spell on loan at Sincil Bank from Bristol City in December 1998. He made his debut for us in the heavy defeat at Wycombe. He then played in a draw against Burnley, and a 1-0 home win over Mansfield before returning to Bristol. He later joined Luton and played against the Imps in two FA Cup 1st round matches in 1999. After leaving the Hatters in 2001 he spent three seasons playing for Northern Spirit in Australia.

Watts, Steve
(2002-2003)
Forward 5 Apps 1 Goals
Born 11th July 1976
1998 Fisher Athletic 5 (2), 1998–2003 Leyton Orient 132 (29), 1999 Welling United (loan) 2 (2), 2002 Margate (loan) 7 (4), 2002–2003 Imps (loan), 2003 Dagenham & Redbridge (loan) 6 (2), 2003 Shrewsbury Town 15 (1), 2003–2004 Dagenham & Redbridge 12 (3), 2004 St Albans City 21 (9), 2004–2006 Fisher Athletic 10 (6), 2006 Bromley 2 (0), 2007–2008 Eastleigh 24 (5), 2008–2011 Sutton United 38 (8)

Watts had made national headlines before coming to Lincoln, he earned a move to Leyton Orient in October 1998 after winning The Sun newspaper's 'Search for a Striker' competition. He was one of Keith Alexander's many attempts to fill the striker's role at Lincoln, joining on loan in December 2002 after scoring 29 goals in 132 goals for Leyton Orient. He made his Imps debut in the tempestuous 2-2 draw with Cambridge that saw three players sent off, and scored an 8th minute opener in a 1-1 draw with York six days later.

He was offered a permanent deal at Sincil Bank but rejected it, stating that he didn't feel a move to Lincoln would be beneficial for his career as he didn't think Lincoln would finish higher than Leyton Orient that season (Lincoln made the play-offs, Leyton Orient finished mid-table). After leaving

Lincoln he spent time on loan at Conference side Dagenham before signing for Shrewsbury, who were relegated to the Conference. As we know City went on to appear in the play-offs five seasons on the spin. Good decision Steve, good decision.

He's most recently been making a living as a professional poker player, his biggest result to date was finishing 59th in the prestigious World Series of Poker. Bizarrely he also managed a singer called Louisa Johnson. She was the winner of the twelfth series of The X Factor in 2015

Weaver, Simon
(2002-2004)
Defender 101 Apps 5 Goals
Born 20ᵗʰ December 1977
1996–1998 Sheffield Wednesday 0 (0), 1997 → Doncaster Rovers (loan), 1998–2000 Ilkeston Town, 2000–2002 Nuneaton Borough 63 (0), 2002–2004 Imps, 2004 → Macclesfield Town (loan) 7 (0), 2004–2005 Kidderminster Harriers 23 (0), 2005–2006 Scarborough 22 (1), 2006 York City 0 (0), 2006–2007 Tamworth 38 (1), 2007–2008 Boston United 13 (3), 2008–2009 King's Lynn 16 (2), 2008–2009 Redditch United 2 (0), 2008–2009 Ilkeston Town, 2009–2012 Harrogate Town 14 (0)

Weaver was a cheap option, signed by Keith Alexander after the club exited administration to survive in the third division at all costs. He was seen as a good, honest pro who wanted a crack at league football.

He made his debut in our 1-1 draw with Kidderminster on the opening day of the season, and although most sources credit Richard Logan with our goal, Weaver claimed it was his. As if scoring (or not) on his debut wasn't enough just two games later he was sent off after eight minutes against Carlisle. Not the best of starts.

From there he went from strength to strength, and alongside Paul Morgan and Ben Futcher made up one of the meanest Imps defences of modern times. He was an uncomplicated player affectionately known as 'horse' by fans and team mates alike. You never expected him to go on a fifty-yard run or to produce 25-yard wonder strike, but he did what he needed to do comfortably. He kicked the ball away, he headed the ball away and when he couldn't manage either Paul Morgan was there to clean up for him.

He scored four times for City in that first play-off season, and three of those goals earned us a draw against Cambridge (2-2), Boston (1-1) and Wrexham (1-1). His fourth and final goal of the season gave us a 15ᵗʰ minute lead in the play-off semi-final against Scunthorpe United. He might have been uncomplicated but he knew when to chip in with a goal.

The following season he was virtually ever present again as we lost in the semi-finals to Huddersfield, but the arrival of Jamie McCombe and perhaps more tellingly Gareth McAuley meant that his day were numbered. He played just seven games of the 2004/05 season before requesting a move due to lack of first team opportunities. He first went out to Macclesfield on loan, and then signed for Kidderminster Harriers. Recently he's been making a fair job of managing Harrogate Town in the National League North, and was even linked with the Lincoln job briefly when Chris Moyses stepped down.

Webb, Danny
(2003)
Forward 4 (1) Apps 1 Goal
Born 2ⁿᵈ July 1983

2000 Southampton 0 (0), 2000–2002 Southend United 31 (3), 2001–2002 Brighton & Hove Albion (loan) 12 (1), 2002 Brighton & Hove Albion (loan) 3 (0), 2002–2004 Hull City 16 (0), 2003 Imps (loan), 2003–2004 Cambridge United (loan) 10 (1), 2004–2005 Cambridge United 33 (3), 2005–2007 Yeovil Town 7 (0), 2007 Rushden & Diamonds (loan) 1 (0), 2007 Woking (loan) 6 (1), 2007 Marsaxlokk 1 (0), 2007–2008 AFC Wimbledon 33 (9), 2008 Chelmsford City 0 (0), 2008 Sutton United 1 (0), 2008 Havant & Waterlooville 3 (1), 2008–2010 Salisbury City 49 (3), 2010–2011, Bath City 29 (2), 2011 Salisbury City (loan) 3 (0), 2011–2012 Salisbury City 0 (0), 2012–2013 Dover Athletic, 2013–2014 Chelmsford City 14 (0)

Danny is the son of former Chelsea legend Dave Webb, but he wasn't able to eclipse the career his father had. He arrived at Sincil Bank with a bit of a reputation for being a 'bright young thing' having come through the ranks at Southampton and earned a permanent move to Hull City. He was the latest in a long line of Keith Alexander striker experiments, and like most of his peers he didn't make a significant impression.

He joined just a few weeks ahead of our first date with destiny at the Millennium Stadium, and he did score for City albeit just the once. He hit a 21st minute opener as we beat Bristol Rovers 2-1 in March, points that turned out to be crucial come the end of the season. That was the total sum of his input though and he returned to live out the life of a mediocre forward at a host of different clubs. He played his part though, and he still contributed more than Kevin Gall and Drewe Broughton put together.

When Webb left Keith characterised his time at the club, and perhaps offered some insight into his search for a striker that was to last his entire Imps tenure; "We've had four forwards in on loan this season and none of them have quite done the job I wanted them to. Although I would like to have kept Daniel until the end of the season he wanted to go back to Hull. I'm disappointed with his decision as I think it's the wrong one but if the lad doesn't want to stay he doesn't want to stay."

He didn't want to stay, and hindsight proved Keith correct in assessing it as the wrong decision.

Weir-Daley, Spencer
(2007)
Forward 4 (7) Apps 5 Goals
Born 5th September 1985
2004–2007 Nottingham Forest 11 (2), 2006 Macclesfield Town (loan) 7 (2), 2007 Imps (loan), 2007 Bradford City (loan) 5 (1), 2007–2009 Notts County 40 (3), 2009–2011 Boston United 79 (35), 2011–2012 AFC Telford United 2 (0), 2011 Buxton 3 (4), 2012–2014 Boston United 87 (31), 2014 Corby Town 47 (27), 2016 Kettering Town 32 (18)

Sometimes a player joins on loan and disappoints only to go on and have a good career (Carl Cort). Very rarely does a player impress so much during his loan spell that you want to keep him, but he goes on to achieve very little. That is perhaps the best way to sum up Spencer Weir-Daley.

He signed on loan having scored twice for Macclesfield during a similar loan spell earlier in the 2006/07 season. We were looking for an injection of goals from somewhere to assist our automatic promotion push, and Weir-Daley looked the part right from the start. He had an air of arrogance about him in his playing style, but also a devastating burst of speed and the ability to finish coolly.

He scored on his second outing for City as we drew 2-2 and then again a couple of games later against Notts County as we lost 3-1. Every time he got onto the pitch he looked like a threat, and two goals live on Sky against Walsall to give us a 2-1 win meant he was getting noticed. After the Walsall game John Schofield was full of praise for the forward; "Spencer took his chances very well and his finishes were excellent. He's taken his chance (in the team) well and his overall contribution was magnificent. He stretched their defence and contested every ball and made sure we had a platford to play from."

He ended his short spell with five goals, and although we wanted him back permanently it seemed the classy striker was destined for greater things.

Only it didn't happen that way for him. He scored on a short loan spell at Bradford after us and the following season earned a permanent move to Notts County, but the goals dried up. He scored just three times before dropping into non-league, and never got another shot at league football. I'll never know how he didn't at least make a regular League One player, the grace and poise he showed to kill off a strong Walsall that night suggested he had so much more to achieve.

Welsh, Steve
(1999-2001)
Defender 47 (2) Apps 0 Goals
Born 19th April 1968
1989–1990 Wimborne Town, 1990–1991 Cambridge United 1 (0), 1991–1994 Peterborough United 146 (2), 1994 Preston North End (loan) 0 (0), 1994–1996 Partick Thistle 55 (0), 1996 Peterborough United 6 (0), 1996–1998 Dunfermline Athletic 17 (0), 1998–1999 Ayr United 24 (0), 1999–2001 Imps, 2001–2002 King's Lynn

Committed and likeable Scottish-born defender who came to City at the tail end of his career to offer some stability to a back line that had been leaking goals. Never really hit the sort of performance levels he had at Peterborough or Partick Thistle, but was never found wanting dedication to the cause. As he entered the final stage of his career some of his pace left him and niggly injuries restricted him to 49 outings in two seasons.

In a testament to his personality Welsh was appointed Football in the Community Officer at Sincil Bank with the role commencing at the beginning of the 2001–2002 season. It meant an end to his professional playing career. Welsh also became manager of the club's under-16 Centre of Excellence side, and later he managed Boston United for a short while.

West, Dean
(1991-1995, 2004)
Defender 119 (28) Apps 23 Goals
Born 15th December 1972
1991–1995 Imps 1993–1994 Boston United (loan) 6 (5), 1995–1999 Bury 110 (8), 1999–2004 Burnley 158 (5), 2004 Imps, 2004–2005 Boston United 24 (0), 2005–2008 King's Lynn 119 (3), 2008–2011 Corby Town, 2011–2012 Lincoln Moorlands Railway 5 (0), 2012 Stamford 0 (0)

Dean West came through the youth ranks at City and scored on his City debut against Carlisle as we romped to a 6-2 victory. He went on to establish himself as one of the better attacking full-backs we've seen at the club, showing bags of promise and attracting attention from bigger clubs. He managed to score 20 times in 93 games for us before he was controversially swapped by Steve Wicks for Bury's Kevin Hulme. Hulme faded into obscurity, but West went on to fulfil his potential. He played over 100 games for Bury before earning a move to Burnley. Another 150 appearances there demonstrated not only what a good player he was, but what an awful bit of business his swap had been for our football club.

He returned to Lincoln at the tail end of his career in 2004 but played just four times in defence before being replaced by Gareth McAuley. It was clear by that stage he'd lost the pace and direct attacking instinct that had made him so successful in his youth.

After football, he invested in a nursery not far from Boston with his wife.

Westcarr, Craig
(2005)
Forward 5 (1) Apps 1 Goal
Born 29th January 1985
2001–2005 Nottingham Forest 23 (1), 2004–2005 Imps (loan), 2005 Milton Keynes Dons (loan) 4 (0), 2005–2006 Cambridge United 31 (8), 2006–2009 Kettering Town 102 (23), 2009–2011 Notts County 87 (21), 2011–2013 Chesterfield 53 (10), 2012 Walsall (loan) 8 (0), 2013–2014 Walsall 59 (19), 2014–2015 Portsmouth 33 (6), 2015–2016 Mansfield Town 24 (3), 2016 Southport (loan) 11 (2), 2016 Alfreton Town 12 (6)

If I had a pound for every time I'd typed 'another Keith Alexander loan striker' then I'd probably make more money than I ever would through writing books. Keith embarked on an everlasting search to find centre forwards who could score goals for him. Sometimes he unearthed a Marcus Richardson or Gary Taylor-Fletcher, and other times he unearthed a Craig Westcarr.

Westcarr wasn't a bad player, far from it. He simply wasn't the quick-fix we needed and after six games and one goal (1-0 win over Bury on his Imps debut) he was gone. He still had a part to play in the history of Lincoln City though. He scored a 68th minute equaliser in the FA Cup replay with Kettering, a game they went on to win 2-1. They always come back and score.

Westley, Shane
(1996-1997)
Defender 11 Apps 1 Goal
Born 16th June 1965
1983–1985 Charlton Athletic 8 (0), 1985–1989 Southend United 144 (10), 1989–1992 Wolverhampton Wanderers 50 (2), 1992–1995 Brentford 64 (1), 1995 Southend United (loan) 5 (0), 1995 Cambridge United 3 (0), 1995–1996 Imps

As a player there is very little to write about. He came in during the short tenure of Steve Wicks. He was initially named as captain and intended as a defensive leader but managed just eleven appearances before calling it a day. He did notch one goal for the club, predictably against his old side Cambridge United.

He joined up as part of John Beck's backroom staff and was a popular figure amongst supporters. When Beck was dismissed he stepped up as manager, and it was under Westley we gained promotion in May of 1998, albeit with the team that Beck built. He didn't last long and was dismissed in November of 1998.

He was later appointed manager of Barrow where he employed Beck in a consultancy role, and when Beck took over Cambridge for a second time in 2001 he brought in Westley as his assistant, proving that there was no hard feelings.

After football he became the managing director of a personal training company called Bodywize, which is no surprise given he was built like a proverbial brick outhouse.

Whitehouse, Elliott
(2016- Current)
Midfielder 0 (3) Apps 0 Goals
Born 27th October 1993
2013–2014 Sheffield United 3 (0), 2013–2014 York City (loan) 15 (0), 2014 Alfreton Town (loan) 4 (0), 2014–2015 Notts County 7 (1), 2015 Nuneaton Town (loan) 5 (0), 2015 FC Halifax Town 4 (0), 2015 Nuneaton Town 54 (20), 2016 Imps

We've not seen much of young Elliott yet, but he's an England C international who served his youth at Sheffield United. He's made a steady drop down the leagues, but after a successful stay at Nuneaton we agreed an undisclosed fee to bring him to Sincil Bank.

He's billed as an attacking midfielder with an eye for goal and the ability to get up and down the pitch, but just three appearances from the bench aren't much to go by. The Cowley's transfer market dealings have been near perfect (Champion aside), so we will have to trust them that this is a name you'll be hearing a lot of in the future.

Whitney, Jon
(1995-1998)
Defender 117 (4) Apps 11 Goals
Born 23rd December 1970

1989-1990 Skelmersdale United 0 (0), 1992-1993 Winsford United 0 (0), 1993–1996 Huddersfield Town 18 (0), 1994 Wigan Athletic (loan) 12 (0), 1996–1999 Imps, 1999–2001 Hull City 57 (3), 2001–2002 King's Lynn 5 (1)

John Beck paid £20,000 for left-back Whitney in October 1995 just a month or two after he took over as manager. He replaced the popular Alan Johnson, and at first his tough and uncompromising style won him few fans. Eventually though that style would be what won him most of his fans.

Let's not make any mistake about it, Jon Whitney was hard. Many a-winger would see him snarling up ahead of them and lose the will for a fight. If they didn't lose it as they approached him, they almost certainly lost it as he kicked them up into row Z. He was everything John Beck liked in a player, instead of getting up and rampaging off with the ball he'd launch it with precision into 'danger alley' and then get back in position ready to go again.

That's not to say he was a bad player, far from it. He knew what he had to do and he carried out his orders to the letter. He was a model pro in that he never shirked a tackle, and never went missing in crucial games. As we beat Man City 4-1 in the Coca Cola Cup, Jon Whitney got on the scoresheet. He epitomised everything positive about John Beck's tactics. He deserves to be discussed in the same breath as Stuart Bimson or Paul Mayo, he was every bit as good as both, if not better.

Injury curtailed his 1996/97 season, coming just after an FA Cup tie with Burnley. He came back better and stronger playing 51 games as we gained automatic promotion under Shane Westley. He stepped up to the next level with relative ease as well, still the uncomplicated full back he always had been. As Kevin Austin slotted into left back he found his chances restricted, and before long he dropped back down to division three with Hull City.

Recently he's surprised anyone who thought him the uneducated hatchet man at full back. In December 2003, Whitney was appointed physiotherapist at Walsall having previously worked as a Sports Therapist in his own clinic and pursuing a bachelor's degree in physiotherapy at the University of Salford. He graduated in 2006, and in 2011 was appointed Assistant Manager at the Bescot Stadium. In June 2016, he was appointed first team manager on a three-year contract.

Wilder, Chris
(1999)
Defender 2 (1) Apps 0 Goals
Born 23rd September 1967
1986–1992 Sheffield United 93 (1), 1989 Walsall (loan) 4 (0), 1990 Charlton Athletic (loan) 1 (0), 1991 Charlton Athletic (loan) 2 (0), 1992 Leyton Orient (loan) 16 (1), 1992–1996 Rotherham United 132 (11), 1996–1997 Notts County 46 (0), 1997–1998 Bradford City 42 (0), 1998–1999 Sheffield United 12 (0), 1998 Northampton Town (loan) 1 (0), 1999 Imps (loan), 1999 Brighton & Hove Albion 11 (0), 1999–2001 Halifax Town 51 (1)

Veteran defender perhaps now best known for managing Oxford United, Northampton Town and currently Sheffield United. Had a relatively low-key Lincoln career, joining on loan as we headed towards relegation from the third tier in the 1998/99 season. After playing for both Sheff Utd and Northampton that season he joined us for a three-game spell that saw us lose to York (1-2), Stoke (0-2) and finally get thumped at Maine Road against Man City (0-4). He returned to the Blades after that.

His stock is rising as a promising manager though having led Oxford to the Football League via the play-offs, and then not only saving Northampton from relegation but taking them to the League Two Championship a season later. Joined Sheffield United in May of 2016.

Wildin, Courtney
(2016)
Defender 1 (3) Apps 0 Goals
Born 30th March 1996
2015–2016 Sheffield Wednesday 0 (0), 2016 Gainsborough Trinity (loan), 2016 Imps (loan), 2016 Boston United 1 (0)

Young defender brought in to help our ultimately doomed push towards a play-off spot in 2015/16. Made a winning start to his Imps career as we beat Southport 3-1. Made just one start as soon-to-be relegated Kidderminster beat us 2-1 at Sincil Bank. Returned to Sheffield Wednesday and was snapped up by Boston United in the summer of 2016.

Wilford, Aron
(2004)
Forward 0 (6) Apps 1 Goal
Born 14th January 1982
1999–2002 Middlesbrough 0 (0), 2001–2002 Scarborough (loan) 10 (1), 2001–2003 Whitby Town, 2003–2004 York City 6 (2), 2003–2004 Worksop Town (loan) 3 (0), 2003–2004 Harrogate Town (loan)

6 (0), 2004 Imps, 2004 Clyde 19 (2), 2005 Stalybridge Celtic 17 (5), 2006–2007 Blyth Spartans 10 (3), 2007–2008 Guiseley, 2008 Southern Stars, 2009–2010 Dandenong Thunder 0 (0), 2011–2003 Bentleigh Greens 43 (2), 2014 Oakleigh Cannons 67 (1)

Wilford signed on a short-term deal to help with the ongoing striker crisis in the run in to the 2003/04 season. He managed just five sub appearances for City scoring once on the final day against Yeovil, and had a brief cameo as we drew 2-2 with Huddersfield Town in the second leg of the play-off semi-final. Most recently found playing in Australia.

Wilkins, Ian
(1997-2000)
Midfielder 6 (4) Apps 0 Goals
Born 3rd April 1980
1997-2000 Imps

A former Youth Team player who stepped up in 1997, Wilkins spent three seasons at Lincoln without ever making the grade. Enjoyed a run in the first team in late 1999, but last appeared in our first 21st century game as we won 2-0 away at Cheltenham.

When he played Wilkins always looked at the very least competent, and along with Craig Stones was viewed as 'one for the future', until the future actually arrived. It frustrated fans to see young talent being wasted whilst we spent lots of money on has-beens such as Dave Phillips.

Wilkins showed that although he may not have been able to hold his own as a midfielder in the Football League, he was more than adequate cover for Jason Barnett at right back. Whatever fans thought was irrelevant though and sadly Wilkins never got a real chance to prove his worth.

Wilkinson, Tom
(2006-2007)
Midfield 0 (1) Apps 0 Goals
Born 29th September 1985
2006-2007 Imps, 2007 Grays Athletic (loan)

Former YTS player Wilkinson made just one appearance for City as a 61st minute sub for Francis Green in a 1-0 away defeat against Carlisle. Unfortunately, a broken leg ended his career before it started at the age of 21, and he was released in the summer of 2007.

He graduated from York St John University in November 2010 with a Bachelor's degree in Physiotherapy, after his studies were funded by the Professional Footballers' Association as part of their programme of post-career training for current and former professional footballers and academy players. He still lives in Lincoln and works as a physiotherapist at the County Hospital.

Williams, Robbie
(2012)
Defender 10 (1) Apps 0 Goals
Born 6th July 1987
2009-2011 Altrincham, 2011-2012 Telford, 2012 Imps (loan), 2013-2016 Barrow, 2016 Newtown

Williams was a tall defender brought in on loan from Telford by the habitual tinker-man David Holdsworth as we plummeted down the National League with Steve Tilson's misfit squad. Williams wasn't a bad player, but he was a measure of how far we'd fallen, taking other non-league rejects on loan to paper over the massive cracks in our squad. It wasn't as much 'Let Me Entertain You', more 'Lazy Days'.

He made his debut as we went down 3-1 to Grimsby Town, and in eleven appearances he only finished on the winning side once as we collected our annual home win over Southport. Played his last game for Lincoln in a 2-2 draw with Fleetwood in which Jamie Vardy scored twice for Fleetwood.

Williams, Steve
(1993-1995)
Forward 8 (13) Apps 3 Goals
Born 3rd November 1975
1993-1996 Imps

Williams was a former Horncastle youth who came through the YTS ranks at Lincoln. He suffered a serious leg break early in his career that perhaps dampened his potential. Scored on his debut in an Autoglass Windscreens game against Darlington to earn us a 3-2 win. Also scored in league matches against Wycombe (1-3) and a third goal for City in a 3-3 draw with Scunthorpe in April 1995.

Willis, Scott
(2002-2004)
Midfielder
Born 20th February 1982
1999–2000 Wigan Athletic 0 (0), 2000–2001 Mansfield Town 0 (0), 2001 Doncaster Rovers (loan) 0 (0), 2001 Carlisle United 1 (0), 2001–2002 Bamber Bridge 5 (0), 2002 Droylsden 14 (3), 2002–2004 Imps, 2003 Stockport County (loan) 0 (0), 2004 Northwich Victoria (loan) 4 (0), 2004 Hereford United (loan) 8 (2), 2004 Halifax Town 2 (0), 2004 Droylsden 1 (0), 2005 Runcorn FC Halton 6 (0), 2005 Stalybridge Celtic 7 (0), 2005 Vauxhall Motors (loan) 10 (2), 2005 Workington 2 (0), 2005–2006 Leigh RMI 31 (9), 2006–2007 A.F.C. Telford United 24 (1), 2007–2008 Leigh RMI, 2008 Witton Albion

Keith plucked Scott from non-league Droylsden after he netted three times in thirteen outings. He'd previously turned out for Carlisle but had drifted into the non-league game. It was just how Keith liked his players, coming up from the non-league and hungry for success. He'd come from good stock having been a Wigan youngster and spent time as a youth at Tranmere.

Scott was worth watching whether you wanted superb goals or biting tackles. His strike away at Carlisle could have won any goal of the season award, but his neck high tackle at home to Cambridge could have resulted in an arrest. His great goal v Exeter had critics applauding, but allegedly spitting at a Stockport defender did him no favours. That 30 a day habit can't have helped his cause either.

He featured in that notable first season that Keith took charge and was a 72nd minute substitute as the Imps crashed out of the play off final 5-2 against Bournemouth. However, his days were numbered as the club had signed Richard Butcher to form a midfield duo with Peter Gain.

He scored three times for City in 33 appearances, predominately from the bench and I suspect his temperament was one of the reasons he was allowed to join first Northwich and latterly Hereford on loan. Two goals for them in eight games wasn't enough to convince them the barmy scouser was worth a punt and eventually he ended up at Leigh RMI and Telford in his native north west. He made just four appearances for Lincoln in 2003/04 before heading to Hereford. His final game for Hereford saw him score in a 2-0 win and get sent off for two bookable offences.

He was also notable for being the nephew of Cilla Black, although I'd wager anyone who saw his kung fu kick would argue he's probably most notable for that.

Wood, Bradley
(2015- Current)
Defender 55 (1) Apps 2 Goals
Born 2nd September 1991
2009–2013 Grimsby Town 113 (1), 2013–2015 Alfreton Town 75 (7), 2015 Imps

In his first season with Lincoln former Grimsby Town player Bradley Wood won Player of the Year, Away Player of the Year and Young Player of the Year. Basically he cleaned up, and he didn't do it by scoring goals, he didn't do it by setting up goals and he didn't do it by keeping a lot of clean sheets. He did it by working hard, and by tackling like a Formula One car crashing into a wall at 200mph.

I'm not going to mince my words here; Bradley Wood is hard. He works harder than a Land Rover engine, and he's tougher than a buffalo. His fair tackles leave players in a heap and he seems to feel no pain himself. He refuses to accept injuries and he plays through not only his own pain barrier, but that of the players he leaves strewn all over the field as well. It's not that Brad is an unfair player either, he's not. He can play a bit too, hismovement is great and he can spread play when he's in the midfield. Like any good attacking full back he comes up trumps with a cross or two when required.

He even weighs in with the odd goal too. He can get his head down and beat people, skills that contradict his label as a hard man. Bradley is an asset picked up by Chris Moyses for the long term benefit of our football team.

Away from the pitch he's a quiet lad, devoted to his family and committed 100% to pushing Lincoln City further up the league. For my money, he is neck and neck with Mark Bailey as the best right back I've seen play for Lincoln, and should he tackle us all the way up to the Football League he has a chance to become a true Lincoln City legend. Will he play right back or midfield for the rest of the season? Who knows? All I know is if he plays midfield there will be an awful lot of relieved left wingers who might just get to play another game in their career.

Woodyard, Alex
(2016- Current)
Midfielder 18 Apps 0 Goals
Born 3rd May 1993
2010–2013 Southend United 8 (0), 2011 Farnborough (loan) 10 (2), 2013 Braintree Town (loan) 12 (0), 2013–2014 Dartford 37 (0), 2014–2015 Concord Rangers 36 (1), 2015–2016 Braintree Town 44 (1), 2016 Imps

When you used to buy packets of cereal there was nearly always a gift with it. Well when Danny Cowley takes over your club you get two free gifts. One is the unproven talent of Taylor Miles, the other is the sublime football ability of Alex Woodyard.

He's followed his mentor from Concord to Lincoln via Braintree, and comes here after winning National League Young Player of the Year last season. He's the England C captain and without me speaking too highly of him he's a cut above many of the players we've had that play in his position. This boy will play football at a higher level, and I believe it will be at least Championship football.

Woodyard is a workhorse, he does all the donkey work and unseen work that players like David Batty had to do at the top level. He plays passes simple, but he is always willing to get the ball and move it on. When we're playing well he sits in the middle of the park dictating play and breaking up opposition attacks. When we're playing badly he chases, harasses and harries every single opposition player, and he always makes himself available for a pass. He wants the ball so much, even in training he has a ball at his feet during talks or warm down sessions. I imagine his Mum had to tie a ball on a rope and leave it in the bath just to get him to clean himself.

He eats, lives and breathes football and he has that special something that you only see once or twice in a generation. He's no fancy-dan with lots of flicks and feints, but he's comfortable on the ball, comfortable moving it about and comfortable getting stuck into hard 50/50 challenges.

He'll have a problem wrestling one of Bradley Wood's player of the year trophies off him, but if I were the engravers I'd already have the first four letters on at least one of them, because a name starting in Wood will take one of them home.

Wootton, Kyle
(2015)
Forward 1 (4) Apps 1 Goal
Born 11ᵗʰ October 1996
2014 Scunthorpe United 32 (4), 2015 Imps (loan), 2016 North Ferriby

Wootton came to Sincil Bank on loan from Scunthorpe as additional cover for Matt Rhead and Liam Hearn. He scored once in a 2-1 away win at Aldershot. Upon completion of his loan spell he returned to Scunthorpe but has found first team chances limited. Recently signed for North Ferriby on loan to get some game time and try to put his career back on track.

Wright, Ben
(2007-2009)
Forward 46 (29) Apps 18 Goals
Born 1ˢᵗ July 1980
1998–1999 Kettering Town 11 (0), 1998–2001 Bristol City 2 (0), 2000–2001 Woking (loan) 3 (0), 2001–2002 Viking 48 (7), 2003–2007 IK Start 68 (29), 2006 Moss FK (loan) 11 (2), 2007–2009 Imps, 2009–2010 Macclesfield Town 39 (6), 2010 Barnet 0 (0), 2010 Newport County 3 (1), 2011 Richmond Athletic 16 (26),

Ben was an imposing striker brought to the club by John Schofield. Steve Torpey and Mark Stallard were preferred and it was only when Peter Jackson took charge that he got a run in the first team. He had scored a European goal for Viking away at Stamford Bridge and had attracted a bit of attention, and his arrival left fans optimistic he might turn out to be a Lincoln great.

Two goals in a 3-1 win over Stockport, and another two in a 4-1 win at Sincil Bank against Barnet quickly endeared him to Imps fans and he went on to make a total of 38 appearances in his first season, scoring 15 goals. He came off the bench in the reverse fixture against Barnet and scored twice in 14 minutes to earn himself a run in the first team. His total haul earned him the position of Imps top scorer, and hopes were high for the following season.

He always looked to have ability and as he got more games under his belt he adjusted well to the physical side of the game. However, in the 2008/09 season his scoring touch deserted him and he frequently found himself flitting between a starting place and the subs bench. He scored just three goals and was released at the end of the season, signing for Macclesfield Town. Six strikes for them was all he could add to his tally of league goals and he wound up his career scoring for fun with non-league side Richmond Athletic.

There's no doubt that Ben Wright was a quality player and for a short spell after he signed he seemed like the answer to our problems. The season after the team didn't perform well, and his loss of form was overshadowed by the exploits of Adrian Patulea and the Magnificent Seven. Had he found his form perhaps Peter Jackson might have pushed the club forward as he so frequently assured fans he would.

Wright, Nick
(2013-2014)
Forward 9 (12) Apps 2 Goals
Born 25th November 1987
2005–2007 Birmingham City 0 (0), 2006 Tamworth (loan) 1 (0), 2006 Bristol City (loan) 4 (0), 2006 Northampton Town (loan) 4 (0), 2007 Ashford Town (loan) 10 (4), 2007 Halesowen Town 8 (3), 2007–2010 Tamworth 87 (28), 2010–2012 Kidderminster Harriers 82 (23), 2012–2013 Mansfield Town 17 (1), 2013–2014 Imps, 2014 Kidderminster Harriers (loan) 9 (1), 2014–2015 Worcester City 25 (4), 2015 Gloucester City 1 (0), 2015 Corby Town 1 (0), 2015 Kettering Town, 2015 Rushall Olympic, 2015 Alvechurch

Six-foot striker who made a name for himself with prolific spells at Tamworth and then Kidderminster at National League level. Whilst playing for Tamworth he scored the goal that earned them promotion to the top flight of non-league football. Scored a ten-minute hat-trick after coming on as a sub for Kidderminster against Newport County to earn them a 3-2 win after being 2-0 down with four minutes of normal time left, and his exploits with the Harriers earned him a move to promotion hopefuls Mansfield Town. He was a bit-part player as Paul Cox led the Stags to the Football League and he joined Lincoln looking to rebuild his career.

It never happened for him at Lincoln either as he struggled to nail down a place in the team. He scored just twice, once against his former employers Kidderminster and once against Alfreton in a 4-1 Imps win. He eventually signed for Kidderminster again in March 2014 on loan, scoring once.

Yeo, Simon
(2002-2005, 2006)
Forward 99 (58) Apps 51 Goals
Born 20th October 1973
1997 Ards 4 (1), 1997 Curzon Ashton 4 (4), 1997–1998 Coleraine 0 (0), 1998–2002 Hyde United 130 (77), 1998–1999 Atherton Collieries (loan) 3 (5), 2002–2005 Imps, 2005 New Zealand Knights 11 (4), 2005–2006 Imps, 2006–2007 Peterborough United 13 (2), 2007–2008 Chester City 35 (8), 2008 Bury (loan) 8 (0), 2008–2009 Macclesfield Town 33 (7), 2009 Droylsden, 2009–2010 Harrogate Town 9 (1), 2010–2011 New Mills, 2011 Macclesfield Town 0 (0)

Players are often referred to as legends these days without good reason. Once every so often though a player comes along so unique and so special that there are no other words to describe him. Step forward cult hero Simon Yeo.

Firstly, the background: After leaving school, Yeo began a two-year YTS as a carpet fitter before, in May 1992, joining the army with the 22nd (Cheshire) Regiment. His army career included tours of Bosnia and Northern Ireland. After leaving the army, he supplemented his semi-professional football career with numerous jobs such as working on building sites, making toilet seats and being a postman in his home town of Stockport.

He arrived at Lincoln having scored a lot of goals for Hyde United in a four-year spell, and was another of the 'cheap' non-league players Keith Alexander looked to rely on after we exited administration. His first thirteen games were eventful, featuring six goals, six bookings and a red card in the first ever Football League Lincolnshire derby between Boston and Lincoln. Yeo came across as a passionate and committed striker who fancied his chances from anywhere. After a brace in the Football League Trophy against York City, the goals dried up. He spent much of the season coming off the bench and not having an effect.

It's written in Imps folklore now that to qualify for our first ever play-offs we needed a draw on the last day against Torquay. We trailed 1-0 thanks to a Martin Gritton goal, and Torquay missed a penalty as well. With 51 minutes on the clock Simon Yeo entered the fray, and just four minutes from time he picked up a slick Peter Gain pass and scored the goal that sent us to a two-legged semi-final against Scunthorpe United.

He didn't start the first leg against Scunthorpe, but he came on as a 73rd minute sub for Dene Cropper with the score poised at 3-3. Two goals in eight minutes from Yeo snatched victory from the jaws of a damaging draw. If that wasn't enough he only repeated his goal scoring exploits four days later at Glanford Park, coming on as a late substitute to steal a 1-0 win, or a 6-3 aggregate victory.

As we know it wasn't to be in the final and even Simon Yeo couldn't fire us to a win against Bournemouth. The next season started in controversial fashion again as he was sent off for kicking the ball away against Oxford in the opening fixture, and then he managed to go 11 games without a goal, a run that cost him his starting place.

In typical Yeo fashion he bounced back though, and starting with a last-minute goal against Huddersfield (3-1) he started to find his form. He scored six in nine as the Imps ascended the league, and despite ending up as losing semi-finalists to Huddersfield Yeo bagged himself 13 goals.

The following season was arguably his best in a Lincoln shirt. Gary Taylor Fletcher stole the opening headlines with goals in the opening five matches, but once Yeo got going there was no stopping him. From January to March he scored 15 goals in 15 games, including a wonderful finish in the televised 2-0 win over Scunthorpe. The goals dried up as the Imps automatic promotion push died away, but once again his goals had fired us to a play-off semi-final, and ultimately another final appearance at Cardiff. That was disappointingly lost 2-0 to Southend, and as the season ended our 23-goal hero moved to New Zealand. It seemed the love affair was over.

Within a few short months he was back in an Imps shirt re-signing on January 1st 2006. Once again he exploded onto the scene with four goals in his first five matches, and the obligatory red card thrown in for good measure as we drew 1-1 with Peterborough. He ended up with five in 12 games, his final goal in a Lincoln shirt coming in the 22nd minute of a 2-2 draw with Rushden.

After Lincoln he could just have been an ex player, but since he left he's often seen in the stands following the club. As recently as the 0-0 FA Cup 4th qualifying round game with Guiseley he has been spotted at the Bank, mixing in with the fans. He turns out in charity games and clearly holds an affection for the club he served so well as a player. In a world of gluttonous footballers without loyalty or honour Simon Yeo stands out as 'one of us', a regular bloke with the golden boots as far as Imps fans are concerned. His name will be forever mentioned alongside the Percy Freemans and John Wards of this world as a bona-fida, 100% time served Lincoln City legend.

Yussuf, Adi
(2013-2014)
Forward 1 (1) Apps 0 Goals
Born 20th February 1992
2008–2011 Leicester City 0 (0), 2011 Tamworth (loan) 10 (2), 2011–2013 Burton Albion 25 (1), 2013– 2014 Imps, 2013 Gainsborough Trinity (loan) 2 (1), 2014 Harrogate Town (loan) 2 (0), 2014 Histon (loan) 6 (2), 2014–2015 Oxford City 39 (27), 2015 Mansfield Town 26 (5), 2016 Crawley Town (loan) 8 (2)

Adi Yussuf's spell at Lincoln was blighted by injuries which restricted him to just two appearances under Gary Simpson. He was an 81st minute substitute in a 1-0 defeat at home to Salisbury, and then last 62 minutes of a 1-0 defeat against Aldershot. He spent time out on loan at Histon, Harrogate and Gainsborough before signing for Oxford City.

He found a prolific run of form at Oxford scoring 27 times in 39 appearances. This alerted scouts from Mansfield Town where he netted five times in 26 outings. He attracted controversy whilst playing for the Stags for urinating behind a stand which attracted a five-game ban and a £700 fine. Most recently he has been on loan a Crawley where he has found the net twice.

Awards

Player of the Year

1993-94: John Schofield
1994-95: Andy Leaning
1995-96: Gareth Ainsworth
1996-97: Gareth Ainsworth
1997-98: Kevin Austin
1998-99: Steve Holmes
1999-00: Lee Thorpe
200-0-1: Justin Walker
2001-02: Grant Brown
2002-03: Paul Morgan
2003-04: Gary Taylor-Fletcher
2004-05: Simon Yeo
2005-06: Jamie McCombe
2006-07: Lee Beevers
2007-08: Paul Green
2008-09: Scott Kerr
2009-10: Rob Burch
2010-11: Ashley Grimes
2011-12: Joe Anyon
2012-13: Alan Power
2013-14: Tom Miller
2014-15: Paul Farman
2015-16: Bradley Wood

Top Goalscorer

1993-94 David Johnson 13
1994–95 G Bannister, M Carbon, D West 8
1995–96 Gareth Ainsworth 13
1996–97 Gareth Ainsworth 24
1997–98 Lee Thorpe 14
1998–99 Tony Battersby, Lee Thorpe 10
1999–00 Lee Thorpe 17
2000–01 Lee Thorpe 13
2001–02 Lee Thorpe 13
2002–03 Ben Futcher 11
2003–04 Gary Taylor-Fletcher 19
2004–05 Simon Yeo 23
2005–06 Marvin Robinson 11
2006–07 Jamie Forrester 18
2007–08 Ben Wright 15
2008–09 Adrian Pătulea 11
2009–10 Davide Somma 9
2010–11 Ashley Grimes 17
2011–12 Sam Smith 9
2012–13 Jamie Taylor 16
2013–14 Ben Tomlinson 20
2014–15 Ben Tomlinson 14
2015–16 Matt Rhead 23

Managers

Keith Alexander
1st August 1993 - 16th May 1994 — P48 W13 D13 L22 — **27.08%**

Sam Ellis
1st August 1994 – 4th September 1995 — P56 W21 D12 L23 — **37.50%**

Steve Wicks
4th September 1995 – 16th October 1995 — P7 W0 D2 L5 — **00.00%**

John Beck
16th October 1995 6th March 1998 — P130 W48 D42 L40 — **36.92%**

Shane Westley
7th March 1998 - 11th November 1998 — P30 W9 D5 L16 — **30.00%**

John Reames
11th November 1998 – 1st June 2000 — P87 W30 D21 L36 — **34.48%**

Phil Stant
1st June 2000 – 27th February 2001 — P38 W12 D10 L16 — **31.58%**

Alan Buckley
28th February 2001 - 25th April 2002 — P69 W16 D24 L29 — **23.19%**

Keith Alexander
5th May 2002 24th - May 2006 — P213 W81 D69 L63 — **38.03%**

John Schofield
15th June 2006 – 15th October 2007 — P51 W21 D12 L18 — **41.18%**

Peter Jackson
30th October 2007 2nd September 2009 — P92 W32 D21 L39 — **34.78%**

Chris Sutton
28th September 2009 28th September 2010 — P51 W14 D14 L23 — **28.00%**

Steve Tilson
5th October 2010 – 10th October 2011 — P37 W11 D7 L19 — **29.73%**

David Holdsworth
24th October 2011 – 17th February 2013 — P71 W21 D19 L31 — **29.57%**

Gary Simpson
27 February 2013 3 November 2014 — P58 W23 D15 L20 — **39.65%**

Chris Moyses
3 November 2014 12 May 2016 — P64 W22 D15 L27 — **34.38%**

Danny Cowley
12th May 2016 – present — P19 W12 D3 L4 — **63.15%**

Interviews

Bradley Wood Interview

Bradley Wood is one of those players that any Imps fan must rate highly from the very first time you see him play. I remember the first time I saw him in action, he clattered a winger in a solid but fair challenge and then set off down the wing in true Mark Bailey style. The similarity between Mark Bailey and Bradley Wood is uncanny. They're both up and down full backs, they'd both run through walls for their team and they're both nice blokes. Mind you Bradley has something Bailey doesn't have: three player of the year awards won in one campaign. It's something he's very proud of.

"Winning those awards, it felt great to know that my hard work was getting recognition. I loved last season. Enjoyed working hard and playing football. First time I can say that for a few years now and to be voted player of the year by 3 different sources was incredible. The lads all congratulated me and were spot on. Great group of men, which a few wouldn't have been far away for the prizes."

It might have been a great group of men, but one man in particular seemed to bring the players together. Success by some is measured by league position, but by this writer success could also be measured by progress and the outgoing manager oversaw a period of progress. He clearly had an influence on Brad as well.

"Moysey understood me. He knew how to get the best out of me. It's always great when you're wanted too. He bought me from Alfreton so I was clearly someone he wanted as a player. I just hope I repaid him."

I don't think there's any doubt that Brad did him proud, but what was it Chris had that made him special to the players?

"He respected the lads. In the changing room the lads knew Moysey's door was always open for anything and he was a genuine top guy. In my seven years as a pro he's the best gaffer I've had."

There's no doubt that Chris was the catalyst for a group of players battling at the right end of the table, despite falling away late on. I was interested to know if anyone stood out as a talented player in the City ranks. The fans and media saw Brad as the best player we had last season, it interested me to see who he thought was talented.

"There are many lads in the squad with different talents. Rheady is the best target man that I've lined up with, 9 times out of 10 you can guarantee he will win a header or hold the ball up. There's plenty of talent at Lincoln it's just playing to everyone's individual asset to get the best out of the player."

I got the impression that this answer was more genuine than an attempt to avoid naming individual team mates for praise. Part of me hoped it was because the players might get to read DF and might even submit to an interview with me!

Brad really came to the fore in the wake of Liam Hearn's departure from the club to go on loan to Barrow. He summed up in an interview how many of the players felt, and although his remarks may have seemed inflammatory they only echoed how a number of fans actually felt. I was interested to know if this caused any friction on Liam's return.

"To be fair to Liam he came back and was fine with the lads etc but you could tell he wasn't himself. I got on well with Liam at Grimsby such a shame it ended the way it did as he is a good goal scorer."

Brad may tell it how it is, but he isn't controversial for the sake of it. Liam has gone and yet the knives are not out. Telling it like it is doesn't always means you have to be undiplomatic. I was beginning to understand there's more to Bradley Wood than the 'heart on sleeve' and 'never say die' attitude he has on the pitch. He's an emotionally intelligent and well spoken man who understands the impact of the things he says. I wasn't going to get any quotes that could cause trouble and I respect that in a player. I thought I'd fish (pun intended) a little harder for some anti Grimsby stuff, I knew he'd had a bad time when he left and I wondered how he saw it.

"I signed for Grimsby when they were in the football league before relegation. My deal was a 4 year contract and if I started 120 games it triggered an extra year. The more appearances I played the more money I was on. I was 1 game away from extending my deal for another year and I fully knew they knew this. They offered me a reduced contract on basically half my wages as they couldn't justify a 21 year old being on the money I was on and I rejected it as it was poor and went to Alfreton."

I knew from some Town fans that he'd been on a decent deal, but even so the way the Cods went about it seemed unfair, especially for a player who would never let a side down. Their loss was Alfreton's gain as Bradley went on to represent England C.

"I'm very patriotic so representing my country was a very proud moment for me and my family. Just signing the national anthem before a game makes hair on the back of your neck stand up. I loved it. It's up there with the best moments of my career."

I was interested in the mention of his family. Those who are on the Lincoln City banter site will know that his other half is very prominent on there, and it's no secret that he is a dedicated family man with very strong family values. I wondered how he felt about some of the stuff on banter, and how Loren reacted to things on there as well.

"Loren is very outspoken and tries to interact with all fans. It's not a case of her opinion is the only one that matters. She's learnt that there are people out there who like me and people who don't. Football is a game of opinions and at the moment I'm liked more than disliked. That can all change. I'm visible on social media as I like interacting with fans as I'm just a normal person like everyone else. I'm down to earth. I'm sure it has an effect on people when there being either slated or praised as football can be a confidence game at stages."

It was fascinating that chatting about a proud moment like England got a shorter response than chatting about his family. I'd always known he was a family man, and when he talks about them it becomes very obvious what drives him. It's the same thing that drives me to get up and go to work: family. Not all professional footballers have family as a grounding in their life, but for Brad it seems to be a priority and that makes him all the more likeable and down to earth.

237

Last season wasn't all roses and sunshine for the versatile full back though. A red card against Tranmere left him gutted at the prospect of letting the lads down, and then in the final game of the season he became a light snack for Cheltenham thug Kyle Storer.

"When I got sent off I was gutted mate. I try and do my best for the team week in week out. I thought the lads were spot on that day and earned a point but last few minutes let it go. Afterwards I just felt it had happened and I had to get up and get on with it."

"Against Cheltenham, he was shielding the ball out of play and I closed him down. He fell down and dragged me down with him. I tried to get up and could feel something on the back of my arm/shoulder like a pinch mark. Then I noticed he was clinching on with his mouth. There was a bit of handbags with the other players but I told the ref and everyone involved that he bit me. I don't mind the physical part of the game at all, but not biting!!!"

Throughout my talk with Bradley I was impressed by his honesty and how down to earth he was. Even when talking about being bitten he was reasonable, and the dejection at his Tranmere sending off was clear for all to see.

Time and space is running out on me here, so I just wanted a few words on Danny Cowley, Clive Nates and where his career goes from here.

On Danny Cowley: "I've met the gaffer once (this interview was done on June 14th, 2016) and he seems to be driven to do well and progress which is a good asset to have. He seems to have his own method which has bought him success so I hope that continues here."

On Clive Nates: "I've met Clive once at a fans forum. He seemed a real genuine nice guy who has a lot of knowledge about the game. He comes across as someone who, if he wants something to happen then he is driven for it to work. In football that is great as we can all go the same way and get this football club back where it belongs which is the football league."

Finally I asked him about his Lincoln City career. With three player of the season awards in one campaign he is rapidly becoming a fans favourite, and in my household he is already up there with Mark Bailey, Peter Gain and Simon Yeo as a firm favourite.

"I'm happy to stay here and finish my career here as long as the management want me. Never ever been so happy playing football. I love the way the club treat my family too. That's the main thing!"

I don't think it's any surprise that the well being of his family comes in as important as the quality of his football. I like that in Bradley Wood, he has values that are in line with most average blokes, he just puts bread on the table a different way. He is far removed from the controversial 'tell it like it is' figure some have him down as though. He's honest but he won't speak out of turn. He's aware how his actions are viewed by people, from comments in an interview to red cards on the pitch. I can tell this isn't just a job to him, he is committed to helping get us back where we belong. I believe another season like the last one will see him a very important cog in the upcoming Cowley's campaign.

Paul Farman Interview

It's fair to say that popular keeper Paul Farman hasn't had the easiest of rides in his career. In amongst the player of the year awards and chants of England's number one there's the odd gaff and spell out of the team. However whatever adversity has been thrown at him he seems to press on through with a cheeky grin and a joke, and he's undoubtedly the number one name on the team sheet these days.

Farms started out at non league Washington and soon alerted the scouts from Newcastle Utd.

"The reason I ended up on trial at Newcastle was both keepers had bad injuries at the time and they basically asked me to come in and see what happens. I do really wish I could have done more when I was there to gain a contract but it didn't work out for me. Paul Dummett was there at the time and look what he is doing now every lads dream to be born in Newcastle and end up playing for them.

The Newcastle boy had his childhood dream shattered, but undeterred he ended up turning out for Gateshead in the conference. That route soon led him to the hallowed turf of Sincil Bank.

"Coming here on loan was the best thing I have ever done. I remember I did a pitch photo with Conal Platt at the time, I looked around and thought 'sh*t this is really a massive club'. I remember telling my pals the ground was huge. I didn't know any of the lads at my first training session. In fact my first 2 sessions I had a bit of a beast to be honest, but on Saturday I had a good game and we beat Barrow 2-1."

The loan spell expired and Farms went back to Gateshead much to the dismay of Imps fans who had been impressed with his performances. However the end of the season came around and he was released. He was once again without a club.

"To be honest I didn't know if any club wanted me but at the time I was young and thought everything would fall together. Then after I started to think about it I began to worry. Luckily a deal got offered to me after few days of Lincoln hearing I had been released. I was delighted with it, it was a big step for me moving away from home but I looked forward to it."

Playing for Lincoln shortly after his move cannot have been a pleasant experience. A succession of weak back lines often led to Farms being the last line of defence. Whilst it meant he saw plenty of action, nobody wants to be a goalkeeper in the wrong half of the table. Eventually whilst looking to sort the leaky defence Nick Townsend was brought in, and when his move became permanent it looked like the popular Farman was on his way. It seemed harsh as many fans thought Farms was doing okay.

"I was gutted but just thought 'it is what it is', and got my head down. I was wanting to enjoy some games. Boston as a club and lads were ledge to be honest. I said if I was going to go down a level I wanted it to be them. I did want to stay in our league but to be real I had no offers, so that's when I said I would like to go Boston."

Despite picking up an injury Farms was kee to make an impression.

"That week I got a shoulder injury in training but managed to get myself fit for their game at Alfreton by taking serious amount of pain killers and strapping up my shoulder until it was more like scaffolding!"

However bouncing back from that hit came in the most spectacular of ways. After starting the season out of favour, he ended it with two Player of the Year awards under his belt.

"I was absolute buzzing when I got those awards. Echo's Player of the Season and Player of Season as voted by the fans, especially after all the shenanigans. It was a very proud moment for me as family were there as well."

Those performances have seen him twice called up to the England C squad and both times he had to miss out. Whilst at Gateshead he was due to play against India, but the opposition pulled out at last minute, then whilst at Lincoln he was due to play against Albania but it was abandoned due to the rain. He'd even got the shirt on

"I'd put the shirt on in the changing room and it felt good, but there's not much you can do about the weather. I've seen the changing rooms flood in Sunday League, , I had my fingers crossed but when the water started coming through the floor we knew there wasn't much hope."

Last season Farms cemented his place in between the sticks and appeared to develop under the watchful eye of David Preece.

"David Preece matured me as a keeper I think his game rubbed off a bit on myself, he got me in a good place playing wise but it was down to hard work and making sure whatever session he put on he got the best out of me at the time."

Although he hasn't featured in too many successful Imps campaigns (until this season hopefully), Farms has played with some very talented players who have gone on to play league football.

"Jon Nolan stood out for me, he has got so much ability and look where he is playing now. Fair play it didn't work out here from him here, he went elsewhere and gained himself a great move."

If picking one Imps nemesis wasn't bad enough, he delved a little deeper in the Imps sin bin to pull out the name of another incredibly talented ex player.

"Also Newts (Sean Newton) was another good signing as people all know his delivery in to the box is absolute northern gravy."

If only his attitude was! Either way Chris Moyses came in and was able to begin to mould the fortunes of the club and set foundations in place for us to kick on.

"I really enjoyed playing under Chris Moyses, another guy like Preecey that got the best out of me. I thought that he brought a good feel around the club to build on. Like now he had all the players playing for the shirt and the club, something the club may have lacked previously. He signed honest lads that are willing to dog deep for each other."

Chris standing down was a bit of a surprise in the summer, but the board seem to have got it spot on by bringing in Danny and Nicky Cowley from Braintree. It seems like things have gone to the next level at Sincil Bank.

"As you read and have seen yourself everything is to the finest details and they have thier own methods and get them across well. We as lads are still adapting to it, but we are all buying into it. We as players all want success and if it is going to be a certain way and a new method to us we will keep doing it."

So everything seems geared towards success this season, and only time and results will tell if the Paul Farman fairy tale is going to have it's happy ending.

"I want one thing in my career and that's a promotion under my belt. If I can look back and say that I'll be a happy man. It's simple which club I want it with!! Some might say I have no aspiration to push on and play higher, but I could happily play my career out at Lincoln. I want to achieve my career goals with this club. We're all imps aren't we.?"

Characters like Paul Farman are crucial to our success this season, not only an accomplished performer on the pitch but a likeable personality off it. Most players would probably have given up after going out on loan to Boston, but like a boss he came back stronger and more determined to succeed. I don't think aspirations of league football shows a lack of ambition at all, I think it shows he buys into more than the 'me, me, me' culture at the top of our game. Paul Farman isn't just a goal keeper, he buys into the club and the fans as if he was sat in the stands with us. To a degree he measures his success by our collective success, and that is refreshing.

Peter Gain Interview

Peter Gain is one of Lincoln City's all-time greats. Voted at number 44 in the centenary legends vote of 2007, and he is amongst the top 30 all-time appearances holders for City with 263, scoring 22 times in league competition. He was virtually ever present in the fateful 2001/02 season and despite his obvious talent he elected to remain at the club through administration and out of the other side, virtually ever present again as we strode on to Cardiff in 2003. Unfortunately he didn't get the heroes goodbye, he disappeared out of the back door under a cloud. Now's he wants to redress the balance.

Peter Gain was also a big personal hero of mine. I've always liked players with a bit of flair and a penchant for the unexpected, and he had just that. He was unpredictable, could glide past players like they weren't there, and although he wasn't prolific, when he hit a shot it stayed hit. Not only did he have ability though, he also ran through walls for the shirt, just like each and every one of Keith Alexanders 2002/03 team. There's no wonder I was so delighted when I stumbled across him on social media the other week, even more so that it was through DF. It transpired that my hero from the Big Keith era was a follower of the Deranged Ferret Facebook page, and he casually commented on one of our picture quizzes. I seized my chance, and whilst chatting to him he told me our humble fanzine was partly responsible for turning Peter Gain into a club legend.

"My first season at Lincoln Steve Holmes had a copy of DF and it had an analysis on all players in squad. I remember reading it and being overwhelmed at my analysis it gave me so much confidence. That was turning point in my Lincoln career."

Gain initially signed on loan from Spurs in January of 1999 and he made his debut in the 3-0 LDV Vans Trophy win over Hartlepool. Three more appearances followed from the bench before the loan spell was up, although his Lincoln City career had barely started.

"Initially Gerry Francis was trying to get all the young players out on loan to gain experience, and I came to Lincoln. Spurs offered me another year but I had made a lot of friends at Lincoln. I really felt part of team whereas, as much I loved Spurs, I was tired of reserve football. I had the option to stay or go back to Spurs, and I chose the option of staying at Lincoln."

It wasn't easy for the young midfielder from Tottenham to force his way into the side, and the year he joined Lincoln wasn't the most harmonious either, signing initially under John Reames. Under Reames he got a bit of game time, and scored his first goal for City against Rochdale in November. Phil Stant took over as manager for a few months, but it was senior players who guided him in those early years.

"Steve Holmes was a great player, it was hard for him when I came because the club did seem to be in disarray. There was no organisation and those senior players had a lot of pressure to steer the ship with no real direction. It was still good being there but there was no stability no direction but big Keith changed all that, he was a great manager."

Keith arrived at the club under Alan Buckley as assistant, and Buckley had a left sided player he liked much more, his son Adam. Buckley frequently picked his son ahead of Gainy, leaving our future talisman to have an enforced spell out of the team. Before Adam signed Gainy was getting game time, scoring in only our second away win in a year as we beat Kidderminster in Buckley's second game in charge. However his son soon took a starting eleven spot.

"It bothered me not playing of course but that's football. I would always confide in Keith Oakes the physio at the time. He's a great man and was an integral part of our good times under Keith Alexander, an unsung hero if you like. I know if he had chosen to manage he would have been very successful and would still be managing today, it's a shame he never did."

I held off jumping to the seasons that made Gain a hero with the fans and gave us such much pride and respect in our football club. Here was a player who had been there as we plummeted towards administration, and a player who had stayed with us during those rough times. It was interesting to find out which other players played a key role before we entered administration.

"Justin Walker and Lee Thorpe were really good players. Terry Fleming was a great leader, as was Steve Holmes. Another leader was Grant Brown, those senior players were great for us younger ones at time."

It's hard to talk to a player who gave fans such great memories without wading straight into those wonderful years under Keith Alexander. Peter Gain was an integral part of that side, producing moments of sublime vision and often awe inspiring technical ability. When Simon Yeo needed an assist to score the goal against Torquay, it came from Peter Gain. It all started in the summer of 2002.

"The start of the good times! Although we never won anything on paper it felt like we were champions those few years especially because everyone wrote us off, but soonpeople started paying attention."

There's no doubt that Keith instilled a confidence in Gain, and although we now know DF played a part the Gaffer built up a good relationship with his talented midfield creator.

"I played quite a bit for Keith in the reserves during Adam Buckley's spell in side. I think I scored in five consecutive matches and so we always had a rapport. He gave me freedom every time I played and it just continued from there. The first season was the same for us players as I'm sure it was for the fans, we were favourites to get relegated at the start!!"

Despite his obvious talent Gainy was unable to fire us to play-off victory against Bournemouth, nor again against Southend two years later. However had it not been for his craft and guile we may not have ended up there at all.

"I remember in particular the assist I played through to Simon Yeo second play-off game against Scunthorpe to seal the final spot. It was a dream to be in both finals but on a personal level I never played half as well as I should. Maybe nerves got better of me, I always felt more pressure when my family watched and they only ever watched me in those finals unfortunately."

Over those three years the team that Keith built defied the odds time and time again. Two play-off finals and a semi-final defeat against Huddersfield followed. I've always maintained the 2003/04 team was the finest side I've ever seen take to the field.

"That's a hard one to call. Obviously Taylor-Fletcher would better any side, but that initial team got the ball rolling. McAuley and Taylor-Fletcher gave us more strength and depth overall."

It's clear to me Peter has an awful lot of affection for that first season and what the group of players achieved. Surely after such a great season players of his ability were in demand, and given administration the year before it was a surprise to maintain most of the players.

"When the club was in administration there was a good three months we didn't get paid. We were promised to be reimbursed, I only got some but I thought fair enough, I moved on and got on with it. After my first season under Keith I signed the same contract I was on at Christmas even though I had two solid pre contract offers from Oxford and Huddersfield for a lot more money. I was loving it at Lincoln and could sense good times were ahead, so I stayed for less money. I really do love Lincoln the fans, the people and the club itself."

The final season Peter played for us culminated in a Millennium Stadium appearance against Southend and ultimately a failure to achieve what the club deserved. I always pinpoint the fall out of the Marcus Richardson and Ciaran Toner affair.

"Maybe, both were very good players. If Yeo's legitimate goal wasn't ruled offside we would have won. Football is all about ifs and buts"

Whether we went up or not that team achieved something that managers have tried for a decade, and that was a restored pride. As a fan you could be proud of your club and of the players, and Peter Gain was right at the heart of that. The Monday after a Gain goal was always the day to get work mates and non-believers to watch Look North to see what this extraordinary footballer had produced yet again. Great goals were a part of his all-round game.

"My favourite Lincoln goals were twice away at Carlisle, we won 2-0 and 4-1. I scored a scissor kick at home to Hull in front of the Stacey West as well, that was a good goal."

That was more than a good goal, this writer remembers spilling half a cup of coke as his 78th minute strike set us up for a 2-0 win over the now-Premiership giants. It was a good time to be a Lincoln fan, with a squad laden with good players.

"There was a lot of players who stood out for me. Probably the ones that stood out the most were Gareth McCauley, Simon Yeo and the late Richard Butcher, but really there are too many to mention. Oh, of course I have to say Gary Taylor-Fletcher! Stuart Bimson was an experienced player who always helped younger pros"

Richard Butcher is another player from that time who is remembered fondly, and between the two of them they formed an iconic midfield pairing. Butcher and Gain were surely the first two names on the Lincoln City team sheet for two and a half seasons.

246

"I want to mention to Gail Butcher and her family. She's a great woman who does so much in Richard's memory to help others. She's a great woman. Richard was the nicest player in football. I know that's a cliche but he really was everyone loved him and playing with him was a pleasure. He was 100% dedicated and, as you know, a great all round player"

Eventually the end came, and when it did there was no fairy tale for our star midfielder. All that was left was a reputation slightly tarnished for a decade, branded (by some) as someone who sold the club down the river. That wasn't the case then, and Peter is keen to put his side of the story across.

"I need to clarify this because I feel my relationship with the fans has been tarnished and I sincerely loved the Lincoln supporters and always will. After two successful seasons my contract came up again and I had three offers from Huddersfield (again), Peterborough and I think it was Rushden. They all offered more money and all it came down to was £50 a week. It broke my heart. I dreamed of a testimonial at Lincoln, but it came down to the principle not the money. My loyalty in previous contracts was not rewarded, and of course I hated way it ended."

The next season Gain scored against Lincoln at Peterborough and celebrated passionately. Some fans turned on him after that, but it wasn't a reaction to scoring past Lincoln, it was a reaction to one or two idiots who had singled him out for abuse.

"I got a lot of stick that day. I was always passionate on the pitch but when I hear personal insults, not related to football I reacted. I hate the fact that Lincoln supporters remember that and the manner in which I left, it's heart breaking."

Just like 1999 when a DF article gave a young player from Spurs confidence to perform to the best of his ability, I hope a DF article can today give an Imps legend the praise he deserved. We saw last season with Chris Moyses how vitriol and abuse can provoke a reaction, and it's clear to me speaking to Peter for a period of time that he has carried a sadness around with him since his departure from Sincil Bank.

"In hindsight I would never have dreamt of celebrating a goal against the fans I loved for so long but like I said during a game so much adrenaline takes over and when I heard personal insults I lost my head. It wasn't football related and I directed my frustration out on that minority, not the real Lincoln fans, although I still feel some were bitter towards me sadly"

These days we see Simon Yeo in the stands as a fan, we have memorials to Keith and Butch and we look on proudly as Gareth McAuley takes to the field for Northern Ireland. Each and every one of those players are 'one of our own', players who cared as much as the rank and file fan, players who battled and fought for the pride and reputation of the football club.

Peter Gain did exactly that as well, and although the manner of his departure upset some, looking back I feel his motivation was understandable. The club had experienced three years of success and arguably our most talented player felt he wasn't being respected. Peter is now a plumber, he didn't have a lucrative career and hasn't been set up for life. After four or five years of dedication to the club, didn't he deserve a tiny bit more security for him and his family? Peterborough offered a three year deal, the sort of security that footballers crave.

Gary Taylor Fletcher hadn't missed out on wages when we went into administration, and not every player subsequently turned down bigger offers to remain a part of the club. Anyone who choose to remember a one-off goal celebration at Peterborough is choosing to remember the wrong thing entirely. I know Gainy hopes this interview will show fans that he wasn't a money grabber, and those years in the heart of Keith's revolution meant everything to him. I asked if he wanted to add anything as we wound things up.

"Just that I loved my time at Lincoln. I loved the city, I loved the people, and those fans will always have a place in my heart."

I know many Imps fans who hold Gainy in the same esteem, after all in 2007 when the legends vote was cast he was a Peterborough players, and yet he still beat the likes of Dennis Booth, Dennis Leigh and Steve Thompson. I hope now that with this heartfelt article he can be remembered for the right things.

Marcus Stergiopolous Interview

Marcus Stergiopolous is the type of player I really wanted this book to pay homage to. I remember his goal against Sheffield United, and the impact hehad in his short stay, but sixteen years on he is nothing more than a footnote, and name in a column in somebodies old programme. Marcus Stergiopolous was much more than that, and still is. He is just the sort of rich and interesting player that makes up the largest portion of Lincoln's appearances holders; the lesser-known short term player.

Marcus arrived after being spotted by former City manager Phil Stant.

"I was on trial at Wimbledon the year they were relegated from the EPL, and played in a few preseason trial friendlies where I caught the eye of Phil Stant. When my contract negotiations fell through at Wimbledon, I was then offered a contract at Notts County and played in another preseason trial game v Sheffield United, and had an absolute stinker."

Luckily for Sterg Phil Stant had seen something in him, enough to feel he was worth a punt at Sincil Bank.

"In the crowd that night was Phil Stant, who approached me in the car park after the game and made me an offer to come to Lincoln City FC. As it turned out, Notts County changed their mind after seeing me play v Sheffield United (I'm not surprised as I was dragged at half time), so I decided to give Lincoln a crack. I'd had enough of trial games, as I had more trials than OJ Simpson that summer."

It doesn't surprise me that Phil Stant scouted sides like Wimbledon and Sheff Utd. Both had reputations for being strong physical sides who liked to get in your face, and that summed Phil Stant up perfectly. It didn't sum up the Aussie midfielder though.

Oz (as he is known) only came in on a short term contract, but he saw enough in that Lincoln City side to convince him that they weren't all that far away in terms of players. What they lacked was direction.

"Off the park I liked Phil Stant, but on the park he and George Foster didn't have a Scooby-Do. Our game plan was direct, which literally killed my style - there were no tactics involved or a plan on how we were going to win, apart from get stuck in and get in their face. If it were me, my principles and overall philosophy would be to produce a group of intelligent, resourceful footballers, who can anticipate situations quicker and react more efficiently than their opponents to ensure whatever is achieved from a match is through design and not by accident."

There were some quality players at the club during Oz's tenure as an Imps player. Off the field the club was beset by financial problems, but that didn't stop us attracting good players.

"Justin Walker and Peter Gain in particular stood out in that squad - they reminded me more of a Spanish player who liked to keep the ball on the ground, tiki-taka style. However, there were some very decent players there like Lee Thorpe, John Finnigan, Gavin Gordon, Paul Mayo and Alan Marriott. We actually didn't have a bad side, we were just poorly coached."

Oz's first match against Sheff Utd hadn't gone well, and he'd been in the Lincoln squad that lost 6-1 at Bramall Lane. His final match against them at Sincil Bank was much better for him though, and he produced a superb free kick to give Lincoln a strong but ultimately pointless win.

"I remember that goal well v Sheffield United, however my 25 yard free kick against Rotherham United and my goal direct from a corner v Southend United in the preseason were better."

That night it looked as if the exotically named midfielder might have a good career at Sincil Bank. We so often lacked dead ball specialists, but in a team that had no direction, flair players simply couldn't flourish.

"I remember the week I left clearly. All week Phil Stant was training me as a left winger (I'm never a winger by the way) for the up coming weekend match. Then Kingsley Black rocks up on a Friday, Kingsley starts that weekend and I'm then dropped to the bench. On top of that, the club were going through some financial trouble at the time my 3 month contract expired. So when it came to renegotiating my stay at the club for the remaining of the season the club then offered me 100 pounds per week after I was getting 500 pounds per week. My rent was 75 pounds per week, it just made it difficult to stay, as much as I wanted to - I couldn't financially. So I was literally forced to leave, which was a very sad time, not just myself, but for my wife too."

That was the end of Oz, the former child prodigy and latterly over-rated lump Kingsley Black cost us the chance of seeing more of the mercurial midfielder. There's no regrets about his time in Lincoln.

"My wife and I thoroughly enjoyed our time there. The club were very good towards me and the fans made me feel very welcome. My wife and I had a nice little one bedroom place just around the corner from the ground, although it wasn't big enough to swing a cat, it was a place we called home. We enjoyed the city environment and spend many hours trying to find a place that served good coffee."

After Lincoln he didn't hang around in England, embarking on a career that took him back home before a spell state side.

"I returned back home to Australia and continued my professional career when not long after I was offered a short 3-month deal at Columbus Crew in the MLS. I linked up with US Internationals Brain McBride and Edson Buddle that season. I thoroughly enjoyed playing in the MLS, it was a very much slow build up from the back, possession style through the lines and very tactical. I came up again Carlos Valderrama at Tampa Bay and Histo Stoichkov at Chicago Fire throughout my travels. Great times!"

He went from being kept on the Lincoln bench by Paul Miller, to pitting his wits against two of the best players of a generation. He hasn't ruled out a reurn to the game at some point.

"I've completed my Advanced Pro Coaching badges here in Australia, which along with Japan, is recognised as the advanced in Asia and is the equivalent to the UEFA A in Europe. However, with only

12 professional clubs here in Australia, it's hard to get a full time job. So it's then a matter of either coaching semi-professionally or casting an eye overseas like Malaysia, China, Japan and India as Australian coaches who have completed the Advance Pro Licence are in demand. That said, I'm always looking at what opportunities are available in England.It's tough as it's not what you know, but who you know over there."

Gijsbert Bos Interview

The giant Dutchman Gijsbert Bos arrived at Lincoln City in 1996 for a fee of £10,000. He was very different to the usual journeyman striker we'd been used to. First off he was tall, really tall. He stood at six feet and four inches, which suited the John Beck philosophy very well. It would do Gijsbert a disservice though to assume he was all height and no ability; he was stereotyped more by who the manager was than his own style of play.

He started out with Dutch side Ijsselmeervogels, and despite a career that brought him to deepest, darkest England, it was in Spain he first looked like securing a contract.

"Coming to England was very surprising to be honest. I never thought about professional football I stopped playing football from age 17 till 20. I only started playing again in a very low division for fun at age 21, before I moved to Ijsselmeervogels. They were in the highest amateur Dutch league, and were my local favourites."

Ijsselmeervogels won their league that year, and as they did things changed quickly for the likeable striker.

"After winning that league in my first year, things went fast. An agent called me if I was interested to play abroad. I rejected the chance to play for Extremadura who were a top Primera B side in Spain. They became champions and played Primera division the year after. I rejected the move because playing on Sunday would probably have cost my relationship with my future wife (still is) because of religious reasons. Spanish football was on Sundays, so I thought that's my professional chance gone."

Despite this set back it is admiral to hear a player prioritising his quality of life, and in particular relationship over and above his football career. However, his chance was still to come.

"When Lincoln came I was flattered to get another chance and jumped at the opportunity."

England certainly isn't Spain though, and even compared to the Netherlands our climate can be quite harsh.

"When I first came over on a trial I wasn't really impressed because the weather was terrible! It was snowing, then raining and windy. Groundsman Nigel Dennis (R.I.P) showed me around that first night when I arrived and even switched on the lights at Sincil Bank, and then I was sold straight away."

Even as far back as twenty years ago our ground was tempting players, and the ethos of our staff was welcoming and accommodating. Nigel Dennis was a wonderful member of staff and it's nice that ex-players remember him fondly.

"Next day I met the players and staff who were very nice and welcoming. I can remember the third day as I called my mother to tell her I was never gonna play abroad as I became a little homesick."

In the Premier League our foreign imports have fixers who look after their every need, but in the lower reaches it seems that it wasn't quite the same. The young man from Spakenburg initially didn't feel he could settle in Lincoln. That all changed;
"After my trial game away at Shrewsbury for the reserves, (we lost but I scored), John Beck called me in his office and asked me if I was interested in signing for little old Lincoln (as he always called them). Surprisingly my homesick melted as snow in August!"

At the time there were some skilful players at City despite us lumping it forward into danger alley, but they didn't always get to showcase their talents. Some were more obviously suited to the game than others.

"Of course Gareth Ainsworth stood out the most as our type of play was made for him as he was fast and strong. Players like Terry Fleming and Jae Martin were maybe more technical, but there was no room for us to play the passing game, the Dutch way. I didn't have any favourite players though, I liked them all. We had a good team spirit."

It wasn't always plain sailing though, John Beck had a clear strategy which didn't always suit the players' strengths.

"I don't have to tell you our style of football under John Beck, it wasn't quite attractive and we were not supposed to pass and play as we should and definitely could. We had to play long ball and go down the channels as he preferred it."

John Beck's tactics pulled Lincoln out of a hole, and goals from the big striker certainly helped. Frustration mounted though as Lincoln continued to play spoiling tactics despite having a strong squad of players.

"I can remember at home against Mansfield, before the game there was a lot of hassle going on in town with their fans, police sirens could been heard at Sincil Bank. With Lincoln 1-0 up, the game was really tight when I received the ball on the left halfway the pitch, I ran past a defender cut inside and scored a screamer in the top corner from about 25 yards. Afterwards John Beck was a little bit angry and told me if the ball wouldn't have gone in he would have subbed me because I didn't play down the channels, in his style. I thought he made a joke but he wasn't joking. the game ended 2-1."

Lincoln were on a date with destiny, and Gijsbert was cast in the lead role. After he scored in the first round first leg against Hartlepool, City secured a 5-4 win and a tie against Manchester City as a reward. Even as a second-tier side Man City were a big draw for any club, and the first leg was to be played in front of 7,599 fans at Sincil Bank.

"The draw was perfect of course, Man City were, and still are a big name to get in the Coca Cola Cup. After 3 minutes I think they scored to make it 0-1, and I thought they would destroy us. As the game developed we got a little more grip and scored the equalizer which was brilliant but surprisingly they didn't speed up the game and that left us with a challenge which we took with both hands. We kept fighting and scored three more goals, included a flick on from me after a long throw to make it 4-1. I still thought this was probably not enough for the away game at Maine Road."

The old Maine Road was a tight and intimidating ground, and John Beck's little old Lincoln City weren't given a hope of snatching a win by pundits. The best we could do would be shut up shop and hope for the best. The pundits were wrong.

"The big night at Maine Road will never leave my memory. Although my goal was a simple tap in we won the game 1-0 and my name would never be forgotten to those who supported Lincoln at that time."

The name Gijsbert Bos will be remembered by more than just the Imps fans of the time. To beat Man City over two legs was a great achievement, and had it not been for a disputed penalty against Premier League Southampton, City might have progressed further. John Beck was hailed by many as a hero.

"John Beck; first I have to thank him, because he was the one who bought me and gave me the opportunity of a lifetime, which I will always remember as one of my best times ever. In those three years in England I became the man I am now."

It wasn't all roses and light though. Beck was a strong disciplinarian and a man whom it was very easy to fall out with. Even the laid-back and amiable Bos could see there were problems.

"He was my downfall as a technical player as we were only allowed to hook and head balls into the corners. Everything I learned in Holland he wanted me to forget, just to play long balls and guide them in the corners. Everyone who didn't do what he wanted got subbed, even players who just came on were subbed after 15 minutes if they didn't play his game."

At first the style was effective at getting the Imps out of the relegation spaces, but as he persisted with the long ball approach it frustrated a large portion of the fans, and the players.

"I did understand this game when I just came to Lincoln as we were bottom of the league and we needed a strategy which would make us like a machine fighting for our lives. The next season we were still playing this style and players started to question this. I really liked Lincoln and I never wanted to leave, but as for John Beck he didn't liked players questioning his style as I did."

Eventually the brash and abrasive manager pushed his player too far.

"I had a bust up with him before the summer break. I told him I was getting married in 2 weeks-time and wanted some more time off, but he wanted me to come back at Lincoln after two weeks' holiday to train twice a week. I told him to ******, and if it wasn't for John Still (Assistant Manager at that time) I would have punched him."

That was the end of his Lincoln City career. He'd hit ten goals from 35 starts, but was cast aside for daring to question his manager. Lincoln City would go on to get promoted the following season, but Beck would be dismissed before that happened. Gijsbert moved on to pastures new.

"That argument was me finished at Lincoln basically, He sold me to Rotherham United in pre-season. Rotherham was not really what I had hoped for, although my personal life became better as my wife came over after our marriage, so I wasn't alone anymore. After a slow start I found my way into the team, only to get injured a lot. It got even more difficult to come back after injury as every time I got injured they took someone on loan. I understood why, but it was frustrating to see that they bought the one who replaced me."

After falling out of favour at Rotherham injuries took their toll again.

"I even went on loan for 6 weeks to Walsall but at the time they were planning to buy me I got injured again. When the second season at Rotherham developed and I still wasn't fit, I decided to quit and return to my home town back in Holland, where I was been able to buy a house. Even though I got the opportunities to keep playing somewhere else, we (my wife and I) decided to call it a day and return to Holland. I know people would think I was crazy to stop being a professional footballer but for us it was probably the best decision. When we came back we both found good jobs and as for playing football I returned to my old club Ijsselmeervogels and became champions again I kept playing first team football till I was 35."

Despite the somewhat auspicious end to his Lincoln career, those goals against Manchester City alone have ensured the name of Gijsbert Bos will always be mentioned in Lincoln City folklore. He was the guy who scored at Maine Road as we won 1-0.

"I am 43 now and I still look back at that time in England and mostly Lincoln and cherish everything. Last year I came over for a charity match for Lincoln legends and met with most of the players. I even stayed with my best mate back then, Shane Clarke and his girlfriend Kerry."

Gijsbert is still happily married to Aleida and they have two children, a beautiful daughter aged 14 years old and a son of nine who he hopes ' be my succesor in 10 years time'. If that means scoring a winner for Lincoln in the cup against Man City, then I hope the same!

It was a real pleasure to chat to Gijsbert Bos. I was just 17 the night he scored at Maine Road, and his goal gave everyone connected with the club something to be proud of. 1996 was the summer of Britpop, the European Championships in England, Cool Britannia and then to cap it all off, little old Lincoln beat Manchester City. Twice.

Contributors

Thanks must go to the small band of contributors who have offered their insights at various points in the book. They've spoken of their heroes and villains, the players that they have been influenced by and cheered or jeered. So thank you to the following people in no particular order:

Chris Gooding:
My name is Chris Gooding and I'm a Lincoln City fanatic I love everything that comes with following our great club but then if you're reading this I know you feel the same...

Oscar Chamberlain:
Oscar Chamberlain is a football, tennis and basketball commentator who works for PSG-TV, the WTA and FIBA. Born in Rome, he became a City fan in 2002 whilst studying at the University of Lincoln.

Mark Whiley:
Mark is the Lincoln City correspondent for the Lincolnshire Echo and a Lincoln City fan to boot.

Tim Priestley:
Tim Priestley is Lincoln-born but now lives in Mansfield. He was taken to his first game in 1981 but wasn't tall enough to see over the terrace wall so his dad made him a wooden step. Tim is a Deputy Head teacher in a primary school and is married. He has two boys.

Walter Senkiw:
Long suffering Imps fan living in Holmfirth......future Imps and England manager destined to lead both teams to incredible success and become a living legend.....

Adam Barlow:
Adam Barlow attended his first Lincoln City match in 1994 aged 15 and has been hocked ever since then going to most home games and about a third of the away matches per season. Adam is also a collecting nut and owns every home match programme since the 94/95 season

Charlie Russell: @ElWriteBack
Charlie Russell is currently a trainee Sports Journalist at Leeds Trinity University. Following previous work experience at Match Magazine and Lincolnshire Echo, Russell has now secured a position with FC Halifax Town during the summer working on their website throughout pre-season. A former Lincoln City season ticket holder, the 18-year-old has a broad knowledge of the Non-League game.

The best Imps side of the last 23 years?

The following was a blog I wrote in March of 2016, and I thought it might be a nice way to end the book. The last great Lincoln City side, until (we hope) the Danny and Nicky Cowley tea of 2016.

A great side has to actually achieve something to be called great. You may have a team packed with wonderful ability, but in order to receive recognition from fans as a great side you need something to show for it. The level of success really depends on the club as well, so for instance a great Chelsea side may win the Champions League but if they qualified for the League Two play offs then the side couldn't be considered as great. However for a success starved team like Lincoln City I think an appearance at a national stadium qualifies that team to be classed as great.

That's why I'd like to end the book by discussing the last great Lincoln City side, that of Keith Alexander's Play Off Finalists in 2005. Arguably the culmination of the hard work that Keith had put in, this season more than any represented a real chance to progress to League One, and to do so with the best Lincoln City squad for over two decades.

I'm not going to talk you through the season, I'm merely going to tell you why I believe this team was a truly magnificent Lincoln City side. I'd like to draw your attention to a particular date, Monday 28th March 2005.

That damp evening we took on our near rivals Scunthorpe United live on Sky Sports. We took The Iron apart with an exquisite opener inside thirty seconds and then we put it to bed ten minutes before the end with a sublime chip that Eric Cantona would have been proud of. There's no surprise we did though, because the starting eleven was one to really fear.

In the sticks that night was Alan Marriott, as he was for most of the years we competed in League Two's upper echelons. He was a great servant to the club and despite being relatively small he was also a very good goalkeeper. He first earned the nickname 'England's number one' from the Stacey West end and he really deserved to pick up the League Two Keeper of the Year award at least twice in his Imps career.

The defence was so ridiculously strong it beggars belief. That's not to say we didn't concede goals, but looking at the names on paper that started that evening you'll find a who's who of good quality defenders. Kevin Sandwith is perhaps one that won't stand out, but he was a competent full back with a great free kick in his repertoire. His team mates that day however were of a very high calibre: Jamie McCombe, Gareth McCauley, Ben Futcher and Paul Morgan.

If you stood McCombe, Futcher and McAuley on each other's shoulders they'd stand somewhere around nineteen feet high, and two of them went on to prove themselves at a higher level. We know McAuley and McCombe went on to bigger and better things, and although Futcher plied his trade around as many of our rivals as he could he has to be acknowledged as a good player for Lincoln. However at the time I feel captain Paul Morgan was more important than any one of them.

In his prime Paul Morgan was a terrific defender. He had pace and a tough uncompromising style that made up where he lacked in inches. After in excess of 200 appearances for Lincoln he never made the step up to the next level, but at that time in 2005 he was the jewel in the defensive crown. He could read a game like you're reading this and tackled with the ferocity of an earthquake.

The midfield was made up of Richard Butcher and Peter Gain, a somewhat iconic pairing for connoisseurs of Imps history. With the style the side played they tried to get the full backs forward and often bypass the middle of the park, but whatever went through the midfield tended to be crafted with guile and speed of thought. Much has been said of Richard Butcher since his tragic passing and I think his legendary status with Imps fans now further cements my proposal that this was the last great Lincoln City side. However at the side of him Peter Gain proved himself as one of my all time favourite Imps with some skill and creativity that should have graced the Championship.

He also bagged over two hundred appearances at City, but struggled when he first arrived. Alan Buckley did his best to further his sons career at the expense of Gain on the left. In Buckleys first game Gain played a blinder against Mansfield, but suffered when left sided Adam Buckley came in and pinched his spot. That wasn't all he pinched though, and soon Gain was able to command a regular place as Buckley trickled into obscurity. When Peter Gain was on song I don't think there was ever a technically better player in a City shirt than him. He could drift around defenders and beat players with such wonderful grace. If he hit a ball properly then fifteen goalkeepers wouldn't have kept it out. Like Butcher he was in his prime in 2005.

Up front that evening against the Iron was a certain Francis Green. He'd come in from Peterborough for a fee which pushed us out of the bracket of relegation fodder and cash strapped strugglers and into serious promotion contenders. He'd hit eight goals including winners against the university cities of Oxford and Cambridge away from home. However his strike partners had considerably more success.

Gary Taylor Fletcher was another who played Premier League football in a successful career. He scored the second against Scunthorpe, a sumptuous chip from a tight angle. He set up the opener and generally had been in the sort of form that would later see him play for Leicester, Blackpool and Huddersfield. He'd scored in the first five games but suffered a little through inconsistency during the season. However he ended with 11 goals and despite the erratic form has gone on to prove himself a top footballer.

Leading scorer that season was Simon Yeo who not only opening the scoring on the night but also notched twenty three goals in total. He hit a hat trick away at Grimsby Town to give us county bragging rights, as well as scoring against Boston to ensure we earned the right to be called Pride of Lincolnshire that season.

We defeated Scunthorpe with ease that evening in a performance that epitomised many games that season. We didn't win every game and it wasn't always great, but results like that weren't rare. It wasn't all plain sailing, but with just two months of the season to go we were touted as potential automatic promotion candidates. The other side around us feared Lincoln City and knew with two years experience in playoff situations we'd be a tough opponent, and that was if we didn't go up automatically.

Of course history will tell you we didn't make it, and history will give you an indication as to why. In 1976 the all conquering Division 4 side didn't go on to greater things because Taylor left with a couple of players. Colin Murphy's side of the early 1980's didn't push on because of Gilbert Blades passion for book balancing. In 2005 I can point to on significant moment that I feel cost us a chance to climb the leagues.

In February of 2005 the Imps had a strong looking squad, as well as the players I've mentioned they also had midfielder Ciaran Toner and forward Marcus Richardson. Both were squad players but both knew the league and had plenty to offer the team. Both would have walked into seventy percent of our rivals teams as well, meaning a well balanced and finely tuned squad. However by the time we played Scunthorpe neither were with us, Toner was at Cambridge and Richardson at Rochdale. Something occurred on the training ground in 2005 that resulted in both being farmed out immediately no matter what the cost to the clubs success. The club simply got rid.

Fast forward to May 2005 and the play off final against Southend. Perhaps with both players in the squad we'd not even be there having potentially won a couple of crucial games in between, but that day the squad needed to be complete. We'd battled hard in Cardiff, but options from the bench were limited. Instead of the cultured Toner or the imposing Richardson we brought on Matt Bloomer, Lee Beevers and Derek Asamoah. Aside perhaps from Asamoah we were never likely to create anything positive with substations like those.

So maybe if Toner and Richardson hadn't had their coming together then we could have gone up that season. I firmly believe it is one of the best Lincoln City sides I've had the pleasure of watching. I also believe had we been promoted Keith Alexander may have got his wish of signing a few new players, with Aaron McClean, Craig Mackail Smith and George Boyd on his radar. Who knows what might have happened?

2005 also saw the arrival of Steff Wright as chairman, a man who in 2011 said he appointed John Schofield because "The fans wanted a better quality of football than had been played under Keith Alexander and appointing John was definitely the right thing to do at the time,"

I didn't. I was perfectly happy with play-off finals and mesmerising players like Taylor Fletcher and Peter Gain. I was perfectly happy with the resurgence the club experienced under Rob Bradley's stewardship. I was perfectly happy in 2005 because deep down I knew I was watching one of the true great Lincoln City sides.

I've had that feeling again, as recently as November 2016. I had it whilst I watched City pull two goals back to win away at Forest Green, or when we confidently put six past North Ferriby. We're very close to having the 'next great Lincoln City' side, and that in itself might spawn another book!

And finally: Daren Dykes

The reason I wanted to write this book as I mentioned in the preface was to honour all of the players who played for Lincoln, not just the club legends such as Gareth Ainsworth and Simon Yeo, but also the other players, who for the grace of god could have been a household name in Lincoln. For every player that made it, there was an equally as talented one who didn't. For every name that conjures up a fond memory there is another that will prompt a blank look. Those players still contributed one way or another to the history of our football club.

Daren Dykes was, for want of a better phrase, 'just another loan player'. He was another name fans were unfamiliar with who dropped down from the academy of a top flight team, managed to secure a contract elsewhere, and then ended up out on loan at little old Lincoln City. He had talent and ability, but luck was not on his side. Now thanks to this book and the memorabilia his parents saved from the time, he can prove to his kids he was a professional footballer.

Daren started out as a youth at Spurs, coming from the same academy that provided us with legends such as Peter Gain and Alan Marriott.

"It was a time when size was quite an important thing, if you were under six foot by sixteen or seventeen you weren't really looked at. I was there from a young age, but I was released around the age of seventeen."

Release from a Premiership club is always tough, but a young Dykes dusted himself down and got on with life.

"I was at Newport for a bit helping out and then I went to Buckingham Town. I played about ten games for Buckingham, and the manager came and said there had been a scout watching. I was asked to go to Swindon Town for a pre-season. I think even though you fall off the radar as a youth people do keep an eye on your name. I'd been told Leicester City were looking at me as well"

Swindon were managed at the time by Andy King who was better known to Imps fans as the former Mansfield Town manager. Swindon were a league above City, and they featured (amongst others) future Imp Steve 'Turbo' Robinson, Sam Parkin and Neil Ruddock. The youngster Dykes felt he was offered a two year contract on the back of the ITV Digital collapse.

"I signed when the ITV deal went belly up, I'm sure Lincoln supporters remember that well! I went pre-season for a couple of games, and they offered me a two-year contract. Unfortunately in a pre-season friendly against Hereford I tore my ankle ligaments. I was out for the first three months of the season, but Andy King still offered me the deal. It came around to December and I needed some games. Andy was good friends with Keith Alexander, he explained a bit about him and the club. He told me he needed me to go and get three or four games as reserve football wouldn't do me any good."

Swindon had a decent set up even back then, and the move down to Lincoln City was a culture shock to a young player more used to the Spurs academy and the better facilities of Swindon Town.

"I remember my first day, I turned up at training and we went to a school! Another day we trained somewhere else. Swindon at the time had really good facilities, and I was a bit stumped by what greeted me! I didn't care though, I just wanted to play football wherever I could."

Back then, just as it is now in 2016, players travelling from distance weren't required to train with the Imps on a day to day basis. For an eighteen year old coming to and from Swindon every day wasn't going to be easy, or cost effective.

"In the end Keith said to just come up for the games. At the time it made sense, I was living in Swindon but it was a really big regret of mine. I remember we played York away and I was just a skinny young lad. I thought I might start as I had trained that week, but I suppose on a cold, wet night in York Keith decided to go with more experience."

He did get a start in the next game away at Macclesfield as City won 1-0, picking up a booking. He started again as we faced Swansea City at home a couple of days afterwards.

"At the time Lincoln played 3-5-2 and I played right wing back. I was a striker or attacking midfielder and it was a tough league. I wasn't used to it, if you couldn't get the ball to Peter Gain it just came back at you!"

It was indeed a tough league and at the time City were a very direct side. With a tight three man defence focus was on the wing backs to get up and down as much as possible. Daren may have been a forward player, but deploying him out of position left a talented young player exposed to the harsh realities of League Two football. For a youth fresh out of a top academy playing out of position and not training with the team just didn't work.

"I spoke with Andy King first and then Keith Alexander and said it was probably best if I went back. I was only coming up for matches and to be honest in my only appearance at Sincil Bank I didn't do very much. It was a hard league and I was basically just doing doggies up and down the pitch! I tell you something though, I really remember the air raid siren that went off at corner kicks!"

Daren looks back on his Lincoln time fondly, and perhaps in another time and place he might have had more success. In that cold December of 2003 City were looking for one thing, and Swindon provided us with something else. It wasn't a matter of the player failing, far from it. It simply wasn't the fit either side had hoped for.

"Looking back I would have preferred to have spent a bit more time there. My big regret is not training with the team as well as playing. It was a lovely club, the people were so friendly and it felt really family orientated. I think I would have felt a bigger part of the team and got closer to Keith if I'd carried on training there. I still say it today he was one of the best coaches that I've ever worked under. He was such a gentleman"

One player stood out from that time, one of the same players that stood out for the fans on the terraces.

"Peter Gain, what a left foot he had! I remember thinking what is he doing here, no disrespect to Lincoln City but Peter Gain was spraying balls left, right and centre on these muddy pitches, I thought he was just different gear. He stuck out more than anyone. I remember thinking he should be playing higher up."

The prospect of a move to Lincoln was never really on the table, and even today Daren is pragmatic about what he expected from Lincoln. He only expected to come and play a handful of games before returning to Swindon Town.

"I knew it was only ever going to be a month or a few games, but you just couldn't be sure where it might lead."

You have to chuckle, at the very beginning of this book you will have read the exact same words from Grant Brown, and he amassed so many more appearances than just a few. It's all about luck in football, and luck wasn't with the skinny teenager from Newport Pagnell.

"I got injured back at Swindon and only played a handful of games before injuries got the better of me. I got taken off in my second game back and then in training I did my cruciate ligament again, not just my cruciate either but basically ripped my whole knee apart. I had a year left on my contract, and even after that Andy King kept letting me come in and use the facilities. I was offered a rolling contract when my two year deal ended, but I was advised I wouldn't play that level again. I remember the doctor even saying you'll never run again properly. It was horrible at the time "

Since that hammer blow the young teenager has grown up and had a family, but he always retains a passion for football and a soft spot for Lincoln City.

"I've done a bit since in and around the non-league game since then, I played for Newport Pagnell and scored something like 100 goals in 120 games, which wasn't bad, a couple of levels below the Conference. I still have my Lincoln City shirt too! I showed my boys and they didn't believe me at first that I'd played professional football! I look out for your results although I was gutted this weekend because I'd got Forest Green on my accumulator (City have just won 3-2 after being 2-1 down with minutes to go)."

Like 99% of the players I've featured in my book, Daren Dykes had to think about life after the game. A total of nine or ten games was never going to set him up for life, and despite living the Imps fans dream of wearing the red and white, he still had to earn a crust just like you and I.

"After the game I started a satellite and aerial installation business which was a success. I sold that and now I run a window cleaning business, we've got a few vans out. I was assistant manager of Newport Pagnell for a while but I had to give that up as the business took off. I run a couple of kids teams, it's great working with the kids. I still love football, despite the injuries. I will be looking to get back into management higher up the Southern leagues once the business calms down a bit. That's the plan."

Daren Dykes might only have made two starts and one appearance from the bench for Lincoln, but he inadvertently spawned three hundred pages of Imps history. His career might have been blighted by injury, but his enthusiasm for the game and his appreciation of the short time he did have as a footballer is still strong. He might be one of three hundred and fifty odd players featured in this book, but his story is one that I'm delighted to be able to tell. He is part of th rich tapestry of our club, and I suspect it came as some surprise when I contacted him! I think his reaction says it all.

"I'm flattered haha! It feels like a million years ago now."

Once upon a time you might have cheered a pass he made playing for Lincoln. You might have winced at a tackle he received. You might have applauded him onto the pitch at York. His presence in a match day programme began my own journey of writing this book, and I think it's quite fitting that it is his story, over and above all the others, that brings it to a close.

UTI

RIP KEITH AND BUTCH

THANKS FOR THE MEMORIES

17063635R00152

Printed in Poland
by Amazon Fulfillment
Poland Sp. z o.o., Wrocław